HIJACK

BY
ANTHONY BRYANT

FREEDOM PRESS INTERNATIONAL

FORT LAUDERDALE, FLORIDA

Requests for permission to make copies of any part of the work should be mailed to:
Permissions, FREEDOM PRESS INTERNATIONAL
3223 N.W. 10th Terrace, Suite 607
Fort Lauderdale, Florida 33309, U.S.A.
(305) 565-BOOK or (305) 565-2665

To order additional copies of this book
TELEPHONE TOLL FREE:
1-800-GET BOOK or 1-800-438-2665

To order multiple copies telephone (305) 565-2665 or write:
ORDERING, FREEDOM PRESS INTERNATIONAL
3223 N.W. 10th Terrace, Suite 607
Fort Lauderdale, Florida 33309, U.S.A.

Printed in the United States of America.
Library of Congress Catalogue Card Number 83-83333.
Bryant, Anthony
    Hijack
    1. Bryant, Anthony. 2. Americans in Cuba - Biography.
3. Political prisoners - Cuba - Biography. 1. Title

ISBN 0-917639-00-6

Other books by the same author:
AB INTRA, A collection of poems and prose, 1983

I dedicate this book to:
Antonio 'Tony' Cuesta, a freedom fighter,
Judge Eugene P. Spellman, a freedom giver,
M. M. Carson, a freedom defender,
And to my mom, Alberta, who gave me life.

My thanks to:
Mother Zeigler, founder of Emerge Inc.,
Ron Laytner who discovered me and helped me in spite of myself,
Carrie Meek, a true representative of the people,
Jose Grinan who was always there too,
Carlos Sigler, 'SDI', and Carlos Guy, my friend,
and to all who believed in me ...

PROLOGUE

This is the story of a hijacking. History records it began just after midnight March 6th, 1969 when I forced National Airlines Flight 97 to Cuba.

But the true hijacking really began many years before when I was a child working with my dad cleaning up bars in San Bernardino, California.

It began the first time my father blocked a door and tried to wash off the word 'nigger' without me seeing it. It began with the sexual assault on a young boy in San Francisco. And it continued with a needle in my arm and a gun in my hand.

I lost my dreams, my hopes and my future on a journey that took me from the back alleys of West Coast America to the cellblocks of San Quentin, Folsom, Soledad and slave camps in Cuba.

In the end I realized it was I who had been hijacked, deceived by those I most admired; Karl Marx, Angela Davis, Jesse Jackson, Fidel Castro, Gus Hall, Jane Fonda, Che Guevara and a whole planeload of others.

CONTENTS

PART ONE

CONTENTS

PART TWO

Angela, you lied!
You never mentioned
Heads gushing blood...split!
Flashing machetes. Slimy
Mucus filled sockets...smashed eyeballs
Hanging...
And
The hunger! The gnawing ache
Day after day, after month, after
year...
You never protested!

You never said a word about the
Terror!
Angela,
Is there anywhere,
In the world,
Where all hands
Are always raised in consent?
They are
In Cuba.

Angela you lied.

Anthony Bryant,
In a Cuban prison, 1976

x

PART ONE

1.
THE HIJACKING

It was a starless night, a quarter 'til two, March 6, 1969. I was black and bitter, armed, desperate and dangerous, at war with the United States of America. A .38 Smith & Wesson revolver was jammed into the back waistband of my pants, pushed against my airline seat. It would give me the courage I needed.

I sat observing the people whose lives would shortly be in my hands and wondered if any of them had the vaguest idea that death was their co-pilot, ready to take us all down in flames.

New York's Kennedy International Airport had long since dropped away beneath the 727 aircraft in which we flew and only I knew we wouldn't reach our destination, Miami, Florida: I was about to hijack National Airlines' Flight 97 and take it to Cuba.

Doubt crowded my mind. What if I had to kill someone? Would there be a federal marshal on board? What if the pilot tricked me by taking me to an alternate destination? I pushed the doubts aside. I had made up my mind. There was no turning back.

I glanced at my watch: 2:20 a.m.; time for action.

The panther was about to pounce.

Though I was racked by a cold and running a fever, I was deadly sober and in possession of my wits. I had kicked the heroin habit to prepare for this moment. It had been a tough battle. But it was worth it. I had vowed to my Black Panther brothers to succeed in this mission or die.

Slowly, I made my way to the washroom and latched the door. A strange face in the mirror stared back at me. It wore a wild Afro, had a Van Dyke beard and crazed and gleaming dark eyes. Suddenly, I was frightened of myself.

Once again I thought of backing off. But, no, I had a score to settle. Before I could change my mind, I took out the .38, flipped the cylinder, shoved the gun back into my waistband, opened the door and stepped out heading for the revolution.

In spite of my determination and resolve, my knees were rubbery as I opened the curtain to the hostess galley. Inside was a pretty lady who looked like Jacqueline Kennedy.

"Yes?" she asked with a soft smile.

I pushed past her and whipped out the long-barreled revolver. There were two others stewardesses in there with her. All three turned pale as cocaine.

"Listen to me and listen good." I heard my voice; it was hard as steel. "This is a hijacking!"

Stunned silence. The Jackie stewardess glanced at the others and whispered in awe, "I told you I had a premonition. I knew we were going to be hijacked!"

"You're right!" I snapped. "Call the captain! Tell him we're on our way to the cockpit."

"Couldn't you hide the gun?" the psychic stewardess pleaded, "If the passengers see it they may panic."

I was surprised by how calm she was. I grabbed a paper bag from the galley shelf, slipped my gun inside and moved with her down the aisle. She did nothing to attract attention. The plane wasn't very full. None of the eighteen passengers looked up.

The stewardess tapped lightly on the cockpit door and it swung open immediately. Roughly, savagely, I shoved her aside, ripped the paper bag away, pressed the cocked revolver against the pilot's head and screamed, "You are dead! Do what I say or I'll blow you away!"

The white man turned whiter. "All right," he said frantically. "All right. Just calm down. I'll do anything you say."

4

The co-pilot didn't move, but sat numbed and staring straight ahead. A quizzical look crossed the navigator's face; he was having trouble coping with reality. A fourth man, who later proved to be a supervisory pilot, stood transfixed to one side.

My voice softened now, soothing, not wanting to create panic in a crucial moment. It was something I had learned as an armed robber.

"We're going to Cuba. I want you to leave on all the intercoms so I can hear every spoken word. You cooperate and nobody gets hurt. Understand?"

The captain nodded.

Then the navigator came alive, warning, "We'll never make it. We don't have enough fuel to reach Havana."

"Then, we'll land in the ocean," I snarled.

"Oh, my God!" Quickly, anxiously the navigator recalculated the plane's position and remaining fuel.

The captain began transmitting a message to Miami Air Traffic Control. "I'm afraid I have to go to Havana tonight..."

Time: 2:29 a.m.

My eyes swept the cockpit.

"Leave the door open."

I stepped outside, no longer hiding the gun, and surveyed the passengers, my hostages.

They stared back in disbelief, stunned by terror. I was the man with the gun and the man with the gun was in charge.

The pretty stewardess took a couple of steps toward me. "May I come closer?"

I eyed her cautiously.

"Sure. Why not?"

"What's your name?"

"Jimmy," I lied.

Wringing her hands in fear, she asked, "Where are you from?"

I motioned with the gun toward the pull-down seat by the cockpit. "Why don't we sit down?" From there, I could keep an eye on everybody.

5

Settling, she asked again, "Where are you from?"

"San Francisco."

She was trying to gain information to turn over later to the FBI. I'd give her all the false data I could. My name wasn't Jimmy, and I didn't live in San Francisco.

I kept an eye on the cockpit as the stewardess continued to question me. Then the strained conversation took a different turn. She suddenly seemed genuinely interested in me.

"I understand why black people feel angry," she ventured. "I can understand why you feel disillusioned. But what you're doing isn't the answer. Why are you doing this?"

I had heard the question a hundred — no, a million times before and it was always the same. I'd thought about it often. The answer lay in a thousand hurts. Maybe it began years before on the first day of school at Mt. Vernon Elementary in San Bernardino, California.

The chatter of happy children had filled the room with the warmth of a bright sunny day. The teacher, Miss Easley, white and grandmotherly, was saying, "Good morning, children. Let's all take our seats and we'll call the roll." Under the magic of her smile and soft voice, we grew quiet.

Soon, she sang songs with us, and afterwards, opened a book and read aloud. Tom Sawyer was a story full of heroes and we all relaxed under the spell of Miss Easley's soothing voice.

I could just feel the slow movement of the Mississippi, hear the boatsmen singing on shore, when suddenly my stomach tightened. Had I heard right? *Nigger*...

The word had slipped from Miss Easley's lips so normally, so smoothly, that it was almost a caress. Slowly Miss Easley lowered the book and stared at me. Then she continued reading. Again the hated word exploded into the classroom dimming the bright colors of the day. Miss Easley's eyes drew into narrow slits aimed at me.

The other children, inquisitive looks on their faces, began to follow her cue and stare at me too. This is what Miss Easley wanted. She read on and once more *Nigger* filled the room.

I sat hunched in my seat, trying to hide. But Miss Easley's eyes never gave up. Her face became disfigured with hate and she sought me out again. The children followed her lead. A giggle sounded. Then two. Finally the whole class sat pointing and laughing. They had learned the lesson she was trying to teach — what a *nigger* was. Me!

It was a long time ago. I shook my head away from the past and stared at the stewardess. 'Why am I doing this?' If I'd had the time I could have told her about the horror of black existence in the United States, a horror she could never understand. But there was more. Much more. I had a personal reason for hating whites, a very personal reason.

It had been born long ago on a night so dark even the trees and bushes in the park melted into each other, moving and twisting with a life of their own. I was thirteen years old and running away from a brutal father and home, tired of being beaten with heavy, leather straps.

I'd taken a couple of hesitant steps down a long, dark path, when, without warning, my way was blocked. I looked up, and in the moonlight saw two fiendish, burning eyes set in a chalky white face. We stared at each other for an agonizing moment. Suddenly a strong hand shot out and grabbed my genitals.

Cold fear swept through me. I remembered horror stories about sex fiends. I was pulled roughly toward the man. To run was impossible.

The weirdly moving shadows surrounding us had already chased me in my younger days; in the small room of a foster home I would pull the blankets over my head to shut out those shadows but in this park there was no place to hide.

The man dropped to his knees, jerking my pants down. I began to sob a hymn. My voice was swallowed by the night... "Jesus loves me, this I know..."

7

I remembered this and much more. How could the stewardess ever understand my reasons for hijacking. She wouldn't. She couldn't possibly comprehend.

For an answer I gave her a slow, thin smile and remarked acidly, "You know something? You got real pretty legs!" Vengeance crossed my mind.

She blushed and lowered her eyes.

"And you know something else? If I told you that in Alabama, they'd lynch me!"

Her face reddened. She stood up and gazed out the window. Finally, she turned and said cooly, "Would you like something to drink?"

"No. But I have a question for you. Who would be responsible for the passengers' money if I robbed them?"

"Why the airline, of course," she answered.

"Fine," I said. "Because that's just what we're going to do." Pointing the gun at her, I stood up. "Come on."

"You don't mean —"

"That's exactly what I mean. Get a sack. You're about to help a poor black boy get a new start in life!"

She found a large paper bag in the serving area and we proceeded down the aisle, from seat to seat, relieving passengers of their cash. I allowed the blacks and those who had little money to keep it. A true revolutionary only robs from the rich. There wasn't a sound or a single movement among the passengers.

Along the way we encountered a swarthy-skinned white, clutching an attache case to his chest.

"Open it!"

He hesitated and pulled the case closer.

"Open it!" The click of the revolver changed his mind. He knew he was close to death. The case fell open and stacks of new $100 bills greeted my eyes.

"Hey Mama, we got a rich one here."

The victim remained silent while the stewardess stuffed a small fortune into my paper sack. Then, as if remembering something, and taking an awful chance on getting shot, he reached into his coat pocket and tried to show me some kind of identification.

"You crazy? Don't waste my time," I growled, and clutching the bag, walked the stewardess to a window near the cockpit.

Nobody had protested. Nobody had moved. It was so easy. It was uncanny. I did it! I did it! I exulted. I'm bad! Bad! Bad! Bad! I hijacked their plane. I ripped 'em off. I showed 'em. This is how you do it, baby. No rest. That's it. You don't give the mothers no rest. You got to hit 'em where it hurts. Ya gotta let 'em know there ain't no hide'n place. And this dizzy fool white girl asking me, 'Why are you doing this?' I'm doin' this to mess you up Miss Legs. I'm doin' this to make you honkies understand it's our turn now. I'm setting an example for my son and all black people.

At this point the supervisory pilot came from the cockpit with a sly smile on his face. He edged closer, babbling idiotic nonsense about putting down the gun. I wasn't even annoyed.

"Take another step and I'll kill you!"

Without a whine or a whimper, he shot back into the cockpit. It was all so easy.

"There it is!" the stewardess said as the plane circled low. She pointed down out a window to gigantic illuminated letters, *JOSE MARTI*, my first glimpse of Cuba.

The landing gear dropped with a dull thud. It was 3:18 a.m. In a few hours it would be dawn in a new world. I was about to enter *Paradise*.

2.
AN ODYSSEY BEGINS

The 727 made its final approach to Jose Marti International Airport.

The huge aircraft tires thudded and screeched as they hit the pock-marked runway. I should have been elated but I felt an almost physical blow in the pit of my stomach. My mouth turned dry and bitter tasting. A sense of doom overtook me. It was as if a black cloud, heavy, and threatening, had settled on and around me. Now that the deed was done, almost over, I was terrified.

When the plane rolled to a stop a young official came on board. He was well-dressed in a tailored gray pinstriped suit. "May I have your gun?" he said in impeccable English, extending his hand.

"*Hasta la victoria siempre!*" I said, meaning, "To victory always," a Spanish phrase I had picked up from Che Guevara's diary. My Spanish must have sounded awkward.

"Huh? What? Oh yeah — sure. Listen. May I have your gun?"

I surrendered the revolver and stood waiting anxiously, wondering what happens next.

"Where are the others?" He looked past me.

"What others? There's nobody but me."

"You mean — you mean you hijacked this plane all..." The words died on his lips when he looked into my eyes. "Come with me," he said and turned away.

We descended from the plane, and under the glow of flood lights and flashing cameras, strolled past lines of soldiers armed with

11

submachine guns and into a small, modest office. Large pictures of Fidel covered the walls: Fidel — submachine gun in hand, gesturing for unseen troops to follow as he charged over a grassy knoll; Fidel — giving a speech; Fidel — waving victoriously from a tank. It was exciting.

The official pointed to a chair and settled behind a shiny desk. I pulled out a pack of cigarettes and offered my new friend a Camel. He accepted one, lit it, and with a luxurious sigh allowed the smoke to filter from barely opened lips.

"What's your name?"

"Anthony Garnet Bryant," I answered. Then, a fit of coughing racked my body; I really wanted to get this thing over and done with so I could go to a hotel and rest. My cold was getting worse.

"Are you ill?" he inquired almost delicately.

"Yeah, I've caught a virus or something."

"We'll make this as brief as possible, then see about getting you a doctor. Okay? Now tell me something. Why did you come to Cuba?"

The man sitting before me was white, and I couldn't tell him how much I hated whites. Had he been black, I would have told him I wanted the white system overthrown, its civilization destroyed. It was time for justice — black justice. It was time for revolution!

This was the country that promised aid to revolutionaries and kept its word. Cuba was creating a true democracy, a place where everyone was equal, where violence against blacks, injustice and racism were things of the past. I had heard a lot about Cuba and Fidel Castro. He and Che Guevera were my heroes. I had come to Cuba to feel freedom at least once and carry back a war message which the racist United States would understand.

I turned to the wall and pointed to the submachine gun Fidel carried into battle. "That's what I've come for!" I reached into my pocket, pulled out a white envelope and passed it over. "This will explain everything."

The official's dark eyes widened as he read the letter written by a Cuban in the United States who had been introduced to me as a relative of Celia Sanchez, Fidel Castro's first secretary and right arm. It was an introduction and a formal request that I be given assistance to foster a revolutionary atmosphere in California.

The turbulent 1960s, filled with shattered dreams and unfulfilled vows of vengeance as well, were drawing to a close. All that was needed to ignite the explosive calm was agitation and armor-piercing projectiles. Heavy caliber arms in a few well-trained hands would paralyze cities.

I leaned forward intently and explained, "I'm a member of the Black Panther Party." I gave my code name, *Kassim,* and the names of other Panthers involved in the operation, as well as plans and routes to be used to introduce the arms into the United States.

"Why did you hijack a plane instead of coming through Mexico or Canada on a legitimate flight?" he asked curiously.

"We decided on a hijacking, because — well, because we thought that it would hit them where it hurts — in their pocketbooks!" He laughed, and I rushed on, encouraged. "Too, we thought it'd be kinda flashy — like giving the system the finger. You know, like telling them, "Up yours!' Anyway, we know that hijackers, revolutionary hijackers, are welcome in Cuba."

He leaned back in his chair, relaxed and evidently pleased with me. "What are the objectives of your organization if arms are made available?"

I outlined plans some of the Panthers expected to carry out; lightning attacks on police stations by urban guerrillas, the paralyzing of major cities like Los Angeles and San Francisco with bombings, the provoking of chaos and economic collapse. "Our final objective is to create a Socialist State. But we need bazookas, heavy arms, if we want to be successful."

He smiled. "Why didn't you guys rob an armory?"

"We figured anything heavy, like bazookas, would have the firing pins or some other vital piece removed and we'd end up with just rifles and we've got plenty of those. What we need are heavy arms. That's what I've come for!" There. I'd had my say. I closed my eyes and leaned back. The virus was hitting me hard. But I felt content.

I had carried out the first step of the plan. I pictured myself being given a warm welcome, maybe by Fidel himself. And the women... I would have all the beautiful women I wanted. When the revolution triumphed in the United States I would be given a place in the new system, perhaps even be a revolutionary diplomat. I smiled at this wonderful future. But precisely at this moment, it began to change.

The door flew open.

A heavy-set soldier burst in, uniform in disarray. He gave me a strange look and rushed to the official's side. Cupping his hand over his mouth, he whispered excitedly; all the while casting glances over his shoulder at me.

The official's feet hit the floor with a thud. He shot upright in his chair. *"Que?"* His staccato-like questions were answered by rapid Spanish and waving hands. Finally the soldier backed away and, after a last furtive look at me, sped through the open door.

The official sat drumming his fingers, gazing up at the ceiling. Moments passed. Finally he looked at me as if for the first time. "Why did you rob the passengers?" Without waiting for a reply he added, "Don't you realize you didn't have anything to worry about in Cuba? I don't know, but I think you made a big mistake. Is that the money?" He pointed to the sack at my side.

"Yes, it is."

The interrogation ended then and there with the confiscation of the stolen cash. Three armed soldiers entered and I was whisked off to a nearby hospital. It was surrounded by a high barbed-wire fence. A barrier at its entrance was raised by a tough-looking armed guard.

I was taken to a room containing a single bed, given a sheet and blanket, and told the doctor would be in to see me after I'd gotten some rest.

That same morning at 8:30, after a few hours sleep, I awoke, hot and sweaty. I wanted a shower. But the water supply was turned off. I began banging on my door trying to attract attention. At last a hospital aide arrived. I told him what I wanted through gestures and pantomime. Wreathed in smiles and stringing a deluge of "Si, Si, Si's," the Cuban hurried off to turn on the water.

I stood in the shower and waited. Finally water jetted out in a cold, rusty spray. I spun the dial hoping for the temperature to change for the better. It didn't happen so I stepped out, toweled myself dry and put on the baggy pajamas they'd given me.

The room was dusty, as if rarely used. A slatted window overlooked a patio filled with plants. The day was sunny with just a tinge of haze. There was movement outside. A thin, dark-haired nurse swept a narrow pathway free of leaves. She was singing. She looked up and for one brief instant our eyes met. I don't know how mine looked, but hers were the saddest I had ever seen. I would never forget that face, that voice, those eyes.

I slipped back into bed, oddly disturbed and was laying there thinking about her, contemplating what I had seen with my soul, when the slow turning of the doorknob drew my attention. The door opened a fraction of an inch at a time, as if the person on the other side had doubts about entering.

Finally a man's head appeared, then a shoulder, and at long last the entire body eased into my room. A tall Latin in a crisply-starched white uniform, stethoscope dangling from his neck and carrying a yellow clipboard pad, moved toward my bed.

I thought: This cat's the heat. No doctor in the world sneaks into a patient's room like he's scared.

"Good morning," he said in fair enough English. "My name is Doctor Hernandez. How are you feeling?"

"Oh, still a little stuffy, but a lot better," I managed.

After a few mundane comments concerning sickness and health, the phony doctor began an intense interrogation. "What's your name? Where were you born? Why are you in Cuba?"

I had had too many scrapes with the law not to be able to

recognize a 'pig' when I saw one. I knew 'Doctor' Hernandez was a cop and after about thirty minutes of questioning, he promised to return the next day and took off.

Lunch came: rice, soup and a piece of chicken that dripped grease. I ate a little and threw the rest away. Later I was to learn how stupid I had been.

That night a soldier armed with a submachine gun stood outside my door. Hernandez told me next day, "You are a very important person. We don't want anything to happen to you." He came to see me once more; then his visits ceased.

Two days later the room was invaded by several plainclothes agents who, with smiles and handshakes, told me to get dressed. "We're taking you to a hotel!"

My spirits soared. I was walking on air. My cold was almost gone, and I was anxious to see Havana, the magic city I'd heard so much about.

Outside, the guard raised the barrier and a few minutes later we sped down an empty stretch of highway in an old American car. We passed through a heavily populated suburban area and finally pulled up before a huge, ancient and forbidding stone structure that must have been built in the days of the Spaniards. A tall, modern cement wall, covered with gigantic posters of revolutionary martyrs in battle, surrounded it.

The agents cast sidelong glances at me. Then they broke into fits of laughter, referring to me as 'the guest'.

"Here you are, Mr. Bryant," one of them gasped. "Hotel State Security. Better known as G-2!"

3.
G-2

They didn't waste time.

I was registered, fingerprinted, and led up a long flight of narrow stone steps by a white-helmeted soldier. Our footfalls echoed off steel doors lining empty corridors, ricocheting and mingling with the warning cries and whistles of my guard. Answering whistles and the clang of slamming doors indicated the message had been received. I learned later that in G-2, no prisoner was ever allowed to see another.

My new quarters were empty except for three metal bunks chained to the wall. A vent made of cement, angled to prevent observation in or out stared back at me from one side of the room. This was Cell 70. I would get to know it well.

The place stank. Searching around in the dim light, feeling as though every pore of my body was being invaded, I discovered why. Human excrement in the corners, some old and hard, others fresh and soft, gave off the putrid odor. There was no toilet, no wash bowl, nothing except the concrete cage and its human prey.

A long, tense week passed. The same man who had masqueraded as a doctor at the hospital, now interrogated me as Captain Hernandez with a fancy office in G-2. After a few remarks about my health, he began. "Now, Mr. Bryant, just why did you come to us for arms?"

I had answered that question several times already. I sighed. "Because this is a revolutionary government and we've been told

17

Cuba is willing to help anyone bring about revolution in their own country."

"What kind of revolution are you talking about? An equal rights movement type of thing? Economic? Social? Just what do you mean specifically when you say 'revolution'?"

I was confused. To me, as well as to most blacks I knew, revolution meant taking whitey's riches and spreading them among destitute blacks.

"Well, for me," I began, "revolution means taking from them that's got everything and making them share equally with the poor. Am I right?"

"Yes," mused Hernandez aloud. "Of course. Yes, that's what the revolution is designed to do. Tell me, what was your position in the Black Panthers and how long were you a member?" He paused. "And, oh, yes, who authorized you to rob the passengers on the plane?"

I moved uneasily in my straight-backed chair. "Well, I've been with the Panthers for less than a year, but I've always fought the system. I always felt racist, capitalist whites had to be eliminated. Everybody's always talking change. My philosophy is that if you want to see change, put a .38 to a man's head and pull the trigger. That's change. As far as my job with the Panthers goes, I volunteered to eliminate anyone infiltrating the party."

His eyebrows shot up. "You mean kill them?"

I nodded confidently. "And nobody told me to rob the passengers. I don't need authorization to do that. I don't need authorization to take what belongs to me. For four hundred years my people have been exploited by whites. We've been robbed and ripped off by American racists, so anything I take is not robbery. It's taking back what they owe me."

"What do you think of Martin Luther King Junior?"

I smiled. "Nothing to think about. He was a pacifist. Never did like him. Mao Tse Tung says 'Political power comes from the barrel of a gun.' I don't believe in praying in the streets while somebody kicks my butt."

"Do you believe in God?"

A momentary struggle occurred within me, but only momentary. God had died for me the night that white homosexual's mouth closed on me in the park.

"No! I believe in the revolution and in myself. Everything else is a pack of lies!" Captain Hernandez threw back his head and laughed. "Ever been in jail before?"

"Yes."

"How many times and what for?"

"I've been going to jail ever since I was a kid and did big time twice. The first time was in Soledad, two-and-a-half years for armed robbery. I also did three-and-a-half in San Quentin for selling dope. There were also a couple of years in some county jails."

He pulled a yellow note pad toward him. "What were you going to do with the money you took from the passengers?"

"Planned to give it to the Panthers or use it to pay off the guards along the Mexican frontier. Mexicans will let you do almost anything, if you've got the money."

"You meant to spend the money on the cause?"

"Yep! It wasn't for me. I'm a revolutionary."

"How do you and your people plan to create a revolutionary climate in the United States?"

"That's simple. We wait until some pig kills a brother..."

He held up his hand. "Wait a minute, Mr. Bryant, what's a pig?"

"A pig? That's a policeman, man. Now like I was saying, when a pig kills or abuses a brother or a sister, we'll set up rallies or marches and turn them into riots. That's easy to do. The cops'll beat somebody on the head or maybe even kill one or two people. It doesn't really matter if the cops do it or not because we'll see to it that somebody gets hurt. Then we retaliate by shooting a few cops. We'll raid jails and let the prisoners go free. That's to create confusion, see? Naturally, Whitey's forces will come out to crush us and people will get killed. That'll create major riots where we'll give the people guns and it'll be all-out war."

"I see. And then?" he murmured, looking out the window and twirling his pencil. Had he heard all this before?

"Then we'll build a socialist government like here in Cuba," I ended enthusiastically.

During many long sessions I was forced to bare my soul. In time Hernandez knew every aspect of my life, and being a true revolutionary, I held nothing back. He was my brother.

After each session I was shuffled back to the cell under the same insulating measures of whistled warnings and exhausted, fall into a heavy sleep. Only the rattle of the food cart roused me. The guards who pushed it had stone faces. I tried to show them my good side, even cracked a joke or two but they remained silent and unresponsive. Each meal was shoved into the cell; then with a crash and bang, the door was locked.

The one substantial meal a day tended to be rice, bean soup, bread, an occasional piece of meat and a slice of guava. After each of the meals I sat dreaming of the fun I would have in Cuba. I was anxious to see the streets. Then I'd fall into a peaceful sleep until the sound of blunt objects striking flesh, mingled with screams and moans, awakened me. This became a common night-time experience. I was surprised, since I knew that all the tales about Communist brutality were just that, tales and lies.

They're probably spies or saboteurs, I reassured myself; Central Intelligence Agency people, maybe. Well, they ought to kill the dogs! Then I'd lie there listening to their cries and laughing.

After the first week, the almost daily visits to Hernandez's office didn't stop. I had expected it to be a brief interlude. But I didn't really mind them. That's to be expected, I told myself; after all, I could be a spy, and like the man says, they've got to be sure that I am who I say I am. Still, I don't like the way those brothers tricked me. They didn't have to lie. I would have understood if they told me they were bringing me to jail and not to a hotel. Well, anyway, I decided, Hernandez says I'll be out of here in no time.

I had finally found my brothers. I hoped they didn't feel bad about me robbing the passengers. I could have used that money! They'd probably set me up though, in a nice pad for awhile, until everything was ready. I was going to have a ball. I'd heard tales of how the women were really liberated in Cuba. I was planning to find me two or three foxes and party down.

After seventeen days I had not taken a shower; neither had I defecated. Not having a toothbrush or toothpaste, my breath was a replica of the cell's odor. I stank. Finally, enraged by this lack of consideration, I started beating on the cell door, a strictly pro-hibited action. Immediately, the small hatch, through which the guards observed the prisoners, slid open.

The guard couldn't understand me. After shouting insults at each other, at least on my part, he left and brought back an English-speaking officer. I shouted, "I need a shower! Can't you people even give me a shower?"

He nodded and gave the order for me to take my first shower, cold, in seventeen days.

That afternoon my door clanged open and a guard beckoned me out. Escorted down the dim corridors, I was taken outside the building and marched across a parking lot filled with anti-que American cars to a section beside a basketball court. A low fence was all that separated me from the street and freedom.

When we arrived at a grassy area spotted with palm trees and flowers, the guard jumped a low stone wall to the left and disap-peared. I froze on the spot. An old con like me with eight years in U.S. prisons knew something was wrong. Warning signals flash-ed in my head: I knew that no prisoner should be left alone, especially under these circumstances.

I lowered myself to the grass, noticing a small hut with a closed door about fifty yards away. I had the sure feeling that if I tried to jump that low barrier, I would be shot. It was a set-up!

Now just be cool, Tony, I told myself; what they're doing is testing you to see if you're going to try to get away.

Fifteen minutes passed; the guard reappeared and marched me back into the building. I was taken out each day thereafter, but on the second day the door to the hut had been left open and I saw a guard with a submachine gun inside. Perhaps he'd been there the first day, waiting to shoot me down if I tried to escape.

Despite the filthy conditions, the cries and screams at night and the guard in the hut, I felt everything was okay. I had complete faith in my Communist brothers.

Late one night I heard a voice crying in English, "Why y'all doin' this to me? I ain't done nothin'. Please. I wanta go home." He rattled the door, sobbing all the while. Then he yelled out, "Niggers! Black niggers!"

Judging from the accent, he was an American from the south. Then I heard the sound of his cell door being opened and the smack of fists.

The American screamed over and over, "Oh, mah arm! You breakin' it." Then the screams came to an abrupt halt. There was a clatter of locks being turned and then silence.

Good, I thought; shoulda killed the dog!

From somewhere in the mausoleum a guard's voice, distorted by echoes, shouted, "Tomorrow you die, Yankee! Tomorrow you die!"

I smiled and fell asleep.

A month crawled by, then two. The interrogations became less frequent. Fighting against doubts that plagued me, I became impatient. Finally, in a fit of anger, I refused food. Nothing was said. I thought they'd hustle right down to see what was wrong like they did in American jails. But nothing happened. To my surprise, the food wagons rattled by the next day without stopping; and the next, and the next...

On the fifth day, as lunch rolled by without acknowledging Cell 70, I got mad. I set up a ruckus, pounding on the door with all my might. Immediately I was shuffled off to see Captain Hernandez.

"What seems to be the problem?" he asked politely.

Trembling with anger, I demanded, "What's going on here? You trying to starve me?"

Hernandez denied any knowledge of my not being fed and promised, "I'll take care of it," while assuring me smoothly, "You'll be leaving soon."

After I had returned to my cell the slot opened and a black hand reached in holding a bag of chocolate candy. What a pickup! Hernandez was a great guy.

The weather grew warm and the cell became hot and muggy and full of vicious mosquitoes swarming around the overhead light bulb.

On some of those hot nights I heard sounds in the corridor. At first it was difficult to make out what was happening. But glueing my ear to the door several nights running, I was able to hear sighs of pleasure and gratification. The guards were engaging in homosexual activities; I couldn't believe it. I didn't know if it was guards and guards or guards and prisoners. But they were doing something sexual.

Since that night when I was assaulted in the park, I had held a strong aversion to homosexuals. Now to hear my communist brothers kissing each other hit me harder than if I'd found out my mother was a lesbian. So what did I do? I refused to believe I'd heard anything and stopped listening at the door.

Sometimes when I didn't even try to listen I'd still hear strange things. Another American was brought in. He was black. I could tell from his voice he was a brother. He immediately set up a ruckus. The guards allowed it to continue for a short while but finally opened his cell.

I heard a voice say in thickly-accented English, "If you make any more noise, I'll cut your wrists and leave you to bleed to death — a suicide." The American didn't make another sound.

One afternoon during my daily fifteen minute walk in the sun, I saw a large homemade rubber raft lying beside the building. I was intrigued and asked Captain Hernandez about it.

"Oh, that," he said. "That belonged to a family who escaped from their government's repression and risked their lives to come to Cuba. When you see the streets of Havana, Tony, you'll find out the revolution has eliminated prostitution and just about every kind of crime. We don't have hunger. That's why people come here. It's their opportunity to be happy."

I always felt stronger and more contented after talking to Hernandez. He used to tell me, "This is only a temporary inconvenience." I accepted his words and waited.

Meanwhile the cell's odors got to me. They obviously had no intention of cleaning it, so I decided to strike a blow for the Cuban health department.

At last I got my idea across to the amazed guards. They brought me a bucket of water and big chunks of hard yellow lye soap. After just a few minutes of wall washing, the water became thick and slimy. Soon it was impossible to wring out the slippery rag. So, holding it at one end, I pulled the rag through a tight grip of my other hand so the filth could slither back into the pail. A gawking audience of guards watched me do the unthinkable.

Four hours and several pails of water later, a few slivers of soap was all that was left. I knocked for the last time and the door opened. The guards stared in wonder at the transformed cell. I laughed. That night I slept soundly.

For days I collected photographs, torn from magazines and other Communist literature they gave me. Then I glued them to the wall with bits of soap, arranged in the form of a gigantic '26' to commemorate the upcoming festivities of July 26th, the day Fidel began his revolutionary liberation. This would show them I was on their side. But on July 18th, 1969, almost a week before Cuba's biggest holiday, my world toppled.

Early that morning I was taken to the interrogation room. My friend, Captain Hernandez, a pile of papers before him on the polished desk, said, "Sit down," and the questioning began with the usual Latin touch, "How are you feeling? Is the food okay? Do you have any problems?" But then, leaning back in his chair, fingertips forming a pyramid under his chin, he added, "Do you remember the guy with the briefcase on the plane, the one with the money?"

"Sure."

Hernandez shifted in his seat. "Do you remember him trying to show you his identification?"

I nodded; a feeling of apprehension crawled slowly over me. "Why didn't you look at it?"

I shrugged and mumbled, "I didn't think it was important."

Hernandez leaned forward, his palms flat on the desk and glared at me. "How long have you worked for the CIA?"

I stiffened and jerked upright. "What are you talking about? I've never seen a CIA agent in my life, much less worked for them!" Was he crazy? I was the guy who was trying to blow up the United States.

"We have information that just prior to your leaving the United States you were in contact with the FBI and the CIA."

My mind whirled. I opened my mouth to deny the accusation.

But Hernandez pounded on the desk, screaming, "No more lies." His dark eyes flashed. "We don't want any more lies." He stood, bracing himself against the desk, his face inches from mine. His voice dropped to a fierce whisper. "Do you know who that man was you robbed? He was a Cuban revolutionary!"

I slumped in my chair, shaking my head in disbelief.

The hoarse breathing of Captain Hernandez filled the room. Outside the office, the birds were singing. It was a beautiful day, the day a dream died.

Back in my cell, completely shaken, I understood now why the passenger had tried to identify himself. Had I taken the time to look at his I.D., I would have seen he was Latin and with me on my way to Cuba, seeking aid, nothing in the world could have compelled me to take his money.

As Captain Hernandez had reminded me, "You're either very smart or extremely stupid. Your action and the subsequent attention brought to the agent has caused a breakdown in a very important intelligence cell." His parting shot really hurt, "You scum. You filthy capitalist agent!"

And so, July 26th came and went and Tony Bryant didn't join

the celebrations. I sweated through the hot, muggy days and tossed and turned during the nights. I was miserable. After a few weeks I tore down the big 26 of July numbers on my wall. And then, on top of everything else, I heard a man go insane.

I knew only a few words of Spanish and these were mostly vulgarities. But I understood a lot of the screaming and shouting when I heard a prisoner cursing Fidel Castro and the revolution. I was surprised. It went on for days, on and on, seemingly without end from morning until late at night.

Then, one day I heard them open his cell. After a short scuffle, the prisoner was dragged to what must have been a trap door in the ceiling. I heard footsteps on a wooden ladder as they climbed. There were curses and shouts, the crash of a steel door being slammed and the prisoner's muffled voice. The muted shouts and screams continued, until the words were no longer intelligible. After a few days I heard the sound of the ladder being dragged back into place. The trap door was opened and demented mumblings burst forth into the corridor. My blood ran cold.

Strange dreams began to crowd my sleep. A scorpion lay embedded in my hair. My mother appeared. After brushing the scorpion to the floor, she pointed and said, "Be careful, son. Watch out for that!" Suddenly the head of the creature leaped to human proportions. It was the face of Captain Hernandez!

I hear these voices. Are they in my head? I've got to stop pacing. Got to stop and sit down. God, I can't. Why have I been here this long with no word? CIA? Me? Are they crazy? It's hot in here. Wish I had some water. Wish I couldn't hear those doors banging. Those boots, those cries and screams. What are they doing? CIA? Me?

I put it down on paper for Hernandez, told him my next mission would be to hijack a plane to North Vietnam. I'd hold the passengers hostage and demand the release of Vo Thi Thang, the girl with the victory smile. But, hey, Tony what would you do if they wouldn't release her? Why, kill every passenger, of course. Boy, I'm hungry. Wish I could get out of here. Please.

I began waking up late in the day with a thick brown taste in my mouth. I could hardly stand, and it was difficult to focus my eyes. Maybe I was being drugged. It frightened me.

I tried to picture a familiar face and the image would grow fuzzy. If the image opened its mouth to speak, swarms of flies came out. Sometimes I'd snap my eyes open trying to stop it but I'd still see the same swarm pouring out of the wall of my cell.

Maybe I looked sick, or if I had been drugged, was giving them the right answers, because not long after, Hernandez informed me, "You are going to be tried for robbery. It's nothing. Just a formality. Then, you'll be released and given all the aid you need to carry out your mission."

The point of all this was to keep others from accusing Cuba of aiding known criminals. I had to be tried. Hernandez even apologized for accusing me of being a spy, and I began to get more and better food. My spirits rose. But the honeymoon didn't last long.

A few days later two guards rushed into my cell and with animated gestures, ordered me to get dressed.

Whisked from the building into a drizzling rain, wearing the same clothes I'd slept in for five months, and heavily guarded, I was taken to the main courthouse in downtown Havana, across from the capitol building. We crowded into the elevator and rose to the third floor. It was supposed to be an open court, but the room was packed with weapons.

Rifles and gun barrels bristled from almost every seat. A few civilians were there but the spectators were almost all guards. I was nudged into a chair and the proceedings began.

A heavyset woman leaned over and whispered nervously, "I'm your interpreter."

The prosecutor opened by saying, "We know this man belongs to the Black Panthers. We've checked and verified. We also know he belongs, or at least is affiliated with, the Peace and Freedom Party, which is linked to the Panthers. He has come to our country asking..." He paused dramatically. "...for arms to carry out the black revolution in the United States. However, is he who he says he is? We also know..."

The interpreter turned to me and said, "He's talking too fast. I hope I can keep up."

The prosecutor ranted and raved for about fifteen minutes and my interpreter kept repeating she couldn't understand him. Perhaps trying to reassure me, she leaned over and whispered, "See that man over there to your right, across the room, the skinny one? He's your lawyer."

This was good news to me. He appeared distinguished and competent. "Can I speak to him?"

"Oh, no!" A shocked expression crossed her face. "That's not permitted. You can't talk with your lawyer during a trial."

"But I've never talked to him at all. Not even a word."

"Shhh! Can't talk!"

I slumped back in my seat. This would all be behind me shortly and I'd be a free man.

The interpreter leaned over again and said, "Your lawyer's about to speak. Listen closely and I'll tell you what he says."

My man stood, glanced at me indifferently and said, "Your Honor, we are ninety miles face-to-face with our imperialist enemy and we must protect the revolution." Then, he sat down!

A guard tapped my shoulder. "Let's go." It was over.

The judge, Armando Torres, beckoned me to the bench. In perfect English he said, "Don't worry about a thing. We'll take care of you. Just don't worry."

As Captain Hernandez had said, the trial had been a coverup. Now the racist imperialists could not say I had failed to face justice. I would be released and given the arms I'd risked my life to obtain. I did, however, have to return to Cell 70, but only until the proper arrangements were made.

It was raining outside the courthouse. I leaned my head back and savored the clean drops of water running down my cheeks. I smiled. Freedom was so near.

Two weeks later I was informed I had been sentenced to twelve years in prison.

4.
OMENS OF TERROR

The day had nothing going for it.

An August morning sun tried to burn through a gray overcast and failed. Dingy, empty streets and broken houses stared back at me as I sat devastated in the back seat of a speeding 1959 Buick sedan.

Two G-2 agents, riding in front, carried on a cheery conversation. The hard, watchful eyes of the agent beside me, hand resting on the butt of his gun, never left me. I glanced at his weapon and turned away. For the first time a gun seemed ugly. I preferred looking at the despairing avenues outside, wondering where we were heading.

This was the saddest day of my life. I'd been betrayed. My faith was shaken and the certainty of my role in life destroyed.

Miles of sugar cane bordered the narrow road which carried me into the unknown. I took my mind off the dreary view and let it slip back to another time and place shortly before the hijacking.

"Dorene!" I had called. "Come here a second."

The mousey-haired woman was no beauty queen, but had a nice body and soft, dark eyes reflecting the generosity of her soul. In the beginning I thought she'd simply been fascinated by a forbidden intimacy with a black man. I was wrong.

Strange, that we should live together or that we'd ever met. She was 23, a university student and white. She had a lovely, little blonde-haired daughter about six years old.

Dorene's parents were respectable White Anglo Saxon Pro-testants who lived in a typical WASP nest. They'd have gone into shock if they knew of their daughter's deep interest in the Black Panthers and of her genuine concern for black mistreatment. Dorene had wanted to do more than just hand out leaflets. She had supported my plan to hijack the plane and even bought my ticket.

"Wait a second, Hon." She walked over to the stereo and lowered the haunting sounds of the Beatles singing *Sweet Lorraine*.

I was kneeling in the middle of the floor, looking down at three tossed coins and scratching notes on a pad. A thick book, open midway, lay in front of me. "Check this out," I told her.

Dorene moved to my side and stared at the open page. Soon, fear crossed her face. *The I Ching,* one of China's oldest books, was giving me a dire warning. In ancient times no emperor made a decision without first consulting its mysterious pages; I believed in it too.

Dorene placed her hand over my notes and looked at me. "Are you still going through with it?"

I nodded slowly. Nothing would stop me now even though the *I Ching* had spoken of a blood-filled pit and the danger of a journey, with a warning not to take it. Everything pointed to danger!

I'd always been interested in the occult. Perhaps we could check my chances another way.

She picked up a deck of Tarot cards and shuffled them, slowly and methodically with a faraway look in her eyes. Electricity filled the air. Dorene seemed reluctant to interpret the cards. She knew we couldn't understand the power we could unleash with a word, a thought or a seemingly insignificant act. I was a deep believer in the occult but also half-fearful of Something I rarely and vague-ly referred to as God. Were we touching the hem of His psychic garments?

The reading was terrifying: judicial problems, prison, death and a trip across many waters. Finally, she reshuffled the cards and, fanning them out face down, said, "Pull one." I did, turned it over and stared in dismay. I'd chosen *The Fool* card...

"Hey, hey, *Americano,* wake up! You like work? Lots of work where you going." I was back in the old Buick, my guards laughing at my misery.

Night had fallen by the time we turned off the main highway onto a narrow trail disappearing into heavy green vegetation.

We bounced and jostled along for about three miles, then the car lights picked up the outline of buildings surrounded by barbed-wire fences. With a start I realized one of the buildings was an old church. A church in a concentration camp? We were entering Guida, a prison work camp.

The guard standing at the barricade, white-helmeted and armed, checked my admittance papers. My body was soaked in perspiration. The night was pitch-black except for several brightly-lit guard posts. I had the feeling of being in the middle of a desert with a candle, total darkness surrounding me.

It looked like *Stalag 17.* The only difference was the main building, housing the officers and living quarters of the Warden. It was the stone steepled church I'd first noticed.

The four of us climbed a narrow staircase to the upper room.

The head of the camp, a slight hawk-nosed man of about thirty, gave a sharp salute to the agents, then dropped stiffly back into a chair. Beads of perspiration broke out on his face as the agents handed my papers over. The man seemed afraid and the papers rustled violently in his trembling hands. The only other sounds came from frogs and crickets outside. After reading the first few lines of the documents, he relaxed a little. What had frightened the man so?

He gave me a long searching look. He seemed to be wondering if I was really the man in the identification papers. And for a long time after the agents left, he sat there, watching me with suspicion. This place was the pits!

A tap at the door and a mangy-looking guard in a green uniform stepped inside. A burst of rapid-fire Spanish and I was escorted down the stairs to the large, open area below which had been the main section of the church.

The walls had been knocked out, the pews were gone. There was no trace of an altar. This big room now served as a mess hall for prisoners and oblong concrete slabs resting on two large blocks served as tables. The stone floor was filthy.

A prisoner wearing greasy denims brought me a bowl of slimy soup with white wormlike spaghetti wiggling around inside. He also provided a prehistoric-looking fish. The soup made me gag and after a half-hearted attempt to eat a piece of the scaly fish, its blind eyes staring up at me, I pushed both aside and got up.

Flanked by guards, I was marched outside and around the corner of the building. It was a beautiful night. The sky was sprinkled with millions of crushed crystal stars. A balmy evening breeze played with my hair. It was warm, quiet and peaceful but I was unprepared and had no idea what was coming.

Apprehension filled me. I took a couple of steps and stopped. The compound was divided in half by a wire fence. I was leaving the side containing the big old church and a small building that looked like a warehouse. On the other side were four barracks resembling barns.

Glued to the fence, packed together, waiting in silent expectation, stood over four hundred prisoners. Most of these men probably had never seen an American before. The intensity of their collective gaze drained me of my strength. For a moment, there was total silence as people from two different worlds, divided by barbed-wire fence, stared at each other. Then, like a hammer blow, a pandemonium of 400 babbling mouths and 800 waving arms exploded. The guards made no attempt to quell the confusion. It would have been futile. I never knew how I made those first steps toward that other world. My feet had no feeling. I'd never been so frightened.

With a click the old Yale lock opened. The chain made a scaly, slithering sound as it was pulled around two posts which held the gate shut. Then it swung open.

Imagine four hundred slathering, hunting dogs leaping and twisting, eyes gleaming with excitement, snarling and held back only by an invisible barrier. The guards pushed me inside. The gate closed. The chain rattled as it was pulled back in place. The lock snapped shut. I was in hell!

The mass of bodies pressed closer and closer. One hand, then two, then three, reached out. The Spanish gibberish intensified to madness. Everybody wanted to touch me. In their excitement, they began grabbing at me. They meant no harm. They just wanted to touch me, but they were dangerous.

I was being pushed and pulled. The prisoners were in a frenzy. The jabber of voices pounded on my eardrums, an angry ocean battering against a reef. Hands clutching, touching. Prison lights spinning, mouths opening and closing. The stars that just a while ago had shone so beautifully above my head, now spun like sparks in a vortex. This went on and on for an eternity. Finally, some prisoners pulled me from the mob and led me to a barn-like building in which I'd live.

My mouth dropped open in shock. Rusted steel beds, stacked four high, with only wire strung from side-to-side for springs, stood packed together. Squeaking rats scuttled over wooden rafters stretching from wall to wall. I hadn't expected to see this in Revolutionary Cuba.

I was given a mattress, so old its insides, which didn't hold enough to stuff two pillows, had sunk down to one end. At last the order was given for silence and, reluctantly, the masses surrounding me retreated. They left with a part of me, a part of my mind, a part of my soul.

I climbed to the top bunk, heeding warning cries as the rickety tower swayed and trembled. I lay there for a while, feeling the wires bite into my flesh. Soon the barracks fell quiet. The whine of night insects filled the air. I was alone and afraid.

I closed my eyes hoping sleep would come quickly. But suddenly, all over again, like an instant replay, there were the screaming mouths and grasping hands. Again, I was thrown into the madness I'd experienced on entering. With a choked cry, I jerked upright.

Silence, absolute silence. Everyone was asleep. The bedlam I was hearing was all in my mind.

My body soaked in sweat, trembling, I lay down once again only to find that as soon as I closed my eyes, I was assailed by this infernal den of insanity. Time after time I snapped upright, shaking, filled with a cold, unknown fear. This went on for most of the night until the gods took pity on me and allowed me to sink into an exhausted stupor.

The clanging of pots being struck together, machetes on bedposts, metal on metal, jarred me awake. It was reveille. The guards seemed to get a kick out of destroying the only peace a prisoner enjoyed, sleep. There was a mad scramble of men dashing to and fro, clutching small tin cans for their morning meal. Everyone rushed outside to be counted.

After an endless wait, a guard made the count. A low groan rose from the assembled prisoners as the official, reaching the end of the line, shook his head and began counting again. This was to be a never-ending comedy. During the long years I was in prison, the guards invariably miscounted.

Finally, joined by a couple of aides, he was able to come up with a number on which they all agreed and the ragged files broke and ran to form a new long line for breakfast; a few ounces of watery powdered milk and a piece of hard bread.

I forced it down, then dropped to the ground, and relaxed against the rickety building, only to be instantly surrounded by prisoners. A couple spoke English, and with a mixture of gestures and broken phrases, made me understand they sympathized with me.

Large cans appeared from nowhere and the morning air danced to the sounds of Afro-Cuban music. Chants from black and white throats alike, accompanied by staccato bursts of improvised drums: "*Asuiro manago iro abacua manango pavio. Efibi tan engomio fo, efibi tan engomio fi."* It was a song from the heart of Africa, mysterious, throbbing.

All morning long, the prisoners danced. Now and then a prisoner would slip through the mass of bodies and present me with a gift. It might have been a little packet of sugar, some crumbled cookies brought by visiting parents or just anything that seemed significant. I later learned no possession was worth nothing. Everything has value when you have nothing. They brought me a spoon, a spool of thread, a roll of damp toilet paper. The prisoners had next to nothing but in a magnanimous way they were telling me they would share whatever they had.

But they were also pranksters. Nobody loves a good joke like a Cuban. Dripping with sweat, discolored with layers of dust, the groups of musicians and dancers finally flopped to the ground. It was getting close to lunchtime and I felt a gnaw of hunger. Almost as if he read my mind, one of the Cubans jumped to his feet and with an impish look, asked, "You hungry?"

I smiled "Yeah!" This was great. Prison room service!

The Cuban ran off and returned a few moments later with a large can filled with a mixture of something that looked like run-over dead dog.

It was called *Golfio* and was actually crushed and ground wheat which was mixed with a little sugar and enough water to make it easy to swallow. It was a treat of the Cuban prisoners.

I took a long, thoughtful look at the offering and closing my eyes, finally took a mouthful. The assembled Cubans gleefully urged me to swallow and I managed to gulp the first bit down. And then someone gave me a sip of water to wash the stuff down. Now there was no stopping the Cubans. I was surrounded and slapped on the back and laughingly urged to devour the contents of the entire tin.

When I finished, the can was snatched away, and a moment later, it came back, filled to the brim once more, and was pushed into my hands. They wouldn't take no for an answer so I finished off the second batch.

When lunch came I couldn't move from the spot. I had absolutely no appetite. But after five days of total constipation I realized what had happened and when I finally succeeded was surrounded at the hole by a crowd of laughing, cheering prisoners. Needless to say, during my entire stay in Cuban, even when I was almost dead from hunger, I never again went for *Gofio.*

The first Spanish phrase the Cubans taught me was, *"No hay!"* There isn't any. A slender, timid Jamaican, serving time for some minor delinquency, became my translator. He told me the phrase, *"No hay,"* was the most used phrase in Cuba. "There isn't anything, Tony. No food, no clothes, and, most of all, no freedom!"

"Aw, come on!" I said. "You expect me to believe that? I've read the papers in the States and I've never seen anything about people here going hungry and all the rest of the stuff you're telling me. I've read just the opposite. So stop giving me that crap. Anytime somebody gets thrown in jail, it's always the government's fault. Sure, you guys are mad at the revolution; you're in jail."

Although sentenced to prison and angry and distressed, at this point I still refused to believe these stories. There was no way anyone could tell me the Cuban people were going hungry, that the revolution, Che's revolution, was a lie.

All of that first weekend the prisoners packed around me and drenched me with tales of hunger and horror.

"My brother and dad were executed because they opposed Fidel... All of my family is in prison, even my mother; they say we're counter-revolutionaries... They execute people every day here in Cuba, Tony... Our sisters and mothers have to be very careful when they come to visit us because the guards will rape them... Everybody except the bigwig goes hungry in Cuba..."

"They're lying, man," I told my Jamaican buddy. "Do they really think I'm going for that?"

The Jamaican, resignation in his eyes, replied, "They ain't lying, mon. They's telling the truth."

"Tony," a Cuban spoke in a low voice and lightly touched my shoulder. The Jamaican translated as I was swamped with questions.

"Yeah, what?"

"Where were you born?"

This would become a ritual that would open a question and answer period that would last until silence was called.

"San Bernardino, California," I replied wearily.

He listened in awe to the exotic name and I began.

"... Well, I was born in 1938 and the first thing I remember is living in an old raggedy house. I think the street we lived on was Dumas."

Other prisoners began to ease closer and squatted or stood nearby, moving in as others drifted up to hear the conversation. The dying sun painted the evening sky red, casting a glow over the group of listeners. It was story time.

"My mom and dad divorced and things were hard. Mom was doing maid's work or whatever she could get. My brother and me fought all the time. He was two years older. When I was old enough I went to a school on Waterman Avenue..."

"It's still there?"

"No. They tore it down. Now there's a gas station there. Every now and then my dad came to visit. You could tell it was him two blocks away. He'd start blowin' his horn, tearin' down the street and come to a screeching halt in a cloud of dust in front of the house.

"Mom would look out and say, 'Here comes that crazy nigger again. There's your crazy Daddy. Go out and see what he wants. I don't want him to set foot in this house!'

"My brother and I would go out to the car, and after talking a while, and casting longing looks toward the house, my dad would give us some loose change. Then he'd jump back into the car and with spinning tires disappear around the corner. But everything changed when Dad took Mom to court."

"Why did he do that?"

39

"Well, according to what my Mom told me, he swore he was gonna get even with her and I guess that's how he planned it."

"Hey, Tony! What kinda cars they got in the United States?"

"Hey, Callate! Shut up!" Growls of disapproval from the others. "Go on, Tony. Keep talking!"

"Well, he brought charges, said my mother was unfit. And after getting members of the church to testify to that, had my brother and me taken away from her. We were left standing one day on the sidewalk downtown and were picked up by my father. He had remarried and his new wife was nice. She really seemed to love us.

"We lived in a big wooden house with a front and back yard shaded by tall, walnut trees. It looked good on the outside but to my brother and me it was a living hell."

The barracks hushed. Every prisoner strained to hear.

"My dad used to beat us all the time, for anything, for no reason."

"Why'd he do that?"

"I don't know. Maybe he didn't like himself and we represented two more failures in his life. You know they went to church all the time, every night. And me and my brother, we'd sneak into the next room to listen to the radio on nights we weren't dragged along. We listened to the *Lone Ranger, The Shadow* and other shows that excited us. When we'd hear the car coming back, we'd snap the radio off, fly to our beds, jump in and pull the covers over our heads.

"Dad would come in, go straight to the radio and touch the tubes. Naturally they'd be hot. He'd go into a rage and come into our room, snatch the covers off and light into us with a leather belt, the kind men sharpened straight razors on. I was terrified of that man. Soon I began to hate him. My brother felt the same. Sometimes the beatings were so bad my stepmom would rush in and plead for him to stop."

The prisoners mumbled among themselves.

"Well, one evening my brother and I decided to run away and go back to mom. My father had us picked up at her home and soon the courts had us placed in Juvenile Hall until they decided which parents should have custody."

"Boy he was mean, that American," someone murmured, "How was it there in this... this hall?"

"It wasn't too bad, except I was just a little kid. It was strange to me; this big building filled with kids who were always fighting and tall, barbed-wire fences surrounding it. My brother was always being beaten up. I tried to be cool; but I was really just scared."

I told them of my first morning when a big, fat, red-faced official, Mr. Michaels, awakened me shouting "Ham 'n eggs!"

"You mean you had ham and eggs?"

"Not at all! That's just the way he woke us every morning. What we really had was cold cereal, toast and powered eggs. There were strange people there. One boy had large breasts and two sets of sex organs, male and female! We all tried to peep at him in the showers.

"The girls lived in the other side of the building. Sometimes they brought us together in the dining room to watch a movie. The girls would sit on one side of the tables and the boys on the other. All during the movie you'd hear girls saying, "Get your toe away!"

"After a few months I started gettin' mad. Here I was locked up for nothin'. I hadn't committed a crime. What was I doing here? So seven of us decided to escape. My fighting brother had already been sent to another detention center to keep us separated. A psychiatrist said we shouldn't live together..."

"Terrible," muttered a man I learned later had killed his wife.

"Anyway, we were gonna get out of there. So one night while the rest of the kids went to the recreation room, we seven remained in the dormitory, one of us in his cell. We had it all planned. Since all the guards, except one, went with the other kids, we only had to worry about overcoming this one man. We did it like we'd seen it done in the movies."

"Go on! Go on!" urged the listening prisoners.

"The kid in the cell began to moan like he was really sick. The guard came and opened the door and all seven of us pounced on him, gagged him, tied him up and grabbed the keys. We locked him in, then dashed down the long corridor to the back door. We climbed onto the roof of a shed close to the fence and, just as sirens began going off, disappeared over the top, jumping to freedom. That was my first escape..."

The day-long story telling served one good purpose. It kept me from thinking too much about my present troubles. I was in shock, but the boisterous, talkative Cubans refused to leave me alone with my thoughts. I saw right away that the camp had adopted me and it gave my spirits a lift.

"Don't go to work or you'll end up like this!" said the small Jamaican showing his hands. "When they tell you to go out with the crews, tell them you'll cut cane but will not pull up grass." His small, brown hands were sliced and deeply scarred. "You're an American, so they won't do anything to you. But once you start, they'll expect you to continue."

On Monday morning when the work crews were called out to go to the citrus groves, I remained in the barracks. The guards finally came and got me, and the Warden, with a worried look, used the Jamaican as his interpreter to find out what was wrong.

I answered with the phrase my buddy had taught me. *"Cana, si; yerbo, no."* 'I'll cut cane, but I won't pull grass'. It was the first glimpse of Tony, the rebel, and the Cuban prisoners loved it.

The guards scratched their heads and the Warden didn't know what to do. The carts filled with prisoners stood waiting. Production and discipline had broken down. I sat on the grass while the Warden held a hurried conference with his men.

He came back, leaned over and said, "You no work?"
"No."

The Warden ran his hand over his face and huddled again with the guards. He called the Jamaican over and sent word to me that I didn't have to work; all he wanted me to do was go and watch the others as they labored. Cool! I went.

They probably thought I'd be shamed into pitching in. But with the encouragement of all the prisoners not to work, I proved them wrong.

After a few days of witnessing aching backs and bleeding hands I made up my mind. "I ain't going for that noise!"

Actually, my rebellion in no way signified I had changed any of my views. It was an angry reaction to what I considered unfair treatment by the Cuban government. I felt I'd been used. I was a patsy, a political pawn, in spite of my revolutionary background.

Hernandez told me on the day of my transfer, "Various countries are accusing Cuba of giving aid to known criminals. To quiet them, you'll have to be sent to prison." So my first rebellious act was just to let them know I wasn't happy about being a scapegoat.

The weather grew colder, the days shorter and the nights longer. I was surprised one morning to find frost on the ground. Still, the prisoners were forced outside to be counted. If the count had seemed to take a long time before, now, in the biting chill of the morning air, it took forever. The first winter I spent in Cuba was recorded as one of the coldest in the island's history. My thin denim pants did nothing to keep out the freezing temperatures. Still the prisoners went to work each day to pull the ice-cold weeds from the near-frozen ground.

Since the barracks had no windows, the cold swept in and trespassed into every corner. I wore all the clothes I had been issued continually, even to bed: two pairs of pants, two shirts, two pairs of socks and any rags I could wrap around my head and hands. Finally, the mercury dropped so low the prisoners were counted wrapped in blankets with only an eye peeking out. The guards, clothed in heavy coats, took their time in making the count and still messed up.

Even though there was a sharp drop in temperature, the food remained the same: a few ounces of milk for breakfast, spaghetti and bread for lunch, rice and soup and maybe fish for dinner. The cold weather crushed the prisoner's spirits and as soon as we had eaten dinner, we dove into our blankets.

A few of the prisoners had been especially friendly to me. Pedro was one; a weasel-faced robber who shared small packages of food with me that his family brought on visits. He asked questions about the United States and finally our conversations touched upon the always-present thought in a prisoner's mind — *escape.*

Pedro was excited by the prospect and together we worked out a plan. He would have his family pay off one of the guards and together we would slip over the fence while the officer looked the other way.

The day before the planned escape, Pedro, waiting until I was alone, eased up to me and said, "Look, I got to talk to you." Speaking slowly and using myriad gestures he made me understand that he was a G-2 informant, a prisoner who worked for State Security hoping to reduce his sentence. The escape attempt, a set-up, would have resulted in my death.

"I can't do it, Tony," he explained. "At first I thought it would be easy, but I've come to know and respect you. Don't go over that fence tomorrow night. They'll be waiting to shoot you." Solemnly we shook hands and went to our bunks.

Still, I continued to fantasize about being taken out of prison. The officials in the camp kept my spirits up by telling me, *"Pronto! Pronto!"* Even the prisoners told me that I could be released any time.

Finally, it turned so cold the prisoners could not work in the fields. Everyone spent about twenty hours a day under the covers.

All during that long, cold winter, under the most adverse conditions, even in icy rain, the prisoners' families came to visit. Every Sunday they brought whatever they'd managed to accumulate to share with their loved ones.

Down the long twisting dirt road, the visitors came to sit for two or three hours, then, once again, they trudged back up the lonely path that led them away from their loved ones. After these visits, the prisoners would come by and give me a bit of happiness that had been brought to them. A small piece of meat, cookies, or maybe just a message: "My mom sends you love." I saw that there was a scarcity of food in Cuba and I wondered if the other things prisoners told me were true.

Finally, in late summer, I was allowed to join in the visits, held in a fenced-in area adjacent to the camp. It had cement slab tables and cement benches sheltered by thatched, umbrella-like tops. As I walked by the visiting families, I'd hear excited whispers. They viewed me with awe, and I knew it. *The Black Panther.* He hijacked an airplane. Alone! My chest stuck out and my back became ramrod stiff, especially when I passed different tables and people called out to me, *Commander!* Great, I thought, they think I'm a commander! When I understood Spanish better, I realized they were saying, *"Como anda?"* meaning, "How're you doing?" My ego sank like a rock.

Of course I had no visitors of my own. In my heart, as I watched the love of these families, I felt shame. Maybe I didn't deserve visitors. I'd used up that family love and wasted it.

I sat in the hot, Cuban sun and drifted back to winter, 1964, where the smoke-clouded Blue Mirror Club on San Francisco's Fillmore Street was filling with patrons. My small group, *The Modern Afro-Jazz Quartet,* was tuning up. Nervously, I ran my fingers over the keys of my flute and stepped up to the mike. The pianist, who had been a child prodigy a long time ago, tapped off the tempo and we swung into a driving blues called *Bags' Groove.*

My mother had forced me to begin trumpet lessons at seven. In time I got to like it and studied for a couple of years. Then I switched to the saxaphone. Over the years I would drop the sax then start up again with the horn. In Soledad prison I'd adopted the flute and now, in San Francisco, they called me the *Madman with a Flute.*

Between one-night stands, women and drugs, my married life was all but destroyed. On this night I was standing on stage, eyes closed, blowing my soul away, when I heard a sharp whisper from the piano player.

"Hey, man, your old lady just walked in."

I gave a nod of acknowledgement and, keeping my eyes closed, continued to play. I had just finished a blazing solo and was lowering the flute when someone pressed me in a frenetic embrace. I opened my mouth to protest and a writhing tongue snaked inside. As I struggled to free myself from the overzealous fan, I saw my wife stand, fling a furious look my way and rush from the nightclub. How do you explain things like this to your wife?

Or when I went to a beach party after work and unfortunately paired off with a pretty young thing who happened to be totally nude. Naturally, as I thought in those days, since we were on the beach, I might as well strip too. Nature did its thing and I lay back on a blanket after and slept. In the harsh dawn I discovered my mistress for the night and my clothes were both gone. I ended up going home draped in the blanket; I told my wife the tide had washed my clothes away. She looked across with anger-filled eyes and shook her head.

And then there were situations I never revealed to anyone:

I should have been thinking of my wife and child and getting ready to go home on the night a couple of women, one white, the other black, picked me up in a nightclub where I'd been playing a gig, and took me to a pad four blocks from Fillmore Street on the second floor of a large building.

Next morning I awakened to the smell of coffee, bacon and eggs. Only the black woman remained and she brought me breakfast in bed. After eating, I smoked a cigarette and smiled in contentment.

Then my friend of the night slipped from the room and returned a moment later with a large packet in her hands. She opened it, extracted a picture, showed me it and asked, "Do you know this person?"

The photo showed a thin, uniformed black soldier.

I took another look and shook my head.

"Look again," she urged, "Take a good look. You sure you don't know him?"

There was something vaguely familiar about the man in the picture but I slowly shook my head and handed it back.

"That's me!" she said.

"What?" I sat up, "What are you talking about?"

The tall, black woman clutched the snapshot nervously to her breast and said in a trembling voice, "Now don't get excited. I can explain everything."

"You sure better!" I cried, shoving the breakfast tray aside, flinging the covers back and grabbing for my pants.

"I'm the first black man in the United States to have my sex changed!"

"Oh no!" I gasped, falling back on my pillow. She went on to explain how it had taken a court order and all types of psychiatric recommendations to permit this *first*. I lay there dumbfounded. How do you explain this to your wife?...

The weather turned hot and again I began daily journeys to the worksite where I would seek out a patch of shade, sit and watch the other inmates work. One day a guard eased up to me and asked in broken English, "What you come to Cuba for?" Without waiting for an answer, he continued, "You *loco*. Everybody here want to go. You come. You be *loco*." Shaking his head, he walked away.

Finally ticked off in the worst way, I sat down and wrote a long letter to my old hero, Fidel Castro describing how my rights had been abused since my arrival in Cuba. Referring to my trial, I said, "Had I known that mockery was going to be made of justice in your courts, I would have defended, not only myself, but those institutions as well."

Evidently the letter wasn't appreciated. Shortly after, G-2 agents came and took me to Havana where I was interrogated thoroughly. Intelligence wanted to know what I thought of Cuban justice and life in Cuba generally. Since I knew nothing of Cuba and my attitude was being colored by the stories I was hearing and since my own trial had been such a farce, undoubtedly the answers I gave were not the ones they wanted to hear.

Because I continued to refuse to work I was no longer forced to go into the fields. Instead, I rebuilt a piano that had been almost ruined by exposure to the elements. It clanked and clanged but at least gave out a semblance of music. American music was prohibited. So the little bit I played and sang jetted me to undreamed heights of popularity.

A few months later, I noticed my hands were swollen. My face felt tight. My feet and legs felt puffy too. A couple of days went by and the swelling could no longer be ignored. My fingers wouldn't bend and my eyes were mere slits in a globe-like mask. There was no doctor in camp, only a prisoner who gave out aspirin when it was available and daubed Mercurochrome on cuts and burns.

By the sixth day, I was very ill. With every step I could feel fluid shake in my legs and currents shoot through my body. Since word had reached the camp of the deaths of two inmates in Havana Prison who had the same symptoms, the Warden decided that it was serious. I was taken to Camp Marquete, which had a prisoner-doctor. After giving me a detailed examination, he prescribed large doses of vitamins plus a special diet of whole milk, vegetables and meat. It looked good on paper, but that's where it remained.

I did receive a dozen vitamin injections, but the protein, milk and vegetables never reached the tin plate from which I ate. Nevertheless, the shots did help. The disease, whatever it was, went away.

When I was feeling better someone came into my life, a man who was to follow me and remain a mystery until the day I left Cuba. Rothrick Allen Brown was a muscular Jamaican bully who was widely believed by the prisoners to be working for G-2.

He claimed he had boarded an airliner filled with a Jamaican sports team and tried to leave Cuba. But, strangely enough, for a crime that usually carried a very long sentence or even death, he had only to serve one year. Naturally, no one trusted him.

He became my shadow. All he talked about was how terrible Cuba was and how much he wanted to leave and go home. Was he Jamaican or Cuban? Was he a political indigent or a clever G-2 agent? No one knew.

But the same clouds of suspicion hanging over Brown covered every prisoner in Cuba. The only person all inmates trusted and used to unload their grievances, doubts and fears, was me. Robert, the little Jamaican who had served as my interpreter when I first arrived, had since been released after serving seven years and I was happy for him. Before he left Robert told me, "You're a man now, Tony. But when you leave here you'll be a superman."

When I had been with the Black Panthers I'd studied Karate but when I began to teach prisoners a few of the moves, guards roughly hauled me to the Warden's office where I was told to back off. I was never to instruct anyone in martial arts and I was also forbidden to speak about Islam, a subject I'd touched on at various times.

At this time I met one of the most fascinating and beautiful women I'd ever known. Kenya was a mixture of an Indonesian-Hawaiian-Indian maiden straight from the cover of *South Pacific* and I quickly fell in love with her.

My weeks were filled with thoughts of this woman and I lived for the moment I would see her during weekend visits. She and her parents came to camp to see her brother. I wrote her a love song and let her know how I felt.

But one day, after the Sunday visit, Kenya's brother warned me, "Tony, I don't think you should see my sister again. You like her and she likes you. But she's a candidate for the *Young People's Communist Party* and if she associates with you they won't accept her." The last time I saw her, wind blowing a wisp of hair in her eyes, filled me with anger and depression.

During the last days of my stay at Guida, a huge hangar-like building was erected in back of the compound. A fence was thrown up around it and soon prisoners were seen changing shifts. Large, iron-spoked wheels for ox-drawn carts were being made there.

Security measures were not as stringent around the hangar-like building as they were at the compound and I decided to get a job. Escape was on my mind. At this time of year, early morning fog was a natural ally.

I still had not lost faith in the revolution. I was just anxious to show them I was sincere. My plan was to escape and then turn myself in. Maybe they would understand I was truly on their side. Somehow it made sense. They'd see my dedication to the cause. The escape would be my way of saying, "Enough! Now let's get down to business!"

After weeks of watching the guards' movements and having picked out a spot that was the least observed by them, I waited for the right weather.

When it came, I folded a small packet of sugar and a couple of pieces of bread into a package and shoved it into my pants. It was nice and foggy, a perfect day for escape. I waited at the gate for the guards to come and search me, wanting to be the first worker into the building.

I waited but no one came. No other prisoners showed up. Finally, a passing guard spotted my lone figure and asked, "What are you doing there?"

"Waiting to go to work."

He threw me a surprised look. "Get back to the barracks. Don't you know there is no work today? You are all going to be transferred to another camp tomorrow morning."

5.
MARQUETE

Transfer!

I'd been on a few, but none like this. The long caravan of tractor-pulled carts bulging with excited prisoners snaked over bumpy roads and a cloud of dust marked our passing. It was the beginning of June 1970, and high above us, Castro's sun beat down in fury.

My mouth was dry and full of dust. And, even though my body was being rocked and bumped from side to side and my ears bombarded by the squeaking of carts and shouting prisoners, my mind wandered back to another day and another transfer.

March 1961. We inmates of Vacaville Prison in California were quiet and subdued. After reading the long list taped to the wall, each of us returned to his bunk and dropped onto a pillow to wait. I'd be going to Soledad and was soon on my way.

With a clash of gears and a rising whine, the overflowing air-conditioned caged bus began its journey to one of American society's human warehouses over smooth, four-lane U.S. super highways. Cars filled with happy families passed by without a glance.

After twelve weeks in Vacaville's processing center to complete a battery of examinations and tests, I was ordered transferred to Soledad State Prison to serve out an indeterminate sentence of five years to life for armed robbery. I'd been arrested on

December 24, 1960, after robbing a combination drug/liquor store with two other guys. During the robbery one of my partners gunned down the other for leaving his post. We were very serious about such things. We fled, leaving our wounded former buddy on the sidewalk.

Police told him, "Talk or we'll let you bleed to death."

He was in shock and angry. Within moments he gave our identification to the San Francisco Police. At my apartment, I was surrounded by detectives aiming shotguns at me and arrested in front of my pregnant, hysterical wife.

I was never to forget the two and a half years I spent in one of the most convulsed penitentiaries in the United States. I was involved in a riot, saw stabbings, killings and came to know people like George Jackson and Black Panther leader Eldridge Cleaver. But anything I'd ever learned in Soledad meant nothing to me now. Cuban prisons were a whole new ballgame...

The clatter of the tractors died and as the dust settled I took a first look at Marquete. Ten-foot high barbed-wire fences and soaring gun towers gave it the appearance of a Siberian work camp. Dusty and sweaty, we were herded behind the camp's ugly stretch of wire and mesh. There was a mad dash for beds. As usual, it was first come, first served. I was lucky. My bunk had all its mattress wires intact.

The camp held 800 prisoners under maximum security. At night we were locked in the barracks and spent our days sitting around talking. There was no work to be done. No one was allowed outside the fence.

After a while, with nothing to do, the days grew long and monotonous. There were no books to read or study and no recreational facilities but there was a lot of excitement. Because for the least infraction of the rules, a beating was administered.

Marquete was the kingdom of a well-known warden, Brazo de Oro. Known as *the man with the golden arm,* he was famous for beating prisoners to bloody pulps. His guards were mean. Carrying clubs and World War II bayonets, they looked for any excuse to attack a prisoner.

And not only humans. One day a small dog wandered into the camp and was quickly adopted by the inmates. He was a sweet little fellow, about a foot long, tan, with a big black splotch over one eye and a stubby tail that blurred happily at the slightest hint of affection.

The prisoners tried to keep him away from the guards but inevitably he would cross their paths and snarl and bark. For some reason the puppy hated them. At these times the camp mascot, for that's what he had become, would run for his life. After a furious chase, and with the help of laughing prisoners, he'd be saved.

But one, warm, beautiful day, a guard caught the puppy alone. Terrified, our little friend froze in fear. With a triumphant shout, the man grabbed him by the neck and called out to some of his colleagues. They brought a rope and slipped it over the dog's head.

The prisoners watched in silence as our little mascot, howling and whimpering at every step, was dragged over the rocky ground. Every now and then the guards yanked on the rope, sending the puppy spinning in the air. They laughed as they pulled the choking animal into a field beside the camp.

Standing where they were sure the prisoners could observe their every move, the guards picked up a large rock... a crush of bones, a final protesting yelp, and it was done.

Just as cruelty was a way of life, the food at Marquete, rancid spaghetti, rotten fish and maggott-infested rice, was a daily ordeal.

Informing, the turning in of prisoners, was encouraged and rewarded. In prisons of almost all countries, the snitch must work in secret. But informers at Marquete operated completely in the open. They were protected to such an extent that anyone attacking them suffered terrible reprisals from the guards.

One of the most deadly was a tall, slender ferret-faced creature, Ortiz. Under the approving eye of this and other prison wardens, he'd formed a group of super snitches named after Russia's infamous one-time secret police, the Cheka.

Cheka had been an organization in Russia that struck terror and so did this Cuban carbon-copy group of cowards. Members thrived on the misery and blood of everyone around them. They preyed on the weak, the defenseless, and answered to no one except G-2 officials or the Warden, if he, himself, was not under *their* investigation.

Ortiz had the run of the camp and walked in and out when he wanted. He ate officers' food and could even take a jeep into town for a day or so. He had complete freedom. Woe to the prisoner who touched him.

I had already heard how, in 1968, at Principe Prison in Havana, several inmates had been executed and many others maimed for life after beatings by guards for killing three informers and stabbing several others. The reprisal was so severe that even the brother of one of the men executed went on to become an infamous snitch.

With all these conditions plaguing me, something else began to pull at my mind. The promises of an early release had proved false. I had tried to have complete faith, but now I began to have real doubts. The last time I had spoken with officials from G-2 they had sworn, "Tony, you'll be in jail for just two years. Have a little patience and when it's up, you'll be released."

But here it was Sunday, March 7, 1971, almost two years to the day since my arrival in Cuba and I was still in jail. I found myself wandering around the camp aimlessly, listening to the happy shouts of prisoners waiting for visits of their relatives.

I sat on the grass and maybe for the first time, really looked beyond the barbed wire at the rocky terrain surrounding the camp. To my right was a banana plantation; a little further out were thickets of sugar cane.

Groups of prisoners were being searched and taken through the gates to another fenced enclosure for their visits. I'd been sitting and thinking for a while when one of my Cuban acquaintances, *The Professor,* dropped down beside me.

"What's happening?" he asked in Spanish and offered me a

pull on one of his harsh-tasting Cuban cigarettes.

"Nothin," I answered, taking a drag. "Just looking."

For a few moments we sat in silence, staring past the barbed wire. Then the Professor, after a cautious look around, leaned over and whispered, "You wanna escape?"

I peered into his eyes, trying to read his mind. It was dangerous to say the wrong thing to the wrong person.

"When?" I asked cautiously.

"Today."

"How are you going to escape in broad daylight?"

"You aren't scared, are you?" Professor goaded.

"Naw," I muttered, not willing to admit fear to another prisoner.

"Then, listen, all we have to do is watch the guards in the tower and when we catch them looking the other way, we just run for the fence, climb over and we're gone."

"But they're going to shoot!"

Professor spat on the ground. "Those dogs couldn't hit their own bellies even with their guns stuck up their butts!"

My stomach tightened; I checked the guards in the tower. They seemed detached and impersonal. I knew they would shoot to kill; gunning down an escapee was worth a three-day pass.

"There's one more guy going with us," Professor added, "if you aren't scared!"

It was broad daylight. It made no sense. But I relented and replied with a sigh, "I'm ready when you are."

"Good man!" said Professor getting to his feet. "I'm going to get my partner."

I suspected they had chosen Sunday for escape because most of the guards would be in the visiting area overseeing prisoners and their families.

This left only the guards in the towers to control the camp. Maybe it wasn't such a bad idea after all. Anyway, it was better to die trying than wither away sitting behind the barbed wire doing nothing. The officials had told me that I would be in prison two years and my two years were up!

After a few minutes, Professor returned with his friend. We walked as close as we dared to the ten-foot high fence, casually strolled back and forth, and watched the guards' every move.

The gun towers were 200 yards apart and it was obvious we'd be caught in a crossfire if we managed to get over the fence. But the rebel in me washed out all preoccupation with life and death.

"Hold it!" Professor whispered. "One of the guards has his back turned! Get ready. I'll tell you when."

Now if only that guard remains like that until the other turns his head, we'll have a chance.

The moment seemed to last forever.

"Go!"

We raced over the thin stretch of 'No Man's Land', the Russian boots they'd issued me, sounding like thunder in my ears. I could see nothing except the fence which seemed to be always one step ahead of my feet.

I was surprised when I grabbed the first strands; there had been no shots, no sounds, only the squeak of wire protesting as we made our way upward. Then suddenly, a prisoner shouted, "Escape! Escape! — They're going over the fence!" A snitch was running to and fro shouting alarms. Immediately the air was filled with gunfire.

We reached the top strands and leaped into space. I hit the other side running. The angry buzz of hot lead tore holes in my sense of invincibility; a loud voice in my head screamed, "Fall! Fall!" I flung myself face down onto the earth. A fusillade of bullets ripped over my head. I lay there a second and then leaped up, running again. The firing had momentarily stopped. Now it renewed with fury.

Half way to the banana plantation I noticed the Professor was not with me. Throwing myself once more to the ground, I twisted around and looked back. He was laying beside a trench just outside the fence. I rose, and once again, under the savage fire of the guards, sprinted for the shelter of the banana trees. The other prisoner seemed to have gotten away. Now all the bullets were directed at me.

I managed to reach a small irrigation ditch. Out of breath, heart pounding, the sound of gunfire urging me on, I tried to leap across. I fell on the slippery rocks with a bone-wrenching thump. Floundering and totally exhausted, I started crawling, pulling myself over the ground.

Other guards from all over the camp surrounded the area. There would be no escape today. Realizing I had failed and knowing it was impossible to run, I raised myself to a sitting position and waited.

First to reach me was a tall, black man. His face twisted with hate, he stopped about ten yards away and raised his rifle.

The moment he fired I jerked to the right.

Instinct? Or was it something else? Death brushed my face in the form of powder burns that stung for days. Another guard, a white man, ran up and wrestled the gun from my would-be assassin.

Jerked to my feet, with a rifle digging into the small of my back, I was herded back to camp. I passed close to where my friend Professor lay and saw guards kicking and beating him with rifle butts. He was screaming in agony.

Couldn't God hear? "Maybe God sleeps over Cuba!" I whispered to myself.

Handcuffed, I was forced to sit on the ground outside the officers' quarters. I had to wait. The orders for my transfer, or punishment, had to come from higher up; I was an Americano.

Nine hours later at 1:00 a.m., I was hustled into an open truck packed with guards and began the long trip to one of Cuba's most dreaded prisons: *El Castillo de Principe,* The Castle of the Prince.

6.

EL CASTILLO DE PRINCIPE

After a long drive down dark highways and through vacant streets, the Russian truck ground up a steep incline to a gigantic structure that looked like an enchanted palace from *Grimms' Fairy Tales*. But there was nothing childish or imaginary about the hard-faced guards who swung the heavy steel gate open.

I was searched and left with only the clothes on my back. Then guards led me to the castle's punishment block. We passed dark, one-man, rat-infested cells, standing side by side like barred coffins.

It was impossible to see into them, but from time to time, in the dim glow of yellow light bulbs hanging in the corridor, I saw hands gripping the bars as though clinging to life itself.

I was not placed in one of those cells; instead, after turning corners and seemingly reversing direction, we arrived at a large cell, twenty feet square. This one was well lit. I was shoved inside and the door was locked behind me. Eighteen to twenty men were stretched out on the floor. Some were clad in shabby shorts, others in dirty clothing; all of them used their boots for pillows.

A powerful black, propped up on one arm, sleep in his eyes, shouted, "Make room! Move over there!" The men squeezed even closer to allow me a place to sit. It took only a few words before they all realized I was *Tony el Americano*, the one they'd heard about. The rest of the night was spent telling them about my ill-fated escape. It was my moment of fame and I basked in it. The tomorrows could handle themselves.

What was I doing here? Why me? An American with an African name belonged here. I'd met him on February 9th, 1969...

"Guns, man. We need guns!" The muscular, dark-skinned black peered earnestly into my eyes. *Kasavubu* was the code name he used in our life-and-death transactions. He had the look of a fanatic.

"It's easy to get rifles and crap like that. But we need heavy arms. And you know what? I got a great idea!"

"Tell me. I'll do anything to help. You know that!"

"There's this guy, this Cuban. He's a relative of Celia Sanchez."

"Who is she?"

"Fidel Castro's personal secretary and right hand, that's all. Hey man, what she says, goes!" His eyes were gleaming. "What we'll do is get the Cuban to write a letter of introduction. Then somebody'll go to Cuba and bring us back heavy arms."

"You mean go to Cuba?"

Kasavubu turned and looked at the crowds of university students moving from class to class. He took a deep breath and swung around studying me intently.

"You know something, *Kassim?* You came to the Black Panther Party and offered your services. You never failed to keep your head in hot spots. You always carried out every mission. Some of the guys are scared of you. But I know you're only dangerous to the enemy.

"You came here as a hit man, *Mr. Eliminator.* But you got more potential and intelligence than to waste yourself on that crap. Anybody can ice somebody. Something like what we got in mind takes a real cool head and steel nerves. You gotta be good for this job!"

Kasavubu was a fighter. He was a real man. And he gave me encouragement. I'd do anything for him.

"We been sufferin' long enough!" His voice grew deadly, "We gotta show these pigs we ready to go all the way. When they come to get us, they gotta come ready! We gonna bring revolution to Uncle Sam. You are the man to help start that revolution. We want you to go to Cuba."

"Me?"

"Shh, man. Keep your voice down. Look, come to the meetin' tonight at nine o'clock and we'll cut up what we got in mind. If you up to it they'll already know you comin'. The weapons are waitin'. All you gotta do is bring 'em back."

"How?"

"Through Mexico. It's already set up. The plan can't fail."

"How do I get to Cuba?"

"You hijack a plane. Castro will honor you with a medal!"

Kasavubu should have this honor, I'd thought on the long ride to Principe. I'd been tempted more than once to grab one of the guards' sub-machine guns and kill as many as I could before they got me. *Kasavubu* should be here with me. He's probably wearing a three-piece suit now, working as a pharmacist and using the perfect English he was capable of...

During those days of punishment I sweltered with my shirt over my nose and mouth, filtering out the stench around me. The toilet was a hole in the floor close to the wall with a small spigot two feet above it. To bathe, you had to squat over the fetid opening, inhaling noxious fumes, and dash water on yourself with a six ounce cup.

The food was horrible! Since the men didn't work, they were allotted only minimal rations. Breakfast was a half cup of thin, watery, powdered milk. Lunch was cold cornmeal mush. And rice, shark meat and a piece of bread was dinner.

After eight days I was taken out, marched across a large marble patio and led to a giant cell that resembled a cavern. It was called a *Company*. Company Sixteen was about eighty feet long and thirty across. Its oval ceiling was close to twenty feet high. A ten-foot high steel door stood at the front. To the rear, almost disappearing in the dimly-lit dome, was a barred vent. There were no other openings.

Rusty iron bunks, missing strands of wire as usual, were stacked six high and ran the length and width of the room. There were 230 men living here. Some slept on the floor in the rear where the toilet was. It consisted of two holes in the floor, one in which to defecate and the other for urinating. To get one of the precious bunks, I was told, cost anywhere from three to five hundred pesos!

I was recognized at once by Juan, a guy I'd known at Guida. He was in charge of the Company. Built like a small gorilla, he promptly threw some unfortunate out of his bunk and gave it to me. Juan labored under the impression that an American should not sleep on the floor.

The stink in the cell was awful. Since there was no toilet paper, we had to clean ourselves with newspaper or anything at hand and throw it into a fifty-gallon drum. It was almost impossible to pass by one of these huge cells and not be overcome by the putrid smell of unwashed bodies, urine and feces, spread in an airless enclosure.

A stranger in a foreign land, I was adopted by the prisoners and allowed to have a full cup of milk for breakfast. Everyone else got half. At lunch-time we lined up outside the building Indian-file and marched a hundred yards to the mess hall. Locked in, and under the guard's watchful eyes, we bolted down our daily fare, before being herded like animals back to the stinking Company.

There were ten of these massive cells. You would think serving food to so many men would take a lot of time. But with the meager meals and guards constantly beating machetes on tables forcing us to hurry, meal-time took less than fifteen minutes for each large group.

After having been in Principe for about a month, I was learning to lie back on my bunk and blank out the din created by two hundred voices in the concrete cave. The only time we were allowed out was for lunch and supper. We spent at least twenty-three hours a day locked behind the steel door, inhaling a stench that tainted flesh and soul.

Fights broke out constantly. Bottles were hurled. There was often an impromptu quiet followed by a scream, then the scuffle to wrench away a blood-stained knife before the attacker killed his victim. Sometimes it was too late. Buried alive... I was buried alive with 230 other zombies. And we were just a tiny corner of the total population. At this time, 1971, the walking dead of Principe added up to more than seven thousand.

Bedbugs! Millions of them infested the old building. There was no escaping them. They hid in the corners and seams of our ancient beds, in our clothes, along cracks in the floor, everywhere! They kept out of sight during the day, but at night, when we sought escape through sleep, armies of bedbugs sallied forth to destroy our only possible moments of peace. Their bite was ferocious and they grew sleek and fat on our blood.

The walls along both sides of the Company were stained crimson where thousand of bedbugs had been crushed. Every Sunday prisoners collected paper and bits of rag and torched the metal frames. Bedbugs crackled and popped.

Blood-fed flames and clouds of blue smoke spread a gagging stink. The floors and walls were washed down with precious water we could have used for bathing. But nothing worked. No matter how many methods we used, that very same night, from God knows where, they'd come again and we'd wake to their fiery bites.

The insects were bad but our main enemy was the guards. On one day which I'll never forget, we were being marched back to the Company from lunch, when a prisoner in front of me slipped from the line and ran to a nearby cell door for a bit of tobacco.

A guard, his face crimson with anger, ran up and began beating the inmate with a machete. The prisoner whirled around and crossed his arms in front of his face to ward off the rain of blows. Finally, in desperation, he lunged and grabbed the machete by its sharp blade.

The guard strained to free his weapon. Convinced he couldn't wrestle it from the prisoner's grasp, he released the machete, shoved the prisoner back, reached under his shirt and pulled out a pistol. Two shots exploded. There was a soggy thud accented by the clatter of the machete, and the prisoner fell face down on the concrete.

Principe was constantly rocked by violence. The small portion of hell I inhabited was no exception. In actual fact, Company Sixteen housed the 'tough guys'. At any time, day or night, I could hear pieces of metal being sharpened into instruments of death. Not a morning went by without a fight, sometimes two or three. Everyone was always in a bad mood in the morning. Who wouldn't be, after being torn from sleep by guards battering on the doors with iron bars?

Youngsters who incurred the wrath or disfavor of officials were thrown into Company Sixteen where only the strongest survived. In the dark of night, in the most obscure corners, we'd hear a child cry out, then a hoarse laugh and sounds of a futile struggle.

The raping of young boys in Principe was commonplace. And sometimes, if the kid fought too hard, he was killed, then raped *cold*. But once in a while rapes had surprise endings.

"My name is Leandro Razo Montalvo." The good-looking, light-skinned young man reached out and shook my hand. He was just seventeen, but we became friends at once. We had a lot in common. We both liked music, wrote poems and had pretty good singing voices.

Many nights, while the others sat around and applauded, we sang. Leandro had a penetrating, haunting voice. He was easily one of the most popular prisoners in the Company. With a tenth grade education, he was qualified to be a teacher in Cuba. He'd been sent to prison for a minor theft and had only eight months left of a three-year sentence. I felt more comfortable with Leandro than with any of the other prisoners. Together we sat around and laughed at the tragedy of our lives.

A few months after we'd met, we were separated. I was transferred to Company Five. I had to admit it was a little better, since it held only 150 to 180 prisoners. It had a back window with fresh air flowing through helping to blow the stink away. The actual conditions in *Five* were much the same as my former Company; the same blood-sucking bedbugs, daily fights and the same hours of captivity. But it was an improvement.

I'd been in my new home a week when I was awakened one night by screams, beds overturning and the slap of running feet. The tumult came from Company Sixteen, a short distance away. No one knew what was happening but, from the cries for first aid, something bad was going on. Next morning at breakfast news filtered in that Leandro, my buddy, had stabbed a man to death.

El Extrano, The Strange One, had tried to molest Leandro while my young friend slept. And so, next night Leandro drove a knife through the Strange One's chest. None of the prisoners blamed him. He'd done what any man would do; defended his honor.

Less than twenty-four hours later the prison rocked with fresh news of Leandro. Placed in the punishment section, Leandro, with one deadly thrust to the throat, had killed the brother of his victim of the night before. Leandro was becoming the talk of Principe.

Later, when prisoners discussed Leandro's double killing their voices dropped in awe and a circle of silence was formed by those standing nearby.

It was happening now. I rolled over in my bunk to listen. Leandro, my buddy, had been given a nickname that would become a legend in Cuba. My friend, the poet and teacher, gentle as a young girl, was now called, *El Pandeado,* The Curved Threat.

"It didn't happen like that!" said one of the prisoners.

"Aw shutup, man! I was there in the same Company!" said another.

"You jerk! You didn't move into the Company until later!"

But then a familiar voice broke in and I sat up with interest.

"I was sleeping by the Strange One that night," said a thin, dark-haired pot-bellied white. A heavy scar crossed his face. Because of his chiseled features which resembled a famous American Indian, he was known throughout the prison as *Crazy Horse*. If anyone had inside information on the double murders it would be Crazy Horse. He was a snitch and extremely dangerous.

The hoarse voice rumbled on, "Pandeado was asleep and everyone knows why they called Extrano, the Strange One." Laughter. He continued, "The creep thought the kid could be turned and decided to go after him, wooing him like a woman.

"One night, as the boy slept, he sneaked over and began to rub his young body." Growls of disapproval.

"You could understand his mistake. Pandeado is a good looking kid and he seems to be soft. He didn't wake up but next morning a friend told him he'd been attacked in his sleep and at that moment, Pandeado turned killer.

"He started asking everybody for a knife. Finally he got one. Everybody, including the guards, knew he had it."

"Why didn't they take the kid out, transfer him to another building?" someone demanded.

Crazy Horse rolled his eyes and shrugged. He knew what everyone else knew, that The Strange One had been allowed to die. Prison officials didn't care.

"Anyway, that night Pandeado reached under his mattress, pulled out a long knife and crept over to Extrano. I woke up just in time to see the knife plunging down and got a look into Pandeado's eyes. They scared me. That body must have jumped two feet.

"Now, here's how he killed Extrano's brother. The man somehow slipped into the punishment block where they were holding the kid. He was coming to revenge his brother. But overnight Pandeado had become a hunter. Nobody would ever catch him off guard again.

"Pandeado spotted him, waited until he got closer, than pulled out another knife and whapped him, killed him dead!"

"Know something strange," mused Crazy Horse, "Pandeado was born under a bad sign. He'll never get out of prison. You see,

Pandeado's mama couldn't make it to the hospital in time. She was standing in the street about to have him when a police car came by. Pandeado was born on the seat of a police car. They gave him life and they're going to be the ones to take it away."

For most of us, life dragged on as usual that long, hot summer of 1971. Without fail, almost every afternoon the sky darkened and gusty winds announced the coming deluge. Lightning split the clouds and high upon a hill overlooking Havana, the walls of Principe shook to crashing thunder. Hissing rain in Seven League boots, swept the city.

Inside the *Prince's Castle* we scrambled to push bunks away from the cell's two openings. The cloudbursts always lasted about fifteen minutes but it took us an hour to mop the flooded floor. While outside, under the glaring sun, it took just a few minutes for the entire city to become dry and dusty again.

On one of these burning summer days I became an unwilling participant in a bizarre spectacle. It began an hour after dinner when the first pains streaked through my stomach. I noticed unusual activity around our small toilet hole in the floor.

I'd been talking with friends when suddenly my stomach was wrenched by a sharp pain. A cold sweat broke out across my face. I thought back to the strange-looking meat we'd been served a few hours earlier. Even boiled, it smelled.

The pains became intense. Hands inside me tore at my guts. My body convulsing, I grabbed a piece of newspaper and ran for the hole, pulling my pants down on the way.

From all around me came cries and moans, and sounds of agonized bowels. Within minutes dozens of men were violently ill. Prisoners stood at the cell door yelling for the medic. One of prison's most dreaded epidemics had struck: dysentary!

There was no way to hold it back. Prisoners let go anywhere but tried to get as close to the hole as possible. I was quickly pushed aside.

A scuffle broke out between two men who arrived at the hole

at the same time. While they struggled, a third party, determined look in his eyes, darted around them and perched gratefully.

It seemed like days, but within hours the prison administration went into action. Trustees arrived with large washtubs, filled with a chalky mixture and ladled it out to each victim.

Hundreds of arms thrust through the bars holding old, bent-up cups, tin cans, bottles, anything. The ten buildings were filled with anguish.

Just as the food, the water and even the sun were rationed, so was the medicine, and it was virtually worthless. I made trip after trip to the hole, now overflowing.

The guards laughed and held their noses as they passed by the stinking masses inside. They were safe. They didn't eat our food.

El Principe was divided into three levels; a lower at the bottom of the hill, a central where I lived and an upper at the top of the hill where the hospital was located. Except for a few inmates, every one of our seven thousand prisoners was stricken. But we survived.

I had other problems that summer. During the day I baked in the heat and at night, because of a new plague — mosquitos, I was forced to wrap myself in a thin blanket and sweltered even more. Between mosquitoes and bedbugs, my body, like those of the rest of the prisoners, appeared to have been struck by the pox.

During those long nights in late September I began to look back over my life in search of answers. I felt I would be in prison for a long time and knew if I didn't face myself now in this crisis, I would be lost.

Who was I?

A psychiatrist at Vacaville Medical Facility in California thought he knew.

"Mr. Bryant, you are a manipulator," he had said.

I smiled.

"You have a tremendous personality; magnetic and charming. You make people like you. Then you use them. Yes, you are a manipulator."

I smiled.

He peered directly into my eyes.

"But that isn't what worries me. The only thing that really bothers me," he paused, "is your smile. I keep asking myself what will happen when Tony Bryant stops smiling?"

I hadn't smiled during my first armed robbery in a San Francisco service station. I'd frowned and pulled the trigger. The shotgun's buck and roar was followed by the shocked scream of the attendant as his legs blew out from under him....

I smiled.

The white girl lay naked and unconscious on the filthy sheet. A squirming trickle of blood shot up into the eyedropper. The needle attached to it plunged into my vein. I frowned and slowly squeezed the bulb. The heroin hit instantly. I nodded and the corners of my lips twisted...

I smiled.

Who was I?

What compelled me to rob, to use drugs, to rebel?

From my childhood, completely destroyed by the violent separation of my parents, I'd felt unsure of myself and everyone around me. I blamed everyone else and mainly my father for my unstable world. I began to hate him. Deep within, subconsciously perhaps, I wanted to destroy him. Ultimately, any authority was a substitute for that hated figurehead.

A needle in my vein, the shootings, the striking out at everything was my way of hurting the man who shaped me in that bitter world.

It was during those long nights in Principe that I finally identified what had driven me so relentlessly — hate!

I began to see myself in a new light. And started studying those who stood between me and freedom — the Communist guards!

They beat prisoners without mercy, murdered in cold blood and took advantage of the weak, forcing them into homosexual activities.

What was the difference between what I had been and what

they were now? Simply that I had acted alone against the law while they acted together within a law created to control or destroy.

I had been supported by one or two bandits. The guards acted with the full complicity of a government. I had acted outside the system. But they were part of an order whose banner insisted *The end justifies the means.* I had been a lawbreaker. But the guards surrounding me stood above all law.

About this time I began to hear stories of another group of prisoners who were rarely seen. They were kept in special sections under extremely heavy guard. They were Cuba's worst: inmates who had committed crimes against the State; political prisoners.

I listened for hours while inmates recounted the rise of Fidel Castro and his revolutionary government. Those who opposed the foreign ideology, Communism, faced execution, imprisonment or exile.

Names like Tony Cuesta, Tomy Lamas de la Torre, Eloy Menoyo, Ernesto Diaz and many others became familiar to me. To the majority of the prison population, these men were demigods. They were the tough ones. The ones who resisted.

I was impressed. What gave them the strength to resist without the possibility of victory? What gave them the fortitude to stand tall, walk straight and command the respect of their countrymen including the mad dog guards?

I had seen one or two of them being escorted to the hospital. They were always heavily guarded and the entire prison population pressed forward just to get a glimpse of these supermen. They seemed to have something I needed — respect. I began to emulate them and soon felt better about myself. My life and even my luck began to change.

The dispensary was short-handed. I volunteered and got a job. It was located in the huge patio facing the *Companies.* I learned simple suturing, how to give shots, and other first aid. For the first time in my life I was doing something useful.

The hours were long but I enjoyed my job. It was a chance to escape the poisonous air of the overcrowded Company. Even more important, it gave me the opportunity to see and treat dozens of injuries each week inflicted on prisoners who had been stabbed or beaten by guards.

It was one thing to hear of beatings and abuse and quite another to attempt, first hand, to staunch hot blood flowing from a split skull. I was sickened by the constant woundings but I tried never to let my disgust show.

I cleansed wounds, sutured and bandaged them and then made out accident reports. I was sorry for the victims. No matter that a prisoner's body was crisscrossed with cuts or that the guards bringing him to me carried bloody machetes; when I asked "How did it happen?" the answer was always the same, "I fell out of bed." To say anything else meant a worse beating and a month or two in the Hole.

To complain to the Warden or any other official was useless. They all worked together. At least fifty percent of all prison accident reports carried the four words: "He fell from bed."

Working in the infirmary also gave me my long hoped for opportunity to sneak into the hospital section reserved for political prisoners only. Using the pretext of delivering medicine, I smuggled myself into a tiny ward where about twenty inmates lay sandwiched together. Most of them had heard about me. They greeted me warmly and one of them led me from bed to bed, introducing me to the occupants.

Finally, I was led to a man who towered well over six feet. His left arm ended in a nub a little below the elbow; when he stood extending his right hand in a direction other than where I stood waiting, I was shaken. I realized then that the muscular, Roman-nosed man was blind.

My guide said, "Tony, I want you to meet your *Tocayo!*" In Spanish *Tocayo* is any two people having the same first name.

The smiling figure facing me was the legendary Antonio Cuesta, hero of dozens of battles. Tony Cuesta's life was like something out of Soldier of Fortune Magazine. His face and arms were marked by tiny blue pocks. Across his stomach ran a jagged scar.

I grasped his hand and said, "Is there anything I can do for you?"

Cuesta hesitated. I represented all he had fought against for so long and with such grievous results. But there must have been something in my voice that caused him to reply, "Yes, there is something. I lost my comb. See if you can get me one. Think you can?"

Cuesta knew that by asking me for a favor, even a tiny one, he was also extending his friendship. It was the beginning of a brotherhood that has lasted throughout the years.

I would sneak by whenever I could to visit the prisoners. But, of them all, it was Tony Cuesta who received the greatest portion of my time. We sat and talked about the U.S., politics, girls, everything. But these visits ended abruptly one day.

I had gone up to visit Cuesta. Upon entering the door, I was struck by the sight of Tony with all his belongings packed, sitting in a straight-backed chair and wearing a tight, hard face. He was demanding to be taken to where the political prisoners were, out of the hospital. He was on strike! They took him away.

Carbon copy days and nights rolled by. The same filth, the same smells, the same faces, the same screams of luckless prisoners being beaten. The same pounding of feet rushing the wounded in to be sewn up, bandaged and sent back into the monster's belly.

The end of October 1971, brought chilly nights. Stars studded the ink-black void stretching over Principe. Cold wind snapped, bit and slithered through the buildings like an invisible monster.

It was my good fortune to be working nights and thus I could catch vermin-free naps during the day. The awful things only came out to bite you at night. And so, I was wide awake one night in December when a prisoner faking an asthma attack rushed in and whispered,

"The Captain of the *Johny Express* is here."

"Where?"

"Right over there in that room." He pointed to a small cubicle which was supposed to be used for classes that never took place.

My pulse quickened. I wanted to see this man. Everyone in Cuba had heard the news about a mystery boat, the Johny Express, and how Cuban gunships had entered International waters to 'capture' it after it left the U.S. mainland flying a Panamanian flag. This was the Johny Express. Was it a spy boat?

A gust of cold wind whipped back my tunic and identified me as a medic. I angled across the patio heading towards the special room. The 'asthmatic' patient had been right. Lights flooded through openings around the door and from inside came voices and movement. The place would be filled with G-2 agents. They wouldn't take my intrusion lightly. But this was important.

I took a deep breath, twisted the knob and stepped inside. An immediate silence fell. A dozen G-2 agents were scattered around the room. Standing at its extreme end was a fiesty-looking grey-haired man of about five-feet, six inches. He probably weighed a hundred and forty pounds soaking wet.

Every eye was locked on me. The surprise was total. All the G-2 agents were struck dumb. Before anyone could react, I strode across the room, extended my hand, grasped the wary-eyed Captain's and quickly introduced myself as an American.

"Well, it's a pleasure to meet you too, Tony, even under these cussed conditions." said the captain of the Johny Express. "But you know son, a man's got to be ready for anything. Know what I mean? I was in the Second World War and I always say if you can't stand bullets don't go on the battlefield."

The agents had been in a trance. The American captain gave my hand a final pump. Now they sprang alive, leaped between us and roughly pushed me to the door.

"Hey, man, don't shove! No need to be rude! I didn't know you were using this room... Hey! Be cool man, I didn't know you all were in here." I was booted, protesting all the way, through the door.

I caught a glimpse of the face of the captain of the Johnny Express. He was smiling. I'd been lucky. I never did find out what happened to the American or his boat but, I hadn't been beaten or thrown in the Hole. I'd met the mysterious American and also had the chance to practice a lesson taught by Tony Cuesta.

"Don't surrender. But, if you do get captured, harass the enemy. Never give him a moment's rest. Molest him, disturb him and when possible, eliminate him."

I was lying in my bed thinking of the American captain and wondering what had happened to him. I was catching bedbugs and squashing them against the wall, when I heard a prisoner moving from Company to Company shouting out names. The walking loudspeaker, beating a padlock against the bars, was met with a volley of curses from the startled, sleepy-eyed prisoners inside.

"*Yo me escupo en la caravela de la madre de Fidel Castro.*" shouted an anonymous prisoner. "Aw, shut up, you sons of the gutter," replied the loudspeaker.

Penguino was his nickname. He had feet pointing in opposite directions resembling, when he walked, that Antarctic bird for which he was named. With a piercing cry he began calling out a long list of names.

The first few names were lost in the conflicting shouts, but upon realizing what Penguino was doing, the prisoners' voices, along with all movement, settled to an expectant hush. After reading many names, including mine, Penguino stood back and with a broad grin, bellowed out, "Load up... you're going to camp!"

Pandemonium broke out. This was the moment for which every prisoner in Principe or any other maximum security prison in Cuba waited, the chance to cut sugar cane. Here was an opportunity to feel the sun, the wind, soft grass and warm earth so longed for in this concrete jungle, a chance to view the entire sky, not just a square distorted by cold steel bars. It was also for many, a chance to escape, or to make the attempt. But most of all it was a change, a relief.

An hour later hundreds of us stood in the patio talking excitedly. Hundreds upon hundreds of names were called until well over a thousand men stood in the expansive patio. We were herded onto tractor-pulled cattle carts, and under the cover of night, driven to the interior of Cuba.

Five hours later we arrived at Aguica labor camp which rose from the ground like an electrical hell. So many lights crowded around the barbed-wire fence that night was turned to day; and two rows of machete-armed guards facing each other formed a long path from the road all the way to a warehouse where we were to be strip-searched.

What was this? A chill swept over me. I didn't like the look of my new home. A feeling of death hung in the air!

7.
INTRODUCTION TO TERROR

A scarfaced lieutenant in pressed uniform and shined boots, sharp fatigue cap pulled low over his eyes, walked slowly toward the first cart, shouting, "If you think you're here to kill time, get it out of your head. We're here to make you work or kill you."

He strolled back and forth in front of the carts.

"If you're lazy, you'll either spend most of your time in the hospital or in the Hole! You're here to work and that's what you're going to do. Now, when I call your name, you get off that cart running!"

The guards forming the gauntlet slapped their machetes against their legs and leaned forward with excitement; you could almost hear their anticipation. Perhaps it was the look on their faces, the way their eyes gleamed or the crouch of their bodies, like animals waiting to fall upon helpless prey, that gave them the form of a silent growl. A guard began to call out names.

"Run! Run! Run! Go! Run!" the lieutenant shouted.

The crack of machetes on the backs of the men fleeing between the two rows of guards was unforgettable.

"Run! Run! Dammit, run!"

My soul hardened. The ever-present rebel in me flared up again. I thought: Well, get ready to fight. I'm not running for him or any other Cuban dog!

The man calling out the list stumbled over my name. With my bundle thrown over my back, I stepped down from the cart.

"Run!" the lieutenant screamed.

Without a glance at him, I began to walk casually toward the long lines of guards. The guards stared in disbelief at the insolent black man; then roared in a collective shout. A slave had disobeyed its master. Like wild hunting dogs, those nearest rushed to punish the defiant one.

The soldier who had called my name raised his hand and the pack came to a halt. "What's your name?" he growled.

I straightened and in my clearest California accent answered, "Anthony Garnet Bryant."

"What? What?" The guard leaned forward trying to identify the strange sounding consonants. I repeated my name. "Where are you from?"

"The United States of America."

It was as though Moses had again smote the water with his rod. Before the magic of the name, the two ranks of guards fell back. The guard with the list stared at me as though I might have arrived from another planet. Then, catching himself, he said gruffly, "Go on through."

I sauntered along between the two lines of guards and into the warehouse where the beaten prisoners were being strip-searched. The renewed sounds of machetes on defenseless backs filled the air behind me.

In search for contraband, bars of soap were being cut in half. I had a five peso note in the carved-out center of a bar of lye soap. I wondered what they would do if they found it.

Another prisoner had done the same thing and was turned over to an ape-like guard with massive hands. Without a word the prisoner was smashed to the ground. In full view of everyone he was forced to disrobe and beaten all the way to a low, cement structure... *the Hole*. Although it was late October and frost covered the ground, the flinty-eyed Warden took three buckets of cold water and doused the prisoner. He left the man in a freezing puddle and locked the door.

They found my money, too. But the status, it seemed, of being a black American saved me from a similar fate.

Why did they treat me differently?

Was it because I was black, American or both?

Already I'd seen that the majority of prisoners were black, so there had to be another reason. Something gnawed at the back of my mind. Some piece to the puzzle was trying to fall into place.

The forced labor camp of Aguica was located in the province of Matanzas. High hurricane fences topped with rolls of barbed wire surrounded a pair of buildings that housed up to a thousand men. Guard towers located at strategic points made the already sombre scene even uglier.

The next morning, thankfully sipping my ration of hot milk, I allowed my eyes to wander over to the small cement box that had swallowed up the badly beaten prisoner the night before and still held him. The shudder that ran through my body had nothing to do with the low temperature.

"Hey, Tony! Buenas dias!"

"Buenas dias!" I replied, swinging around to face a buddy. We turned and, conversing guardedly, ambled back toward the barracks.

"You see that walkway from the barracks to the dispensary?" asked my companion.

"Yeah. What about it?"

"Well, if you look close, you'll see a red marker somewhere alongside. Look! There it is!"

A very small triangular shaped flag attached to a stick in the ground was about halfway between the barracks and the dispensary.

My friend shot a wary look toward the gun towers and, though no one could hear him, lowered his voice, "If you ever have to go to the dispensary, always be careful to see where the flag is. See? They move it every day or so. If you step past it without getting the okay from the guard in the tower, he'll shoot you."

"What!" I exclaimed.

"Oh, but don't worry," the Cuban blurted out. Placing a reassuring hand on my shoulder while nervously glancing around, he added, "They don't try to kill you. They always aim for your legs!"

The tip of the sun peeping over the horizon slowly painted gently swaying palm trees. Farther away, low rolling hills took on discrete crimson hues. The air tasted fresh and clean. I hurried to join the long line of prisoners; after being searched to make certain no one carried tobacco or matches, we were herded into tractor-pulled carts in which armed guards sat.

The caravan of shouting prisoners then bumped over a dirt road which led to the highway. A thirty-minute ride and the tractors pulled off the main road onto a patch that took us into a seemingly endless expanse of sugar cane. While the prisoners sat in the carts, the area to be worked was surrounded by guards. As your name was called, you descended from the cart. After being lined up and recounted, then and there, the inmates were issued machetes and assigned a long row of cane as the day's quota.

The camp foreman, astride a spirited horse and wearing a ten-gallon hat, patrolled the area constantly to insure the maximum effort. Soon the morning air resounded with crisp whacks and thuds.

I paused and stared at the evil blade in my hand. I took a light swing at a cane stalk. The machete passed through it like a hot knife through soft butter. Hey, man, I thought, this thing is dangerous. These fools must be crazy if they think I'm going to go swinging this sword around; I'll probably cut my own head off! I sank deep in thought for a moment, then a bright idea flashed across my mind.

Since sugar cane was one of Cuba's principal exports, and a chief source of foreign revenue, cutting of the cane was high priority. Throughout the sugar cane season, Cuban radio and television stressed the importance of getting the most out of each stalk. The people were urged to cut the cane as close to the ground as possible.

With an impish gleam in my eye, I took a firm grip on the

machete and lit into Cuba's economy. Standing straight, I began moving down the row. Hardly glancing at the cane, I began slashing left, right, left, right. Cane stalks flew like seeds being thrown through the air by a madman. Ten minutes passed and, quite naturally, I had outdistanced my nearest competitor by a country mile.

Suddenly, across the field at a dead gallop, clutching desperately at his ten-gallon hat, came the foreman. He brought the horse to a sliding halt near me. Eyes bulging at the catastrophe I had wrought, he choked out, "No, no, no! Americano, no!"

A long line of tall stumps jutting out of the earth marked my passing. I stopped with a quizzical, innocent look on my face and said, "*Que pasa?* What's wrong. I'm doin' okay, ain't I?"

Wringing his hat and only daring to observe the cane massacre from the corner of his eye, the foreman fought to control himself. "Look, *Americano*. Don't cut another stalk. You hear? Not one more stalk! You go find a place to sit and stay there. Do you understand? Stay!"

I allowed a hurt look to cloud my face; then, in an indignant voice said, "Okay, if you don't want me to cut cane, I won't!"

As the foreman rode away shaking his head, I heard him mumbling something about *"Bel ladron de azucar."* The sugar thief had struck!

Lunchtime found me sitting at the foot of a tree chewing stalks of sugar cane. As I watched the sweaty, dirt-encrusted men lower their aching bodies to the ground, I knew I had made the right move.

"Hey, *Americano,* what happened?"

"They fired me!" I replied with a grin.

The men burst into laughter. For weeks after, they recounted over and over again how *Tony el Americano* had beaten the system.

During my stay in Aguica, I asked questions about the country which Fidel Castro declared as *The First Free Territory of America*. Before the onslaught of personal testimonies by the prisoners, the myths of that *free* territory began to crumble. The inmates seemed to sense that here with them was a man who would someday take the awesome truth of 'The Cuban Experience' to the *Outside World.* They never missed a chance to explain to me what they thought I should know.

They all agreed Fidel Castro was a highly intelligent man, that he hated his own people and that he was the biggest liar alive. They all wished to see him overthrown.

"But I thought the majority of the Cuban people stood with Fidel!" I argued.

Patiently they explained that this had been true back in the early 1960's when the masses believed he was their liberator. But as time passed and murder, destruction, and abuse of the population became the norm, they began to see him for what he was, a crazed killer! Almost all of the people blamed Kennedy's betrayal of the Bay of Pigs invaders as being one of the prime causes for Fidel Castro's being in power. They referred to Fidel Castro as *The Mare*, possibly because of the tale that he had only one testicle.

Late at night, while the others slept, I stared up at the dimly-lit ceiling, pondering the things I had been told. From the many prisoner-abuses I had witnessed, I could not find room to doubt their stories. If just a few men had made the same accusations about the scarcity of food, for instance, or the brutal murders cloaked in courtroom jurisprudence carried out around Cuba, I would have had doubts. But when ninety-nine percent of those I met repeated the same tales of terror, hunger and debasement, I had to accept the allegations as truths.

For example, I had yet to meet a man who did not agree that Raul Castro was a blood-lusting homosexual. Not one! They told me the story of how, after the triumph of the revolution, Raul began to have so many men executed by the firing squad that even Fidel became upset and ordered him to shed no more blood. So freaky, little Raul began to have the prisoners hanged.

I remembered the first prison work camp I'd been sent to in Cuba, Guida, and the Warden who seemed terrified when G-2 agents delivered me. Now I realized why his hands had trembled.

He was another Cuban victim of terror. Fear is a necessary tool under any dictatorship. Only terror can make the wishes of a few the will of the masses. It had taken me years to learn how Cuba had been reduced to malignant fear.

When the revolution triumphed in 1959 positions of power in the new government were naturally taken by those who had fought, sacrificed and shed blood. They had earned their positions and made decisions of policy based on what they felt was right.

But this didn't sit well with Fidel Castro. He intended to have absolute rule and power and become Cuba's only voice. A slow, weeding out process of people in high places began. They were replaced by others who had never fired a gun but who could be controlled. Mysterious accidents and trumped up charges were used against strong-willed revolutionary leaders and they were replaced with pliable civil servants.

Many of those original leaders who had been replaced without execution explained phase two of Castro's post revolution to me years later as we sat and rotted in his prisons. The civil servants were at first loyal to money but Castro wanted to control them by other, less costly means.

A reign of terror in government began, a campaign of infiltration by G-2 agents who inserted themselves into Cuba's work force. From menial factory jobs to the highest positions in government, they sowed dissension, unrest, suspicion and destroyed trust and faith.

An agent would strike up a conversation with someone like a warehouse chief and with whispers and furtive glances, denounce Fidel Castro or the revolution. If the tested man agreed, he would be arrested, tried and publicly executed. If he didn't denounce the defamer he'd lose his job. Soon Cubans distrusted one another and life-long friends betrayed one another.

To cause complete social and moral breakdown, Castro next began to control the food supply with ration cards. As rations decreased, there was a mad scramble for positions that promised food. Hunger forced betrayals never imagined. Loyalty disappeared. Children were taught not to trust brothers and sisters. In his final consolidation of power, Castro eliminated people like Che Guevara and Camilio Cienfuegos to become Cuba's only spokesman, policy-maker and god.

I realized later the camp official trembled because he didn't know if he'd been denounced and the agents had come to take him away. A thousand thoughts must have flashed through his mind. Had he done or said the wrong thing? Had they found out some of the prisoners' food was being sold on the black market? No wonder he had been terrified and had sat nervously in his chair studying me for long after the G-2 agents left. I was learning a lot about the Castro system.

Almost every Cuban I met throughout my time in Castro's prisons felt the same way about the Russians who occupied their country. "They stink! Tony, they must never bathe. You can smell them a yard away." As for propaganda that the Communists were mankind's saviors and that they were concerned about what happened to other people, the prisoners gave this simple rebuttal: "If the Russian Communists murdered their own people by the millions, how could they love or care about foreigners?"

So I learned, and my attitudes, like my job, changed. I didn't have to cut cane; I became the medic for the workers in the field.

"Medic! Medic! Americano, urgente!" The cry was taken up by every man in the cane field. I snatched up the small first-aid kit, and shielding my face with one arm, stumbled through the cane in the direction of the excited voices. "Where is he? Where's the hurt one?"

"Over there, hurry!"

I elbowed my way through the cluster of cane-cutters to a frail prisoner. His face was white as a sheet and the bony hands clutching his thigh in a tourniquet-like grasp resembled dirty marble.

The man's machete had glanced off a slippery stalk and

embedded itself in his tough Russian boot. "No, no, don't touch it!" The terrified prisoner screamed as I dropped to my knees.

Although dreading what I might see, I had to remove the machete. "Now just take it easy. I'm going to try not to hurt you, but I've got to see the wound, so stop acting like a sissy." That always got a positive response. Being true *macho* no Cuban man wishes to be considered less than a combination of Casanova, James Bond and Superman.

"Up your..."

"Shut up," I growled as I gave a tug on the machete. The blade came free.

The man blanched and fell back.

Prepared to see a gush of blood, I unlaced the boot and slipped it off. Nothing, not even a drop. The machete had gone through the top of the boot and nestled itself between the two large toes of the man's foot. Only a tiny scratch marred the skin.

An explosion of relieved laughter went up from the on-looking prisoners. The wounded man, peeping through one eye to see the joke, was struck in the stomach by his destroyed boot as one of the prisoners threw it at him. He was jeered to his feet by the others and given solid kicks in the rear by his happy friends.

"What a life," I groaned, picking up my kit and heading back to my resting spot. I had no sooner settled myself on a mat of leaves when the dry cough of rifle fire snatched me to my feet.

Grabbing the first-aid kit, I ran back to the clearing. There, under a shower of blows, the prisoners were being forced to lie on the ground. I too was ordered to get down. Turning to face a wide-eyed man sprawled alongside me, I asked, "What happened?"

"Escape," was the tense reply.

One of the prisoners had taken advantage of the momentary distraction caused by the machete-struck boot and had slipped into an adjacent field. A guard had spotted him and now search-and-capture proceedings were underway.

While two submachine gun-armed guards stood watch over the

men stretched on the ground, the other fifteen or so began fanning out on all sides of the area where the would-be escapee had disappeared. The foreman, dashing up and down on his mount, shouted out clipped orders. The trap was set. The example given was to be short and brutal.

On three sides of the squared area, the guards lay on the ground with their guns pointed toward the field. Three others, walking abreast, about five yards apart, began advancing into the dense vegetation raking the area with submachine gun fire. If the prisoner attempted to escape the fusillade by running out on any of the other three sides of the field, he would be shot down. To stand and even attempt to find a possible exit was to be exposed to the spray of bullets of the advancing guards. Very simple, very efficient, and very deadly!

The cry of "Don't shoot! Don't shoot!" was heard almost immediately. Shortly, screams filled the air as the crack of machetes on human flesh sounded. The beating seemed to last forever. Then, a momentary quiet swept the area only to be broken again by the clatter of hoofbeats.

I turned my head toward the approaching sound. A horrible sight slammed into my brain. The foreman crouched low over the horse's back and was urging the beast on at breakneck speed. His thick fingers gnarled and twisted in the escapee's hair, he dragged the man over the razor-sharp stumps of sugar cane. Reining the animal to a careening halt, he hurled the bleeding mess of flesh to a tumbled heap in front of the prisoners. "This is what happens to people who try to escape. Nobody escapes from Aguica!" He glared at the inmates; there was no doubt in anyone's mind that he would rather see you dead than have you escape from this watchtower of hell!

This was the same foreman I had tricked into preventing me from cutting sugar cane. It was no longer funny. Suddenly, I realized how dangerous the man was and how close to death I'd been. I shivered. What I had just seen was the most methodical, brutal and cold-blooded act I had ever witnessed and I became silent and withdrawn. Days passed and weeks took their place. Mile upon mile of sugar cane bowed to the flashing machetes wielded by suffering, desperate men. Beatings and hunger were constant. I observed and took note.

From the beginning, the officials had attached one of their best snitches to me. His name was Amore. He followed me everywhere. Since he had pull, he used it to get favors like extra food, which he forced on me. Dwelling on the possibility of another escape attempt, I ate the extra food to keep up my strength. Did I feel guilty? Yes! But rebellion was once again boiling in me and I was preparing myself for the battle. Up to now, I had rebelled only to tell the authorities I was alive and kicking. But soon something was to take place that would put me forever on the opposing side. It was to be my introduction to terror. It happened like this.

The day had been long and hard. The prisoners had been cutting cane in a weed-infested area. At quitting time the cars usually bristled with conversation, but today they were strangely quiet. The men were exhausted.

After a skimpy dinner of fish and rice and upon completion of count, we stumbled off to bed and fell into a coma-like sleep. A heavy thunderstorm passed and hardly a person gave heed to the lightning or rolling thunder. Around three o'clock in the morning, the door to our barracks was flung open. Guards, led by snarling dogs straining at the leash, poured in. What followed was a slap of machetes, the sounds of beds being overturned, and the bewildered cries of terrified prisoners.

"Oh, God! Wait... please! No! No!"

The dogs, their eyes blood red, snapped at the men's testicles! Screams of terror mingled with the blows and snarls. The grim-faced guards, lips pressed together tightly, never uttered a sound. Their eyes shone with the same thirst for blood as that of the leaping dogs!

Whipped out into the rain-soaked fields, trembling from both the cold morning air and the horrifying experience, we waited, clad only in shorts. A full moon slipping from behind a fast-moving cloud gave the near-naked bodies a strange hue. Silver rays sparkled on the blood dripping into puddles of muddy water around our feet.

My world shook. I had witnessed a debased, evil and diabolical thing. I had seen the human being stripped of its human condition. I had felt Satan's presence. For the first time in many years, I dropped my head and prayed.

The fear I felt that morning became my closest companion. I was never again to hear the rattle of keys or the thud of approaching boots without my mouth going dry and my stomach twisting into hard knots. What was the reason for the attack? What could possibly be gained by such insane abuse? The answer was simple; to instill terror, to make you so afraid you would not question any order given. Their masks had slipped. I had glimpsed the true nature of the Red psyche. I stopped talking to anyone, and I withdrew into the safety of myself.

My next rebellion held clear political overtones. I wrote a declaration where I denounced the abuse to which I had been subjected. At the same time I informed the officials that in the almost three years I had been in Cuba, all communication had been denied me. I had not been permitted to send or receive a single letter, not even to or from my mother. For those two basic reasons, I declared myself on a hunger strike and demanded to be taken to the Hole. Within minutes of reading the declaration to the men in the barracks, Amore, my G-2 buddy, informed the camp Warden, and, seconds later, they took me to an eight-by-four-foot cement cell.

The Warden came by to talk with me. After hearing out my complaints, he said, "If you weren't American, I would flood this cell with water and leave you to catch pneumonia and die." The steel-plated door clanged shut, bars were shot home and, following the sound of locks being set, silence filled the tiny cell.

I glanced at the cement vault and stretched out over the unyielding springs of the bunk. It's almost like being buried, I mused, but at least I have privacy. I let my mind wander back over the almost three years I had been in Cuba, the lies, the truths and the lessons learned.

During one of my first interrogations, Captain Hernandez had declared, "Since the triumph of the revolution, delinquency, prostitution and racism have been eliminated." Well, three years and thousands of testimonies later, I knew such statements were lies.

Prostitution and its shadow, venereal disease, were rapidly reaching frightening levels. A large percentage of newly-arrived prisoners had syphilis because prostitution was no longer controlled. Before the revolution, my Cuban cellmates explained, there were many houses in sectors of the city that lent themselves to the lucrative trade and whose professional girls submitted to regular, weekly, medical checkups.

Now, practically every Cuban woman, in one way or another, practiced the age-old profession. For a pair of panties, a scarf, a pack of American cigarettes or even a small can of milk, a man could have almost any female he wanted. And if that man was from any of the free world countries, he was accosted by fresh *Lolitas* and aged matrons alike. A thick doughy pizza and spaghetti could buy a memorable night. Meanwhile, the boast that crime was a thing of the past was pitifully ludicrous. Estimates of up to one-half million prisoners packed in work camps and prisons around Cuba belied these claims.

"Everyone steals, or wheels and deals," a prisoner told me. "It's all a part of life here. The system forces you into situations that make you break the law. That way you can't accuse them of being crooks. The pot can't call the skillet black. Lenin said that there was no better revolutionary than a rehabilitated criminal. Well, there's hardly a family in Cuba who doesn't have some relative who has either been in jail, is in jail, or on his way to jail."

These and hundreds of other stories made my blood run angry.

The statement that racism was a capitalist ill was simply another lie. When I arrived in Cuba, I had been told to fill out a document in which a space was provided for *Race*. I had innocently written, *Black*. The officials were aghast. "Oh, no, Tony, you aren't black. You're mulatto."

I had insisted, but they prevailed. Tired of arguing, I allowed them to replace *black* with *mulatto*.

They were all smiles, and I had gotten my first lesson in Socialist-Cuban racism. I had been so naive then, just like most Americans.

I would never forget how shocked I'd been when I found that only a few people in Cuba owned refrigerators, television sets and other commonplace household appliances. When I told my Cuban friends that I knew no one in America who did not have a telephone they stared at me in frank disbelief. I was just as skeptical upon being informed that cars were so scarce that a 1955 model American car could cost up to 20,000 pesos, and only if you could find someone who would sell one, even if you had the money.

But the most shocking thing of all was the food shortage. Cuba, supposedly an agricultural country, should have an abundance of food, yet after years and years of revolution, the people still had ration books and were going hungry.

"After the middle of the month," a Cuban friend explained, "You don't have nothing in the house. You come home and you got your kids looking up at you saying, 'Daddy, I'm hungry.' So what do you do? You do what any parent would do. You go out and buy on the black market, and if you get caught, you end up here. It ain't right, Tony, it just ain't right. They send all our food to Russia in exchange for iron and guns. Who are we afraid of? We got no borders to defend. Nobody's attacking this island. Why all the guns except to use against the people. The Russian big shots eat all our food and what do we get? Iron! There ain't no food, Tony. *No hay nada!* There's nothing here except hunger, misery and abuse!"

They told me that if I walked down the street with a bag I would be stopped and searched. "You don't see people in Cuba walking around with bundles, Tony." Over and over again I heard the same stories. Time and again I met men thrown into jail for buying food on the black market.

I'll always remember one case. It occurred during the time I was in Company Five in Principe. A nineteen-year-old youth had been caught with meat hidden under this jacket. He was brought to prison and thrown in with the rest of Cuba's dispossessed. The next morning, since I was an early riser, I was the first to notice what seemed to be a set of clothes on a hanger dangling from the bars at the rear of the building. Something made me take a closer look. The bulging eyes and lolling black tongue in the purple, swollen young face burned into my brain. I rushed to the hole in the floor and vomited.

8.
PRINCIPE AGAIN

"Couldn't take it, huh?" A sneering guard, sucking on a ragged cigar butt and seated, flipped through the papers that had accompanied me from Aguica. After only two days on a hunger strike, they'd transferred me back to Principe.

I clamped my lips together and stared into the middle distance. I heard him mumble something unintelligible, then, with a grunt, he heaved himself from behind an old desk.

"Wait here. I gotta find out where we gonna put you."

While he was gone, I glanced at the papers on his desk. One was a death certificate. A prisoner had hanged himself in the Hole. The shocking aspect was that it stated: the prisoner had shown great disrespect toward Fidel Castro and the revolution. To hang oneself was an impossibility. You were stripped of everything in the Hole.

The guard returned and I was taken to Company Eight where I was surrounded by a group of curious prisoners. I brought them up-to-date about friends and relatives still in Aguica and told them of prevailing conditions. The question and answer period went on endlessly.

There was no bed for me this time. Like dozens of others, I was forced to find a space on the cold cement floor. With my boots as a pillow, I lay listening to the snores of my fellow inmates and to the dry scuttle of rats racing around inside the cavern.

Once in California I had said, "I'd rather be a prisoner in Cuba than a free black in the United States!" I must have been out of my mind. Compared to this, San Quentin was a country club.

I thought about the differences in food. When food is denied, plus being locked up, plus being terrorized, then one's body and mind become atrophied. At least in Quentin we had steaks once or twice a week. No one went hungry. I had never seen a guard assault a prisoner. There was recreation. While home wasn't perfect, I was beginning to reminisce about a country that respected the *human condition.*

"What about racism in the United States?" a cellmate asked. "Isn't it true that black people don't have the same rights and protection as whites? Don't tell me they don't sic dogs on you. I saw..."

"I know what you saw," I interjected.

About every six months the Cuban Communists published in their government-controlled newspaper, *Granma,* old pictures of American blacks being attacked by policemen with fierce killer dogs. It was always the same picture. They never missed a chance to point out and underline the sad reality of white on black repression in the United States.

"But they don't show the world how Cuba turns dogs on you and beats you with machetes for no reason, do they? What they did to us in Aguica won't ever be known by even the Cuban people, much less those outside this country," I explained to my Cuban cellmate.

"But is it true?" insisted the Cuban. "Here they put dogs on anybody. But there it's mostly blacks who catch hell!"

"Here it's mostly blacks too," I retorted. "It's mostly blacks in prison. It's mostly blacks who have the worst jobs. It's mostly blacks who get the worst beatings. Here it's called Social Orientation or some other crap. But when it occurs in the United States, the Communists call it racism. It's all the same thing."

"Well, at least they don't lynch us," broke in an older black. "And we can marry a white woman if we want to. I'll bet you've never had a white woman in your life. They'd hang you if you went out with one!"

The prisoners broke into laughter.

"Okay, okay, it's true," I admitted. "There is still racism in the U.S. It's true that there are still lynchings going on..." I paused searching for words to explain the phenomenon that was undeniable. I felt extremely uncomfortable. I sensed the need to defend the U.S. and yet I still blamed whites for much of what happened to me. "But there is something else happening. Someone or something is playing games on the people and it's more than just a thing about black or white. And as for white women..."

Sure, I'd had white women before... As I talked to the prisoners, I let my mind steal back over the memories of some of those liaisons.

My first experience had been with a little white girl named, of all things, Barbara Ann. I thought this was funny because she lived in the rear of the store where Barbara Ann bread was sold. She was about ten, had saucy blue eyes and liked to show herself. I was around the same age.

Barbara sat on the steps across the street, pantyless, and opened and closed her legs slowly. Dry mouthed, I stood at the window staring. The very first sexual thrill in my life was peeping at Barbara Ann. In my mind, she belonged to me.

Once a white boy, Barbara and I slipped into a cab of an abandoned truck that sat alongside the store. We hung rags from the windows to block any view. Barbara Ann only let me look, but she allowed the white boy to touch her.

I understood now that this might have been one of the reasons for my hatred of white men. Aside from all the other factors which were part of my black reality, a white boy had gotten what I had been denied.

My next experience was at sixteen. A black pimp escorted me to a back room in a shabby hotel. Stretched out beneath a dingy sheet lay a dark-eyed brunette. Throat dry, hands trembling, I handed the pimp ten dollars. He left, and she helped me off with my clothes. She was soft and exciting.

From that day, I was infatuated with white women. At the same time, I harbored a growing resentment toward the white race in general. The contradicting emotions plagued me for years. There were other relationships, some intense, some not. As far as I was concerned, I enjoyed any woman, white or black. I found it hard convincing the Cubans that neither blacks nor whites were as interested in sexual as they were social contact.

But I didn't tell them about Kitty. October, 1968; the Greyhound Bus station in Sacramento had been packed. Trying to take advantage of precious minutes during stops to gobble down food or relieve aching bladders, passengers dashed to and fro, bumping into each other and spilling coffee over everything. Loudspeakers blared notices of arriving and departing buses and competed with the whine and roar of the big vehicles. The air inside the building shook and vibrated.

I had a job, was earning a living, was out of jail, off drugs and off the streets. It wasn't anything special but it was keeping me straight. I was filling trays with dirty dishes, pushing them into one end of a steaming dishwasher and snatching them out the other. As they appeared, I'd stack the dishes on a shiny, aluminum table for waitresses to grab as they needed them. I picked up two plastic containers holding clean dishes, put them on a busboy's cart and wheeled out into the terminal dining room.

The starched collar of my white jacket scraped my neck as I twisted to get a better look at a woman who had just walked in. She was tall for a woman, close to six feet, and the blonde tousled wig she wore, made her taller. The Asiatic slant of her dark eyes and high cheekbones gave credit to an American Indian heritage. She had a small bust that tapered to a narrow waist and a lovely bottom. Long, perfectly-shaped legs would have made any magazine centerfold model jealous.

Just below the hem of her mini-skirt, large enough to draw attention to her sexy legs, was a tatoo; *Kitty.* She was what we called, a *fox — a diamond fox!*

A couple of times, as I bussed the tables, I'd been close enough to read the tatoo. She usually came in around ten at night, drank a couple cups of coffee, crossed her legs showing more than advised for *nice* girls, and idly moved her foot up and down while looking every passing man straight in the eye.

Kitty was a prostitute.

Tonight was no different. The tatoo girl carried a cup of steaming coffee over to a table by the wall and crossed her legs. She must have seen me watching her in the mirror. She turned and gazed into my eyes, a slight smile touching her lips. I felt myself blushing and turned away. When I came out again to clean off tables, her face wore a deep, thoughtful look.

Arriving at her table, I felt a tiny kick on the shin. Surprised, I looked down. She had a mischievious look in her eyes and her lips made a sexy pout.

"Hi! You haven't been working here long... Have you? My name's Kitty."

"Nope. Started a week ago." I looked down at her thigh, "I already know your name. I'm Tony. I'm just outa' the joint and my parole officer told me I had to become a slave so here I am."

"Welcome back," said Kitty, "What were you in for?"

"This last trip was for possession and sales. I did three and a half, got out, and now I just got back from a six-month dry-out."

"Oh! Naughty boy! Here! Take this." She reached into her purse, pulled out a vial of pink pills and passed it over. "Take three of four. It'll make your night go faster."

"And happier," I said, slipping the speed into my pocket, "Let me bring these dishes into the kitchen and I'll be right back."

But she was gone when I returned to the dining area.

I told my Black Panther brothers about her and immediately got into trouble. "Hey Tony, don't go gettin mixed up with another white chick..."

"But she's not really white. I mean, her skin is, but that woman's got a lot of Indian in her!"

"So she's mixed-white. So what. She's still white and the brothers down at the party offices don't dig it!"

"Wait a minute! The Black panthers are one thing. I'm gonna always take care of business for them but there's nothin' wrong with me seeing this girl."

"Did you see her look at you? Man, that woman is dangerous!"

"I can handle it Jones. I can handle it!"

But I couldn't. And neither could she.

Two days after arriving in Sacramento in October, 1968, I'd visited the Black Panther offices and asked to become a member. A couple of brothers gave me the rules and bylaws, plus other study material including *Mao's Red Book*. I explained I'd just gotten out of prison and was ready to do anything to help bring about the Revolution.

I told them I was sincere and to show how serious, proposed, "I volunteer for the most dangerous job you've got! I'm ready to eliminate anybody you know has infiltrated the party or anyone that's an informer. I don't care who he is, whether he's an FBI agent or anyone else. Just tell me who, when and where. I'm ready!" I was in. I belonged.

Every night when Kitty came to the bus terminal we'd sit at an empty table. There was nothing to talk about, just everyday things people discuss when they're feeling each other out. She did not treat me as a John and I treated her like a lady.

One night at quitting time a week later, I surprised her sitting in a booth crying. I sat beside her and she burst into a fresh flood of tears and put her head on my chest.

"I'm sorry. It's just that I've got problems with my old man. I left him a few days ago and he keeps bugging me. I have to talk to somebody." She took out a pen and paper from her purse. "Here's my apartment number. Come by tomorrow. I want to discuss something with you..."

Something told me not to go and that night, for the first time, Kitty didn't stop by for coffee.

But next night Kitty stepped into the dining room at eleven-thirty and surprised me as I stood behind the cash-register. They trusted me. I'd been promoted!

"You kept me waiting."

"That's okay. No need to explain. I'll be waiting outside when you get off work tonight." She raised her hand. I poured her a coffee, fluffed up my Afro and smiled, heading for trouble and knowing it.

It was a beautiful night. Clusters of stars filled the sky. Warm puffs of breezes tugged our clothes. We were silent all the way to her hotel.

"Like me?" she had asked.

"I like you very much," I whispered.

Next morning she pointed to her purse and said, " It's yours, just like me. I want to be your woman. Can I? You make me feel like a woman. And I don't want you to work anymore. I can't have *my baby* working!" It was a new low. I finally had become what my mother warned I could become, a pimp.

We moved into a bungalow on the outskirts of town. There was a color TV, a vibrating bed and a small microwave oven we never used. Breakfast, lunch and dinner were ordered by phone from a nearby restaurant. Her ex-pimp had kept the Caddy so we travelled everywhere by cab. A lot of money was spent but Kitty didn't mind. She was earning over two hundred dollars a night.

During the days we lived for each other. We went on picnics and long walks and kissed beneath the open sky like any two young lovers. At night, around nine o'clock she would take a cab and disappear into the dark.

During this time there were many secret meetings with members of the Panther Party. We decided that because of my work with them, it was best that few people as possible knew about our collaboration.

So, I lived two lives.

One was the life with Kitty; I didn't want my black brothers to know I was living with a white woman. The other was my secret connection with the Party, some of whose members I was spying on. Belonging to the Panthers meant a lot. Perhaps the long emptiness I had felt could be filled. And yet, torn by the conflicting emotions of living two lies, I felt more alone than ever.

For about a month things were fine, then Kitty began overindulging in drugs. She seemed intent on killing herself. We started having arguments about her drug abuse but she refused to bend and finally one night the inevitable occurred.

Kitty overdosed. An ambulance rushed her to hospital where she remained for three days. Upon her release she continued taking large amounts of pills. Naturally this affected her behavior. She was now being arrested often and a large percentage of the money she earned was paid out in bail bonds and fines. But there was no doubt she liked me. Besides money, Kitty gave me a gold Ronson lighter and a diamond ring. But by then, with all the time Panther Party affairs were taking, things between us had become strained.

The first time I threatened to leave, Kitty cut her wrists. I still moved out and she pulled through it. Though we were separated, she came by every day to see me.

At this time Ray, a white pseudo-revolutionary I'd met in San Quentin, came into my life again. He was determined to prove he was not racist and one of the first things he did was take me to Richmond, California, to meet a friend.

It was Dorene, the white WASP with the six-year-old daughter who later bought my hijack ticket. We fell in love almost immediately and I decided I'd stop seeing Kitty. I told her everything was over between us, packed my things, left Sacramento and moved in with Dorene.

A month later I heard Kitty had been found lying in a pool of blood. She had rammed both arms through the plate glass window of her living room, jammed them down on the jagged edges and bled to death. I tried to feel sorry for her as I suffered in Principe; but I felt nothing. Maybe I was here because of such things.

I wasn't proud of the life I once had led in the States. The only person I confided such stories to was Tony Cuesta and he refused to pass judgement. "Only God can do that," he said.

Other conversations with Cuban prisoners and discussions about America pleased me but we never discussed the ugly aspects of our life, like what happened next.

The long line of prisoners shuffled through the iron-barred door into the mess hall. The sound of spoons scraping on metal trays was similar to chalk being raked across a blackboard. Rumbling conversation and the shouts of guards slapping their machetes over the tables filled the air. The crash of empty trays thrown into a pile by prisoners at the exit added to the maddening racket.

The mess hall was huge, about five to ten thousand feet square; more like a huge cave. Sometimes in the rush to get the prisoners fed, three or more Companies would be packed inside. Then, the ensuing clamor heightened to a deafening roar. And since enemies were brought in close contact with one another, there was a greater possibility of serious problems arising.

"Move it! Move it! Get through and get out!" The men rushed to slurp up the mush and soup. It was best to get out of this dangerous area as quickly as possible.

I stepped through the door and let my eyes wander over the mass inside. I had learned that here it was not always a case of the strong surviving, but rather he who was most alert. A seemingly innocent bulge under a shirt or in a waistband could be, and often was, a knife or a hand-made machete. The way a prisoner walked told you if he had a two-foot sword jammed down his pant leg or not. Gestures and expressions were an open book of a person's intention and if you didn't learn to read them, it could cost your life.

Yta, a buddy of mine, was telling of the arrival of two other Americans to the prison. Allegedly, they had been trafficking in marijuana. Actually, their plane had run out of fuel and had made an emergency landing. They had been arrested on the spot and taken to G-2. Tried and sentenced to four years, they were now living in the hospital section. The food and living conditions there were a thousand times better than here. Of course, they were white. Once again the not so subtle racism that Communists swear does not exist was made clear to me.

For myself, after almost three years in prison, it was next to impossible to get up to the hospital section that lined the peak of the hill on which Principe sat. It angered me because it was such an obvious case of discrimination. Aside from that, of the dozens of workers in the hospital, only a couple were black.

I had decided to make an effort to see the new guys. At the same time, I hoped to talk to the officer in charge of hiring to see if I could get a job there.

I turned to make a comment to Yta when a movement toward the center of the mess hall caught my eye. It was Chini, a soft-spoken black who captured my attention.

Two things were wrong. Chini carried no tray; he was moving too fast. Slipping stealthily between the rows of tables, he came to a stop behind Jabao, another prisoner, who, completely unaware, continued eating. With one deft move, Chini drew a razor-sharp, two-foot long sword from his pants leg, and clasping it in both hands like a priest about to make a ceremonial sacrifice, he raised it, point down, high over his head.

Everything stopped. All eyes locked on Chini. If Jabao had a friend there, it was too late to cry out a warning. The sword flashed down; a solid crunch followed.

A loud "Oh!" exploded from the lips of the onlookers as the cold steel drove through Jabao's back, destroyed his heart and tore a gaping hole in his chest. His face dropped into the plate of mush. He appeared to hiccough once; then from his mouth, ears, eyes and nose gushed all his life's blood.

It was no big deal. After the mess had been cleaned up, the long line began moving forward again; the sound of spoons scraping food into hungry mouths could be heard.

A few days later, using a faked hospital pass, I made my way up a narrow, almost perpendicular flight of cement stairs to the hospital. I was certain the Swiss Embassy, which handled U.S. affairs in Havana, would be out to see the two new Americans, and I wanted to send a message asking for an interview. I hoped the Americans would help me. Moreover, I wanted to talk to another American, even if he was white. For three years I had been completely out of touch and the longing to talk about what was happening outside Cuba was a near obsession.

I met only Richard, a blonde, blue-eyed, typical All-American boy, who hailed from the Bay Area; at least we had something in common. We were from the same neck of the woods.

Nervously, Richard told me of their capture: "Man, was I terrified! This one guard told me to raise my hands. Then he pointed his pistol at me and pulled the trigger. The hammer fell on an empty chamber. They all stood around and laughed. Man, I thought it was all over! They kept us in G-2 for over two months, then tried me. What a farce! The judge slept through the whole thing."

We only had a few stolen minutes together. But Richard expected to see the embassy representatives in a few days and promised to tell them about me.

From there I went over to a small office where a black lieutenant, in charge of hiring and firing, sat. As I stood waiting to talk to him, I wondered if he understood how he was being manipulated in the overall racist scheme. Here was the man who hired the workers and he was very black, and if all the workers happened to be white... well, you couldn't call that racism, could you?

I decided to gain my objective by using the same arguments they employed, only against them. He finally called me in. "What is it?" the stiffly-starched lieutenant asked.

I gave him my angriest look, then replied: "You know, ever since I've been in this country you people have been telling me there's no racism. That everybody's equal. But, you know what? I've found out you're just as racist, or maybe more so, than the whites in the U.S."

The black lieutenant's mouth dropped open. He was genuinely shocked. "What do you mean?" he sputtered. "We don't have prejudice. We treat everybody the same. The revolution doesn't permit racism in our country."

"You say there's no racism here? Well, look around you. Here in the prison, right here in the hospital, almost everybody who works here is white! That's because the best living conditions are up here. If it's digging ditches or chopping weeds, that's where you'll find all the blacks. And you say there's no discrimination? Besides that, as soon as two whites from the U.S. arrive, they're given the best treatment you can offer. But me, even though I've had a little medical experience, I can't get a job in the hospital area. If that's not prejudice, then I don't know what is!" I had given it to him hard and fast.

He sat there stunned for a moment, then parroted some flimsy jargon about the blessings of the revolution. Finally, he wrote a note, gave it to me and told me to take it to Sergeant Barrios, who would see to it that I was given a job.

Walking on air, I left his office. And so, I began working again in the central infirmary. Evidently my talk sparked a change in hospital policy; soon afterwards, blacks could be found working all over the place!

I had chosen the night shift because, having no bed, it was better to catnap on the emergency cot in the infirmary than bed down on the dirty cement floor in the Company. The infirmary, prior to the revolution, had been a snack bar. Now it housed rows of bottles filled with first-aid supplies.

A shiny treatment table, a few wooden chairs and an old-fashioned machine to sterilize syringes and needles gave it the necessary qualifications to be classified as an infirmary. In the rear, behind a yellowed sheet that divided the small room, were two bunks. Those were for the non-critical cases; usually they had an asthmatic or two wheezing and blowing, stretched out on them.

Medicine was scarce. Although it was supposed to be for prisoners only, the guards and officers all the way up to the

Warden, came in and took what they wanted. The vitamins and best medicines disappeared into their pockets almost as soon as the infirmary was stocked.

"Hey, Reinaldo, how're things going?" I saluted the Cuban medic.

"Boy, it's been a mess," he replied. "We had over 150 cases today. Lots of dysentary. A few cuts and things."

"Nothing serious, huh?" I dropped some dirty needles into the sterilizer's bubbling water, warily eyeing the drops jumping over the side.

"Nah! Just the same-oh same-oh. But I'm beat. Oh! There's a cup of sugar-water and a bun for you in back. I'm going to hit the sack. See you later!" Reinaldo went out, slamming the door behind him.

I sat down, reached into my pocket and pulled out a small package of cigarette butts and the end of a well-chewed cigar which was still damp. These came from prisoners who'd had visitors that day. They collected butts off the ground and smuggled them back in.

I tore the cigar butt into tiny pieces, put them on a strip of paper torn from the wrapper of a roll of cotton, twisted it into a near-perfect cigarette, then licked it together. The first drag went down like sandpaper.

I had been sitting there enjoying the balmy night breeze flowing through the door, hoping not to be confronted with an emergency, when a prisoner, groaning and holding his back, staggered in. Well, so much for that, I thought, blowing out a cloud of blue smoke.

"What happened?"

"I was being transferred and the truck turned over. My back feels like every bone is broken."

I stubbed out my cigarette carefully and with a resigned sigh told him to sit down. The prisoner appeared to be in pain. I said, "I don't want to take chances. I'm calling the doctor."

An immediate change came over the man. Jerking upright in the chair, he said, "No! Don't do that. I'm starting to feel better. Just give me something for the pain."

I fished out a couple of aspirin tablets, then turned to fill a cup of water.

"Anthony Garnet Bryant!" The pronunciation was perfect, without the slightest trace of accent.

I turned off the spigot and spun around. I studied the man. His legs were crossed now; there was no evidence of pain. "What?"

"Anthony Garnet Bryant. That's your name, isn't it? Listen, let me ask you something. What do you think about Cuba?"

Suddenly it was all very clear. I knew who the fake patient was; G-2! When I answered my voice could have chilled water. "What do *you* think I think about Cuba? All I've seen are prisons. To me, Cuba is a cement cell with bars. Do you expect me to feel any differently?"

The man reached into his pocket and pulled out his wallet. "Look, Tony. See that? I work for G-2. Now listen. You've got to get smart. I can do whatever I want and nobody can say a thing! That's all you have to do. Just fake it! You can have everything. All you have to do is just cooperate!"

Under my angry glare, the smile on his face slowly died. He slid the wallet back into his pocket. We looked at each other for a moment, then he stood. I ignored his outstretched hand. "I guess it's too late, huh?" he asked softly.

"Yeah," I rasped. "Too late."

Although the majority of cases treated in the infirmary were of a semi-serious nature, minor stabs, cuts and abrasions from beatings and the like, there were times when tragicomedy took the spotlight. I had long since thought I was prepared for and had seen about everything, until Jose!

It was a hot, humid evening. An April shower had fallen, leaving a sticky feeling in the air. Soft rolls of far away thunder trembled on the air, then died.

As I passed one of the Companies, someone yelled to me to bring some aspirins. I gave a wave to show I had heard and stepped back inside the infirmary.

I opened my mouth to greet Reinaldo when a howl that sounded like a cross between a lovesick wolf and a hound dog hot on its tail, jarred me to a stop.

"Ohh! Ohhh, help me! Ohh! I can't stand it. Oooh!" Then came a loud sneeze.

I gave Reinaldo a startled look, but he just smiled; since conversation was impossible over the yowling, he rolled his eyes heavenward and turned back to the patient he was attending.

There were two other men sitting in the wooden chairs waiting their turn and who, judging by the looks on their faces, wondered what the screeching was about too.

"Ahhee! Ohh, No! No! Ohh! Please help me. I can't stand it!"

Boy, he must be hurtin', I thought as I headed toward the curtained section of the infirmary. I had taken a couple of steps when, without warning, the sheets parted and a muscular black man, nude to the waist and holding a pillow against his face, stepped through.

"Ohh please, gimme... Oh no... gimme a shot!" The man was bent almost double and genuine misery was etched on his face whenever he took the pillow away to breathe. I stopped dead in my tracks. The other two prisoners in the room tried not to laugh and quickly turned their heads, pretending the howling man did not exist.

Howling all the while, and sneezing violently, the man lowered himself to his knees, trying desperately to keep the pillow over his face, trying to keep his eyes from bulging out of his head with every explosion from his nose.

"Good Heavens! What the..." At the look on my face, Reinaldo burst into laughter. Gasping for breath and holding his sides, Reinaldo managed to point to a syringe.

The man rocked back and forth. "Ohh. This... Ohh... ain't... Please! It's not funny! Oh!..."

I managed to snap myself out of shock, run over, grab the syringe and inject the drug into the man's arm. The pain-killer took effect and after a minute Jose, for that was his name, was able to drag himself, still moaning and sneezing, back behind the curtain.

Reinaldo had pulled himself together somewhat. "You won't believe it. Tony, you won't believe it! This guy... Ouch!" he muttered as the needle he was trying to unplug jabbed him in the finger. "This guy was brought in last night. He's been in a street jail hospital for twenty-six days. That's how long he's been sneezing!"

"What!" I exclaimed. "I don't believe it. You mean... "

"Yep! Twenty-six days and the doctors don't know if they'll have to operate or not. If they do, he'll never breathe properly again."

"That's incredible, incredible! I've never heard of anything like that in my life. What caused it?"

Reinaldo explained that Jose was a peeping Tom. He had been spying through a window, when he was caught by the victim's husband and brothers. He'd sneezed in excitement and hadn't stopped since.

I went in to talk to the poor guy. "Twenty-six days!" I marveled. "I bet you don't want to see a woman undress ... "

"Stop!" screamed Jose. "Don't mention that word to me."

Jose kept sneezing a total of thirty-seven days before the sneezing suddenly stopped. He spent two more years locked up, mildly famous as the *Peeping Nose*.

All days were not so hilarious and interesting as those spent with Jose. Most were hot, muggy hours I spent practicing French, working, thinking of home, and dying a little. Then one evening, I was told that the following morning I was to be dressed and clean shaven. *Embassy visit!* Richard had kept his word.

On the morning after, two guards came and escorted me through the tall double gates and down a narrow road to a stately building where a room had been set aside for the visit. After a short wait, the door opened, and with my heart pounding, I stepped inside.

Four men were in the room. Two, behind the desk, were the Swiss representatives and stood and extended polite handshakes; another man sat behind them to their left and the fourth man sat on my right. These two were G-2 agents.

The heavier of the two men behind the desk introduced all of those in the room, stressing the fact that two G-2 agents were present. The embassy representatives were plainly nervous.

After we were seated, I was told that the U.S. State Department had authorized them to see me and look out for my welfare, to see to it that I was not being treated unreasonably, and to help me maintain contact with my family. I felt like shouting. Never before in my life had I felt proud to be an American.

"We're here to try to see to it that while you're here, you receive proper treatment. Tell me something, Mr. Bryant, what are your future plans for when you're released? What do you plan to do?"

"Return to the United States," I blurted anxiously.

"You realize that the law is very harsh in this type of case!"

I didn't care about that. I had a message to give. I looked him in the eye and said, "If I knew that the electric chair was waiting for me tomorrow in America, I would still want to go back today."

The two agents began scribbling madly and the fellow on my right turned a dark red and looked as though he would explode.

The two embassy visitors glanced at one another, then back at me as though pleasantly shocked. "Well, in that case, would you like to sign these papers? They are for your passport and..."

"Just hand them to me. I'll be happy to sign anything you want me to!" I grabbed the papers, pulled them toward me and swiftly wrote my signature. After some pleasantries, I was dismissed.

Later, when I'd returned to the Company, the prisoners crowded around me. One said, "You know, black people aren't supposed to do anything except kowtow to these people because the revolution was supposed to have done so much for them. And in your case, it's even worse. They're always telling us how they lynch and abuse you; how they sic dogs on you, and still you'd rather go back to all that than stay here. Boy, you sure made liars out of them!"

The prisoners were dumbfounded that embassy personnel had come to visit and had brought me a bag filled with personal items, some, things they had heard about but never seen: Colgate toothpaste, socks, shorts, vitamins... I shared all I could with them. I knew I had a powerful weapon in these items and from that day on used them as such.

I went to see Richard as soon as I could and thanked him. Although we would have our differences in years to come, I was always grateful for that one gesture which established my only link with the U.S. and my family in over three years.

Communication with my country and those I loved had begun but my personal feelings in prison remained at zero. I was still alone in Cuba, unable to share my feelings as a caring and loving human being. I existed, a disgusted non-participant in an atmosphere of open homosexuality, never forgetting the attack on me as a child.

Though Principe was rife with rumors about who was going with who and what man had taken what young boy as his *wife,* I didn't gossip, talk or even joke about sex.

Then something strange and wonderful happened. Somebody or some group decided *Tony El Americano* should get married. Maybe the trouble-maker would calm down.

On September 27, 1972, I was visited by Rothric Allen Brown, the mysterious Jamaican I'd met earlier in the prison at Guira de Lelena and who had been suspected of working for G-2.

"I heard you were here, Mon!" he grunted, producing a happy bear-hug. "I took a chance to come see you, a really big chance. If they catch me oooh!" His eyes stretched wide and he whispered. "Don't tell nobody you saw me. I ran away from the last jail I was in and now they're lookin' for me!"

"Aren't you afraid somebody will recognize you?" I asked. His story seemed a little far-fetched.

"Oh no mon! That's why I got the beard. I told them you was my cousin." He stared hard, searching to see if I believed the story. How could I? It was difficult for anyone to get into the prison for a visit and almost impossible to see a foreigner.

Rothric rattled on about nothing at all and then dropped his bombshell. He had a woman for me.

"She wants to marry, and for you it's a good deal. She'll take care of you, come on visits... Oh, and you know, mon, when you get married you can have the *special* visit for all night.

"What do I have to do for her?"

"What she wants is to leave de country. So you promise to take her with you when you leave. That's all she wants, mon!"

I was desperate for the feel of a woman in my arms and wasn't about to turn down this strange gift. Rothric would bring her next day.

On Friday the 28th of September, the Jamaican was back with my bride-to-be's sister. My future wife had arrived wearing slacks and been turned away by guards. I had no idea what she looked like. My cell-mates were astonished at two visits in two days. "Don't trust any of it," they warned. "This woman's a G-2 agent. She's a spy!"

Next morning I was escorted to a small room next to where the Embassy visit had taken place. Roberto Crespo, the Warden, sat behind a shiny desk, smiling. There was a fat woman notary public. Beside her was a thin, young woman with fair skin but curly, almost kinky red hair fluffed out in an Afro and a very pleasant face. A couple of guards stood in the room grinning foolishly.

My fiancee was Zaide Hernandez and we exchanged light kisses on the cheek, then answered the notary's questions. In as much time as it took us to sign our names; we were married.

It must have been the fastest romance and wedding in Cuban history. From start to finish it had taken less than three days! Prison marriage was normally a three to six month process. My friends were dumbfounded and highly suspicious. But whatever the reason G-2 or anyone else wanted me married, I decided to lean back and enjoy it.

There were rooms set aside inside Principe, apart from the Companies where married couples were allowed visits, something most Latin countries have almost always allowed, something which I knew in 1972 was still not permitted in America.

After the ceremony we were escorted by a broadly smiling guard to our honeymoon room. He grinned, locked us in, and said, "Pace yourself, *El Americano.* Don't fall asleep."

Zaide blushed and I laughed. There was a dumpy bed in the room covered by clean sheets. I was excited and couldn't decide what made me happier, the prospect of being with a woman or the chance to lay down on a real bed. I hadn't slept on a bed in more than three years.

My wife and acquaintance of one day, undressed with her back to me and I learned the meaning of conjugal in a visit that lasted eight hours. The new Mrs. Bryant visited me faithfully once a month and held my hand affectionately as we were escorted to the building of our marriage, filled with shabby little cement rooms and caved-in beds in which we clung together and shared what love we could.

There was a strange feeling in the little room. Once, I heard a soft cough coming from a window looking down on us. And many times, after our husband and wife visits, we would be escorted back by smirking guards. I had the feeling they had been peeping in on us but I never mentioned it to my Cuban wife. No matter what, I didn't want my prison marriage to end.

A year of considerable happiness passed quickly by. The strange marriage might have endured but it was based on a lie. Zaide was obsessed with leaving Cuba; I had been warned to never let on I had more than two years of prison sentence ahead of me. When we weren't making love, my prison wife told me of her dreams of America. She wanted to see Miami, New York and Disneyland. We'd go to Hollywood and watch Frank Sinatra sing. She was certain we'd soon leave together for the United States.

It might have continued and we might have left together but one day, as we sat in the visiting area, tragedy, in the form of a happy prisoner, rushed over.

"Tony, Tony. Did you hear? They took seven years off my sentence. I'll be getting out soon. Isn't that great! Maybe the same thing'll happen to you. Maybe they'll take off seven or eight and you'll be able to leave too."

I frowned, but it was too late. My Cuban wife sat stunned. I really felt sorry for her. She must have felt used. I never did find out what she thought. She just stopped coming by.

I expected her to show up on the monthly visiting day, but nothing happened. Then I just hoped she would appear. Finally, I knew I'd never see her again. I was alone in Cuba once more.

Thoughts of her filled my mind for a couple of years. Then, finally, she began to fade. Several years later, it ended as it began. I was taken to the Warden's office, faced the same notary, who had gained even more weight over the years and was pecking on the same old typewriter. I signed a piece of official-looking paper and was granted marital *freedom* once more. I'd tried Cuban marriage and this was Cuban divorce. I never did find out what happened to this girl who gave me happiness. I always wished her well.

9.
NIGHTMARES BEGIN AT DAWN

"Mr. President, it is natural to man to indulge in the illusions of hope. We are apt to shut our eyes to a painful truth, and to listen to the song of that siren, until she transforms us into beasts. "

Patrick Henry pronounced those words, but had they been stated by anyone else at any given moment, the same truths would be self-evident. For me, a man who had tried to violently overthrow the government of the United States for something vague and better, the sense of that statement took on a deep and soul-stirring meaning in June 1972.

There was no doubt that my feelings concerning the revolution, Communist-style, had changed drastically since my arrival in Cuba. Too many tales of terror reached my ears and I also had felt its touch. Too often had I seen Big Brother's ever-watching eye strip and destroy individuals of the last vestige of the human condition, turning them into traitors and killers of the sacred dream. Up to that point had the Communists been anything less than beasts; forgetting that the soul is a rebel, and thinking that by terror and starvation any animal can be controlled, had they possessed a bit of human dignity and love or respect for humankind and demonstrated it, not just to me but to anyone around me, then there was a chance I could have been tricked into believing they were truly concerned about mankind's salvation. I had many lessons to learn, but what I was about to experience overshadowed all that I thought I knew about the Cuban

Communists. It was early June 1972, when the drama began.

I was at work preparing for the normal influx of prisoners, actually ill or faking, who flooded the infirmary at night. It was around eleven o'clock when the iron door was pushed open.

Three guards, highly nervous and excited, burst in. They made a quick search of the place, then slapping their machetes on the stainless steel treatment table, ordered me to close up and go with them.

They had a wild look in their eyes, and all the way back to the Company they cursed and beat the walls of the buildings as though stones could feel and cry out. I knew better than to utter a word. I had seen them in their near mad-dog frenzies before and could tell that something had driven them to the killing level. For once I breathed a sigh of relief when the barred doors slammed shut, locking me in the relative security of the Company.

Conversation inside was low and tense. An air of electricity filled the room. No one knew what was wrong but the constant slap of machetes on stone sounding all over the prison alerted everyone to danger.

Prior to that night, the guards struck their machetes to emphasize a point or to hurry prisoners along. But we had never before experienced the constant clatter and bang which assailed our ears. A new practice had been born; the constant slapping of steel on concrete. This sound was to become a part of every prisoner's waking moment. No more would a moment's peace be allowed.

That night the deadly crack, similar to the sound of pistol shots, filled the air. Everyone spoke in whispers. The feeling of fear was like some *thing,* invisible yet alive, which crawled over and smothered you in its irreversible embrace.

Then, as though borne on the gentle breeze itself, came the rumor. How it arrived I'll never know...

"Escape! They say three guards have been killed!"

"Who says?"

"I don't know, but the whole prison's locked down!"

116

The rumor gained intensity and the mere fact that no guards came by ordering us to bed gave it credence.

At around 1:00 a.m., a trustee working in the Warden's office was brought in and locked up. Everyone crowded around him to get the facts. His eyes reflected the terror that had been sparked that night.

It was true! Three prisoners had somehow gotten over the wall and into the minimum security section of the prison where the bakery and a few workshops stood. They had killed the old guard in charge, taken his clothes, and made their way to a side exit. In the struggle that followed they had killed two more guards. One of the escapees had been slightly wounded but managed to get away.

Absolute silence engulfed the Company We all knew the repercussions from those killings would be terrible. But no one dreamed what had happened that night was to change Cuban penal policies from mere abuse to brutal slaughter.

The slap and ring of machetes rose to a frenetic level. The sound of the guards running past the Companies augmented the tense atmosphere. They were shouting, to no one in particular, "They've caught one! They've caught one! Hah! They've caught one!" Their voices were choked by something between a snarl and a savage bloodthirsty laugh. Then word filtered in and swept from building to building: The wounded escapee had gone to a nearby hospital, *Calixto Garcia,* and was captured there.

Scores of guards were called in from other prisons. The tramping of their hard-heeled boots resounded up and down the narrow streets between the buildings all night. Nobody slept.

I had found a space by the large barred window at the back of the Company and with a thin ragged blanket propped behind my head, sat against the wall and watched the inky blackness outside turn into an angry-looking crimson dawn. The usual rattle of iron carts bringing cans of milk at five o'clock did not sound; no one expected it.

Around six-thirty, frenzied activity began in the patio. All around the huge square, which was the size of two basketball courts, loudspeakers were being installed.

Guards, sweaty from the early morning heat, dashed to and fro as though preparing for a fiesta. Only they weren't happy; they were grim. The prisoners were being completely ignored; there were better things to do than worry about a few thousand hungry men.

Soon, flocks of people began streaming through the tall gates beside the patio. Civilian and military personnel by the hundreds swarmed over the patio opposite the Companies where scores of prisoners had jammed against the bars to observe. Guards with rifles and fixed bayonets lined up in front of each window.

My friend, *El Griego*, the Greek, and I stood watching the drama in the patio, mashed by the press of bodies around us.

"What do you think's going to happen?" I asked.

"I don't know, but it looks like they got something big in mind."

"Look! They're bringing in TV cameras!" someone shouted.

Sure enough, movie and TV camera crews were setting up at different points around the patio. A hot sun beamed down from a cloudless sky overhead. It promised to be a beautiful day.

More and more Communists flooded in. By nine o'clock thousands, chatting and pointing at the prisoners inside the Companies, filled every niche of the patio and perched on the roofs. Then, a couple of impressive cars pulled through the gates, eased over the crowded patio, and stopped in front of the seldom, if ever, used classrooms.

Three men, obviously judges in long black robes, descended from one of the cars. From the other stepped a group of top brass, and in their midst, like a bewildered lost sheep, was a thin, dark-haired prisoner who stood, hands cuffed in front of him. He was shoved roughly into a classroom and the door slammed shut.

"Look! There's Lemus!" shouted a prisoner.

Lieutenant Lemus was the man in charge of all prisons in Cuba. It might seem strange that such a low-ranking officer would hold such a powerful position, but you had only to look at his face to understand why. It was cold and deadly. His eyes were made of glass. He and a group of men and women entered the classroom. From the loudspeakers on the roofs sounded clicks and distorted voices as last-minute checks were made.

El Griego said, "They're going to hold court there in the classroom!"

Over the loudspeakers the trial began. After the charges were read; murder and escape, the fiscal, or state prosecutor, as we would call him, began his diatribe.

He started in a low, dramatic tone, speaking as though he could hardly contain his emotions. "Your Honors. There have been many times that the revolution has been confronted with anti-social elements which are remnants of the capitalistic system under whose yoke we no longer labor. Many times have our valiant people stood over the coffins of the motherland's brave defenders against filth such as that which cold-bloodedly and with premeditation, snuffed out the precious lives of three defenders of the revolution. A revolution that has offered to the people the chance to rise above man's exploitation by man." His voice rose a bit. "A revolution that is benevolent and caring. Many times have our hearts burst as we saw those yet living in the past, seek to destroy what our Commander-in-Chief Fidel Castro Ruz created." A round of applause. "But few times have we seen such cowardly and dastardly murders as those that took place here in this prison last night!" A low, menacing rumble sounded from the audience.

Now the prosecutor had warmed up; pounding on the table to emphasize his points, he began to shout and rail.

He pointed out that the accused's mother was a traitor to the revolution; she had fled the country for Miami. What else could be expected of a child except that it be a carbon copy of a traitor and murderess? Those who deserted the revolution were the slime of the earth!

By now the people in the makeshift courtroom were at a frenzy. "Firing squad! Firing squad!" they screamed.

The prisoners around me had been turned to stone. Each of

them must have felt the same chill that invaded my body.

At this moment, the iron gates swung wide open again and an open bed truck pulled into the patio. The soldiers on the truck bed began tossing down sandbags.

I felt my arm caught in a steel-like grasp and turning to face the Greek, found myself staring into a face which terror had made almost unrecognizable. He choked out, "Oh, my God! They're going to kill him, Tony. They're going to kill him right here!" The Greek was shaking and trembling as though on the verge of convulsions.

I looked again at the busily working soldiers, then back at my friend. "I don't believe it."

"Yes, they are, Tony!"

"But the trial isn't even over yet," I protested. "And besides, anybody's got the right to an appeal!" I stared at the Greek's slowly-shaking head. "But at least they're going to..."

"To what?" strained out the Greek. "They're going to kill him; that's what they're going to do!" And he collapsed at my side, weeping. Friends took him to his bed and I returned my full attention to the drama unfolding in the patio.

After more minutes of raging against the accused, the prosecutor ended by asking that the *people's wishes* be carried out, that the man be executed by firing squad.

Now it was the defense lawyer's turn. His voice never rose above a ho-hum level. We could hear him stand up and rustle papers near his microphone. He coughed a few times. Was he studying the angry faces in the 'courtroom'? All we heard him say was that although this *assassin* had struck a blow against the heart of the revolution, the judges should take pity. Then he added, "He's young, your Honors. There may yet be some chance for him; he's so young!" That was the accused man's defense!

The room was rocked by cries: "Firing squad! Firing squad!"

The truck pulled away from the mound of sandbags and the courtroom audience flooded into the patio. Walking at a stiff, controlled gait, came the prisoner, escorted by Lieutenant Lemus.

It took them a full thirty seconds to cross the patio. The TV and movie cameras whirred as Lemus casually talked to the condemned man while the crowds on the roofs shook their fists and shouted down insults.

The two men reached the pile of sandbags. A lost expression swept over the prisoner's face as Lieutenant Lemus stopped and pushed him against the mound. The full realization of what was about to take place struck him. I could see his mouth working, as though praying.

I stood rooted to the spot, unable to tear my eyes away from the lone figure standing against the bags. A dead quiet closed over the crowd. Then the crack of marching boots ripped the silence apart. What I saw next burned itself into my memory forever.

Six soldiers, automatic rifles carried at chest level, filed in at a stiff-legged half-step from behind the iron gates where the sack-laden truck had entered not long before. Their faces wore hard, implacable expressions, like robots or zombies. They made a column left to where the prisoner stood, marched in place about five feet in front of him, then, on orders from Lemus, halted and faced right.

"Ready!" The sharp rattle of bolts pulled, released, and sliding home, sounded with a definitive crack.

The prisoner's lips moved at an even faster rate.

"Aim!" The rifles were snapped up and the soldiers gave the impression, with the forward lunge of their bodies, of actually leaping at their victim, as though wanting to shove the barrels of their guns through his chest. At that moment, a woman watching the execution, who appeared to be about six months pregnant, screamed out, "Shoot him in the face!"

"Mother! I love you!" shouted the prisoner.

"Fire!" The automatic rifles roared and the force of the bullets lifted the prisoner from his feet and flung his body away from the sandbags. Lieutenant Lemus stepped across the man's head, bent down, and fired a bullet into his brain, straightened, kicked the cadaver's face, then walked away.

I was horrified. But the show was not yet over. The firing squad, rifles held high over their heads, began to dance like savages around the body. Urged on by the spectators, they leaped and jumped about as though they had just conquered a deadly foe or won a great battle; I dragged myself away from the window and dropped to the spot on the floor where I had spent the night. I was sick and drained.

How could they make a spectacle out of killing a human being? The guards standing in front of the barred openings of the Companies, suddenly turned on the watching prisoners and began thrusting their bayonets through the windows, sticking and cutting those not fortunate enough to get away.

An hour later, a dull red spot in the patio was all that remained of the Communist festival. There was no lunch, but it is doubtful anyone could have eaten. We were filled with terror.

Around six o'clock that evening, a prisoner pushing a cart and escorted by three guards, passed each Company and handed out a few ounces of sugar. Each man got his ration and quietly went back to his bed or place on the floor. That was supper.

This was the loneliest night of my life. Surrounded by filth, far from home, hungry and afraid, I felt as though even God had abandoned me.

"Oh, God, my God, don't leave me!" I murmured as I fell asleep.

Had I been forced to point out a certain time or situation that stood out as a dividing line between all that had been and all that would be, I would definitely classify those moments as *The Dawn of the Apocalypse,* a time when the four horsemen rode hard and fast, crushing with their passing, lives, hopes, and dreams; a time when nightmares began at dawn.

The following morning a fierce quiet blanketed the prison. There was no reveille, no breakfast, no noise. Just a graveyard silence. Most of the prisoners remained in bed. Others, including me, only moved to allow some fellow inmate the right to pass over to the floor space that each night was loaned to them. The prisoners' stomachs, reduced by months and years of meager intake, contracted even more. We were hungry, but to complain now could bring only devastating results. So we sat, feeling guilty, but not really knowing why. Perhaps it was because we belonged to the same species who had performed so atrociously the day before.

I could see a deep shame reflected in the eyes of the other prisoners. They had been living this debased existence for many years, but to have a foreigner witness their disgrace was equal to that of a man inviting guests to his home, only to have it dishonored by a drunken, whorish wife exposing her disgusting private life to his best friends!

In times like these it was common knowledge that marshal law prevailed. Havana was under siege. Police with photos of the other two escapees stood on every corner scrutinizing every passerby. Every taxi and bus displayed a photograph of the men. House-to-house searches were underway and anyone who had known the two were kept under surveillance. Roadblocks cut off all exits to the city. The dragnet drew tighter and tighter. Escape from Havana was virtually impossible. Two days later the men were captured.

Once again loudspeakers were tested. Again the prison was packed by those desirous of blood. Only this time it was to be a double feature.

Once again I stood at the barred window of our cell and watched while vengeance, not justice, was meted out. The identical procedure was followed; nothing varied.

After the bodies had been tossed into the back of a pick-up truck and the crowd had departed, the prison sank once more into a sombre silence.

All during this time the inmates had not been allowed to leave the large cells. No milk was served in the morning, but at noon and suppertime a little soup or hot sugar water was passed out.

This went on for a few days, then a guard came to the Company and told everyone to get dressed. Outside, the prisoners' view stood scores of guards armed with machetes and clubs. The iron door was opened and the prisoners were ordered to march in a straight line to another patio-like section.

This patio was about thirty feet across, three hundred feet long, and sat between two gray buildings. It was closed in at both ends by tall gates. Streams of other prisoners were being herded into the same enclosure. It's probably a search, I thought hopefully. Soon, well over a thousand men were jammed like sardines into the restricted space.

Slight movements at the top of the two buildings caught my attention. Suddenly, all around the edges of the roofs, guards with submachine guns pointing down at the prisoners, appeared.

I thought: My God, they're going to massacre us!

The low conversations that had been in progress died away. There was no movement. It seemed that time had stopped, locking each protagonist in his respective pose. Minutes ticked by. What are they going to do? The silence was unbending. What are they going to do?

Some tiny voice in my head told me to move to the center of the crowd, and although that placed me in the middle of the patio where the sun was hottest and where most of the guns were pointed, I slipped and squirmed my way to where my hunch led me.

There were loud clicks as the guns overhead were cocked; almost in the same moment the two gates at each end of the patio flew open. Dozens of guards rushed in and threw themselves over the prisoners, striking and chopping with machetes, clubs and iron bars.

The crowd recoiled toward the center. I was nearly crushed by the panicked mass of bodies, but those caught on the periphery suffered most. They were chopped and beaten down like wilted weeds. Old men and those of frail build were knocked down and trampled by the terrified rush of others in their search for safety. For the majority of us that day, there was no hiding place.

Faces laid open by machetes and iron bars glistened red in the afternoon sun. The blows by the guards were so savage that the walls were spattered with blood. The beatings and pleas for mercy went on and on.

The soggy crunch as heads were bashed cut into my soul as deeply as the machetes cut into the backs, arms, and legs of the convulsed mass of men. The massacre continued. But just as the sword cannot be eternally lifted, and the wounded in body and soul must someday find respite, the guards finally tired and slowly retreated through the gates.

Moans and cries of pain filled the air. The armed guards overhead had also disappeared. About an hour later the gates were opened and the men ordered to line up and march back to their respective caves. Those too badly injured were left lying where they had fallen.

The rest of the wounded, aching and bleeding, struggled back to the Companies where others, less hurt, helped them to cleanse and bandage the wounds as best they could.

That night, stretched out on the floor, I thought about that strange voice which had prompted me to move. I was reminded of the time I had tried to escape from Marquete and the same still voice within had told me to throw myself to the ground saving my life. Something was happening in my life. I seemed to be always protected.

Barely warm, watered down powdered milk appeared the next morning, but no bread. There would not be any for a long time. That was part of our punishment because the escapees had killed the old man in charge of the bakery.

At lunchtime the order to file out was given. It's easy to imagine with what fear the prisoners dressed. Those who had extra shirts and pants, thinking that another beating was in store, put them on. The additional clothing would at least absorb some of the force of the blows.

The aura of fear was so powerful I could feel, smell and taste it. I was terrified too. I had never in my life witnessed such cold-blooded terror tactics. Sure, I had done a lot of things in my life, but not once had I purposely and with malice, tried to destroy anyone.

Outside, guards with their shiny machetes, filled the narrow streets leading to the dining hall. There were faces I had never seen before, which meant that the guard force had been increased. They smacked their weapons against the sides of the buildings, glaring at the prisoners.

"Hey, you! Keep quiet there!" Crack! The flat side of the machete caught a man full in the face. The prisoners were ordered not to say a single word and woe to anyone who even leaned out of line. The inmates were marched in single file into the dining room.

Rows of trays with a smear of mush covering the bottom was the fare. The guards beat on the table tops all during the meal. Marched back in the same fashion we had come, no one dared even to yell a greeting to a friend as we passed by the Companies. Inside once again, we all breathed a sign of relief and settled down to wait for the next meal. Conversation was sparse.

About four o'clock, the doors clanged open and again the silent march to the dining room. Such a pitiful amount of rice was in the trays that I could not believe my eyes. A thin pea soup, splashed into another compartment of the tray, made up dinner. I counted the spoonfuls of rice as I ate: one... two... three... That was all. Three spoonfuls of rice!

We felt hungrier after leaving the mess hall than before going in. The rations had been cut to starvation level. For months and months that was to be the prisoners' diet, except for stray cats that wandered into the prison. Only the bag of products sent every three months by the Swiss Embassy saved me.

I traded the articles for food and even with this I lost so much weight that one day when Richard, being taken to see the doctor, passed by; he didn't recognize me. I spoke to him; he kept on walking. Then Richard stopped and whirled around suddenly. "Is that you, Tony?" he gasped. "Man, I didn't even recognize you! My God, what are they doing to you?"

I shrugged. "Everything they can!"

Since the escape the staff of hospital workers had been reduced to a minimum. I, along with the majority of the orderlies, was not permitted to leave the cells. The same went for the sick. It was almost impossible to see one of the inmate doctors. At any time of day or night you could hear prisoners yelling for the medic. But no one came.

Now with practically no medical attention, poor food, filthy sanitary conditions, and little or no water in which to bathe, a type of rot or fungus attacked the men. I watched their toes and fingers swell, turn gray and burst open like rotting sausages. Sometimes the disease crept up their thighs to their testicles, backs, and even into their eyes, causing a slimy yellow pus to flow.

If the Companies stank before, now the smell of bloated, decaying flesh added a putrifying odor that kept one always on the verge of vomiting.

Moans and cries of impotent rage sounded night and day. This was the revolution at work, grinding and pounding to dust the will to struggle, trampling under hard-heeled Russian boots, the hope for nothing except a quick death.

We were being starved, barely kept alive. We were callously subjected to interrogations where icy-eyed doctors, either Russian or Russian-trained, visited the prison and calmly asked the decayed bits of flesh, "What kind of dreams do you have? Do you sometimes feel afraid for no reason at all? Why? Do you masturbate? How often? Do you think about your children? Why?" Endlessly.

Teeth decayed and fell out. Eyes grew faint and accepted a darkness that only death should have brought. Hearts grew weak and sometimes, luckily, stopped.

What was happening in Principe, the national prison in Havana, I would find out later, was also taking place in every other point of detention throughout Cuba. The same mass beatings, starvation and diabolical experiments!

All the while this went on, weak American politicians, aided and egged on by International Communism, sought to drive the U.S. government into establishing diplomatic relations with Cuba. It was clear, at least to me, that the Russians wanted a change in geo-political strategy. Why not let the western powers support a Communist dictatorship?

And while the men, women and children of Cuba drowned in the vomit of Communism, in the U.S., the Kennedys, the Church, and the Carters, sought desperately to give a veneer of respectability to *Fido* Castro, the Russian lap dog!

Where was Amnesty International? Why were the *peaceniks* demonstrating, clogging streets, stopping production and demanding that the U.S., not Russia, halt nuclear experiments? Where was Jane Fonda, Sidney Poitier and Angela Davis? Where were you Jesse Jackson, when under the cover of darkness and muffled by the cannons' roar at nine o'clock at the back of the Cabana, black and white bodies perforated by hot lead, slumped and bowed before the always-ready firing squad? Where were you?

Who protested the beatings and murders I witnessed? Who protested when Fidel Castro shipped his dogs of war to Africa to help subdue black people, enslave them and turn them over to the white Russian masters?

My eyes were opening. I was learning.

Months passed and I grew weaker. I was not alone. Even the Cubans were silent. Anyone who knows a little about the Latin temperament is well aware that they love to agree or disagree in loud boisterous voices. In fact, just sitting in a Latin home with three or four of them is like sitting in a dug-out with a ball club that has just won the pennant. Well, here in these dark caves lay thousands of men and all you heard now and then was a feeble groan.

Too weak to talk, all our energy was saved for one thing, to struggle to our feet and down to the mess hall for one more meal to give us the strength to get up for the next.

The cement floor sapped my strength, the bedbugs my blood, and the animal abuse around me, the will to live. Many nights

I prayed for God to let me die in my sleep.

If there was one thing that gave me the will to go on, one thing that gave me the strength to push myself to my feet and totter to the greasy, smelly mess hall, and carefully count each spoonful of rice or force down the rotted shark meat, it was *Hate!* Hate for the Communist system and its progenitors. I had to survive!

I began to understand what the prisoners meant when they said, "If this government goes down, the street will be turned into rivers of blood! Indonesia was nothing, Tony. Here in Cuba, at least two million people will die... and they know it!" I watched and learned.

One day I saw Fermin, a Communist guard, give lessons to new recruits in the art of beating a prisoner. He picked out any one at random, called him over and then demonstrated to the goggle-eyed fledglings, with rapid blows to the head, legs, back, and arms of the inmate, how to keep the victim off balance by alternating the region to be struck. The students learned fast. Sometimes they made errors, but so what? That's what doctors and graves were for.

These were young men who had been raised by the State. They were devoid of all feelings except those inspired by the shock of their machetes striking human flesh or the flow of red, hot blood.

There was no resistance. Even the rebels were too weak to fight back. Most of the prisoners were now dangerously anemic.

Doctors in the U.S. might say, "It's impossible to remain alive with a count of three thousand white blood cells." Yet, Dr. Alvarez Tejeiro, one of the best Cuban doctors I knew, told me he saw and knew of scores of cases brought in with a count which dipped below that...

They were horrible walking nightmares; these men, who hung their scarecrow bodies from the bars with strips of filthy clothing when the pressure became unbearable, these holders of terrible, broken dreams who cried, "I give up!" and preferred to confront hell's fire for self murder than face another day in that *Communist Apocalypse.*

10.
SIGN OF A REBEL

In early August 1972, after being in prison over three years, I awoke to find I could hardly move. My body was stiff and sluggish. My vision was blurred and I had trouble focusing my eyes. My hands and legs were swollen.

The Greek took one look at me and declared, "Hey, Tony, you better get a doctor. Something is wrong with you."

I thought, at first, that I was just a little bloated from sleep. I had noticed a tingling in my legs for the last few days, but dismissed it as being something trivial. It seemed to be a repeat of the same sickness I'd had when I was in the first concentration camp at Guida.

"Yeah! Okay!" I replied. "Tell the guards!"

Within twenty-four hours I could no longer stand. My eyes were swollen almost shut; my arms and legs resembled overstuffed sausages. Breathing was difficult too. I felt rotten. I knew I was sick. Really ill. I tried to get up and fell on my face.

My friends, alarmed, began to beat on the bars. A guard came to see what was the problem. He took one look at me and sent for a stretcher. I was admitted into the infirmary. They still would not take me upstairs to the hospital.

The inmate doctors, always sympathetic to our dilemma, took one look at me and said, "Borderline starvation." The doctors managed to get me a diet consisting of fish, cows' milk and, at times, a piece of meat or chicken. It wasn't long before the swell-

131

ing reduced and I could begin helping in the infirmary again. Since workers were scarce, my aid was welcomed. I worked hard. I knew that if I didn't, as soon as I was a little better, I would be sent back into the dungeon.

Because I had worked there before and the inmate doctors liked me, they kept me on. Within a month I was well on my way to recovery. Even when my diet was discontinued shortly afterwards, I still received workers' rations and I could walk into the patio where the executions had taken place, and soak in a few of the sun's rays.

In December, a bed in the upstairs hospital workers' dorm became available and I moved in. For the first time in years, I slept on a clean sheet in a semi-clean room. I felt blessed.

Following the arrest and incarceration of Richard and his partner, many more innocent Americans were plucked off the high seas or forced by MIG jets to land their aircraft, then put in jail. They were given the option of confessing to smuggling drugs or spying. It was better to confess to smuggling, better than being shot. By February 1973, there were seven white Americans living in the workers' dorm and four black hijackers in the hospital ward itself.

It was apparent the Cuban government was doing everything in its power to drive the U.S. to the bargaining table. The men being captured were to be put on ice and used for ransom or political exchange, the Cubans told me.

One evening while I was on duty in the infirmary, the door banged open and three black Americans surrounded by guards stormed in. They were Louis Moore, Henry Jackson and Melvin Cale. They looked tough! "They're the ones that hijacked that plane for thirty hours!" whispered one guard to another.

The trio had hijacked a Southern Airways flight from Memphis, Tennessee to Birmingham, Alabama. Moore and Jackson had been suing the City of Detroit for four million dollars on charges of police brutality and were angry when the city offered to settle the case for $25.00. During the hijacking the boys demanded a ransom from Detroit. Later they threatened to crash the jetliner into the nuclear reactor at Oak Ridge, Tennessee. News reports at the time said relatives described them as 'disturbed.'

Now, Melvin had stomach pains and no wonder! After I gave him a shot, they left. They had not been too talkative and seemed suspicious of everything around them. I was to come to know them well in the years ahead. More Americans came; none as dramatically as these three, but we began having harder times. Castro caused a lot of it. He was perennially raving about U.S. imperialism and an always-imminent invasion of the island. Secretly, Cubans hoped he was right but his anti-American ravings also had their effect on the prison.

Guards and snitches, in an attempt to solidify their positions as true revolutionaries, laughed at and mocked the American prisoners and the U.S. government. It was all right for me to talk about my country and the fools who ran it, but I was an American. It wasn't okay for these sick, enslaved animals to criticize anybody. They referred to Nixon in the foulest possible terms. I tried to keep away from them so I wouldn't cause trouble for myself. But fate had ordained otherwise.

On the morning of March 30, 1973, Jesus, one of the four black hijackers in the hospital, called me into a small patio that separated the wards from the workers' dorm. "Say, Bro. You believe in dreams?" Jesus paced back and forth, bounding on the tips of his toes at the length of each stride.

"Yeah. Sure. I believe in them sometimes. Why?"

"Uh, well, I had this dream last night. It seemed like we was all out here on the patio an' there was blood everywhere! All over the steps an'.." He stopped and stared at me. "An' then I saw you come out. You was covered with blood!"

I shrugged it off. By evening I had forgotten all about my colleague's dire prediction. I was coming into the patio, heading for my dorm, when I saw a guard nicknamed Long Sleeves, for the oversized shirts he wore. He was standing in the midst of a group of prisoners. I drew closer. Long Sleeves was indulging in his favorite pastime, talking about the U.S. and President Nixon. I started to pass by when I heard the phrase, *"Nixon es un hijo de perra!"* Nixon is the son of a bitch dog! Before I could stop myself, I made a lewd remark about Longsleeves and his mother.

The guard's head snapped up. "What did you say?"

I kept walking, hoping he would let the whole thing drop. I had made a serious mistake.

"Hey, *Americano!* What did you say?" he yelled after me.

"I said balls," I threw back without turning.

A shocked silence followed me to the dorm. Knowing I was in for it, I snatched up a piece of paper and began writing a poem. Sometimes it helped to relieve the pressures. The poem was about storms, blood and death.

That night I dreamed of running through steamy, mud-filled wastelands. Something with sharp teeth breathed hotly on my neck. The sky was blood red and empty. When I awakened the next morning I tried to recall the strange dream, but only vague images flickered across my mind. Finally, I took a pencil and dashed off a finish to the poem, which seemed appropriate. I had just written out the title, "The Angry Dawn," when Long Sleeves walked into the room, and stopped about ten feet from my bed.

"Get up and get dressed."

"Why?" I asked, knowing full well.

"You have to go to the Hole. Yesterday you used 'balls' in my presence. That is a grave lack of respect. Get your things together."

My heart raced. If I went to the Hole, I would be kicked out of the workers' dorm and sent back downstairs into hell.

Well, if I got to go, I may as well go big, I thought.

"Yesterday you called the President of the United States a son of a bitch," I replied, all control over myself going. "You're the one who has shown disrespect." I tossed back the covers and got out of bed; Long Sleeves took a quick step backwards.

"Now look, Bryant..." He pronounced it Breean.

"No, you look!" I shouted. "If you don't get out of here right now, I'm going to show you what disrespect really is!" I took a step forward.

Long Sleeves scuttled to the door. He gave me a dirty look and sped toward the hospital director's office.

I turned to the other workers, most of whom were still in bed, and said, "You guys better get out of here. I think there's going to be trouble."

I had disobeyed an order. The guards would be here soon; I made up my mind to rebel. The prisoners threw on their clothes and abandoned the building in haste.

G.A., another black hijacker, and Jesus heard that I was about to have a problem and came over. "What's happening, Bro?" asked G.A.

I slipped a heavy padlock off the door and dropped it into a sock. This was my weapon. "I was told I had to go to the Hole, and I've decided not to. Look, this is my fight. Don't get involved! You hear?"

They agreed and after a minute or two they left. My hands perspired and sweat rolled down my face in streams. It was too late to turn back. I was committed.

A few minutes passed and then I heard approaching voices and the crunch of Russian boots on gravel and cement. First to ease around the door was Fereiro, head of the guards. *El Bizco* was the nickname no one would repeat to his face; it means cross-eyed. Actually, one eye peered straight ahead while the other veered off to one side. He was like some strange animal, able to see in two directions at the same time. He was also referred to as *The Shadow* because he seemed to appear out of nowhere. His guards feared him as much as the prisoners. Slender and tall, he had the stealthy gait of a feline.

Behind him came one of the most dreaded guards in the prison, Pedro O'Toole. He was six-foot-one of wiry corded muscle. He resembled a deadly snake, always coiled and ready to strike. No other guard in the prison had beaten as many men. He had a long narrow face filled with pock marks and his eyes were sunk into his head, giving it the appearance of a death's head skull. His hand rested lightly on the handle of his machete as his hooded eyes flicked over me.

Fereiro stepped up close to me and calmly asked what was wrong. I was in the process of telling him what had happened and protesting the injustice of being sent to the Hole for voicing an opinion since they were doing the same thing. Suddenly, Pedro, the back-up man, reached around Fereiro and snatched up the sock holding the lock. "What's this?" he said, jiggling the homemade blackjack up and down. He unknotted the sock and let the lock drop to the floor. Quickly he bent low behind *El Bizco* and in one swift movement, slipped the shiny machete from his waistband.

"What are you going to do with that?" I asked, "I know you're not even thinking about hitting me!" For an answer, the machete flashed and sliced into my arm.

Without hesitation, I grabbed up a large I.V. bottle and hurled it into my attacker's face. Cross Eyes grabbed my arm. "Just wait a minute! Calm down here! Calm down!"

Mad with pain, I kicked him in the groin, karate-chopped him on the side of his neck and then caught him going down with a solid kick under the collar bone. I was whirling around to face the other guard when I was knocked off balance by Jesus who ran in to fling a kick at the fallen man. That was just sufficient time for Pedro O'Toole to line up on me and, with all his force, swing his machete.

Lights exploded in my head. The last sounds I heard were machine gun fire and the rattle of falling bottles as my head struck a night table, scattering medicines onto the floor. Then everything went black...

I was being jostled up and down. I opened my eyes; I was being carried on a stretcher. The stretcher-bearers were running. I caught glimpses of faces as we passed through the patio. Then I was shoved into the back of an ambulance and everything went black again...

People were stripping me of my clothes. I felt a little embarrassed because a couple of the *strippers* were female nurses. I knew I was in the hospital and badly hurt. My clothes were blood-soaked and my body, sticky red. They washed off the blood, shaved around the wound in my head, put me on a gurney and wheeled me to the X-ray room. As I drifted between sleep and wakefulness, I heard someone say something about a fractured skull.

They stitched me up and sent back strict orders that I was to have absolute bed rest for thirty days, then more X-rays. Under no circumstances was I to be moved. It wouldn't do for an American to be beaten to death at this moment; Fidel Castro was trying to establish relations with the U.S. If something like this got out, it could prove detrimental. I was taken back to the prison hospital and placed in a special ward. Actually, it was just a small room with three hospital beds in it. In the other two beds were G.A. and Jesus.

G.A. looked like a mummy. He had so much gauze around his head that all I saw were his eyes, nose and mouth. Both hands were also heavily bandaged.

Jesus had a bandage around one arm and a few facial bruises. "What happened to you guys?" I whispered through my pain.

Jesus explained that after the guard struck me, G.A., thinking the man was going to keep chopping me, ran in, grabbed a small bench, and began beating the guard on the head. "Man, he was beatin' the mess out of that guard. Pow! Pam!" Jesus jumped around giving a blow-by-blow description of the fight. "I mean, he was really whuppin' him... then the bench broke and the fool guard had a chance to get his stuff together." He paused, looking over at G.A. "He cut G.A. all in his head, and in his hands too. But G.A. really gave it to him. Man, he really socked it to that sucker!"

A glow of gratitude flowed through me. Here were two brothers who, without really knowing me, had risked themselves to protect me.

They had decided my life was worth guarding.

11.
INTERLUDE

Toom Pa! Toom Pa!

The men's bodies swaying from side to side under the dim bulbs of Company 8 resembled intermingling shadows. Stripped to their shorts, dripping sweat in the humid atmosphere, they crowded around a man beating on a makeshift drum and chanted to the saints they worshipped.

Sitting on the edge of my bunk, I leaned forward so I wouldn't hit my head on the bunk above. Trying not to miss a beat, I clapped and chanted along with the others. After a month in the hospital I had been sent back downstairs to the *Pits*. It was early June 1973.

I had been in Company Eight for over a month; although my head was bandaged, I felt few ill effects from my first encounter with the *Beast*. In fact, I was proud. The Cuban prisoners practically worshipped me. I had done something the majority of them would have loved to have done. But, as bad as things had been for me, had a Cuban tried it, he would have been left maimed and crippled for life. In a way, I carried in me the embodiment of one of their dreams.

I leaned forward to eavesdrop on a nearby conversation. "Ochun is the mightiest of all warriors! All of your enemies are plucked up and tossed away. She is the saint of saints, the black warrior of warriors!"

The speaker's voice was convincing and a shimmer of pride could be noted in reference to Ochun. I was surprised that the speaker was white.

139

He went on talking, telling about the black saints of the dark continent, of their powers, how they could protect or destroy. The Cuban beliefs seemed to be a melange of Catholicism and age-old cults blended to form a challenging concept of religious practice. They believed firmly in Jesus Christ and the divinity of the Virgin Mary. At the same time, huge serpents crawled between machetes gingerly fixed point down so that a touch by the snake tumbled them, forming patterns from which divination could be made; these were considered as much a part of their beliefs as God Himself. They were the *Babalao*, who were able to see into the future, and *Spiritualists*, who communicated with the past.

Se Acaba el Mundo was the most feared spiritual power known to those who practiced witchcraft and black magic, and yet all confessed that God was above all! *Dios es todo!*

A guard gave a rap on the bars. The chanting and throbbing beat of the drum died away. The men shuffled to their beds, those who had them, and soon, like a gray mantle, quiet settled over the room. I had a bunk. The prisoners refused to let me sleep on the floor. I stretched out and after putting my boots in a comfortable position under my head, closed my eyes and fell peacefully asleep; I was beginning to like myself more.

The months rolled by. Neither the food nor the treatment of the prisoners had changed. The starvation diet remained, and it was commonplace to see an entire Company of men, chased by guards, run over each other to reach the safety of the building where they themselves slammed and bolted the door.

I met a man who told me how the Communists had tortured him. "They took fish hooks, pushed them through my eyelids and taped them to my forehead, forcing my eyes open. Then a bright light was turned on inches from my face. I was beaten and interrogated all night long." As a result he was left almost totally blind.

I managed to get a bag of cornmeal stolen from the kitchen. When I opened it, the contents wiggled with maggots. That was the same corn mush we ate every day for lunch. We laughed. That's our protein!

The civilian population was experiencing practically the same terrors as the prisoners, I was told by many. Everywhere in Cuba, and for no reason, people were being picked up and disappearing for months. Entire streets were cordoned off and all those caught within the confined area arrested and taken to jail. Only card-carrying party members escaped.

Fidel was demanding more sacrifices, which meant more work and less food. Also, he wanted more prisons built to house the controlled work force. He needed more free labor.

There was talk, though, of closing Principe. It was a sore thumb, sitting as it did, in the middle of Havana. There was a drive to complete the massive Russian-styled prison, Combinado del Este, where the seven or eight thousand prisoners from Principe would eventually be housed. Aside from that, dignitaries from other Communist countries could not be taken to Principe and shown how well prisoners lived under the mandate of that savior, liberator and lover of mankind, Fidel Castro. Even Communists might have been shocked. So now there were plans to close the ancient Spanish fortress and turn it into a museum, a tourist attraction, refurbished and freshly-painted to hide blood stains.

I could just imagine how it would be. A pretty, starchly-dressed militia lady leading the goggle-eyed tourists from attraction to attraction, pointing out the 'facts' concerning the prison in a smooth, well-trained voice: "Now here we have the Companies where the prisoners were housed. As you see, there were showers, fans to extract the hot air to make it as comfortable as possible for the men, and forty beds so each man had the sufficient area needed as a human being to function in the necessary air space. Contrary to imperialist propaganda, our aim, the aim of the revolution, is not to take vengeance on a man who has committed an error, but rather to help him. Rehabilitate him. Make him see that the revolution is benevolent! I beg your pardon?... No! No prisoner sleeps on the floor of any prison in Cuba! Of that you can be sure. That is an imperialist, capitalist lie! That's their

141

way of treating those who made a mistake. We are not animals and the revolution was made to eliminate the horrible humiliation of man by man. Here we show the offenders love and consideration so he himself can see the blessings of the revolution and transform from a negative to a positive element for the State. Now we see the dining hall. The redwood topped tables seated four men. They were served three hot meals a day. You say you would like to see a menu of the food they ate? Well, of course. We just happen to have one right here. Let's see... eggs, toast and milk for breakfast. Hot stew, vegetables, bread and dessert for lunch." The lies would be swallowed up, and the tricked and confused tourists would go home lauding the wonders of the revolution. If they came from a capitalist country, where protests are allowed, they would take to the streets at the drop of a hat, denouncing U.S. intervention and blockades of peace-loving, happy Socialist Cuba!

Well, they can listen to the lies, believe and be cursed for all I care, I said to myself, picking the last grain of rice from my plate. If you told them the truth, they'd call you a liar. I carried my tray over and dropped it on the stack by the door, then joined the long line of drooping shoulders and bowed heads, struggling to reach in safety, the putrid, overpacked confines of the Company.

In September 1973, the infamous, bloody prison, Castillo de Principe, closed. Only the hospital section overlooking the silent monolith remained operational. Prisoners were shipped to various camps where they were to stay until other facilities, such as Combinado del Este were ready.

All the foreigners were grouped together and transferred in steel-plated trucks resembling World War II ambulances, to a maximum security camp, *Quivican.*

12.
QUIVICAN

The ride to Quivican was torture.

The heat inside the armored truck sucked my breath away. The special-built Jaula or van bumped and swerved over seldom-used roads; the prisoners bounced to the hard roof, cursing loud enough for the driver to hear if he hadn't been travelling near the speed of sound.

I sat staring at the walls of the steel-plated cage. There was no doubt my already very unstable world had been shaken and totally uprooted. Out of sheer desperation, I struggled now to do the impossible: create something out of nothing.

I could have drowned in the sea of problems in which I existed; but perhaps it was the very essence of my adversities which kept me afloat. In seeing so much negativity and evil, I began to realize positive good did exist. If there was wrong, then right had to exist! I began to believe in the positive because I had witnessed the negative; I believed in good because of the bad. I began to truly believe in God, because I had come face to face with the essence of Satan.

As to what was occurring around the world, there was clear evidence of a vast conspiracy. I saw, not a struggle between two superpowers, but rather a tacit agreement to control the masses by any and all means. To me this answered a riddle: Why the government of the United States kept, and continued to keep, Russia, its arch enemy, alive with food and technology, while in

143

Africa and Latin America, poverty and starvation were the norm. Communism was sweeping the world and America, although crying out at the brutal nature of the *Beast*, continued to sustain it. It seemed that world politics were the results of a strong spiritual and racial conflict.

It reminded me of the times I had been in jail in the States. There was the good cop and the bad cop. The bad cop knocked you around then the good cop rushed in and defended you, but only if you agreed to confess. Both were working for the same thing: your confession.

Everything was going as planned. Countries were being lost to Communism and the U.S. taxpayer took on the burden of supporting them. I was forming a concept. But there were pieces of the puzzle that still had to fall into place. In fact, there were pieces of the puzzle yet to be made. They would be formed by experiences waiting for me down the road.

"Hey, Tony, what're you thinking about? Your old lady?" Lonnie, an American, cursed as the truck hit a bump and his behind struck the seat with a sharp slap. Lonnie was some kind of Dennis the Menace. He had a James Bond complex that had caused him to be dropped on his head more than once. But he retained a childlike quality which made me like him.

Lonnie had kind green eyes set over a long nose and a tough-guy mouth that nobody took seriously. A lock of brown hair, slicked back in the best Bogart manner, topped his five-foot, nine-inch frame. He was always in some kind of mess. But he had spunk.

His true name was Allan Schwandner, but he liked to be called Lonnie. Lonnie had hijacked a plane to Cuba, married a Czech girl and spent most of his time in Havana hustling on the black market. A stolen radio had caused his fall. Sentenced to three years, he was deserted by his wife, and now was just one of seventeen men who made up the group of Americans being transferred to Quivican that day.

I smiled at Lonnie. "Nope. Not thinking of my old lady. Just wondering what kind of place we're going to. It can't be worse than the rat hole we just left, that's for sure."

There couldn't have been many who thought differently. Though the men in the four-truck caravan were nervous and unsure about what was ahead, we all felt glad to get away from bloody Principe Prison.

With us was a foolish-looking Mexican, a very emotional Venezuelan, a Puerto Rican who wanted to show he was homosexual, and two young Arabs who didn't care one way or the other. All the foreigners had been grouped together in what seemed a new policy.

Three hours passed in the hot, bouncing trucks before we arrived at our destination. A double row of barbed wire-topped hurricane fences surrounded the five barracks lined side by side, each enclosed in another circle of wire. Guard towers stood like sentries around the perimeter. A line of guards searched our belongings, confiscating anything they wanted.

Crowds of men behind the double fence waved and shouted at us; a few quiet Cuban prisoners had been transferred along with us, but the Americans were nervous. Most of them knew no one behind the fences and the shouting, waving mass of men must have given them the same impression I received when I was sent to my first camp years before.

The search completed, we picked up our remaining belongings and headed through the outer gate into a wired-off section that separated the infirmary and the mess hall from the barracks. There, the guards stopped. Pointing to another gate that led to the interior of the camp, they told us to go through.

We looked at one another quizzically, wondering why the guards didn't want to go into the wired enclosure.

We soon found out.

A trustee ran over with a key, opened the gate and stepped back. We were still bunched up at the gate when pandemonium struck. *Fearless John*, a lanky Cuban who looked like he had just escaped from an insane asylum, charged through the group swinging a machete. The Americans, thinking he was after them, scattered like leaves.

I had been talking to a couple of my buddies. I turned in time to see the machete flash a foot from my face and land with a wicked thud on the upraised arm of one of the Cubans who had come with the Americans.

Fearless John was raging. "Cut me on my butt, will you? I'll show you!" The attacked man tried in vain to run. Every way he turned was cut off by Fearless who energetically swung his machete while screaming at the top of his lungs, "You cut me on my butt! You remember? You cut me on my butt!"

To cut a Cuban man on his backside is a grave insult. It's tantamount to saying the man was running away and thus categorizing him as a coward. The man under attack had dashed by Fearless one day in Principe and slashed his buttocks on the run. I remembered that day well for I had sewn up John's wound. But now the coin had flipped and Fearless, with his trusty machete, was chopping away relentlessly on his newly-arrived and recognized enemy.

The problem was that the machete was dull and only a few drops of blood were visible. Suddenly, Fearless stopped, and to publicly show what a gentleman he was, drew a short knife and threw it in the dust at his enemy's feet. "Pick it up! Pick it up," he ordered, "Pick it up and die. Today you gonna fight me like a man!"

Each time the man tried to grab the knife Fearless was on him like white on rice. The poor guy wasn't being cut much, but he was taking a terrible beating.

This went on for awhile and not one guard appeared. It was impossible for them not to know what was happening. Here was a cloud of dust, yells of encouragement from the onlookers, Fearless John's bellowing, and the frantic cries of the man attacked, and yet not a guard came to see what was happening.

Friends told me later the guards hardly ever came inside. If there was a killing, they waited until the body was dragged to the gate, then picked it up. They didn't care if the prisoners killed each other off, but Heaven help us if we touched a guard.

The battle raged on. Finally, the man made a desperate lunge and snatched up the knife. To me the fight still seemed a little one-sided. Fearless was almost twice as big as his enemy, and his three-foot machete gave him a reach over his adversary's knife. But somehow in the thick of the back and forth thrust and parry, Fearless John received a small cut on the inside of his arm. His friends decided his honor had been defended and leaped in and stopped the fight. The other guy, knots and bruises over most of his body, was glad to call a cease fire. The Americans, never having seen anything like this before, were about ready to fly over the fence.

They called a war council and, gathering me near, declared, "We've decided we're not going in those barracks. Did you see what happened as soon as we get here? These people are crazy! We'll wake up tomorrow morning dead or with our underwear stolen! You got friends in there, Tony. You can go in and nobody's going to bother you, but you know what will happen to us!"

They were right. "So what do you guys have in mind?"

Richard, the main spokesman, said, "We've decided to refuse to go in. They'll have to let us sleep out here on the ground or take us to the hospital section. They'll have no other choice!"

I didn't mention it, but there was a third possibility. The guards could come out and beat us into the barracks!

"Thing is, we've got to stick together!" Richard thumped his fist into his palm. "We've got to show a united front!"

"Okay," I sighed. "I'll talk to a few of my Cuban partners and explain the situation. That way they won't feel all pushed out of shape. Plus, we're going to need arms, just in case!"

Swarms of Cubans surrounded us, jabbering and pointing at the Americans' Swiss Embassy sacks. I could hardly get through, with all the shaking of hands, back pounding and hugs. I had just broken away from the crowd when I heard someone say in

147

perfect English, "What are you running for?"

A man, the spitting image of what cartoonists conceive as the typical con was standing there. He weighed around two hundred pounds of flab which might have been muscle at one time. His skin was white and untannable. Square jaws carved out of a large square head, thin lips, cold, watery, blue eyes and a nose that had probably been broken a couple a dozen times, faced me.

"What?"

"Are you a politician? I saw you shake just about every Cubans' hand out there and kept askin' myself, now what's he running for?" There was a mischievous twinkle in his eyes as he reached out to shake my hand.

"My name's Lester E. Perry, Jr. You're Tony!"

"Yep! Tony Bryant. Glad to meet you!"

"Say, what are those guys doing?" He pointed to where the Americans were spreading blankets on the ground. Some were even rigging up tents.

I explained the situation, then promising to talk with him later, hurried off to the barracks. We'd meet again and be cellmates in Cuba's toughest prison.

The same overpacked, squalid conditions I had seen too often were present. Filthy prisoners with dead looks on their eyes lay around on the floor. The lucky ones sat in silence on their beds. I had hardly entered the barracks when I was grabbed by one arm and dragged to where a little guy waited. He had a head so big it seemed impossible for his tiny body to carry it. *El Martiano*, The Martian, stood there with a smile wreathing his giant face. He hugged me and pounded my back.

His nickname told you all you wanted to know about his appearance. Five-five of guts and determination, the Martian was feared and respected. He promptly handed me a very long machete.

El Martiano doubled over with laughter when I told him how scared the Americans were and what they planned to do. He did agree, however, that it was a good idea. "But you, Tony, you're not going to sleep on the ground. That's out! What kind of friend do you think I am? No! no! no!" His upraised palm permitted no objections. "Here!" He wrestled his own fat mattress from the bunk, and almost falling under its weight, directed me to grab the other end. It would have been an insult to refuse his offer. We carried the mattress to the area where the Americans had set up camp, and telling Lonnie to keep guard, stashed the machete beneath it.

"Hey you! Open the gate!" We had decided to raid the infirmary for alcohol. Martiano snapped his fingers and the trustee gatekeeper, without a word, ran over and unlocked it.

Twilight had settled and the air was warm and soft. We chatted like two kids as we made our way to the infirmary. I found out Pandeado had knifed about ten more people, the guards were now more brutal, the snitches more open, food was scarcer than ever, and in general picked up the latest news and gossip; biggest one then making the rounds: everyone was sure Fidel would not last another year. Sabotage and absenteeism were on the rise. There was even talk of an invasion.

At the infirmary, Martiano shouted, "Hey, *Matador* look who's here!" Martiano pulled me into a small green room stacked with bottles. Behind the treatment table, seated at an old desk, was a plump man whose nickname must have been given to him as a joke. On seeing me, he jumped up, ran around the table and flung his arms around me. Without prompting, he told us to wait a moment, then disappeared into an adjoining room. He reappeared a moment later with a stack of small boxes. "Ahhh! Here we go!" he exclaimed, like a New York bartender, slipping out a tiny vial. "I knew you came for the real stuff!"

He had several dozen glass containers holding surgical needles and thread. Each was filled with alcohol to sterilize and preserve the suturing set inside. Matador popped the top from the glass vial, dumped the alcohol into a nearby cup, then threw the needle and thread into the trash. "Come on, you guys, gimme a hand!"

A lot of shiny new needles would have to be disposed of, and the catgut thrown away that evening could have filled three cats. But the three cats who stumbled out of the infirmary an hour later couldn't have cared less. The stuff wasn't Courvoisier, but it sure got you high! I almost forgot the fight ahead.

The Warden didn't, however. At count time he showed up with a couple of guards to talk with the Americans. He knew everything. But he faked a concerned look on his face and listened. He tried to be very diplomatic, but after an hour's debate with the Americans standing firm, he shrugged his shoulders and said, "Okay. If you guys want to sleep on the ground, go ahead." He started to walk away, stopped and with a cynical smile, head cocked to one side, remarked, "It looks like rain!" He was right. A light drizzle fell on the men all that first night.

The next day, Lonnie and I wandered from barracks to barracks, talking to prisoners and making deals with the Cubans for the Americans' embassy products.

The camp was teeming with dope. Pills, marijuana, and even alcohol, had been brought in by guards who had seen the products and were determined to get their hands on something, anything, marked, *U.S.A.* Needless to say, the bags shrank and the drugged Americans, lying out on their blankets under the warm sun, didn't really care.

Lester came around every now and then to talk. He told us about another American who had recently been killed. He had been shot trying to go over the fence. They had left him hanging from the top strands of wire, head down, blood gushing out, for hours. But nobody cared. The victim had been a notorious snitch.

We were fed separately from the Cubans and given more food than was normally allotted. The Cuban prisoners were on starvation diets. They showed me how they could put all their food into a container the size of a small Carnation milk can and still have room left over.

"Nobody outside of Cuba would believe it, Tony. That's how they get away with this. Nobody would believe it!" Martiano said.

"That's why they put walls and barbed wire around Communist countries. It's not to keep people out, it's to keep people in! And besides, since you can't see or know what's going on inside, they can mistreat the people and still tell others anything they want. When somebody escapes and tries to tell the world about the abuse and terror, the people who influence or control the news media in the free world brand you as a CIA agent or a liar. Or, even worse, they won't even print what you say!" The average Cuban prisoner was more politically astute than many a U.S. businessman or politician.

Martiano got me thinking. He explained that Cuba operated on a basis of fear. I remembered the Warden at Guida who had been so frightened when I arrived with two G-2 agents.

Now I knew why. Fear is a necessary tool under any dictatorship. Only terror can make the wishes of a few the will of the masses. Martiano explained that it had taken years of punishment for him to understand why Cuba had been reduced to an island of malignant fear.

When the revolution triumphed in 1959, positions of power in the new government were naturally taken by those who had fought, sacrificed and shed blood. They had earned their positions and made decisions of policy based on what they felt was right.

But this didn't sit well with Fidel Castro. He intended to have absolute rule and power and become Cuba's only voice. A slow, weeding out process of people in high places began. They were replaced by others who had never fired a gun but who could be controlled. Mysterious accidents and trumped up charges were used against strong-willed revolutionary leaders and they were replaced with pliable civil servants.

Many of those original leaders who had been replaced without execution explained phase two of Castro's revolution to me years later as we sat and rotted in his prisons. Cuba's civil servants were loyal first to money, but Castro wanted to control them by other, less costly means.

And so a reign of terror in government began, a campaign of

infiltration by G-2 agents who inserted themselves into Cuba's work force, from menial factory jobs to the highest positions in government. They sowed dissension, unrest, suspicion and destroyed trust and faith.

An agent would strike up a conversation with someone like a warehouse chief and with whispers and furtive glances, denounce Fidel Castro or the revolution. If the tested man agreed, he would be arrested, tried, and publicly executed. If he didn't denounce the defamer, he'd lose his job. Soon Cubans distrusted one another and life-long friends betrayed one another.

To cause complete social and moral breakdown, Castro next began to control the food supply with ration cards. As rations decreased, there was a mad scramble for positions that promised food. Hunger forced betrayals never imagined. Loyalty disappeared. Children were taught not to trust brothers and sisters. In his final consolidation of power, Castro eliminated people like Che Guevara and Camilio Cienfuegos to become Cuba's only spokesman, policy-maker and god.

I realized now that the Warden at Guida had trembled because he didn't know if he'd been denounced and the agents had come to pick him up. A thousand thoughts must have flashed through his head. Had he done or said the wrong thing? Had they found out some of the prisoners' food was being sold on the black market? Was the prisoner before him really a G-2 agent? If it was this bad for officials of the revolution, I'd better watch my step.

Next day I took a walk to the one-room hospital and was surprised to see how clean it was. The floor shone and dust was minimal. A sallow-skinned patient, breathing laboriously, lay in one of the beds. His eyes were closed and a thin sheen of perspiration covered his brow. The doctor was on pass and the male nurse, who doubled as janitor, knew absolutely nothing about medicine.

I was no doctor but I could see that the man was seriously ill. I told the nurse to bring me a stethoscope, and listening, discovered the man's lungs were filled with fluid. Questioning the nurse, I learned he had poured milk down the patient's throat although the man was unconscious.

Checking for reflexes and muscle control and finding both absent, I told the nurse to run and call the Officer of the Day.

"From the little I know about medicine," I told him, "all symptoms point to meningitis and possible pulmonary complications that could present an irreversible trend leading to death within forty-eight hours. We've got to get this man to a hospital now!"

The Officer of the Day looked at me as if I were speaking Chinese. He dug at his nose, "Well, we'll see what we can do. We ain't got no transportation right now."

"But this man is dying!"

"Now listen, *Americano*, the doctor ain't here, and I'm just a guard. I can't authorize this man to go to the hospital!"

"Well, who can? Aren't you the officer in charge of this madness?" My troublesome reputation must have preceded me because the guard began easing toward the open door, mumbling something about getting a tractor to transport the patient.

Hours passed and nothing. I sent message after message to the officers and even to the Warden. The man died the next day. We had been in Quivican just three days and had already witnessed one death and a stabbing.

The evening of the third day, the Warden came and told us to collect our belongings. We were moved in with Lester. But from the look on his face, Lester was not too happy about it.

I felt sorry for him. The man had been in jail about three years without trial. He was being kept on deposit. He had committed no crime but his past record was such that the Cubans refused to allow him on the street. One could feel sympathy for him, but the rest of the Americans had the right to a roof too. We were packed in like sardines, but at least everyone now had a bed.

Although we were all American, Lester continued to get his food apart from us, and we still received ours apart from the Cubans. It was clear to me that the only things distributed equally in Cuba were poverty, abuse and inequality. The following day there was a search. All prisoners were corralled in a fence-enclosed field in which sat a solitary cement disciplinary building, *the Hole of Quivican*.

The sun beamed hot and not a breath of wind moved. Clouds of gnats swarmed around our heads. Every now and again, a stream of curses erupted as someone's knife or machete was found. The guards were tearing the buildings apart. Forty or fifty machetes and knives were confiscated. But that night the sound of steel being honed to a razor's edge once again drifted through the air.

The next day the Swiss Embassy brought bags to the Americans, but the Warden refused to distribute them. The day after, he told us our bags would be given to us the following day, and they were, just as we were being loaded into the steel cages. We Americans had worn out our welcome at Quivican and were being transferred. No one knew where we were going and everybody felt a little sad. It had been a nice holiday and to face the unknown again was unsettling.

13.

LA CABANA

La Cabana was an old fortress built by the Spaniards when they were lords and masters of Cuba.

It sat on a cliff beside Morro Castle, overlooking Havana Harbor. An old drawbridge marked its entrance and the moat below, encircling La Cabana, hadn't been used for ages. Its dry, rocky bottom was covered with grass, weeds and plants.

The towering walls, ending in jagged breaks against the skyline, were awesome and frightening. At first I couldn't see the gun towers. The old structure was too massive and mind-absorbing to allow a close look at any of its parts. But as soon as I crossed the bridge and passed through the outer walls, everything changed.

The inside of the prison bristled with guns pointing at us. It was 10:00 p.m. when we arrived, hot, tired and thirsty. We stood still for a long time waiting to be searched.

The night was warm and every now and then, faint streaks of lightning brightened the horizon. The far away roll of thunder was just a murmur when it reached our ears.

Finally, a group of guards led by a slender lieutenant came and very thoroughly began to go through our property. Everyone, including the guards, was silent and depressed.

At last it was over. As usual, a small mound of things confiscated were left behind and we were escorted deeper into the prison.

We walked for about a block, then turned a corner of a building that had been added to the original structure. Although the building was old, its design was less ancient.

The lieutenant stopped and rapped on a steel-plated door. A few moments passed before it was opened by a wary-eyed guard. We stepped into a large room filled with cement slab tables. This was the dining room. It looked cold and ugly.

Leading off to the left was a long corridor. Inside the hallway, to the right, three Companies housing about one hundred men each, sat side by side. At the extreme end was a low, arched gate made of bars which opened into a small stone foyer. To the right was a large cell with a steel gate that reached eight to ten feet to the ceiling. On each side, running from the walls to the gate, thick bars rose from the cement floor to a stone block ceiling.

There was a loud crack as the slide latch was pulled. The first gate screeched open. Then, with a rumble and moan, the tall door separating the two rooms was flung wide.

All of us, with shock written over our faces, stepped inside. The gate closed with a crash. There was the clatter of locks being set, then silence. We were in the most isolated section, La Cabana's infamous *Cell 34*.

The room was large, about thirty feet wide by sixty feet long. The ceiling was supported by huge stone blocks that made up the dirty gray walls.

Mounds of trash scattered over the floor gave it the appearance of a dump, and standing in the center of the mess, clad only in shorts, was one of the three blacks who had come into the infirmary in search of a pain-killer that night in Principe. He was one of the three hijackers who had tied up a plane for thirty hours and demanded millions of dollars from the U.S. government. His name was Louis Moore, alias *Lou*.

Lou was about five-feet, eleven-inches tall, muscular with heavy, negroid features. He stood staring at us and we, in exchange, studied him. I walked over and put out my hand. "How're you doing, Bro? Remember me?"

156

"Oh, yeah! You that brother that gave Melvin a shot that night." His face broke into a grin. "Yeah, man. I remember you now. What y'all doin' here?"

"We just got transferred from a place called Quivican."

"Yeah," Lonnie broke in. "They didn't like us there, so they sent us to this dump. Man, this place stinks worse'n a pack a junkyard dogs."

"Well, I'm sho glad to have some company. These dogs done had me here for over a month now. Me'n my brothers," Lou added, disgruntled.

"Where are they now, your brothers?" asked Richard.

"Well, Flip is in the Hole. An' Melvin had to get an operation on his stomach. But hey! Put down your stuff and make yourself comfortable."

We busied ourselves pulling the single bunks into line and making them up. Lou went around looking closely at each man and introducing himself.

"Don't they have a broom to sweep up this mess?" asked Phil, one of the newly-arrived Americans who still hadn't grown accustomed to filth.

"Man, they ain't got nothin' here. I tol' you I been here for over a month an' they ain't never give me nothin'. I ain't worried though, 'cause they tol' me we ain't gonna be here very long. I don't know what they think, but I know I'm gettin' outta here."

"You got water in this joint?" Phil asked.

"Yeah." Lou scratched his head. "That's about all this place's got. The shower's over there." He pointed to a tall pipe curved over at the top with a spigot at chest level.

"Well, this isn't going to make it," I said. "Tomorrow they'll just have to bring stuff to clean this mess or I'm going to blow the roof off."

Early next morning, the guards taking count came by banging on the bars. No one moved.

"Hey, *Americanos*! Hey! Stand up for count!"

It was a good thing the two guards could not understand

English. A variety of colorful obscenities was flung at them. Finally, seeing the crazy Americans were not getting out of their beds, the guards came in and walked from bunk to bunk taking count. They slammed the steel door hard as they could as they left, making as much noise as possible.

A volley of curses followed them as they disappeared down the hall. The Americans had defined and established their own set of prison rules and without the help of the American Civil Liberties Union. We were prodding the Cubans. What would happen now?

Soon, a Cuban prisoner, escorted by a nervous guard, brought a pail of milk and twenty-five hard buns. The Americans staggered out of bed, took one look at the pail, and went crazy.

"You dumb Cuban slob! Take this stuff out of here! You dirty red! Get out and take this crap with you. What do you Commies think we are, dogs?"

I looked. The pail was bent and crumpled. Black greasy dirt was caked all over it, inside and out. It had been used either for scrubbing floors or dipping out sewage water.

Pushing the Cuban trustee ahead, the guard slammed the gate and beat a hasty retreat. The pail hit the bars, splashing milk over the floor of the next room. Guard and trustee ran.

We were fighting mad. Here we were in a super nasty cell and with nothing to clean it: we had been awakened by an infernal beating on the bars, which in the cement confines, crashed in our eardrums like thunder; and now having our milk brought to us in a dirty slop can was just too much. We were riled and we had a right to be.

Lonnie leaped up on the tall bars and using the weight of his body, began rattling them with all his might. The rest of us grabbed up whatever we had that would make noise and began banging on the bars.

After awhile, the lieutenant who had brought us in the night before appeared. Everyone was yelling and talking at the same time. The lieutenant held up his hand and when the clamor died down I explained to him the reason for the outbreak.

The lieutenant promised to send a broom and rags to clean the cell and a breakfast pail that was clean. He kept his word. Less than ten minutes later, a shiny new pail filled with hot milk arrived. Along with it were two old brooms, old but good enough, and several large cloths to use as mops. We labored for three hours scrubbing the place down. By lunchtime most of the stink was gone.

"Hey, Tony! Come look at this!" Lonnie beckoned me to the window.

The square aperture, about four feet deep, was the thickness of the wall. Covering the opening were four sets of bars, a foot or so apart, stacked one behind another — four sets! Fifty feet or more below lay the moat and directly across from our window, on the other side of the ravine, stood a small guardhouse.

"They sure don't want to lose us!" Lonnie quipped.

We were buried alive behind tons of granite rock, two iron gates, a steel-plated door, and all of it, fifty feet above a rock-bottomed moat. We were in for a hard battle.

A few days later, Flip, in reality Henry D. Jackson, was brought back from the Hole.

I was knocked back with surprise. The last time I had seen Flip was the night he, along with his two brothers, had stormed into the infirmary at Principe. At that time he had weighed well over two hundred pounds. The man standing before me now would not have tipped the scales at one hundred fifty.

I wondered about Flip and Lou being brothers. They shared no resemblance whatsoever and their last names were not the same. I decided they weren't related at all, and when the third member of their group showed up, my suspicions were borne out.

Melvin Cale only slightly resembled Lou and his attitude toward Flip was somewhat cool. Melvin was the musclebound pseudo-intellectual of the three. Though he had problems using correct English, he really saw himself as a very intelligent man. Of the three, Flip was by far the shrewdest and most dangerous. All the Americans quickly came to the same conclusion.

In general, for the first couple of weeks, everyone managed to cooperate. Whatever racial, ethnic or personal hangups existed were kept in check and the mixed group whiled away the time talking, playing cards or sleeping. But the pressure of being locked in one room twenty-four hours a day began to take its toll. Nerves were raw and everyone stayed on edge. Contact was made with Negro, a male nurse who worked in the hospital. Escorted by a guard who turned his head while business went on, Negro was soon bringing Antitusin cough syrup and anything else to get one high, in exchange for American products, of course. The rotgut drugs, along with depressing living conditions, caused a definite deterioration in our morale. It was natural that suppressed angers and anxieties led to an explosion.

Days passed and first to crack under the pressure were two of the brothers. Flip and Melvin bickered constantly and some insignificant word was spoken. Although Melvin's stitches had only recently been removed and Flip could hardly hobble on his barely-healed ankles, broken in a recent escape attempt, they suddenly tore into each other.

Both were too weak to do much damage. They threw a few blows, then tusseled each other to the floor. Lou and I jumped in and pulled them apart. After that first explosion, things settled back to the normal, zombie-like existence of before.

Practically everyone took something to stay high and escape, via drugs, from the coffin in which we lived. But I sought release from my anxieties through writing prose.

I had an obsession to expose all I had witnessed to the naive Americans back home. I had already decided that upon my return to the U.S., I would write a book. With that in mind, I began playing with phrases. Like most poets, I tackled the questions of life, love and death.

In late October 1973, as I lay on my bed lost in thought, an idea began to stir. I picked up my pencil, and at the end of an hour, I read to the others what I had written:

I can still hear if I listen hard
The creaking moaning mast.
The smothered exhausted cries of pain
That echo from the past.

I can still hear if I listen hard
The swish of falling whips,
The dripping blood that stains the decks
Of nocturnal phantom ships

I can still hear if I listen hard
The metallic rattle of chains
The frantic feet... a rifle blast
The sound of spattered brains.

I can still hear the cries of rage
Of a virgin ripped and torn
The crack of rotted rope that snaps...
Rotted corpse... too long borne.

And I can hear swell from my chest
Like a rose breaking through the earth
A cry for justice; precious gem,
That adorns the sweet rebirth.

Then we'll not hear, even though we listen
With all our heart and ear
Nothing except the blessed song
Of love forever near.

"Hey, man, that's not bad! You wrote that? Man, it's out of sight!"

I felt pleased that others liked what I had written. I didn't expect them to understand it because, frankly, I didn't! It was as though I had written in a semi-trance, and it was difficult for me to claim authorship.

After that, they treated me with some deference. Naturally, due to my length of time in Cuba, I spoke Spanish better than they, and in some respects considered myself more knowledgeable. But I had been beaten and battered about for so long that my self-esteem and confidence were practically non-existent. I needed their praise, and like a weary desert traveler guzzling water after a long day's walk, drank it in.

Through my poetry I learned about myself. I saw hidden, in the sometimes stormy, sometimes tender phrases, a sensitive and yet extremely violent personality. A typical Pisces, I was torn between two extremes: overly kind and gullible to the point of dupery, yet cruel and insensate to the limits of destruction. I understood more than ever that if I were to survive, I would have to find a cause bigger than myself so that, at the same time, I could love and hate with equal passion. I had to find *someone* or some *thing* worthy of my tenderness, and some *thing* or *someone* deserving of my wrath!

Also, I realized that anger for anger's sake was pointless and only brought about self-destruction. My hate, like my love, had to have a universal context. No longer would I stand alone; I would have history, if possible, on my side.

Arriving at this point, I had only to decide what the human worth was. What were its aspirations, dreams and illusions? And mainly, what was the human condition? In time I'd learn.

The food had become impossible to eat. Garbage was a superlative for the unidentifiable mush they gave us. And over and above that, there was little of it. Meanwhile, everyone was desperate to savor a touch of sunlight and feel a patch of grass tickle the soles of their feet, if only for five minutes.

We awoke to the echoes of a cave, walked its interior to the degree that we knew exactly how many lines were in the cement floor, and then closed our eyes and sought a deeper darkness than that of our concrete tomb.

Tension was so thick one could feel a pressure around one's self night and day. It was like walking under water. We had voiced our complaints to the officials several times; our pleas were in vain. Letters were sent; still no answer. Or, if an answer came, it was always, "We'll see about it." *Vamos a ver!*

This was the atmosphere when, one morning at count time, the guards began banging on the door. As usual, the Americans didn't stir.

"Hey, *Americanos*, get up! *Oye!* Hey, get up in there!"

The guards yelled for a while, then opened the gate and rushed in. They began kicking beds and snatching off covers. For some reason, they didn't say anything to the blacks. Maybe it was something they saw in our eyes. At any rate, still not getting what they thought was proper respect, the guards began grabbing the men by their legs, trying to pull them out of bed. It was hilarious and tragic at the same time. One guard was insolent enough to hit Phil in the head with his count-board. That did it.

All the Americans jumped out of bed yelling and cursing. It was a free for all. The guards ran through the gate and closed and locked it just as a couple of cans crashed a few inches from their heads. After that, it was pure, unleashed rage. Some of the Americans grabbed their bunks and began crashing them into the bars. The huge gate was sturdy but under the concentrated assault, it began to sway.

After almost ten minutes of pandemonium, a group of officials, uniformed and in plainclothes, dashed into the small outer room facing the cell. Andres, a G-2 official, was with them.

He stared at the Americans as if he wanted to throw a grenade into the cell and call it done. For a second, he and I locked eyes, then he raised his hand. Little by little the noise died down. He nodded to me and said, "I want you to translate. This situation is very grave. We all should have a talk and discuss things. This can only get worse if we don't. You better understand that we are not going to be pressured into anything." His mouth was hard and uncompromising.

I translated for the Americans, who immediately began shouting and slamming the beds against the bars again.

Andres raised his hand. But the Americans continued booing him and trying their best to drive the beds through the iron bars. Now Andres was shouting to be heard. "Listen! Listen, you guys. This is getting bad. It's going to get out of control!" He leaned close to the bars and shouted to me, "Tell them to hold it a minute. Maybe we can work this out."

I held up my hand and the noise died away. I figured it was time to talk. "Okay, what's the story?"

"That's what I'd like to know," Andres snarled. "I want to know what this is all about. And I'll tell you one more thing. We've got over a hundred guards in the hall, and if we can't come to some solution, we're coming in!"

I told the others what had been said, and bedlam broke out again. Andres screamed out for us to send a spokesman, and after thinking about it for a moment, I decided he was right. I quieted the men again and told them what Andres had said.

"Don't believe that sucker!" shouted Lou. "He's tryin' to get you out there so's they can jump you!"

"That's a possibility. But we're going to have to talk to somebody sooner or later. I agree to make trouble night and day, but now they're here, it's time to try and get our points across," I reasoned.

"Well, I ain't goin' out there. They gonna have to come and get me!" Lou was adamant.

Andres broke in, "Tell them I want everybody who's not mixed up in this to move to the back of the room and whoever comes out as spokesman isn't going to get hurt. I give you my word."

I translated, then added, "I'm going to talk to him and give him our list of complaints. If he doesn't straighten things out we'll continue."

164

Lou was against talking.

I didn't see any value in arguing. Common sense told me that if we didn't talk, our problems would never be resolved. "Andres, you give me your word?"

"That's right. I give my word as a man!"

His word wasn't much but I hoped the Cuban *macho* syndrome would subdue the Communist in him for a moment at least. "Okay. Open the gate. I'm coming out."

I stepped through the iron gate into the corridor. Lined shoulder to shoulder, armed with clubs, bayonets and machetes, were more than 150 guards. A shudder ran through me.

The other three Companies had been emptied. The officials wanted no witnesses to the carnage they had planned. I followed Andres between two lines of poker-faced soldiers to the dining room, then outside. The sunlight hurt my eyes. I had been inside the building too long.

"Okay," Andres said abruptly, "What's the problem? Why are you guys raising all this hell?"

I spelled out to him the complaints: The food was horrible and insufficient. We never had a chance to get sun. We couldn't eat in the dining room. We were forced to stay in one cell twenty-four hours a day. There was no infirmary for us; when someone was ill, all the guard did was bring a couple of aspirins.

"We want our own first-aid station in here," I told him. "You know it's impossible for us to go to the hospital or get medicine when we need it. The only remedy is to put a small infirmary in the dining room!"

Andres took notes as we talked. A small commotion was heard and I caught a glimpse of Lou, Lonnie and Flip being taken to the Hole.

Andres looked up. "They brought it on themselves. I don't often give my word but when I do, I keep it!"

For once he told the truth. Throughout all the years I knew Andres, he never again gave his word or told the truth. In fact, the very next thing he said was a blatant lie.

"And I'm going to let you in on a little secret. There is an order to get rid of all the Americans by the end of the year. I can tell you that by the end of December, there won't be one American left in Cuba." He forgot to tell me which December. January 1, 1974, found us still in Cuba and still in prison.

The little riot brought some changes, though. Once or twice a week we were taken outside for thirty minutes of sun. We also began eating in the dining room. Our food was served apart from the Cubans and it was a little better. A small infirmary was set up in the rear of the dining room and I was put in charge of taking care of, not only the Americans but the three Companies of Cubans as well. I did not mind; it gave me an opportunity to stretch my legs.

I noticed a definite change in Lou's attitude toward me, however. I had acted as I wanted during the crisis and Lou never forgave me for that. He said we should have stayed together. Lou wanted to be head man in everything. It was an obsession that was to cause an almost complete breakdown in our relationship.

The guards did business with us for our American goodies and only minor skirmishes over food disrupted our existence. But I was of a different breed. Although I had more movement than the others and could hustle extra food, I was interested in one thing and one thing only. Escape!

Lou managed to get hold of half a hacksaw blade which had been smuggled in. Lou, Flip, Lonnie, Melvin and I began cutting the bars of the window overlooking the moat. Each time we cut through a pair of bars, which made an opening large enough for a body to slip through, we mashed rice into a gummy lump and stuck the bars back together. A little dirt rubbed around the *glue* gave it the same color as the bar.

We worked for days. Getting through the first set of bars wasn't too hard. The second set gave us a little trouble and we were almost through the third set when the bust came down. It happened just before lunchtime.

166

A group of guards carrying iron bars irrupted into the cell. They walked straight to the window and one of them, a husky lieutenant, ran his piece of iron across the first row of bars. A large hole appeared as an entire section clattered to the floor. He repeated the action on the second set. Another crash and our *freedom hole* grew larger.

Now the lieutenant was almost in a frenzy. He wriggled his body into the opening and began hammering furiously on the other bars. One more fell. After soundly beating on the remaining ones and being satisfied they were intact, he backed out and, livid, turned to face the giggling Americans.

"All right," he bit out. "Who did this?"

I rolled my eyes upward, shrugged my shoulders and said, "You know how Russians make things, man! Them is Russian bars; they fall down all by themselves!" The Americans roared.

The lieutenant turned a deep blue. "Fall down by themselves, huh? Get out of here! All of you! Get out! Out! Out!" He was on the edge of having a stroke.

We were taken to an empty Company while the welders repaired the damage. A couple of hours later we returned to the cell. So many extra bars had been added that the window was almost a solid sheet of iron. Lou walked over and running his hand across the bars, drawled, "Boy! You talk about pumpin' sunlight to a niggah."

Everybody rolled.

A few days later another white American was brought in. He refused to tell his name or where he had lived in the U.S. and he was constantly praising Castro's revolution: now wonderful things were on the streets of Havana and how bad things were in the United States. For a few days I tried to ignore him. But to be truthful, everybody was getting a little up-tight with the guy. Besides, he was filthy and he stank.

It all came to a head one day when he started bragging, "You're all a bunch of jackasses. I've been sent here to watch you, so you better watch your step. Stupid fools! Watch it with me!"

Now, this guy really didn't now how sensitive an area he had touched. I picked up a short iron pipe I'd managed to keep hidden from the guards and, shielding it behind my body, walked over to Mr. X. In a low, tight voice I said, "You know something? I don't like you. You talk too much, you stink and you're a Commie." I took a deep breath, fighting for control. "I don't think you'd better say that again. And I'm telling you now — don't watch me too much. It makes me nervous!"

Still hiding the iron pipe, I turned and started to walk away. Suddenly I spun around. Mr. X stood glaring at me.

"I thought I told you not to watch me."

I took two long strides, brought the iron pipe up and crashed it down on the man's head. About the same time, Flip hobbled over and broke his cane on X's back. There was a screech and the man, blood flowing from his head, took off.

"Help! Help! They're killing me in here! Oh, guard, help! Get me out of here!"

I was right behind him. We jumped beds, knocked over our wooden box tables and now and again I took a swing, but the guy always managed to move his head just in time.

"Guard! Guard! Help!"

"Hey, Tony, get rid of that pipe! Here comes the man!" cried Lonnie.

I stuffed the pipe into the shower and rushed back to the door just as the guard arrived. Throwing my arms around the wounded man's shoulders, I said, "Hey! You better get this guy to a doctor. He fell on top of his head."

"That's a lie! That's a lie! He hit me with a pipe. They're all against me because I'm a revolutionary. They tried to kill me!"

I turned to the rest of the Americans, "Hey, fellows, isn't it true that this guy fell down?" There was a chorus of "Yeahs!" plus a few "Dirty Commie scum!"

The guard took him to the hospital. Needless to say, X never returned to the cell again.

One day, Lieutenant Crespo, the former warden at Principe,

came with a group of officers and guards. He told the long-haired Americans they had to get haircuts. While it is true some of the Americans had gone to extremes with their barbering, or lack of it, we objected strongly. Lou had shaved his head to stylish Mohawk but some of the others were imitating hippies.

There was no reason for haircuts. We didn't have visits. We spent practically twenty-four hours a day buried under tons of rock and steel; no one expected to be going anywhere soon. To us, haircuts seemed unimportant. Nevertheless, an order had been given. So when the guards inquired later as to who needed or wanted a haircut and no one came forward, the prison officials became upset.

Again word was sent that we had to cut our hair. We ignored the dictum. A confrontation was looming. Once again Lieutenant Crespo sent word: if by the next day all the Americans were not cropped *military style* they were to be held down and barbered. That made us mad.

"Hey, man," Lou complained. "Who do they think they are, telling me that I got to cut my hair! It's my hair an' I'll do what I want with it!"

Lonnie agreed. Boy, he looked like Moses just down from the mount. "Ain't nobody tellin' me when to cut my hair!"

"Wait a minute, guys," Flip said. "You know if we don't do somethin' those fools are comin' in here and we're gonna have a fight on our hands. What we got to do is beat 'em at their own game!"

"What are you thinking about doing?" I asked.

"All of us ought to shave bald! They can't accuse us of not cutting our hair 'cause we won't have no hair to cut!"

"Right on, man!" cried Phil. "Break out the razor blades, boys!"

We were careful not to let the guard who came the next day to inquire about haircuts see us. The guard went back to report that the Americans refused once again to cut their hair. All of us, except a few of the smugglers, had shaved off our hair and then doused our scalps with mineral oil.

About one o'clock that afternoon, the Warden, backed up by a dozen guards, stepped up to the gate, unlocked it and ordered all the inmates out.

Everyone knew what was coming so we had all remained hidden under our mosquito nets. Told to get out of bed, the Americans, yawning and stretching as if wakened from deep sleep, emerged from beneath the nets—bald heads shining!

The Warden's eyes bugged; he swallowed several times, searching for his voice. When it finally came, it was a thin squeak. "Get out of here, all of you! Smart guys, huh?" The veins in his neck stood out rigid. "Get out! You're going to the barbers anyhow!"

With our heads sparkling in the noonday sun, the object of curious stares, we were marched to where over fifty machete armed guards stood waiting. Those Americans with moustaches were brutally clean-shaven.

The guards were hopping mad. They milled among us, purposely bumping into our bodies. One shoved Flip, whose legs were still healing and unsound. He stumbled and fell against a guard and that was the pretext for another guard to slash Flip across the forehead with a rod made of interwoven wires.

The situation became explosive. The rest of the guards whipped out their machetes and stood glaring at the prisoners. No one moved. Flip was taken to the Hole for 'hitting' a guard and the rest of us were marched back to the cell — smiling. Castro's guards had drawn blood, but we had won the battle!

14.
REBEL IN REBELLION

Cuban prison authorities had now classified me as a troublemaker. Maybe so, but I had motives of the highest order based on my respect for the suffering but defiant political prisoners.

My reasons for rocking the boat might not have been totally pure. Perhaps I felt my position as leader was threatened by the presence of the three brothers and wanted to reaffirm it. But deep inside, I reasoned that if the other Americans were to survive they would need someone to demonstrate raw courage, even to the degree of foolhardiness. Maybe they could draw on that strength.

I had decided to expose to the Americans the *Beast* as I knew it, by provoking it with audacious and dangerous actions. Whatever the reason, it prompted in me such an aggressive attitude that its keepers were confounded as to how to control and, or, break the rebel I had become.

Also, there is the possibility that my future hazardous escapades were prompted by a growing belief in my destiny and in God. I began to believe so firmly I had been destined to undergo these tests, trials and tribulations and someday return to the U.S., that I believed myself invincible.

When I stopped believing in death for myself, I began seriously testing the powers I believed had been sent to protect me. Sent by whom? By God! By everyone who loved me. By every person who felt the need to know the truth. By those who, without ever having known me, sent their vibrations of love and protection, to a kindred soul in hell.

I was part of a powerful scenario, no longer black or white, just a man; a man who believed in his God and his cause, facing conditions designed to mangle and destroy, created by an enemy attempting to make the myth of its immortality and invincibility accepted as reality to all men.

Could one man taunt, tease and wound the *Beast* sufficiently to force it to react and, in reacting, to unmask itself? Certain who the enemy was, I planned my battle lines, asking no quarter and giving none. Like a dog edging backwards to get the utmost power in its attack, I began to retreat into myself.

For days I had been morose and withdrawn. The limited recreation of card games and sitting around swapping lies had lost its attraction. Now, after passing out pills or treating minor infirmities, I headed back to the cell. Disregarding everyone, I slipped under my mosquito net and lay in bed with my thoughts. Each day I grew more quiet.

Then in March 1974, when the guards came in to take count early one morning, I got out of bed, dressed, picked up a bundle of personal effects I'd packed the night before, and without a word, walked out of the cell, the guards racing after me.

"Hey! Where do you think you're going?"

"I'm on a hunger strike. Take me to the Hole!"

Their eyes widened. People didn't put themselves in the Hole. Everyone, in fact, tried desperately never to see that part of the prison.

We stood in the dining room arguing for a few minutes; then, left with no other alternative, they took me to the punishment section. They opened a steel-plated door that led into a narrow hall about forty-five feet long. On either side of it were five side-by-side concrete cells, each capped by a steel door. They were nothing more than cement boxes into which air could enter only through cracks beneath and above their heavy doors.

Pena, the hard-faced guard in charge of discipline, separated one of the keys on his noisy key-ring and snapped the lock. The door squeaked and groaned on its hinges as it swung open. The dank odor from the filthy cell rushed out and blanketed me. I stepped inside and with a crash, the door was slammed shut, isolating me in silence and the dark.

They had taken all my clothes, except the shorts I wore. Not even a thin blanket to throw over the floor was allowed. After a while my eyes grew accustomed to the darkness. The walls were green and slimy and covered with mildew. The rank, foul-smelling cell was only six feet long and four feet wide.

The floor sloped down at about a thirty-degree angle from back to front. The eternal hole in the floor, half full of feces, was at the back of the cell at its highest point. This meant that if I didn't want to lie on the cement with my head lower than my body and blood rushing to my head, I was forced to sleep with my face beside that opening and breathe in its noxious pungent fumes.

Breathing through my mouth, I checked the walls of the cell. They were marked and scratched where others before me had feebly tried to leave behind some evidence of their existence. The prisoners had used spoon handles to carve slogans, images of patron saints or their own names on the hard surface.

The childish outline of an airplane had been scraped out near the ceiling and as I looked closer I could make out an American flag. Underneath the flag was the slogan: *"Communism sucks, Lonnie."*

So, this is where they put the poor kid the time we had that little riot, I thought. Well, that's good. All of them need to be thrown in here for a while after being beaten just a little. That way they never forget and maybe when they go home they'll fight and not just sit back saying, "It'll never happen here."

As the day wore on the cell grew hot and humid. Dripping sweat, I sat with my nose pressed to a crack at the door's edge, like a dog locked in a hot automobile, trying to catch every wisp of less fetid air.

There was no water in the cell and that was fine with me. I hoped to escape and this cell was the first door of my journey. If I refused the food but drank water I would be in the Hole for a month or more. But if I turned down the water I would become dehydrated within a matter of days and the officials would be forced to send me to the hospital where I hoped to find a way to break out. I would be running the risk that my blood could turn thick and sluggish, maybe stop flowing, but I had decided to embark on an all-out war.

The noisy food wagon brought some wormy white spaghetti and a cup of water. I refused the food and the water. I did the same at dinnertime. I promised that night, "This is it, Castro. From here on I'm going to fight you with everything I've got. I'm going to cause so much trouble, you'll wish I never came to Cuba!"

I lay crossways in the cell with my knees drawn into my stomach and my forehead pressed against the bottom of the door. I had tried lying with my head sloping downward but after only a few minutes in that position the blood flowing to my head caused a tight, pressurized feeling. But no matter what, I had no intention of sleeping with my face up high near the toilet hole at the back of the cell.

The cement bit into my flesh and every few minutes I had to move so that the same centimeter of skin and bone would not be constantly under the weight of my body. I folded my arms under my head to keep my face off the floor and meditated.

If the officials thought that by putting me in this particular cell they could soften me up, they were completely wrong. As I lay there, my resolve grew as hard as the cement digging into me. The following day was a replica of the first, and the next, and the next, exact copies of each other.

Roaches, slipping under the door or up through the filthy hole in the floor, bit me in the face while I slept, leaving large knots which turned black and burst, oozing yellow pus. Mosquitos stung and tortured me constantly.

I grew angrier and angrier. When the guards opened the cell to ask if I wanted to break the strike, I merely glared at them. I must have looked crazy and dangerous; they hurriedly dropped the tray outside the cell, along with the previously rejected meals, and clanged the door shut.

On the fifth day I began feeling weak. The hot cement cell, plus the lack of water, were draining my strength. Under somewhat normal conditions, by drinking only water, a person can go up to thirty days on a hunger strike and suffer few ill effects that are lasting.

Many have gone blind or been left crippled by a hunger strike, but usually they had gone over thirty-five days without eating. But when one stops drinking water, death usually occurs within twelve to fifteen days. And that's under normal circumstances that include a bed and clean surroundings.

Lying on a filthy cement floor, tormented by insects, listening to the rats fight over my food on the other side of the door but close to my ear, were the conditions under which I began my first serious hunger strike. It was the most dangerous kind of all, the rejection of all nutrients, both food and water.

On the sixth day my tongue felt thick and dry. Pieces of parched skin hung from my lips and when I pushed myself to a sitting position, the dimly-lit cell went completely black for a minute. I breathed hard from that slight movement. My muscles ached but I seemed to be slipping into a state where I really didn't care.

The seventh day, when the guards came by, I did not move from my fetus-like position. A male nurse was sent over from the infirmary to take my pulse. A few minutes later a doctor came in and examined me. Then once again I was left to use my last energy and strength to face another night.

The next morning the doctor checked me again. In less than an hour, two prisoner medics, carrying a stretcher, came in, loaded me on, and hurried me out to a waiting ambulance. With a guard to escort me, the old vehicle rushed out of the prison.

After a short ride, we pulled up to my old home, the now deserted prison of Principe. I was carried up a nearly perpendicular stairway to a hospital ward directly facing the dorm where some of the Americans and I had once lived; the same place I had fought Cross Eyes.

A bulbous-nosed Arab doctor, a total incompetent who knew nothing about medicine, was in charge. I knew him well. In the past he had disconcerted patients by giggling and laughing for no reason at all. He was screwy.

"Well, Tony, my boy, how're you doing? Hee-hee! Looks like you haven't been eating. You're not hungry? Is that it? Hee-hee. You're not hungry?" He moved around, jabbing my stomach with a thick, hard finger, then ran that same finger around the inside of my mouth. "Hee-hee. Kinda dry!" He decided I needed dextrose and ordered an intravenus bottle set up. After missing about five times, the Arab finally hit a vein and giggling every now and then, taped the needle in place.

The 5,000 cc's of dextrose was replaced by the same amount as soon as the bottle emptied, and then by another, over and over, all night and into the following day. I felt much better. By that evening I could stand without getting dizzy. I drank some hot broth and slept like a baby.

The following morning the Arab came in, and after a brief examination announced, "Well, my boy, you seem to be in fine condition. Hee-hee!" He poked around a bit more.

"I'm discharging you."

"You're what?" I cried, sitting upright in bed. "You're discharging me?"

I knew the man was a poor doctor and terrified of officials, but I was shocked that he would even think of putting me out of the hospital after only two and a half days following an eight-day hunger strike. Besides, I'd gone through all that suffering so I could escape from this hospital. I needed time.

The doctor jumped about two feet, and rubbing his fat hands together, stammered nervously, "Uh, well, you're okay and besides, there are three guards from the Cabana who've come to pick you up." He danced from one foot to the other as perspiration trickled down his brow.

I threw back the sheet and with eyes drawn to narrow slits, slowly stood. "Now you listen. You're out of your head if you think

176

that after being almost dead I'm going to let you throw me out of the hospital." My voice rose and I trembled from the effort to control myself. The other patients in the ward followed the conversation with interest; they were in for some entertainment.

"I'm not going anywhere. Do you understand me? Nowhere!"

"But the guards are waiting for you."

"You go back and tell them I said I'm not leaving this hospital until I'm okay. Now you just run and tell them. Hear?"

He was moving at top speed by the time he hit the door. You could have shot dice on the white smock streaming out behind him. Certain that action was on the line, several of the sixteen patients in the ward crowded around me to get all the details.

I explained briefly, while collecting empty I.V. bottles and lining them up on the night table. All the patients had retreated to a safe distance and I had collected about thirty bottles, when three guards walked in. They stopped by a low wall which formed a kind of walkway for the patients and which ran the length of the ward.

Looking first at the array of bottles, then at me, they shuffled around a bit. Sergeant Leva, an even-handed cool-acting guy of about thirty, not known to be too brutal or too nice, either, took a step forward.

"Don't come any closer," I whispered coldly.

Leva paused, looked around at the watching patients, then turned back to me. "Look! You've gotta come with us. The doctor released you and we gotta take you back with us. We've got our orders, Tony."

"I'm not going anywhere. And if you take another step, I'll smash this bottle in your face!" I snarled. "I told you once. Now, if you don't get out, somebody's going to be in trouble and that somebody won't be me!" To let them know I was serious, I drew back a bottle. I must have been a little crazy. I couldn't face being locked in a concrete box again. And besides, I planned to escape somehow from this room.

The three uniforms pulled together and headed for the exit.

They had taken about three steps; three more would have gotten them through the door, but Leva stopped and turned around, probably to voice some new argument that had popped into his head.

Because I had told them there was nothing more to be said and Leva was totally disregarding my pronouncement, I hurled the 5,000 cc bottle at the cement wall. There was a splintering crash as the bottle broke into dozens of razor-sharp projectiles on the cement wall, a foot from Leva's head.

A geyser of blood shot up from the sergeant's bare arm. He clamped one hand over the wound, spun, and ran for the door. But not fast enough!

Another bottle shattered over them as the guards fought to get out of the building and away from the madman. Another guard cried out and slapped his hand over blood streaming from his head. There wasn't time to get off a third bottle so I replaced it on the stand, turned around and gave the astounded prisoners a nervous smile. One little guy, Juan, ran around collecting bottles for me but the others, wiser, got as far away as possible.

I had no idea what the repercussion for my action might be. It would certainly be bloody and devastating. My heart pounded, cold tremors ran over my body. Everyone waited. There was nothing said or to be said. The die was cast. I was in the eye of the storm!

It wasn't long before the tramp of dozens of Russian boots could be heard approaching. I stepped closer to my *ammunition* cache and picked up two bottles.

I stood ten feet from the only door and watched as the small patio between the dorm and the hospital ward filled with *bottle-carrying* guards. I was shocked! This was incredible! I was a prisoner and had resorted to the first thing at hand as a weapon, so I had grabbed the bottles. But to see the brave revolutionary guards with them blew my mind.

Well, I decided, this is going to be a real trip.

A couple of guards began Castro's assault. Running low and zigzagging in the best military fashion, they streaked to the door, hurled their empty bottles in and scurried off before I could retaliate. The bottles smashed against the wall close to my head. A ricocheting piece struck my ankle. I didn't have time to check if I was bleeding. Suddenly, all the guards were hurling bottles into the hospital ward. The patients began shouting and running from one place to another.

I fired back, through and around the door, as fast as I could lift my arm. The smash and tinkle of breaking bottles sounded as though someone had gone crazy in a china shop. Shards of glass sprayed the air around me. But it was as though an invisible shield covered my body. Bottles shattered around my head, close to my feet, in front and behind me, but not one piece cut me.

"Don't you hurt my guards!" A white-faced lieutenant peeped his head around the door. "*Americano*! Don't you hurt any of my guards."

I flung a bottle at the spot where his head should have been. "Move fast, don't you, sucker?"

There was a momentary lull; then, a barrage of bottles came flying through the door. They were trying to sneak a man inside behind the low stone wall so he could gun me down. I knew what they were up to but the onslaught of bottles drove me back toward the spot where the patients now were huddled. That set off a stampede. Yelling and screaming at the top of their lungs, the prisoners scattered, ducking and dodging flying bottles at every step.

One patient was in a wheel-chair; his buddy was pushing him like he was trying out for the Indianapolis 500. I caught a glimpse of them making a high-speed turn. The wheelchair was tilted to one side, riding on one wobbly wheel and I couldn't hold back a wild burst of laughter.

Actually, the situation was not the least bit hilarious, just dangerous. I ran back toward the door in time to see a blur of green pass through and disappear behind the stone parapet. One of them had gotten in! Would he shoot me?

The lieutenant bellowed, "Watch it, there! Don't you hurt one of my guards. If you do, we'll kill you!"

"That's what you'll have to do. You have to kill me!" I ran from one end of the room to the other, hurling bottles over the top of the low wall into the cement behind it. The guards outside renewed their barrage with a fury. Bombarded by bottles, I was forced to take my eyes off the walled walkway where the guard hid. At that moment, he rose up a little to the left and rear of me. There was no sound of a shot. Instead, he made a perfect pitch. A fist-sized rock caught me behind the left ear.

My legs gave away and the floor rushed up. The bottle I held lay in pieces around my right hand. Only the top, which I still clung to, was intact. Blood poured from my head. My arms collapsed and I fell face down. I could hear shouts and the pounding of running boots.

There was a swish and a crack. The hot pain of the first machete blow brought me struggling up to my hands and knees. Scores of blows from many machetes drove me to the floor again. They kicked me in the face, in the sides, everywhere that a machete was not already striking.

I managed to flip over on my back and striking out at the legs surrounding me, screamed, "Kill me, you cowards! C'mon, kill me. Kill me and get it over with! Kill me!" And they might have, but the lieutenant unexpectedly, jumped in and yelled, "Hold it!"

Soaked in blood, I was kicked to my feet. A guard on either side grabbed me beneath the armpits while another twisted my arms behind my back, almost breaking them. They dragged me to the stairway and down to the section between two large prison entrance gates, beating me with their fists all the way.

They called a medic from the infirmary to stitch me up and while one guard pushed down on the side of my head with his booted foot, the scared medic, who had been ordered not to use anesthetic, sank a large curved needle into my flesh.

I was too weak to move, and so angry and frustrated, the pain of the needle was nothing. Tears, mixed with blood, formed a puddle beside my head. I was so enraged I felt a ball of fire inside my chest where my heart should have been.

The medic was gouging the needle into my head when the hospital director, Lieutenant Campos, ran up. "Hey, you! Hold it there!" Campos pulled the medic up, and shoving the guard's foot from my head, shouted angrily, "I don't allow this kind of treatment. As long as I'm present you can't do this. You should be ashamed!" He glared at the guard, who muttered and wilted. Campos turned to the medic.

"Go and get the stretcher. You'll take this man to the infirmary. You'll admit him under my orders and you will treat him as a patient. Sew up those wounds. And do it with anesthesia! What are we? Animals?"

Later, with the blood washed off and bandaged up like a mummy, I stretched out over the bed and closed my eyes. Hearing a noise, I jerked up.

"You just relax and don't worry." It was Lt. Campos. His eyes were sad and his voice compassionate. "I've given orders that no guard is to come in here unless he's with me. So lie back and try to get some rest. You've been beaten pretty badly."

I reached out to shake the man's hand. "Thank you. At least there are still some human beings here. Thank you."

Campos waved my thanks aside, and turning to leave, gave me a wry grin, "Boy, you sure tore my hospital apart!"

"I told them I wasn't going anywhere!" My lips were cracked and swollen but I drifted off to sleep chuckling,

A few months later, I was tried and sentenced to an additional year and a half for assault and battery. News of the bottle battle went far and wide. If, prior to the hospital assault, people had treated me with deference for simply being an American, afterwards it was an honor to be seen with me and counted as one of my friends. And though I had not managed to escape while in the infirmary at Principe, I felt contented. Again I had drawn blood from the *Beast* and survived. And now the guards gave me a wide berth; I had established my position as a leader.

15.
REUNION IN DISCIPLINARY

May and June were hectic months. There were constant rejections of the food and subsequent reprisals.

Lester Perry had been transferred from Quivican to the Cabana in April. With twenty-five people in it, the cell was a sweat box. The days were long. Petty squabbles became a daily occurrence. Most of the time I lay on my bunk, mad at the world. The lack of sexual release also played a part in the bottled-up feelings that had me on the brink of an outburst. I sought refuge in sleep only to find myself plagued by nightmares and dreams of romance that awakened me soaked in sweat.

Constantly I played with the idea of escape. I had heard of a couple of attempts made from disciplinary, and after going over in my mind the pros and cons of that possibility, I decided to get myself thrown in there.

July is the most important month of revolutionary Cuba. The twenty-sixth, the same *26* I had naively hoped to celebrate in my first year of imprisonment, is the island's big national holiday. Christmas and other pre-revolution religious holidays have been outlawed and abolished. Since religion is the *opiate of the masses*, there is an all-out war against God and His believers. So much emphasis has been placed on the twenty-sixth of July that it has become a *holy* day for Cuban communists. Children are taught to revere it, anti-Communists to fear it, and Marxist-Leninists to worship it.

On July 15, 1974, I committed an unforgivable sin: I took the name of Fidel Castro in vain.

A lone guard wandered back to our cell, and after ogling us for a few moments, struck up conversation. As usual the prisoners were telling him about some of the horrible things they were living and seeing and he was trying to point out the wonders of the revolution and its leader, Fidel Castro. I sat listening to the exchange for awhile, then suddenly grew angry. Something came over me. Out of nowhere I struck a bolt of lightning:

"Oye! Me escupo en la caravela de la madre de Fidel Castro!" I'd heard other prisoners mutter this secretly.

"What?" The guard stared at me as though I had just stepped out of a nightmare. "What did you say?"

"I said I spit on the skull of Fidel Castro's mother."

Although it loses a little of its poetic beauty in the translation, one can understand the impact. I was glad the other American prisoners didn't know enough Spanish to be alarmed.

The guard backed away from the bars, staring at me as if expecting me to be struck down by a dozen sickles from the sky and pounded into the dust by as many hammers. Then, with disbelief written on his face, he dashed down the hall.

I began collecting the things I thought they might let me keep during a stay in the Hole: blanket, comb and toothbrush.

"Hey, Tony!" Lou yelled. "What'd you tell that guard? He's real mad!"

"Oh, I just reminded him that we're Americans. You see, they've got a funny thing going on here. They think everyone is as big a fool as they are."

"But what'd you say to get him so riled?"

"I told him I'd like to spit on the skull of Fidel's dead mother. I don't think he liked that! Oh, oh! Here they come!"

Two guards, in best Gestapo fashion, stomped to a halt, unlocked the cell and stepping back, ordered me to come with them. They looked plenty mad.

I grabbed my belongings and called over my shoulder, "Well, fellows, see you around."

"What kind of flowers d'ya want?" cracked Melvin, nervously.

"Any kind — as long as they're not red!"

They marched me to a small, low-roofed building nearby. No sooner had they pushed me inside than they were transformed into the monsters they truly are.

A guard slammed me into a chair. Before I could react, another whipped out a long revolver and pointed it at my head. A lieutenant leaped on me and began choking me, screaming like someone gone mad. "You dirty American pig. You think you can come into our country and talk about our leader like that, huh? Who do you think you are?"

I would have been glad to tell him, but I was having a little difficulty breathing. The guard holding the gun kept shouting, "Move out of the way! Get back and let me shoot him."

A guard appeared from a side office. He was glaring at me and swinging a baseball bat back and forth. The only thing that saved me was they all wanted a piece of me at the same time. With one choking me, another pointing a gun at my head and the other waving a baseball bat, the situation was critical. I had to do something fast before I got badly hurt.

So I gave a loud death rattle gasp, rolled my eyes to the top of my head and slumped limp in the chair as far as the lieutenant's choke-hold would allow. As the hands left my throat, I breathed a sigh of relief.

Somebody slapped me a few times on the cheek to bring me around. In true Hollywood fashion, I revived. I was jerked to my feet, and with a long-barreled revolver held at arm's length pointing at my head, was marched to the Hole. All the way, the gun-wielding lieutenant, the same one who had choked me, kept repeating over and over, "Just make one misstep. Just one! Just stumble... anything!"

I walked very, very carefully.

They were so anxious to get me locked up that I was shoved,

blanket and all, into a cell. The outer door crashed closed and silence filled the cement room. Luckily I had been put in a cell about twice the size of the one in which I'd gone on the hunger strike. At least I could spread my blanket, lie down and not have my face near the hole in the floor. Another thing, the steel-plated door had a square opening where the food was shoved through; I could see other prisoners when they passed by and stand at the opening while talking with my neighbor.

I had just spread my blanket over part of the floor when I heard a vaguely familiar voice.

"Hey, Tony! *Tony, El Americano!*"

"Yeah! This is Tony. Who're you?"

"El Pandeado! You remember... Leandro Montalvo from Principe."

Great! It was my friend who had killed the two brothers in less than twenty-four hours and had gone on to become one of the most feared prisoners in Cuba.

"Hey, Pandeado, my brother, how are you? What are you doing here? I thought that you were up at Cinco y Medio Prison."

I could tell from his voice that Pandeado was glad to hear me too. He explained he'd been brought back from *Cinco y Medio* to stand trial in Havana for a couple of old cases of attempted murder. Since the last time we had seen each other back in Principe, El Pandeado had accumulated a fearful record of stabbings. He was rapidly becoming a living legend who would die unmarked!

We talked about old times and then serenaded the rest of the cell block inmates, just like before.

"Hey, Tony!" We had eaten supper and the closing door at the end of the hall signaled a couple of hours that the guards would not be in the front office of the punishment section.

"Yeah, what's up?"

"You know how to make a key to open these locks?"

The padlocks hanging outside the doors looked more effective than they were. Simply by sliding a thin piece of metal down into the top where the U-shaped bar entered and pressing downward on the lock at the same time, would make it spring open.

"Sure, you want to get out?"

Five minutes later Pandeado and I and his cell-mates, Pepi and Betancourt, met me in the corridor where we all hugged one another and shook hands like lost brothers.

It was eerie, hugging Pandeado, because the killer was holding a long, deadly knife in one hand. We were friends, but he now never took a chance on anything. He had been set up too many times by so-called friends to really trust anyone.

"You know I've got a death sentence on me for a killing a little while back."

That news bothered me. I might be getting out someday but my friend would surely face the firing squad. As we walked up and down the hallway, talking about the possibilities of Pandeado being executed, a plan began to form in my mind. I studied the hallway. "Hold it! Look up there."

There was a square opening in the ceiling. It was shaftlike, and just large enough for a person's body to wriggle into. Then, of course, one would have to inch upwards, keeping one's back pressed firmly against the side or, from a height of at least fifteen feet, come tumbling down. The length of the shaft from ceiling to roof was another six to eight feet. It resembled a small tunnel.

"If we could get somebody up there," I ventured, "tie a rope or a sheet or something to the bars at the top, then dig around them, we might have a chance of getting out. It's better than waiting till they come to stand you in front of the sandbags!"

Pandeado stared at the opening overhead. "You know, I think you've got something. We could get somebody to stand on this." He tapped a narrow shoulder-high ledge that ran along each of the corridors. "And then one of us could get on that person's shoulders, get a handhold and pull up inside. Listen, there's a big guy in the first cell. He's strong. Let's get him out!"

A minute later a powerful-looking black, *El Calvo* was out of his cell and the five of us, whispering excitedly, made plans for the climb. El Calvo found balancing on two ledges no trouble at all. With one foot on each side of the hall, and by pushing out against the walls with his hands, he was stable as a rock.

Pandeado and I helped Pepi climb onto Calvo's shoulders. When Pepi straightened, he found he could get a firm hold on the rough bricks inside the shaft. After a brief struggle, he pulled himself up into it.

"Okay," I said. "Jump down. That's all we need to know. Now we've got to make a rope so that whoever is digging can tie themselves to the bars." A row of thick bars sealed off the shaft outlet to the roof. When everyone was safely back on the floor, I explained that I thought the digging should begin the following day. "The guards will be checking back through here in a little while, so let's lock up."

The next evening, as soon as the guards left for supper, I opened the cells. It was Pandeado who shinnied up into the shaft this time. He had torn his sheet into long strips and braided them into a strong rope. He tied one end around the bars and a length of the extra around his waist. Now, with both hands free, he began digging like a man possessed.

The rest of us stood below, holding a blanket pulled taut to catch the pieces of rock and cement that plummeted down.

The first good-sized brick that fell took us by surprise. It hit the blanket, wrenched it from our hands, and struck the floor with a loud crash. Right away, the sound of a guard opening the outer door was heard. We had to get back into our cells fast!

"Pull the rope up! Quick! A guard's coming in!" I threw Pandeado a whispered warning, grabbed the rock that had caused the noise and sped for my cell.

Pandeado did not have the chance to descend. He pulled up the dangling bit of rope and waited. The only way the guard would notice him was if he happened to look up. For a moment the hallway was filled with the clang of doors being slammed shut, followed by nervous rattles as my fellow captives snapped the locks in place, then silence.

Pandeado waited above, long knife held ready in his hand. If the guard looked up, Pandeado would leap down and kill him and we'd all be shot.

It took the guard a full thirty seconds to open all the locks and bolts on the door that led into the Hole. He had heard the doors slam and it was common knowledge that the locks could be opened easily. "All right, wise guys. Just let me catch you outside." Not once did he look up at *Death* waiting above him. He mumbled a few stock threats, then went out.

The long process of setting all the locks and bolts was ludicrous. The departing guard would not go through the trouble of opening all those locks again soon. It was too much work. Furthermore, he knew that by the time he got in, everybody would be in his cell again. No sooner had the guard's footsteps died away then the cell doors popped open and the five of us, in whispers, talked about the close shave.

"I could have dropped a rock on his head," said Pandeado. "But I figured if he looked up, I'd just spit in his eyes!"

We laughed nervously.

About ten o'clock the next morning, Lou was brought to the Hole and put in the cell with me. "Hey, Bro, what's happening?"

"What're you doing here? Hassle with the guards?"

Lou yawned. He had a habit of doing that when he needed or wanted a few extra seconds to think. "Aw, man, you know how these jerks are. Man, I'm tryin' to tell this fool guard somethin' an' he keep runnin' off at the jibs, so I..."

The crash of a chair overturning and the slap of machetes on flesh interrupted our conversation. I moved to the food slot in the door and peered out. The outer steel corridor door flew open and a prisoner, clothes ripped and torn, dripping blood from various cuts, dashed in.

Three guards ran behind him striking him at every step. There was no place to go. The prisoner fell to his knees, drew his face into his chest and doubled his arms over his eyes. The guards kicked and beat the man, grunting as they put all their force into each blow. Tired, finally, of beating the unresponsive piece of flesh cowering in front of them, they opened a cell and threw him inside.

No sooner had the door slammed shut than a handful of filth, taken from the toilet hole in the floor, splattered all over the guard who was about to put on the lock. He snorted like a bull, leaped back and started beating at his clothes as if they were on fire. The other two guards, fearing the second volley, took off at a dead run, taking the lock with them. It would have been funny had not the air been poisoned by the putrid smell of the thrown feces and the bestial behavior of the Communist guards. The man inside the cell was raging. His strangled sobs echoed throughout the building.

A new group of guards appeared and slowly began advancing toward the cell. The prisoner inside reached out through the food slot, pulled back the bolt and stepped out. He was naked. His body was covered with excrement! Slimy filth dripped from his face, neck, arms, chest; all over his body! Foam dribbled from the corners of his lips and slithered down, mixing with the feces. In his right hand was a rusty razor blade which he held pressed to his temple. He must have found it inside the toilet hole. "You're not going to beat me anymore. You hear?" shouted the man. "If you come near me, I'll slice open my face!"

In the Cuban super macho society, throwing feces on a man is a deadly offense. Blood has to be drawn by the assailed if his honor is to be redeemed. If not, he automatically falls to the level of homosexual; nothing can restore his manhood. He becomes an outcast, despised and disrespected by everyone. It is a disgrace to even touch dirty shorts, but if one is doused with either urine or human wastes, blood must flow. But on top of all this, it is considered cowardice to force a person to disfigure himself.

So, here we had a strange deadlock. The guards wanted to attack and draw the necessary blood to defend the honor of their brother in uniform; their honor was at stake too. It was their uniform that had been desecrated.

And yet, who was going to be bold enough to grab the stinking mess facing them? Also, there was the razor, poised and ready. There was no doubt the man would cut himself.

Guards and prisoner stood looking at each other. The stink was unbearable. Minutes ticked by while the guards talked the situation over. Then the door opened. The soldier who had been splattered walked in.

The disgraced guard had washed up and changed clothes. He elbowed his way forward and then, as his comrades stepped back, drew his machete. Crouched over, grasping the weapon with both hands, he eased toward the nude, debased prisoner.

The inmate's arm grew stiffer. The edge of the razor made a slight indentation at his temple. "If you come any closer, I'll do it! I swear I will!"

The machete rose. There was a blur and the inmate stumbled backwards clutching his bloody face. The man's teeth and jawbone showed through the deep cut.

The guard straightened up and lowered his sharp weapon. His honor had been defended. He turned and walked out.

The prisoner allowed himself to be hosed off and taken to the hospital for sutures. He returned a short while later, bandaged and slumped over, staring at the floor.

Lou came out that evening to observe the escape proceedings and gave us a hand with holding the blanket to catch the falling debris. We worked hard that night and the next. A fairly large hole had been made in the roof, and we estimated a couple of days of quiet excavation would be all that was needed for our breakout. There had been minor setbacks, such as Pandeado breaking his knife and the day's wait to get another smuggled in. Also, the alarm runs back to the cells were more frequent. We always made it, but I suspected the guards were on to the escape attempt.

It was late on a Friday evening and we had locked ourselves in to await the next day and a final assault on the opening. I had decided to catch a few winks when the main door opened. Mentally I followed footsteps until they reached my cell and stopped.

I looked up to see a young black guard, with whom I was friendly, standing there peering through the food slot. "Hey, Tony, how's it going?"

"I think I'll make it. How about yourself?"

The guard fished for his key, then stuck it into the lock. "I'm okay. Listen, would you step out here for a minute? I want to talk to you." He pulled the lock off and opened the door. Then we walked to the end of the hallway where none of the prisoners could hear our conversation.

"Tony, they know that you and Pandeado are digging a hole up there!" His eyes rolled upward. "They're waiting to shoot you. Forget about the escape. They know all about it and they plan to kill all four of you!"

There was no doubt in my mind that this guard was telling the truth. We turned and headed back to the cell. I thanked him for the warning and fell into a disappointed sleep. The next morning, I informed Pandeado of the bad news and the escape plan had to be chucked. A couple of days later, Pandeado and his two cellmates were taken out of the Hole and sent to a Company. Lou, who had been in the Hole for a few days, was taken out, and I found myself alone once again.

Days and nights slipped by but I refused to acknowledge or accept their passing as a loss. I'm here for a reason; to learn some lesson, I told myself. When I've learned what I need to know, nothing on earth can keep these doors closed!

August 1, 1974.

Pena, the tough overseer of disciplinary opened my cell.

"Okay, Tony, roll 'em up. All of you foreigners are being transferred to another prison!"

"What? You're kidding! Where to this time?" I leaped to my feet and rolled the few things I had brought with me inside the blanket.

"I don't know. All I know is your buddies are waiting. So step it up."

Outside, the Americans and the other foreigners crowded

around. They hadn't seen me since I'd cursed Castro's mother and gone to the Hole.

"Hey, man, they beat you?" asked Phil.

I shook my head. "Nope!"

"Hey man, you're kiddin'." Richard gave me the fish eye. You're telling me that they didn't lay a finger on you. I don't believe it."

"I didn't say they didn't lay a finger on me. I said they didn't beat me. The fact is, one of them laid ten fingers on me — all around my throat!"

They roared with laughter at my recital of the dramatic events that had taken place. But their laughter turned to murmurs of disgust and pity as I recounted to them the drama of the man who smeared himself with excrement. And their disgust gave way to a wondering silence as I told them of the life-saving warning to me, and who had given it.

It promised to be a hot day. Already the burning sun had turned the two steel-plated trucks into hollow chambers of suffocating heat. We managed to get all our belongings loaded and boarded the trucks.

Happy to get rid of the American problem group, the guards applauded and cheered as we roared off.

It was always a bad trip in a Jaula. The hard seats, bumpy roads and drivers who thought that the brakes, like cows in India, were too sacred to touch, made for very sore behinds.

As we sped through small villages, I caught glimpses of pretty peasant girls walking to and fro. They had an air of soft sadness covering their innocent faces.

Small open-front stores with empty shelves were a common sight. The houses were falling and dilapidated. Out in the country, the shrubbery, the flowers, and even the stately palm trees seemed to droop in mourning.

16.
GUANAJAY

About six hours after leaving La Cabana, the Jaulas turned off the highway onto a wide lane that led through an open field.

We came to a stop in front of the gate of a tall chain-link fence and after papers were checked and the underside of the Jaula given a quick once-over, were passed through and came to a stop in front of a large semi-modern building.

My breath caught as I stepped from the Jaula. Two-story cement buildings stood like evil guardians behind the fence. At first sight, there appeared to be at least a dozen of the large structures. They were so positioned that the guard towers surrounding the prison could completely monitor all of them. A six-foot high white wall encircled the prison. On top of its white-washed length, rising another six feet, was another fence of meshed barbed wire.

Fifteen-foot high gun towers with powerful searchlights stood a hundred yards apart. Between each tower huddled a couple of small guard shacks. Armed guards patrolled from tower to tower constantly.

"Well," I commented to the others, "take a good look. This is a prison! All the rest have been a cakewalk, but this one is for real. Here's where we separate the men from the boys!"

"Man, I sure don't like the looks of this joint," grunted Phil. Everyone else mumbled agreement.

"Look over there," whispered Lonnie. "Them is some hard-nosed lookin' suckers, ain't they?"

A group of about twenty, clean, sharply-dressed, very cold-eyed guards stood watching us. They meant business.

A heavyset man with captain's bars walked up, gave us a cool, impersonal stare, then ordered the guards to search the new arrivals.

The guards were well trained. They scanned each page of the few books we had miraculously acquired. Some were confiscated, others not. They ran their fingers along every seam of every piece of cloth we wore or carried. Soap was cut in half, medicine bottles emptied and each man was made to strip naked, run his hands through his hair, open his mouth, lift his scrotum, bend over and spread his cheeks, lift each foot and wiggle his toes, then hold his hands out in front of him while a guard inspected them.

After that, we were allowed to put on our clothes and a few minutes later, marched across a wide stretch of well-kept grass toward a building marked with a large yellow *E* painted on the outside.

Bright lights along the white wall, on the roofs and all over the prison, turned the area into day. The only way one could tell that night was falling was to look beyond the wall's perimeter into the darkening shades that swallowed the outlying hills in the distance.

On reaching *E*, we were led up two flights of cement-block stairs to the second floor. Our new home held grubby two-man cells sitting side-by-side. Each had a wash bowl, toilet stool and two wire bunks that let down from the wall. Between the line of cells and the containing wall ran eighty feet of five-foot wide corridor. At its end, where windows had once been, were barred openings.

There was one large six-man cell that Lou quickly grabbed for his 'brothers', saying, "Since there are three of us we need the biggest cell!" All the other cells were six feet wide by ten feet long and Lester and I decided to share one. I took the bottom bunk and Lester, the top.

"Well, we's here!" he said as we entered, "Home, sweet home!" He gingerly pressed the wire spring of his new bunk and growled,

"Yep. We here all right an' I got a funny feelin' we gonna catch it! Man, dis place is filthy. Look at dat facebowl!"

"Yeah. But at least we got one. I still can't believe I'm looking at a real toilet. Can you believe it, a real toilet stool? I didn't think Cuba had any!" I gazed in wonder at the strange sight.

It seemed too good to be true and it was. We should have tested the toilet before using it. As it was the thing didn't flush and even though we placed paper over its top, the stink that seeped out into the cell that night was gagging.

The following morning, I heard the guards go by making count. They didn't awaken the Americans by beating on the bars; instead they whispered as each cell's occupants were counted. What a luxury!

The air was cool. A dewy smell collaborated with the morning quiet to embroider a mantle of peace that was almost heavenly. In the distance, a rooster crowed and from a nearby farmhouse the bark of a dog could be heard.

I opened my eyes, and after a moment rolled over and slipped out of bed. Taking a deep breath of invigorating country air, I stretched and walked over to the cell door. From there I could see through a window on the other side of the corridor. It had no glass or screen. Instead, steel bars, like those that made up the cell's door, criss-crossed its opening. The barred window had once held shutters but they had long since been ripped out and now probably decorated some communist official's home.

The sun in all its glory peeped over rolling hills, splashing them in warm tones. The palm trees and countryside shrubbery wore a myriad of golden colors. Shouts of early morning risers in the prison and the rattle of carts loaded with cans of milk peppered the morning air.

Lester choked on a snore, tossed about for a moment, then turned over and puffy-lidded, asked, "What time is it?"

"I don't know. Must be around six or six-thirty. The guards have already gone by and I can hear milk cans coming up. It must be getting close to breakfast."

Lester stretched, then lowered himself from the top bunk. "Too bad about the toilet," he muttered as he approached the sink. "Hey! Ain't no water in the face bowl either," He angrily turned the squeaking faucet handle back and forth.

Just then, from outside the building, the putt-putt of a small motor gasping and sputtering, sounded. Suddenly, a gush of yellow water shot out into the sink.

"Here it comes!"

Alas! I spoke too soon. The motor died and the rusty gush slowed to a thin trickle then stopped. Again the motor was cranked and this time, after spits and coughs that shook the walls, water spewed out in a steady stream.

"Oowee! Hey boys, we hit water!" Lonnie cried from a few cells down.

Someone else yelled, "Man, look at that stuff. In the last thirty seconds it's turned five different colors!"

"Somebody missed the toilet and it's coming into my sink," shouted another.

"You mean we got to drink this?"

"It's water ain't it? What'd you expect, champagne?"

We Americans and our five foreign compatriots were awake now. The sound of splashing water and shouting filled our portion of the building. About ten minutes later there was the rattle of keys and loud clanks as one by one the cell doors were opened.

The man opening the doors was one of the sloppiest guards I had ever seen. He was a direct contradiction to the smart professionals who had searched us the evening before. He had a fat, rubber eraser-colored head, topped with thin, graying hair. Stupidity was written across his face and his olive green shirt hung unbuttoned, down to an over-hanging pot-gut.

Perspiration stained his armpits and although he was making an effort to appear casual, he was clearly nervous. The man opened my cell, then moved on to the next.

No one knew what was up, so we stood around talking quietly and looking out at the countryside until the last cell had been opened. Then the disheveled guard told us to follow him.

We were taken to the other end of the hallway through a barred door and into a dining room. Five concrete slab tables, with hard concrete seats, filled the room with seating for about thirty people. Our group was told to sit and a few minutes later hot milk and buns were passed out by a Cuban prisoner.

The Cuban, who knew me from another prison, eased over and whispered, "I'm the one in charge of the workers here. I'm going to talk to the sergeant and get you put on the work list. We do nothing and at least you'll be able to have your door open all the time. That way you can come out when you want and walk the hall!"

"Thanks. I appreciate that." The chance to walk around was priceless. "Listen, is that fat slob over there the chief?"

"Yeah, That's Ciprian. He's all right, just stupid."

"How're things here? I mean, the food, the guards, everything?"

"Well, the food's better'n a lot of places I've been and as far as the guards go, they don't mess with you too much. Some'll even fight you. And if you win they'll shake your hand and walk away. Course, it's not too smart to win. They get you later."

The sergeant cleared his throat from a nearby table, then rose and walked to the center of the room, "Anybody here speak Spanish? I need a translator."

The prisoner I'd just talked with moved over to Ciprian and whispered in his ear. The sergeant swung around and looked blankly at me, "You want to translate for me?"

I nodded.

The Americans were given the rules. No fighting. No swearing. No contact with Cuban prisoners. No walking the halls. No buying, no selling, no trading... No... No... *No nothing!*

"Can we masturbate?" piped Lonnie. Everybody laughed.

"What'd he say?" asked the sergeant, a frown clouding his face.

"Uh... he asked if we can play golf." I managed.

"Golf! Golf! What's golf?"

"Uh, it's a game with little balls and long sticks!"

I translated and the Americans rolled with laughter.

"Baseball!" concluded the sergeant with a happy shout.

"This guy's so dumb we got it made," announced Lonnie.

"If you people cooperate with us we'll get along fine!" The sergeant smiled, pleased.

The cells were open all that morning so we could clean them and just before lunchtime the sergeant walked by whistling happily. He probably thought the group he had was a piece of cake. He just didn't know!

At noon we were locked up for a few minutes while the Cuban work crew served the trays for lunch. After the Cubans had been ushered out of the dining area, we were released. But the gate leading into the dining room was still locked. Since the process of opening the cells was somewhat lengthy, the first Americans out packed around the gate staring at the food on the other side.

First of all, lunch consisted of boiled grain mush, and not much of it at that. And, as we soon discovered, it had grown cold. Second, hundreds of flies were settling on the ugly paste and instead of appearing yellow, the goo was beginning to look like a moving, black mass. The Americans started shouting for the sergeant to hurry up. That only made Ciprian nervous and letting us into the dining area took even longer.

"Hey, man! Tell that fathead fool to come open this door!" someone yelled.

"Yeah. Hey! Hey monkey! Get your butt over here!"

"Tell that sucker, if he don't open this gate, we gonna tear it down. Look man, you see all them flies?"

"Hey, stupid! You heard me, get over here!"

We emphasized our demands by beating on the door with tin cups. That brought Ciprian running and I translated for him:

"What's the problem fellas? What's all this noise about?"

"Do you see those flies all over our food? You expect us to go eat this dog mess? It ain't fit for pigs."

"Now hold it, fellas. Just hold it!" As he opened the heavy door, Sergeant Ciprian decided to establish his authority. He lifted

200

both thick palms in the air, and putting on his hardest face, forced his eyes to flash a bit and growled, "I've told you that you don't make no ruckus in the building and ..."

All shouting at once, the Americans stormed through and converged on the fat man, shaking their fists.

Unnerved, Ciprian rapidly switched to game plan two. He forced his face to go soft and a cajoling grin touched the corners of his lips. "All right, all right, all right fellas. Let's talk it over!"

He agreed we were fully justified in objecting to flies in our lunch. Then he allowed us to choose who we wanted as workers. Slowly, we calmed down. Then we picked off the flies and ate the cold mush.

Very impressive! Ciprian had avoided a direct confrontation. He was not as stupid as he looked. He was a snake in the grass and if you played his game he swallowed you up.

The evening meal consisted of fried fish, rice, soup and a bun. I had to admit it tasted better than anything I had eaten in a long time. The fish was crispy and salty, the rice well cooked and the soup, fish heads.

All in all, when we went to bed that evening, we weren't full, but with a cup of sugar-water to help, we weren't too hungry either. Things were looking up.

There was a shower room and we used it most of the next day washing clothes. The water was cold but for once there was enough for all of us. Bars of lye soap had been given to us when we entered the new prison and now we put them to good use. We made our clothes and cells liveable and laughing like children, splashed water on each other.

A type of comradeship was holding us together even when deep dislikes coursed through the group. Many difficult days lay ahead, days that would try our souls. We had to stick together!

But that evening, after all sound in the prison had died away and complete calm had descended from the hills outside, the night was rent by sub machine-gun chatter and automatic rifle bursts from the towers. Tracers streaked across the sky. The deadly rattle spelled out a warning, "We are here!"

No one had attempted to run away. We later learned the demonstration had been ordered for the American trouble-makers, just to let us hear the sound of death in case any of us were planning to escape. No one had ever escaped from Guanajay.

After the firing died down, the night became still and quiet. Soon, I was deep asleep, locked in a nightmare, running from machine gun bullets and the dry cough of rifles.

We had been in Guanajay prison for only a short time when Jesus, Richard, Hamilton and a dark-skinned, tough little guy, Rocket, arrived. After talking to Rocket and checking him out, I concluded his nickname was correct for the shape of his head and condition of his brain. Rocket had been a professional boxer and too many blows had left him permanently spaced out.

Jesus immediately started hollering and performing what he called singing. Jokingly, we wished we could put him on the radio so we could turn him off. Richard was his normal self, withdrawn. Hamilton didn't seem to be quite sure of where he was or who.

These four men were black hijackers who had lived in Havana in a place called *La Casa de Immigracion*. I had heard many tales from Lester and others about Immigration House where most of the hijackers, male and female, were housed. They described it to me as Peyton Place.

Within days after our arrival in Guanajay, the guards, were dealing with us through other prisoners. None stood exempt from the allure of a product marked: *Made in U.S.A.*

It was, and continues to be a status symbol in Cuba to use Johnson's Baby Powder, Right Guard, or, wonder of wonders, Colgate toothpaste. Colgate was one of the hottest sellers; a tube would go for 100 pesos any day of the week. I saw thermal-knit T-shirts sell for as much as $400, and even for a pair of socks that wore out after a couple of months one could get 60 pesos. Multi-vitamins were exchanged at the rate of five pills for a pack of cigarettes. Cuban cigarettes at that time sold for 10 to 20 pesos a pack! Since all that one could legally buy was four packs a month, the Americans were forced to deal on the black market just like any of the Cuban population.

We had a thriving commercial operation. All of us had fifty or sixty packs of cigarettes in our cell. The same guards that screamed, "Down with the Yankees," when Fidel made a speech, did undercover business with us Americans and secretly cursed the revolution. The Cuban population was hungry for food, hungry for freedom and hungry for life.

I felt compassion for the Cuban people. They were generous, fun loving and caring. Some relatives of prisoners traveled hundreds of miles to visit them every two weeks and the little bit of food they brought to share with their loved ones was at the cost of great sacrifice in rationed-plagued Cuba. Neither rain nor long dusty walks under a burning sun could keep these visitors away. I admired them. They were a tough people!

17.
PROTEST AND DIE

We had been in Guanajay for over a month and fallen into a daily routine that rarely varied. After breakfast we were locked in our cells until lunch, then after eating, put back into the cells until about two o'clock. At that time, if it wasn't a day for patio, sun and exercise, we were permitted to walk up and down the hallway for an hour. After dinner, we stayed out for another thirty minutes and were locked in for the remainder of the night.

Since most of the day was spent under key, we devised ingenious methods to amuse ourselves. Large potato sacks were taken apart and the string rewoven into long lines. Tying a bar of lye soap to one end and holding the other, we threw the line to adjacent cells, dragging back books, notes or even a carefully-pulled cup of homemade wine, a concoction we brewed unceasingly. We carved two tiny chess sets out of soap and, by calling out the moves to each other, played games that thankfully lasted for hours. But most of the time, we lay on our bunks and reminisced or slept. During this period, boredom and frustration were enemies we all fought.

Communication between the U.S. and Cuba was terrible. We received letters from home that were up to six months old. A letter arrived for me one day from my dad postmarked December 1973. Almost a year had gone by since it had been mailed! But what could we do? There was no one to complain to except the floor chief, Ciprian, and he was useless.

Seldom did we see an officer, except a short skinny, black guy, bumming cigarettes, or the perennially half-drunk Warden. We complained to him while he stood glassy-eyed, swaying back and forth, looking at us through the fog of his alcohol-clouded brain. He would give us a *"Si. Si. Vamos a ver.* Yes, yes. We'll see," then disappear until the next time.

It rained almost every afternoon and the dismal atmosphere created by the moaning, mist-filled wind was depressing. One night, after silence had been ordered, I heard a familiar voice, from far away in another section of the huge building. It was my friend, Pandeado!

Barely able to hear each other, we shouted greetings back and forth. Pandeado had just arrived at Guanajay. Over the next few days, through bits and pieces of information gleaned from other prisoners, I learned what had brought my friend.

After the frustrated escape attempt with me at the Cabana, Pandeado had been removed from the Hole and thrown into Company Eleven where an enemy lived. Pandeado's foe, *Carabela*, was a killer and as evil as he looked. He was known to club young boys senseless and rape them. Since both he and Pandeado were highly dangerous, they watched each other like hawks and plotted against one another's life. They even had a tacit agreement to always shower together. This was to prevent one from being attacked by the other while naked and defenseless.

But one day, while Carabela stood at the shower room entrance, arm propped on the door talking to a couple of other prisoners, Pandeado stripped and announced he was going to bathe. He tied a towel around his waist, which was normal, and headed to where his enemy stood. Masked by the towel, a razor-sharp knife lay tied to Pandeado's stomach. Carabela never suspected a thing. As Pandeado ducked beneath his arm to enter the shower stall, Carabela glanced at him then turned back to his conversation.

Pandeado's first thrust pierced Carabela's kidney and dropped him to the floor. A stream of stabs directed at his vital organs, followed.

A year later, during the time we were together in the top security death row cells, Pandeado recounted the inside story to me through a hole in the wall.

"When he hit the floor, I straddled him and started stabbing him all over. Blood was flying everywhere! My hand was going so fast... it was like I had no control over it. Carabela fought. The blood on my hands made them slippery and he couldn't hold them. He grabbed the knife and I cut his hands open. He still tried to resist but he had lost too much blood and finally, while I kept sticking my knife into him, he moaned, 'All right, Pandeado, I'm dying. Let me go to the infirmary... please!' I kept stabbing him!"

Pandeado took his enemy's blood and bathed himself in it. He then dragged the disemboweled corpse by the feet into the center of the Company and dripping in blood screamed to the terrified prisoners: "This is what happens to rapists and snitches. If anybody's got anything to say, speak up now or hold your peace!"

Pepi, who had been in Pandeado's cell while in the *Hole* at the Cabana, and had hoped to escape with us, was murdered by mistake along with Carabela. He heard Carabela cry out and headed that way to see what was happening. Another friend of Pandeado's stabbed Pepi to death. Thus, two corpses left Company Eleven that night. Carabela's cadaver had seventy-two punctures. Now Pandeado had two sentences of *Death by the firing squad!*

The days passed into a haze of inseparable yesterdays and we were doled out just enough food and water to keep us alive. We were not physically abused during that time, but the sounds of Cuban prisoners being beaten echoed through the building at any time day or night and the scars left on our minds were just as deep as those left on Cuban backs. September went and finally, October with its quiet rainy days, set in.

We were in the hall taking our one-hour walk-around. Jesus and a group of hijackers stood bunched together talking. As usual, it was Jesus who did most of the vocalizing. Today he appeared over-hyper and jerked spasmodically.

"Man. Something bad is about to happen! I had a dream last night." His arm twitched.

"Oh. Oh! Here we go again!" Melvin said half joking.

"Man, this cat is somethin' else!" Flip said uneasily.

"I know. He had a dream about me once and it came true!" I murmured.

"You remember?" asked Jesus, "That was when you got your head fractured by that guard at Principe!"

"What'd you dream?" Melvin asked fearfully.

"Well, all I remember is that I saw my grandmother in her coffin. She was laying there an' there was blood all over the ground around her. Then I saw this calendar's pages flipping, you know, like in the movies. Every page was marked the 28th. The pages kept turning an' the number 28 was on every one!"

"Did you see the month? What month was it?" asked Richard.

"I couldn't see no month. Just the date... the 28th. Somethin' bad is coming. Y'all jes' watch. Somethin' bad is comin'!"

That was reason enough to spend the next two days talking about the occult and psychic phenomena. However, as time passed, the conversation was forgotten and things went on as usual.

Lester ate part of a diet I had managed to wrangle out of the prison doctor and slept. I wrote poetry and stared at the open fields on the other side of the fence. The rest of the American prisoners, depending on their legal status, talked about the U.S. or of a way to immigrate into a third world country. Most of the 'jackers' living in Cuba believed the Cuban government sooner or later would permit them to migrate to some country in Africa. Others, like Jesus and Rocket, wanted to return to the U.S.

Lonnie was our joker and we needed one. He played pranks and in general gave the guards headaches. If he wasn't trying to slip out of the building during the times we came out to eat, he was lowering strings out the window to the cells below and pulling up contraband; pills, books, anything edible or stolen. Some of his pranks didn't turn out to be funny.

On October 27th one of Lonnie's jokes backfired. We had

finished dinner and were taking our habitual thirty-minute-before-lock-up-stroll, when Lonnie, with a mischievous gleam in his eye, began to jam the lock of the gate that led into the foreigners' section with bits of metal and debris.

"Tonight we're going to walk the hall!" he chortled, rubbing his hands together. "They're not gonna lock us up now!" He leaned back clapping his hands and laughed. For a finale, he stripped pieces of wire from the bunks and tied them around the gate and the steel column supporting it.

The other Americans applauded his ingenuity.

"Stick it to 'em, Lonnie. We'll show these fools!"

"We're on broadway tonight, baby. We gonna stroll!"

"Hey, man. Check them bad broads on the conna!"

"Yeah, man. See that one with the mini-skirt?"

"Yeah. The one with the kinky hair?"

"Uh huh! Well, tha's my woman. I tol' her to wait there 'til I get off the set. I can't be seen wit' no ball-head woman!"

We joked and walked around, unaware Death strolled with us.

Finally, there was the stomp of boots. A guard had come to lock us up. Amazed, he stopped short and stared at the gate. After inspecting it further, he spun and headed back downstairs. It was a good joke.

The Americans laughed as they discussed how the guard's face had looked when he saw the gate. Since all of the cells were locked, it was impossible for us to get inside; we had a perfect excuse to continue promenading in the hall.

Ten minutes had passed when steps sounded ascending the stairs. First to appear was the Warden, half-drunk, as usual. He walked to the gate and with his hands clasped behind his back, stared, not at the door, but at the grinning Americans strolling up and down the hall. A group of guards came up behind him, including one carrying a wire cutter and other tools and after fifteen minutes of labor the door was unjammed and clear.

The Warden called all of us to the gate and demanded, "Who's responsible for this?"

No one answered. We weren't going to snitch.

"All right. If the guilty one doesn't come forward, you'll stay locked up twenty-four hours a day!" Granite-faced and unusually steady on his feet, he waited and glared at us.

The Americans shuffled around.

"Hey, man, that ain't right. It ain't right for all of us to suffer for what one person did!"

"Yeah. Now everybody's got to pay!"

Lonnie's popularity had dropped. We had enjoyed the extra minutes in the hall, but we weren't ready to pay the cost.

Lonnie shouldered his way through the crowd and facing the Warden with a friendly smile announced, *Yo lo hice.* "I did it."

The man's drunken eyes narrowed. He ordered the guard to open the gate. I didn't like the look of things so I tried to include myself when the Warden told Lonnie to come out.

"No, no! It's okay. I'm just going to talk to him!" said the Warden, stinking of alcohol, and pushing me back inside, "He'll be right back. I promise you."

Too ashamed to look at each other we waited in the hallway, staring at the floor.

A quarter of an hour passed when steps sounded up the stairs. Lonnie, held up by two guards, was returned. He collapsed in my arms as they pushed him through the outer door and we carried him to his cell.

Since I was the one with the most medical experience, the others stepped back while I examined him. The back of the poor kid's head was bruised and swollen. Red streaks around his throat testified to the stranglehold that had been used on him. Portions of Lonnie's skull felt soft.

"What did they do to you, Lonnie?" I asked, already knowing the answer.

"They beat me up!" he quivered, "They beat me bad! Two guards held my arms and the Warden grabbed me by the throat and beat my head on the bars!" He stared up in shock. "They beat me bad!"

Putting Lonnie to bed, I promised to come by early next morning to check on him. I was still boiling but next day when I stepped inside Lonnie's cell I was greeted by a sight that made me shudder.

The entire left side of his body was convulsing. It was evident that serious damage had been done to Lonnie's brain. Whatever the cause of the abnormal contractions, I knew we had to get him to the hospital quickly.

I called Lou and a couple of others and together we ran, carrying Lonnie, all the way to the prison hospital. Naturally, we had to leave him and were returned to our cells by a downcast Ciprian.

As soon as the fat man disappeared back down the stairs, we began a heated discussion of the cruel beating.

"Man, did you see that guy? They tried to kill that boy!" shouted Lou. "Hey, Tony, what do you think about it?"

"First of all, I think we ought to blow the roof off. But it won't do any good to just do something that won't get further than the front gate! If we're going to do something, we have to make sure the Ministry of Prisons hears about it!"

"I think we've got to do something drastic," agreed Flip. "Something that'll get some brass down here quick."

"Flip's right," said Lester. "What're you thinkin' about doin' Tony?"

I outlined an idea. We would soon be outside in the general walking area. We were due to get sun that day. In the center of the big field we'd be in, facing the buildings, a water tank towered twenty feet above ground on a steel platform. There was a ladder leading up to its top and once we got there, no one could climb up without being repulsed by those in command of the summit.

I told them I would write a letter of complaint, including a formal accusation, against the drunken Warden and the two guards for abuse of authority and brutality. The letter would be kept, while we were on the tower protesting, until someone from the Department of Internal Affairs arrived. Then the complaint would be turned over to them. We would then come off the water tower and go back to our cells; totally pacific, totally harmless. It would be a typical American prison demonstration, the kind that usually didn't even hit the papers back home.

There were cries of assent and I wrote the letter.

But when I asked who was going up on the tower, a troubled silence fell and dragged on uncomfortably long. Until:

"I'll go!" said Flip.

Lou and Melvin nodded. They were with me!

"Well, I don't know what you into, but if y'all goin', me too!" yelled Rocket.

Jesus declared, "I'll go, if Tony goes!"

"Me too, man," smiled Lester.

The only other foreign prisoner who volunteered to protest the beating was a little Colombian hijacker named Hymie. So there were eight of us; eight crazy souls ready to stand up against the *Beast* and its keepers.

I felt a little downhearted. I believed all the Americans would stick together over this very serious mistreatment of one of their own. But only the black Americans, all hijackers, felt affronted.

All of the others, whites in the majority, excepting Lester Perry, tucked their tails and like snails, slithered back into shells of cowardice.

As I walked through the door into the sunlight, I touched my pocket to make sure the letter was there. My knees were rubbery. It was as if I were back in time hijacking National flight 97.

The yard was filled with a thousand shouting Cubans. A few guards sat in front of the buildings watching them. I was followed by the six other Americans and Hymie, the Colombian. A hollow feeling hit my stomach as I looked up at the water tower. It was far away, very high and completely exposed.

I took in the positions of the guards, then started toward our objective. My heart was pounding. I knew our plan was extremely dangerous. I grasped the rail and started up, staring at the sky overhead.

Jesus was the second to reach the top. He sat down on my right. The others arrived and stood looking down at electrified guards herding Cuban prisoners off the yard and into buildings. Other guards in olive-green uniforms carrying rifles and submachine guns went up on the roofs of surrounding buildings and aimed at us.

Dozens more, armed with machetes, surrounded the base of the water tower, which now seemed pretty low to the ground. Three lieutenants I'd seen on various occasions, worked their way through the ring of guards and stepped up to the ladder. They wanted to know what was going on.

I had written a letter to be given to the prison officials explaining the reasons for the protest and asking them to call the Ministry and explain the situation. Now I threw the letter down and the officers read it.

One lieutenant started to climb up but Flip balanced a large concrete slab above him and the officer retreated. There was a hurried conference and a guard headed toward the Warden's office at a trot.

The soldiers on the roofs, submachine guns pointing at us, seemed to have turned to stone. The sun glared. There was no movement. Even the breeze had died away.

"What d'you think they gonna do, Tony?" asked Jesus.

"I don't know. You can never tell. I don't know."

"I wish Amnesty International was here!" Jesus whispered.

Minutes ticked by. Then we heard the sudden sound of motors racing and grinding as three fire trucks swung through the gates and into the prison. The trucks slammed to a halt around the tower, revved up their engines and firemen directed a solid wall of high-pressure water at us.

To stand was to be knocked over the side of the tower by the water's force. Instantly, we were choking and coughing. I picked up a rock and prepared to throw it.

"No, Tony! Please. No! That's what they want you to do. That's why they've got all them guards up there with machine guns. We said this was going to be peaceful — an' that's how it has to be! If we do anything else, we lose!"

213

"You're right, Les!" I dropped the rock.

All at once the drenching stopped and over the edges of the platform swarmed machete and club-waving guards who had come up under the torrent's cover. Soggy thuds and sharp slaps filled the air. The guards screamed, "Get off. You're finished! Get off!"

There was only one ladder and, although closest to it, I was stunned by the swift, brutal attack, and sat entranced. Then, there was a blur; someone had jumped. I didn't know who. But I did see Rocket, struck by a club, fall headfirst through the roof of a small building alongside the tower.

A black soldier charged, swinging a machete. Crack! Jesus grabbed his head and doubled over.

Galvanized into action at last, I rolled toward the ladder and groped blindly for the rail. The black man's machete flashed again and again. I threw up my hand to ward off the blows. Blood spurted. Desperate, I threw my feet over the top rung and started down.

I was moving quickly but my mind was moving faster. I knew the guards spread around the tower were waiting their chance to mangle me. Since I wore no shirt, I smeared blood over my body as I descended. Reaching the ground, I collapsed holding my stomach. Blood pouring from my hand made it appear I had been stabbed.

As my feet hit the ground, a horrible *crump* sounded to my right. It was Hymie. He had been thrown from the tower and had landed flat, face down. A friend of mine who was a stretcher bearer and his co-worker dashed toward the tower. I was lifted onto the gurney. The guards, momentarily confused by my escape, leaped forward to punish Hymie who lay helpless on the ground. As I was wheeled away, I glimpsed machetes falling in torrents on the Columbian's back. The beating was senselessly brutal. Cuban prisoners, watching from the buildings around the square, were booing and shouting, "Killers... Assassins!"

Lester came down the ladder and was terribly brutalized. Ordering him to run, the guards began beating him savagely. He refus-

Hijacked Captain Edmond Buscher and stewardess Madeline A. Emmel tell of ordeal.

Cuba Jails Air Pirate And Discloses Identity

HAVANA—(AP)—In an apparent move to stem the tide of air piracy, Cuba announced for the first time Thursday the arrest of a hijacker and identified him by name.

The Communist party newspaper Granma said the National Airlines jetliner from the U.S. to Cuba Wednesday was hijacked by a man it identified as Anthony Garnet Bryant.

The paper said Bryant was a U.S. citizen and had been arrested in the United States for robbery and drug traffic. It added that he robbed one

Garnet Bryant
. . . former convict

National Airlines passenger James Tucker, said, "The man came up to me and asked me if I was a rich man or poor man. I said, 'I'm a poor man' and he said, 'Well, I won't rob you.'"

intended to crack down on hijackers.

To me, as well as to most blacks I knew, revolution meant taking whitey's riches and spreading them among destitute blacks.

"I lost my dreams, my hopes and my future."
Tony at 16.

Soviet, not Castro communism, dominates Cuban life.

Cuba's future leaders, super-intelligent boys taken from their parents and placed in a special school on Fifth Avenue, Havana.

Mission: Kill Fidel Castro

CLEWISTON, Florida One thousand heavily-armed men, 14 to 45 years of age, have been training in the Florida swamps for an assault on Fortress Cuba and their number one target — Fidel Castro.

The uniformed commandos are members of the Internal National Liberation Front, tough Cuban soldiers on American soil who plan to rush to Cuba when a revolution erupts.

Anti-Castro Cuban commandos are leaving their heavily-guarded base in the Florida swamps and moving to a large new training site close to Miami. They're preparing for a coming internal revolution in Cuba, they say, but observers believe they are actually teams of hit men and women training to infiltrate Cuba and assassinate Fidel Castro.

Photos : Ron Laytner

Back home in Miami, blinded and lacking an arm, Tony Cuesta, after serving 12 years in Cuban prisons following a attempt against Fidel Castro.

Photo: Andrew St. George

*ung Antonio Cuesta in-
tes Communist Cuba to
up Soviet shipping.*

Tony Cuesta's bodyguard shot

SHOT/*From 1A*

Cuesta said he felt Friday's attack was a reprisal for his continued anti-Castro agitation.

Bello, armed with a .357-caliber revolver, moved to the kitchen and waited in ambush.

Cuesta, who also carried a revolver, waited nearby against a wall.

The would-be assassins failed to budge the apartment door. Bello moved from the apartment kitchen to a hallway and pulled the door open.

The gunmen fired twice, Cuesta said.

One slug hit Bello in the chest and exited through his shoulder.

Bello fired twice. He then chased the gunmen down a flight of stairs before returning to the apartment.

"Don't shoot. It's me. And I'm wounded," the bodyguard told Cuesta.

The two men agreed before-hand that Cuesta would open fire if he didn't hear Bello's voice after the door opened.

Photo: Ron Laytner

An eyewitness report from refugee boats

By RON LAYTNER
News Special Writer

WITH THE RESCUE FLEET, MARIEL, Cuba—Fear has begun to grip 8,000 Americans who rushed to Cuba in small boats to take advantage of Fidel Castro's offer to let dissidents leave his country.

Members of the rescue fleet realize they are virtual prisoners of the Castro regime, unable to leave for the United States without Cuban permission.

Although many dozens of boats arrive daily, only about 25 get to leave, either through bureaucratic slowness in boarding refugees or calculation aimed at preventing panic and keeping the dollar-spending fleet in port.

Most boats in this massive fleet, which has grown to more than 3,000 vessels are radio-equipped for the 90-mile crossing of the Florida Straits and are anchored in three bays of Mariel Harbour about 25 miles west of Havana.

FRIGHTENED CREWS heard radioed cries for help as a Greek ship, leaving Havana with three Cuban girls, was threatened with cannon and machine-gun fire by Castro gunboats.

"Some of those leaving were among the worst killers in Cuban prisons."

Carter: Deport all Cuban criminals

The Associated Press

WASHINGTON—President Carter ordered the Justice Department yesterday to try to return to Cuba any refugees known to have serious criminal backgrounds or who have violated U.S. laws since their arrival.

"What concerns most Americans is the prospect that some of the people who have committed crimes might be relocated in American communities," said White House press secretary Jody Powell. "That will not happen."

Powell said the administration has evidence that Cuban President Fidel Castro dispatched "this undesirable element to the United States in a calculated effort to disguise the fact.

"There is a desire on the part of...law abiding citizens (among the Cubans)...not to be associated with those criminals who, by all available evidence, were placed, forced, put into this flowing out of refugees by Castro·

Photo: Ron Laytr

Executions, torture are charged to Cuba in human rights report

RIGHTS/*From 1A*

Administration officials said the information came from intelligence sources, the U.S. Interests Section in Havana and the State Department's Bureau of Human Rights and Humanitarian Affairs headed by Assistant Secretary of State Elliott Abrams.

The report said that in 1983 at least 15 executions of religious believers and dissidents were carried out in Cuba an that at least four suicides and one killin could be attributed to human right abuses.

According to the report, Cuban polic "commonly" round up persons in nigh arrests.

"In 1983, several Cuba-American 'disappeared' while in Cuba visitin relatives. No information regarding the relatives who inquired about them."

*This is one of the last publicly viewed executions in Cuba, when hund-
reds died after the revolution and were allowed last rites by a priest.*

Federal Judge Eugene P. Spellman

Black Panther Hijacker Gets His Freedom After 12 Years

By MARY VOBORIL
Herald Staff Writer

An accused hijacker who once said he would rather live as a prisoner in Cuba than as a free black man in the United States was released from federal custody Monday after nearly 12 years behind bars.

Anthony Bryant, who surprised a courtroom audience last week by declaring that "communism is humanity's vomit," was released despite a four-page rap sheet that dates back to 1956 and includes a conviction for armed robbery.

His attorney, assistant federal public defend Larry Rosen, said Bryant intended to plead guilty to piracy charges stemming from the 1969 hijack. Thr passengers were robbed at gunpoint in that incide

BRYANT, 42, a former Black Panther based in S Francisco, was one of 30 Americans freed from Cub prisons Oct. 27. Federal agents promptly rearrest him.

U.S. District Judge Eugene Spellman releas Bryant to the custody of three men who met him Cuba. They are Tony Cuesta, a well-known anti-Cas exile; Jose Perez, another exile who spent 11 years

Exile Hero Vouches For Hijacker He Met in Jail

By MARY VOBORIL
Herald Staff Writer

Tony Cuesta, a well-known anti-Castro commando, offered to put his liberty on the line Friday to help an accused hijacker who says his mission in life is to combat communism.

"I would be willing to give something more than money" to guarantee Anthony Bryant's court appearances, Cuesta said. "I would give my freedom in this country."

The two met in a Cuban prison 10 years ago. They were reunited at a bond hearing Friday in U.S. District Court in Miami.

Cuesta is a veteran of more than a dozen commando missions. He was captured in May 1966, after landing a raiding party in Cuba. In that mission, he was blinded and lost his left hand above the wrist when a grenade exploded. He

3orn-again' hijacker finds a new mission

By LIZ BALMASEDA
Herald Staff Writer

Tony Bryant is a man with a mission.
The one-time Black Panther who spent 12 rs in a Cuban jail for hijacking a plane nts to "break down the walls" between blacks 1 Latins in Miami.

Tonight, Bryant will unveil his plans for Emerge Corp., a non-profit organization to be based in Liberty City.

He has invited prominent Latin leaders like Miami mayoral candidate Manolo Reboso and Abdala spokesman Ricardo Aparicio and black leaders like Marvin Dunn and Cleveland Bell.

Photo: Ron Laytner

Tony Bryant struck a responsive note across America when he appeared on the CBN Network's "700 Club", left, and below, being interviewed by Jim Bakker on the PTL Network.

FOR MY ENEMY

I would stalk across the face of the sun
And leave a blazing trail
And hurl my anger in its path
to make the sunlight pale
    Away and die!

I would with the hate that's in me
Tear fistsful from the sky
To mar that celestial beauty
And thus my enemy deny
    God's heaven!

To deprive him even a sip of water
I would drain the seven seas
And have the wind sing mournfully
To answer his fervent pleas
    For love!

The only music he would hear
Would be the siren song
Of "pain" the constant singer
With "Woe" as constant song
    Forever!

And then I'd take away his tears
So that never could he cry
Have death sing always in his ears
But never let him die
    Not ever!

Anthony Bryant

For the first time in my life I had a friend who was white and for the first time also I realized that any man can be whatever he wills himself to be. The only limits are those we place on ourselves.

ed to obey! A guard drove the butt of an iron pipe into Lester's kidneys, dropping him to his knees. Under the frenzied beating of about ten guards he struggled to his feet and once again started walking. He walked slowly, beaten every step of the way, all the way to the building.

Lou and his two brothers were chased by firemen and guards. The firefighters used their hard helmets as flailing weapons hitting them about the head.

Poor Rocket had gone straight through a hole in the roof and landed on his head. Momentarily stunned, he was not able to get out of the room before a dozen guards stormed in and began beating him. Our peaceful demonstration against brutality had turned into one of the most vicious prison carnages long-time Cuban prisoners had ever witnessed.

I was lifted onto the treatment table and the blood washed from my body. The doctors were disgusted when they saw the small cuts in my hand. They had imagined me to be mortally wounded, but they bandaged me up and told me to lie down on a stretcher and keep still.

I didn't have the chance to lay there for more than a few minutes before the sound of someone being brought in made me twist my head around. It was Jesus. He was pushed inside between two guards clutching him by both arms. A smashed eye hung out of his head!

The Americans had been beaten all the way to two small cells. There was no need for anything larger. The critically-injured Hymie and blinded Jesus were sent to the hospital in Havana.

Lester, Rocket and I were in the same cell. Rocket's head was swollen to twice its normal size. His body carried the angry outlines of machete blows. Of them all, except Hymie, Lester had been beaten worst. His body was covered by a mass of bruises and cuts and purple lumps and black and blue marks. And now, stripped to his shorts, as were we all, he was forced to stretch his aching frame over a cold cement slab. He never uttered a sound.

That evening, the prisoner medic in charge of the night shift in the hospital came by. The guard allowed him to put a little iodine on the wounded men. As soon as the guard walked away, the Cuban said, "Lonnie died... "

"What!"

"Shhh!" cautioned the prisoner. "He died! But the doctor brought him back. It was close. Real close!"

"How's he now?"

"Well, he's better, but it looks like he's got a blood clot on his brain, and if one breaks away..."

He told me Jesus had lost his eye and Hymie was in serious condition. Hymie's legs had been broken and his lungs pushed together by the force of the fall. He also had sustained internal injuries caused by the beating. Lou and his two brothers had only minor bruises. He gave Lester a pain killer and left.

So, they had killed Lonnie and brought him temporarily back to life. My insides turning to ice, I banged on the door until a guard came. I asked him to bring a pencil and a sheet of paper; I had a very important official letter to write. Even the guard had been shaken by the massacre. He brought them to me.

"Senor Director," I wrote, "Few times has humanity witnessed anything as brutal as that which was unleashed on us today. Hitler would have been proud to have you and your guards as storm troopers. If you are a man, which I doubt, then accept this challenge. I challenge you to a duel. You may have the choice of weapons, bare hands, machete or guns. I anxiously await your reply. Tony Bryant."

I made three copies and the next morning, to assure their arrival, sent them to the Warden by way of three different lieutenants. Lester and Rocket looked at me as though I had gone crazy.

"You're out of your mind!" Lester groaned. "They'll kill you, Tony. You see what they did to us already."

"Yeah, I know, but I can't let this go by just like that. That man is a cowardly punk and if he accepts my challenge, I'm going to kill him. It doesn't matter what happens to me, but I've got to get him!"

216

The Warden did not accept the challenge, but he did send Lonnie back to the building after only six days in the hospital. On his second night in his cell, Lonnie died... permanently.

"Do you remember what date it was when we got beat up?" asked Lester.

I thought for a moment. Then the realization of what Lester was saying struck me. It had been on the 28th of October! Again, Jesus had been on target with his grisly foretellings!

A couple of days after Lonnie's death, a full scale investigation was launched — not into the cause of his murder, but instead, into who had instigated the protest. Word filtered down that top brass from Immigration and the Ministry of Interior were visiting and questioning the Americans upstairs. Then, on or about November 10th, we six protestors were thrown our clothes and under heavy guard taken to a building where the prison's official business was handled.

The three brothers were interrogated first and, as each one left, taken back to the stinking waterless cell. Because Rocket did not speak Spanish, I went in with him to translate.

Three men sat behind a long shiny table. Papers and files on the *rioting* prisoners were spread out in front of them.

Although I had come merely to help Rocket, I became the object of their attack. "So, you're Tony, huh?" a weasel-faced lieutenant said.

The room was quiet as the three officials studied me.
"Who do you think you are?" barked a big, fat officer, straining forward as if he wanted to leap across the table.
"First of all a human being, a man and an American!"
"We don't want any smart guy answers out of you!" snarled *Fatso*.
"What he means," broke in the third officer, his voice and eyes as cold as ice, "Is who do you think you are challenging an official of the revolution to a duel?"

My voice was strained with anger: "Frankly, he's not much of an officer or a man, and I still maintain what I wrote."

They stared at me as though they couldn't believe this skinny, underfed black was actually willing to challenge one of them. "I don't believe it!"

Fatso sank back in his chair in shock and swiveled around to face the other two.

Now *Cold Eyes* spoke: "You've been a problem ever since you arrived in Cuba. We're going to have to do something with you!"

"You can start by sending me back to the United States!"

"We decide what becomes of you!"

"You're the one who started that riot the other day, didn't you?" a voice thundered.

"No. The Warden did when he came in drunk and took a man out and beat him to death!"

"You be careful how you talk or we'll take you back before the tribunal and charge you with making false accusations," hissed the third officer.

"Who instigated that protest, uh, that riot?"

"I don't know."

"Who was the first to talk about going up on the water tower?"

"I don't know!"

"Who wrote the letters?"

"I don't know!"

"Well, we know more than you think we do!" said the third officer, leaning back and giving me a piercing stare. He turned to the others, "He's the one!"

"You may go now." said Cold Eyes, "Get out!"

Rocket and I headed for the door.

"Mr. Bryant!" A voice called after us.

I stopped.

The third officer looked me up and down and then said softly, "We'll be seeing you again, Mr. Bryant... Take care of yourself!"

Three days later, around nine o'clock at night, we six *rioters* were taken back upstairs to the Americans' quarters. Lester and I had barely gotten inside our cell, when three guards walked up and ordered me to pack up all my belongings.

The night air had a cool nip and on the other side of the fence crouched a solid black wall of darkness. The guards escorting me were sinister. Only the crunch of our boots as we headed toward a waiting Jaula broke the silence.

I felt a throbbing fear. I wondered if I would arrive alive at my destination. It would be very easy to stop the van on some lonely stretch of highway, put a bullet in my brain and write it off as an escape attempt.

I looked up at the sparkling stars overhead and, murmured what was becoming a habit when faced with the possibility of death, "Ok. I'm ready. It's a good time to die!"

The Jaula's motor roared into life and a moment later I was rushing into the unknown.

PART TWO

18.
SQUARE ONE REVISITED

It was a long apprehensive ride.

When the Jaula swerved onto a road that led to a familiar outline, I gave a deep sigh and breathed heartfelt thanks to God. I was at La Cabana. I was taken in, booked and led straight to the Hole. The stink of the cell enveloped me immediately, but I was just glad to be alive. I spread my blanket over the floor and lay down. I managed to block out the sound of rats scuttling around in the hallway and with my arms under my head, fell asleep.

The days drifted by and no one came to tell me if I was to be taken to trial for something or if I was in *the Hole* indefinitely. As it turned out, it was neither. On the morning of the tenth day, my cell was opened and I was taken to a small office where the Warden, Lieutenant Crespo, sat. The Warden, sweat beading his forehead, waved me to a chair. "Sit down." He extended a pack of Cuban *Popular* cigarettes to me, then plucked one out for himself. "Tony, I want to help you. You can't keep going like this. You just can't win." He leaned forward. "You're one against an army. You've got to have patience and wait until our governments work something out."

I listened, studying the man facing me. From Principe, I knew him as a diplomatic type who used force but not as a primary option. I felt that he was leading up to something, so I sat back and waited.

"How would you like to work here in the infirmary? You would live in the workers' dorm, get extra rations and be out in the patio whenever you wanted. In fact, you would be living with the military prisoners!"

I almost fell out of my chair. It was a fantastic opportunity. The chance, not just to work, but to be among a segment of the prison population, kept apart and almost hidden, was too attractive to pass by. I would be able to talk to ex-soldiers and guards and find out what was discussed among military personnel concerning Castro, Communism and the U.S.

I tried to act nonchalant as I answered, "I'd like that!"

"Well, all I want you to do is promise that you won't fight with the guards or try to escape — at least, while I'm here as Warden. Give me your word, and I'll take you out right now and put you to work."

I didn't have to think about it. I stood and held out my hand. "I give you my word."

The Lieutenant smiled. "Come on. Let's get you to your dormitory."

The Cabana was divided into three sections completely separate from each other. One section was for political prisoners, another for common criminals and the other for military offenders. Each of the sections was fenced-in and had its own cement yard or patio, as they called it in Cuba, its own dining area, infirmary and from six to ten Companies.

The workers' dorm was no different from the regular Companies, except that the bunks were stacked only two high and it was much cleaner. Also the door was left unlocked. The dorm, like the Companies, was maybe sixty feet long by thirty wide. There were two shower stalls and three fifty-gallon drums of water for bathing. These were the best living conditions existing, and men coveted the positions that allowed such luxury. Lieutenant Crespo took me to the infirmary and the doctor in charge was given orders to put me to work.

The infirmary was nothing more than another Company that

had been converted into a makeshift hospital ward. Anyone entering the building walked immediately into the emergency section. There were the usual trappings: a stainless steel treatment table whose sides sloped to the middle so that blood and wastes ran into a hole in the center and drained into a bucket hanging underneath, a sterilizer, a desk, and a couple of chairs. Leaving that room, one stepped into the ward. Twenty hospital beds, ten on each side, lined the gray walls.

Doctor Lorenzo was average in size with gray hair and an overly white complexion for a Cuban. He was serving a sentence for incompetence. It seems that he had pronounced the famous singer, Roberto Faz, as dead; later when the family of the popular artist demanded an autopsy and the cadaver was exhumed, the corpse lay face down in the casket. The curved fingers showed that in his last moments Roberto had tried desperately to claw his way out!

There was no need to ask if the doctor was a snitch. The fear in his shifty eyes when he saw Lieutenant Crespo or any other guard told me that here was the one who had sold out... a destroyer!

Five or six patients always occupied the ward, and when I was on duty, I gave them my best. I worked hard. I did have a dual motive for my actions. I wanted to hear, firsthand, how those in the military really felt about living under Communism and too, I hoped to destroy the lies about Americans and the U.S.

Tony Bryant, the ex-Panther, hijacker, dope addict, armed robber had changed greatly. I still distrusted whites, but now the focus of my anger was on a specific white—the Russian. I would gradually change even that concept but that too would come with the passing of time and lessons learned.

With the officials and guards, I was firm but respectful. I told them, "Never ask me to inform on anyone." I told them, "No monkey business will be permitted while I'm working, but you have to leave that up to me."

As the prisoners' faith and trust in me mounted, I began to

hear terrifying stories. They were hard to believe at first, but they were repeated so often that I had to accept them as true.

As one ex-guard told me, "I worked as a border guard between Guantanamo Base and the Cuban territory. There were always people trying to get to the U.S. base, but there is only one road leading there and it's got three check points, all with machine guns. If you get past one point, you've still got two more barriers to run."

"Why can't the people go through the hills or forest to get to the base?" I asked.

"Because there are mine fields, so if anybody tries to sneak by like that they get blown up. When we heard an explosion, we just went out and picked up the body!"

I recalled the case of a young black child in the hospital at Principe. Only sixteen years old, he had tried to go across the mine field. Now he had no legs!"

"How many people get killed or maimed trying to escape?" I asked.

"Whew!" The ex-guard threw his hands over his head shaking his fingers as though ridding them of something distasteful.

Those who had been in the Navy told me chilling tales of high speed torpedo boats coming upon Cubans trying to escape by water; the order was given to open fire, and the raft or boat sunk. The PT then criss-crossed the area running down any survivors. When the PT's struck, mothers held up their babies and begged for the child's life, only to be ripped apart by machine gun fire. Often their bodies washed up on the beaches — if the sharks didn't get to them first.

I learned that there were scores of secret camps in Cuba where guerillas were trained. After completing the courses, they were then infiltrated into different countries, including the U.S., where they spread Communist propaganda, death and destruction. Logic told me the U.S. government knew about them, yet did nothing to stop them.

"I think they're scared, Tony," one Cuban told me. "Fidel has missiles that can hit a few major cities in the U.S. and he's got jets that can be in U.S. territory in minutes. For the first time in history, there's an enemy country in this hemisphere capable of killing innocent American people."

I asked, "If you don't like Fidel, why don't you conspire?"

"You've seen them execute people here, Tony. You know they don't fool around. You don't conspire because nobody knows who anyone else is. You might be an agent, an informer or a Communist. Everybody's afraid to talk, much less conspire. So, they either accept the seven pesos a month they get paid and follow orders or they run away and end up like me — in prison."

"If there was a war, would the people fight?"

"Against the U.S., no! Against anyone else — to the death!"

I learned much and thought even more. By the new year, I was on my way to a 180 degree turnaround.

The food, though much the same, was better prepared. There were the usual fights, cuttings and self-mutilations. In that, the military and common prisoners were equal. They too lived in the same overcrowded squalid conditions. Only the beatings by the guards were less, and that too had its reason.

Quite a few of the prisoners had families or friends who were members of the Party and the pressures executed by the hierarchy, if a jailed relative was beaten, could cause serious repercussions. But the fears, intrigues and hates were equivalent to any other prison I had been in. In fact, deadlier. Case in point...

"Tony! Come over to my office. I want to talk to you."

Doctor Lorenzo and I got along because we had to, not because of any particular likes or common interests.

I followed him to the emergency room. After closing the door, he turned to me and said, "Listen, Tony, there's something that we want you to do. We think that you're the man for the job!"

It was only by a supreme effort that I kept my composure as the doctor outlined what was desired by the prison officials.

A patient, an ex-official of the Army, was no longer wanted around. The man had a coronary condition and had to be injected with a powerful pain killer when his attacks hit. He also had high blood pressure. When the morphine-derived injection was given he had to be administered another medicine to keep his pressure stable. The two medications were combined and injected intravenously.

"We want you to give him a shot," said Lorenzo. "It's not the regular one but no one will question what happens and the officials and the revolution will be indebted to you. Well, what do you think?"

I didn't know what to think. In the past I would have killed for the cause had I been ordered. But now I could not bring myself to murder anyone in cold blood and much less someone who was a nuisance to my enemies. Still I wanted to know, just for the records, if he was serious.

"Leave me the stuff," I told him. "I'll handle it."

Lorenzo took a small ampule from his pocket. Careful not to let me see the label, he snapped off the top and drew the liquid into a syringe. "As soon as you give him the injection, put the needle and syringe into the sterilizer," he said. "I'm going over to the Warden's office. Give him the shot in—let's say ten minutes."

He was convinced I would murder the man. If the shot was lethal, they could hold that over my head forever; if it was not, they would still know that I could be used. After the doctor left, I emptied the syringe and dropped it into the sterilizer.

The patient lay sleeping, unaware that his life was being conspired against. Why didn't I warn him? Because I would become involved in accusations and charges that could result in additional years tacked to my sentence; for all I knew, it could be a plot with that end in view.

When Lorenzo returned a half-hour later, a questioning look in his eyes, I just shook my head and kept working as though we had never discussed the macabre plan. He said nothing. A week later the patient was transferred to Calixto Garcia Hospital in Havana. A couple of weeks after that the same hospital returned the man's hospital record. Stamped across the front was one word: "Deceased."

I wasn't a doctor, but in emergency situations I was good. In fact, I gave a course in emergency procedures to the other guys working with me which might have saved a few lives.

I gathered the four other aides around and then yelled out, "Emergency!" Each one dashed to carry out a pre-appointed task. This was to avoid confusion and also render the greatest help to the doctor. Meanwhile, I became well known for my suturing. Many times I was dragged out of bed to sew up some patient who refused to allow anyone else to work on him. Then a situation occurred that elevated me to a level that was almost untouchable.

I had been puttering around when a commotion broke out in the yard. I paid no attention to it and had just stepped back into the emergency room when the door to the infirmary bust open. I swung around and stopped — stunned. Carried by three other prisoners, blood gushing from his chest, was a buddy of mine.

"Emergency!" I yelled, running to grab the surgical instruments. I was joined at once by Lorenzo and the other aides.

"Get his shirt off," Lorenzo ordered.

Two deadly wounds came into view. One, about the fourth rib up on the left side, the other, beneath the armpit in the region of his heart!

In a flash two bottles of plasma were hooked up. While the doctor struggled with forceps in hand, trying to clamp off the destroyed arteries, I busied myself preparing adrenalin injections. It was impossible to stop the bleeding. It gushed out hitting the floor in a continual spatter.

A guard ran for an ambulance. The officials didn't like their record marred by prison deaths. Thus, the concern for the man's life. The Warden and other officials packed around the door watching the proceedings. Lorenzo, a foreigner to emergency situations, was almost hysterical under their scrutiny.

I had a great amount of experience in emergencies. I had worked with Dr. Tejeiro at Principe when stabbings and cuttings ran about one a day, and I had worked with a young surgeon prisoner who was good too. I learned a lot from them. I was a good aide. I could diagnose with accuracy. Without my help, Lorenzo could not handle the situation. I had no intention of letting the man die if it could be helped. But I meant to destroy, once and for all, the white-haired man's credibility. I stepped back.

Suddenly the patient's breath went out in a loud whoosh!

Lorenzo looked up, shrugged and said, "Well, it's all over!" and started away from the patient.

"Why you dumb jerk," I shouted. "Now is when you have to fight for his life!"

Before the startled eyes of the officials, I leaped forward, administering intense heart massage. A long moment passed; then miraculously the patient started breathing.

An exclamation of amazement broke from the onlooking officials.

Lorenzo turned pale. "You go ahead, Tony, and take care of the patient," he stammered. "I'll get his medical records together." He scurried off.

Meanwhile I worked ferociously to keep the patient alive. "Fight!" I whispered in his ear. "You've got to fight." I like to think he heard me. Once again, before the ambulance arrived, the man gave up the ghost, and once more I brought him back to life.

As the patient was being rushed into the ambulance, the Warden said to me, "Go with him, Tony. See to it that he gets to the hospital alive. You won't try to escape, will you?"

"I gave you my word. Remember?"

"Okay, Tony. Take off!"

With siren screaming, the ambulance sped out the gate toward downtown Havana. This was a first. No prisoner, not even a doctor, was allowed to leave the prison with a patient, no matter how grave the situation. We were met at Calixto Garcia by a group of doctors and nurses who rushed the patient into the operating room. An hour later the poor guy died.

I had entertained the idea of escape, but only briefly. I had given my word.

A guard was sent by the prison to ride back with me in the ambulance. I was met at the infirmary by the Warden and some other officials. They were all smiles. It did not matter that the man had died. He had not died on prison premises.

As a result of this event, the Warden came to see me with an interesting proposition. "We're getting rid of that doctor. He's to be released, and we want you to take his place. You can live in the hospital and get guards' rations, but mainly: be free within the prison." I would have to give consultations, write presciptions, admit and discharge patients just like a doctor.

I couldn't believe my ears. I opened my mouth to accept as the lieutenant raised his hand. "Before you answer, I'll have to tell you that if anyone dies while you're in charge of the hospital, you can be given up to twenty years for manslaughter. Are you willing to accept that responsibility?"

This was a golden opportunity. Lieutenant Crespo would not be Warden always. People in positions such as his were transferred frequently. If I accepted the offer I would have unlimited movement and the opportunity to escape might present itself. I realized that the possibility of a stabbing victim was always great, but it was too good to pass up. I'd have to take my chances.

I settled back and waited for the vacancy. Lorenzo had another two months to serve.

During this time I met a man who had been interned in *Mazorra*, Cuba's national psychiatric hospital. The hair on both temples had been burned away by numerous electric-shocks 'treatments'. He was a pitiful vegetable. Later, when he improved, he told me scary tales of the horribly fearful buildings where men were caged and treated like animals. Forced to defecate on a piece of paper or whatever was at hand, some of the more deranged used the plates from which they ate. The tin plates were only splashed through a little cold water. Some of the excrement remained, appearing on your plate at your next meal.

According to this patient, there had been a thick-skinned man with red eyes who — grinning fiendishly — gave the shock treatments and a huge gorilla of a black who held down the patients for the other to shock into limbo. Men flipped around the floor like grounded fish, bloody foam bubbling from their champing mouths.

He told of cold water being hosed into the cell to wash away wastes that one could no longer hold and the shock of it hitting your body; of the insane screams of terrified souls clasped to Satan's bosom. He told me how they burned people's minds out on orders from the government.

I believed him. I had known an American who was sent to Mazorra. They had turned him into a mindless freak. In his more lucid moments, the American had told me the same stories.

Rumors that the military prisoners were going to receive some special dispensation from Raul Castro were everywhere. To show how benevolent the revolution was, they were to be released, if they had no common crime, and returned to their outfits. Of course, they might find themselves on the next shipment to Angola, but at least they could seek a glorious death.

Lorenzo left and I took over his duties. The responsibility was tremendous. Everytime I prescribed a treatment or medication that could produce adverse effects, I would be caught up in doubt and fear for days. Gray hairs began to sprout over my temples.

The military prisoners were released and I was sent to another section of the prison. I was told to put the infirmary in shape because the juveniles, then residing in Morro Castle Prison, were to be transferred to this, their new home, La Cabana, Patio One.

19.
SIBLINGS

Patio Number One held the largest complex of the prison.

Five cave-like Companies, joined together by cement and stone, sat side by side, facing replicas across an expanse of concrete twenty yards wide. Dark and foreboding, they resembled small caverns which the earth had vomited to its surface. Thick bars slashed across their fronts like wounds. The buildings to the left sat on the edge of the ancient moat. The back of the others formed a solid windowless wall on top of which an armed guard patrolled, observing all that took place in the patio below.

It was late April 1975. I had managed to maintain my sanity since the arrival of the juvenile offenders two months earlier. Over a thousand of them had been jammed into quarters that should have held no more than four hundred. No need to describe the living conditions. Suffice it to say — they equaled most of Principe or any of the other human warehouses in Cuba.

The great difference, of course, was the age of the inmates. In other places I had been, the majority of the prisoners were adults, therefore they handled the restricted quarters with a resignation that was completely foreign to these children. Not one was over twenty. Fights and stabbings broke out from the first day they arrived. I had only the help of a couple of kids, Artimes and Jorgito. It was work; night and day.

The stabbings, rapes and cuttings were always vicious and taxed me to the limits of my medical training and physical endurance.

231

Over and above that, I had to be a Guapo, a tough guy. The siblings of the revolution were as close to savages as anything I'd ever seen. They were creatures formed by Marxist-Leninism. They snitched on each other, raped and abused the less fortunate, fought anyone except a guard, and stabbed at the drop of a hat. So it happened at times that a patient whose life I had helped save, found himself looking at a two-foot sword held by me and being told to get out or suffer the consequences.

It was about 9:00 p.m. and I was taking an evening stroll before turning in. Someone from one of the Companies hissed and called me. Twisting and grinding to the hypnotic beat of an improvised drum, danced two blacks.

One, by *her* feminine movements, was clearly the woman. The other, a powerfully-built youth, exemplified by his strutting, the *macho* that every Cuban male is supposed to be. They were nude. From time to time, *She* brushed her hip against him. Urged on by applause, the two fell to the floor and copulated.

Later I talked to Jorgito, my aide, about that. Here's what he said to me: "I'd say that at least eighty percent of young people in Cuba practice homosexuality. They've lost their family life. Either the dad is in the army, some work center or jail; and the mother is somewhere too. So, the kid gets thrown into a state school. Just about everybody here has gone there. The teachers rape the students, and the students do it to each other. They see their parents sometimes once a month, so the only direction they get is from the teacher. What else can you expect?"

They were the ones who would take over the reins of government in Cuba some day.

Children were primary targets in the war against religion. From the moment a child entered school, I was told, there was a determined effort on the teacher's part, to separate the child from any notions about God and religion. One method used was to first point out that God is a fairy tale and that the revolution and Communism are the answer to everything. The teacher then tells the children to prove it for themselves. They are told to close their eyes and pray to God to put an orange on their desk. Naturally after a minute or so of prayer, when the children open their eyes, the desk top is as empty as before. Then the teacher tells them, "I'm going to prove to you that Marxist-Leninism is the true power. I'm going to prove to you that the revolution is the only power that will make our dreams and prayers come true. This time, I want you to close your eyes and ask Fidel Castro, our Commander-in-Chief of the revolution, to put an orange on your desk."

While the little innocents prayed, the teacher darted around the room placing an orange on each desk top. Oranges were seen rarely by Cuban children; the impact upon opening their eyes was twofold. A miracle! An orange! Given, not by God, but by Fidel Castro and the revolution.

A relentless battle was waged to turn the child against the false teachings of its parents and against God. The siblings, dominated by the teacher's powerful arguments, had no one to turn to for answers and ended up being shaped and formed in the image that the teachers wanted.

One would think that with such a ferocious repression the church and religious beliefs would soon be extinguished but that was not always the case.

A group of young Jehovah's Witnesses was brought to the patio. There were about fifteen of them. They had refused to bear arms and had been given eight years in prison each. They lived in the same Company. They were quiet and well-mannered. The other prisoners held them somewhat in awe. No one bothered them except the soldiers. One night they were taken out of the Company and mobbed by a bunch of guards. The kids never murmured.

These young people later told me, "The Communists hate Jehovah's Witnesses. Seventh Day Adventists and Pentacostals." They had to hold secret services in different homes in an effort to escape from the watchful eye of State Security. To be caught in one of those *unauthorized* meetings could mean jail, torture, and sometimes even death.

There were stories of a special cell in G-2 that was flooded with human excrement. Anyone caught practicing one of the renegade religions was thrown into it.

The urine and feces slithered around one's knees and it was there that you were kept until you renounced God and denounced others or went insane. Those who escaped with just a beating considered themselves lucky. Catholics were frowned on but tolerated. All religions and their practices were discouraged.

One of the things that weighed most on my mind during this time was my preoccupation over Eunice, my first wife, my parents and naturally my son. I felt guilty for not having been the husband and father that I should have been. After all the years apart, I realized that I still loved Eunie, perhaps more than when we first married. I wanted to make her and my son proud of me.

At night, alone in bed, I created mental pictures and fantasized about my return to the U.S. I pictured myself going to trial and being released because the man on the plane that I'd robbed turned out to be an international spy hunted by the CIA for years, and due to my action was ferreted out while an entire espionage network was destroyed. I saw myself being wined and dined in grand style. Then, I would write a book exposing to Americans what Communism and Castro's Cuba really signified. My book would be hailed as a literary gem and the Pulitzer Prize would be mine. I fantasized, but perhaps reality's essence is fantasy itself. I held firmly to the ancient Chinese adage that a man must accomplish three things in life: father a son, write a book and plant a tree.

Well, I had a son. I was creating the material for my book and someday, when I owned the residence that I pictured in my mind, I would plant a tree; an oak or redwood that would embrace my spirit when I had passed on, a towering reminder to posterity that a man's soul is unconquerable. One can give it away, but if one struggles, it can never be conquered.

I fantasized and fought whenever I could.

20.
ONCE A REBEL

I had been dropping hints among the snitches that I was interested in renouncing my U.S. citizenship and adopting another. Word reached prison officials who started coming around and treating me like a long lost sheep. Soon, the order was given that I receive a special diet; guards' food was no longer good enough.

When the national holiday, July 26, 1975, rolled around, a messenger was sent with a jug of beer for me from the officers' kitchen. And soon after I was informed that officials from Immigration and the Ministry were coming to talk to me concerning my desires. A few days passed, then a guard came to escort me to the Warden's office.

Inside the plush room, seated around a golden oak table, sat several important-looking men. When I walked in they stood and cordially shook my hand. This was a long-awaited day for them. The problematic, thorn-in-the-side, *Tony el Americano* had finally come to his senses. He was ready to embrace the cause and become their ally.

"Sit down, Mr. Bryant. Here, I'll just move these documents out of the way... there! Well, how do you feel?"

"Great! Really great!" I gave him my most dazzling smile.

"Good! Well, Mr. Bryant, your discontent with your present status has been brought to our attention. You're not satisfied. Is that correct?"

"Yes, sir," I answered, bobbing my head up and down. "That sure is correct."

A different official took over and in a soft voice purred, "Tony, we know you've had a pretty rough time here and... oh! Just a moment." A female guard brought in a plate of ham and cheese sandwiches, a soft drink and placed it before me.

"Go ahead. Bite into it. You're among friends. Um! As I was saying," he continued, "you've had it tough and it was necessary that it be that way. But we always hoped you would finally see the light. You see..." He leaned back and looked at me like a benevolent father. "You're different from those other Americans. You're brave, a man of your word and respected."

I gulped down my sandwich and tried to say, "Thank you," with my eyes. The ham sandwich was good but I would have to hurry if I was going to have time for seconds.

"We don't ordinarily accept petitions from foreigners to become part of the revolution. There are many who'd give their right arm to become Cuban citizens, but you can count on your fingers the ones whom we've allowed to take part in this historic endeavor of forging a new world and..."

"But, sir," I interrupted, gulping down my soft drink, "I think there's some mistake!"

"Mistake!" The official stiffened. The room full of smiles whithered and died. "Did you say mistake? Isn't it true that you want to become a Cuban citizen?"

"Oh, no, sir!" I choked out, barely able to keep from rolling on the floor at the shocked looks on their faces. "I just wanted some help from you so I could become an African citizen. Then maybe you'd let me go!"

Back in the infirmary I laughed until I cried. "Jorgito, if looks could kill I'd be in the morgue right now!" Within a week my special diet and the supplement from the guards' kitchen stopped and once again I was eating the same garbage as everybody else. Somehow it tasted better than officers' food.

If the officials had any sense at all they would have seen in that stunt the red flag of danger. The rebel in me was still kept in check by my promise not to attempt to escape or cause trouble with the guards, but it was getting itchy.

And then in September the Warden was transferred. I had made no promises to the tall, lanky captain who replaced him and took charge of the prison. I could now put my heart and soul into breaking out and immediately bribed a guard into smuggling in two hacksaw blades.

Jorgito, though only a minor, had decided to come with me. He had nothing to lose. He had more than a hundred years to serve for various crimes. He gave the blades to some youngsters in Companies 5 and 6 to cut the bars of the windows facing the moat. The two Companies sat at the edge of the ravine and we planned to lower ourselves into it from one of the windows, climb up the other side and try to make our way across the prison reservation without being seen. The land surrounding La Cabana teemed with guard posts and military barracks.

The hacksaw blade being used in Company 5 broke in pieces after cutting through two of the four sets of bars that blocked the window at the rear of the building but the boys in 6 succeeded. A couple of days later however, a guard making a routine check, came across the severed bars in Company 6 and the escape attempt was foiled. But by now we were revved up, determined to find a way out.

Jorgito and I spent every free moment walking the patio, slipping into the dining room in search of an outlet, watching the guards' movements and studying the fifteen-foot-high wall that sealed off the far end of the patio. Even though a guard patrolled the other side, we contemplated going over it. We could always run for our lives. Maybe the bullets would miss their mark.

During one of my never-ending searches, something caught my eye. It was just a shadow at first, then it solidified. I couldn't believe what I was seeing. Jorgito and I had walked the patio a thousand times and never noticed our escape ticket! There, running from the roof of Company Five, down the side, ending in a faucet two feet from the ground, was a two-inch pipe!

I ran and got Jorgito. Casually strolling back and forth, studying the tube, we decided the pipe could hold our weight. An armed guard patrolled over the row of buildings to the right but the roofs of the buildings that sat on the moat were unattended, mainly because armed guards kept watch on the other side of the deep trench.

Still, we estimated, we could wait until the guard making rounds turned and went the other way, giving us time enough to shinny up to the roof before he started back. We would worry about other guards when we reached the opposite side of the moat.

We went right into action and began to make a rope from long strips of dyed gauze. Intertwined, the gauze made a tough line which could be rolled up and stashed until the day chosen for the escape.

Next the most sensitive problem of all had to be solved, clothes! I had a blue king-size blanket that the Swiss Embassy had brought me. We decided to make two pairs of pants from it. Thanks to the embassy, I had needle and thread. Now, all we needed was a tailor.

It happened that Jorgito had a friend in one of the Companies who knew something about tailoring. I admitted him to the infirmary, drugged the other patients every night to assure peace and tranquility and stood guard while he worked.

Sometimes our labor had to be halted because of the impromptu arrival of a guard or patient during the night. But, a week or so later, the pants were ready. Did it matter that both pair were greenish-blue?

We removed the white *prisoner* bands running down the sides of our shirts and restitched them in such a way that one quick snatch would liberate us from the tell-tale markings. We were ready!

The day of the planned escape dawned overcast and dull. It was a muggy day, tense and uncomfortable. We had chosen this particular day, Saturday, because there was a national celebration going on and the number of prison personnel would be decreased with many guards attending different functions in the city.

After dinner, almost as a joke, I took out three Cuban coins, jiggled them up and down like dice, then tossed them on the floor. "Tails, I won't make it; heads, I will!" I watched the coins tumble and spin to a stop. Three tails stared me in the face! Was it the Tarot cards all over again? I decided to make it the best two out of three tosses. Once more I threw the dice. Again three tails came up!

I refused to believe it. Once again I tossed the coins to the floor. The chance of the same thing happening again was remote; I needed to dispel the nagging sense of doom I had felt all day. "Come on, baby," I whispered.

The first two coins settled quickly — tails up. The third spun awhile then quivered down to match the other two! I leaped back. My elbow struck a book which hit a bottle scattering everything on my desk. I already felt the escape would end in disaster.

Later, Jorgito and I put on our escape clothes underneath extra large sets of prison garb a friend had obtained for us. After everyone had been locked up and the night count taken, we walked out into the patio and waited for the changing of the guard. The same man who had smuggled in the hacksaw blades was supposed to be on duty patrolling the roof that night. A tacit agreement had been made that he would look the other way when the escape was made.

When the relief guard showed up my heart dropped. "What happened to our man?" I asked Jorgito.

"I don't know. They've changed something. Probably they put him on another shift." He looked as disappointed as I felt, "But that don't mean a thing. We can still try it!"

"I'm game if you are," I said, without confidence.

We watched the guard make a few rounds and decided that when he turned and headed toward the other end of the patio, we'd make our move—twenty feet straight up!

"Think you can do it?" asked Jorgito.

"I'll be right behind you. Don't worry about me."

"Okay. Let's walk over to the pipe so that as soon as he turns we can go for it. We'll only have a few seconds."

Loud talking spilled out of the dimly-lit Companies into the patio and a few curious prisoners observed us as we stood by the pipe. The guard turned and started back the other way.

Jorgito grabbed the water pipe with both hands and began fighting his way to the top. My hands were clammy. I had to make two attempts before I managed to get a firm hold and start up the vertical ascent. Jorgito disappeared over the top and whispered a warning, "Look out! There's an electric cable."

Too late. My arm touched the heavy wire and a jolt shot through me almost making me lose my grip on the pipe. I pulled myself a little higher. The roll of gauze needed for the descent slipped from the string around my shoulder and fell with a plop to the cement below.

I threw my arm over the top again and another dull thud of electricity hit me. Desperately, I glanced to my left to see where the guard was. A disheartening drama was unfolding.

A Chilean prisoner stood shouting to the guard and pointing my way. The guard looked and headed toward me at a run. I made one final effort and tumbled over the top beside Jorgito.

Although a low parapet shielded us from the guard's view and thankfully from his gun, we could not move across the roof without being spotted. He had us trapped!

"Hey, you, over there. Stand up! Get up and put your hands behind your head. Stand up I said or I'll fire!" Then, he yelled down to the quarters of the Officer of the Day, warning that an escape was in progress.

"Don't stand up until someone else comes," warned Jorgito, "He'll shoot you and claim you were running."

About three minutes passed, then a lieutenant whom I had known in Principe came up on the roof. He was half drunk. "What're you guys doing up here?"

I invented a story on the spot. "The TV in the ward broke down and we came up here to see if we could fix it. Then that guard started yelling at us."

"But you guys ain't supposed to be up here." He gave us a bleary-eyed look and told us to return to the infirmary until he had talked it over with the new Warden. He escorted us safely down and back to the patio gate.

Once inside the infirmary, and before the startled eyes of the patients, we tore off the incriminating street clothes and sent them, along with the few pesos we had, to a friend who would dispose of them.

About ten minutes later, the lieutenant returned with the order to take us to the Hole. The coins had not lied.

Next day, Jorgito and I were interrogated. I stuck to my guns and denied attempting to escape. I knew they didn't believe me but my fate had already been decided. I would not give them the pleasure of feeling totally justified with their punishment.

That evening, chained and fettered, I found myself bouncing over the rock-hard seat of a speeding Jaula. The ride was almost identical to the one I'd take a year before, only this time I was heading in the opposite direction.

Although it was late when I arrived at the prison of Guanajay, there was a welcoming committee waiting. It was made up of the Assistant Warden, the Head of Penal Security, a G-2 official and Ciprian, the snake in charge of American prisoners. A half dozen other guards gathered around as I stepped down from the Jaula.

Ciprian strutted up and with a grimace said, "Well, here's our little problem child again. What'd you do this time? Stab some guard? Hee-hee!" Then, with a mocking smirk, he added, "Seriously, what happened?"

"I don't know. I didn't do anything!"

"Why we heard they caught you up on the roof of the Cabana trying to escape," he guffawed. "Is that true? Were you really trying to get away?"

"I wasn't trying to escape. I was fixing the TV antenna."

I waited until their laughter died down, then said, "I wasn't trying to get away. " I looked squarely at them, "But now I'm going to!"

The gauntlet had been thrown. The group fell silent.

"So, you're going to escape, huh? Guards!" yelled the security head. "Put this man in maximum security upstairs in Building E. I want him watched carefully." He turned. "See if you can escape now!"

Although Guanajay prison had recorded only one escape from inside the compound, and that one with the aid of a uniform which allowed the inmate to walk unchallenged through the gates, officials were extremely sensitive about escape. There was a certain myth that had to be kept alive and Guanajay wasn't about to let one person put it in jeopardy.

As we headed for Building E, Ciprian strolled alongside, trying to prod me. "You still haven't learned a thing, have you? Still trying to play the tough guy. Why don't you get smart like..." And he named one of the Americans. "He works with me. Nothing happens that I don't know about. You ought to listen to him. He could teach you a lot!"

"The only thing either of you can teach me is how to die and I demand a personal demonstration first." That shut him up. He gave me a stony glare, then spun away.

The second floor of Building E was where we had lived when we first arrived in Guanajay a year or so ago. Now all of the foreigners had been relocated in the left half of the building. Extra locks, nuts and bolts had turned the right side into maximum security cages that were opened only when you walked in and only when you left, a period that could range from a few months or up to a year or more.

The clatter of our feet must have awakened inmates. Tips of mirrors suddenly appeared around cell bars monitoring my progress. We stopped at a cell midway along the corridor and after extracting wrenches, hammer and keys from his pocket, the guard began opening the door. The hallway echoed with dry squeaks as rusted nuts were twisted off. He hammered back the bolt, then with a rattle of keys turned two other locks.

After removing my handcuffs, the guard locked me inside.

"Hey! *Tony el Americano!*"

Climbing down from the upper bunk, all smiles, was Hector, a man I'd met in Principe. He was serving a twelve-year sentence for theft and been in prison seven years. Although he was only twenty-five years old, the hard time made him look fifty.

I threw my things on the bottom bunk and we backslapped. Then, as though remembering something, Hector snapped his fingers.

"Hey, you know who's in the death row cell underneath us?"

"No. Who?"

"Your buddy, Leandro Razo... El Pandeado!"

We stomped the floor a few times to get Leandro's attention, then called down from a barred window in the rear of the cell.

When he answered his voice sounded strange and distorted. The two-foot-thick stone walls surrounding him created an eerie echo chamber. Hector said there were three, two-inch holes in the rear of the stripped cell through which a little air seeped in. It was through those that Pandeado shouted. We talked to each other for awhile, stopping only when a guard approached, then yelled good nights.

"Pandeado has another death sentence," said Hector.

"What happened?"

"He killed another guy!"

"Oh no!" Now, for sure Pandeado would be executed. This made his third death sentence.

Hector showed me how to get notes, cigarettes and small articles down to Pandeado. Taking a long length of string, he tied a piece of soap to one end then dropped it from the window.

Pandeado had a wire bent to a small hook at one end. When the string swung past the three holes in the wall, he reached out with the wire and fished the string in. Two tugs let Hector know the package was ready to be received. Whatever was being sent was then tied to the string and lowered.

This arrangement with Pandeado would prove invaluable in the future. Meanwhile, we swapped stories about our past experiences in escape attempts and finally began a game of *How could we break out of here?*

Plan after plan was gone over and rejected for some flaw or other. It was fun, though, just imagining an escape from this escape-proof prison. Slowly, the game turned into serious contemplation.

When January 1976 rolled around we had hyped ourselves into believing that not only could an escape be attempted but that we were going to accomplish the impossible.

At night the prison was lit up like day. Guards patrolled the walkway between the gun towers. Those in the towers could scrutinize not only the roofs of the buildings but just about every foot of ground inside the prison as well. Also, there was the whitewashed stone wall and a barbed-wire fence on top with which to reckon. Just to reach the wall one would need a miracle. But we dared to believe in that miracle!

21.
THE IMPOSSIBLE ESCAPE

By January, 1976, we had decided to do or die!

Everything would depend on a hacksaw, so I sent word to Richard, the hijacker, to keep quiet about it, but to try to buy one. There were always blades in the prison. Prisoners used them to cut out pieces of metal to make knives.

While we were waiting for an answer we began to weave together strings taken from smuggled-in sacks. They were taken apart, then, string-by-string, rewoven into several long cords. On the day of the escape they could be quickly tied together into a long rope.

The basic plan was to cut through the bars, pull up onto the roof, crawl to the center of the building, fifteen yards from the nearest tower, tie the rope and go down the side. We would be inside the prison, of course, and would have to cross that brightly-lit path to get to the wall, but the worst that could happen was; we'd be shot and killed.

A few days later word came from Richard; he couldn't find a hacksaw blade. We weren't going to take the chance that a careless conversation might ruin our plan so I sent word back that we had discarded the idea.

The long-woven cords were strung across the cell as though being used for a clothesline. We took care to always have something dangling from them.

The hacksaw blade now had the highest priority. I decided to ask Pandeado if he could get one.

245

The answer, when I pulled back the line, came wrapped in a small package — a three-inch piece of hacksaw blade. Along with it was a note, saying, "You got to have it back in twenty-four hours." The blade was old and worn. We would have to make a Herculean effort if the extra-thick bars of our cell were to be cut in such a short space of time.

To mask the sound of the sawing, and watching for guards with the tip of a mirror at the same time, one of us stood at the cell door singing or talking as loudly as possible while the other worked. Hector had melted down a toothbrush and made a handle for the blade. But it wasn't long before blisters popped up on our hands and our unused muscles cried for rest. And yet, we couldn't stop. We had committed ourselves. Neither of us would show weakness.

We stopped only for dinner. As soon as the guard had disappeared with the food cart, we fell to the task again. When night came, we tied a couple of towels over the outside of the window — this was permitted to keep out the cold air—and we continued cutting.

Only short strokes could be made. The handle bit into our hands. Blisters burst and the flesh underneath turned red and angry. Seventeen hours after the first scratch had been made, we peeped through the cut and shook hands gleefully. Then, we tied a string around the cut to hide it. Exhausted, we flopped into our bunks.

Later that morning, after we awoke, we sent a note to Pandeado telling him we needed the blade for another day. There was no way we could give it up now. One more bar had to be cut. Pandeado said, "I'll tell the owner it's still in use, but you gotta get it back by tonight."

In the afternoon we started sawing on the other bar. The towel still hung over the window, hiding from view the activity taking place inside the cell. We stopped for dinner and took a short break and then, after a couple of cigarettes, tackled the obstinate bar again. Late that night we were only three-quarters through and decided to rest and finish up next day. Pandeado agreed the work was too far advanced to stop; he'd stall on the blade a little longer.

On January 6th, the third day, I made a bad push and the blade snapped. I cursed until I was blue in the face. "Will you look what I've done!"

"Oh, no!" groaned Hector. "Of all the rotten luck." He took the two pieces and shook his head. "What now?"

I had blown it! If a search came, and we were due one any day now, the bars would be checked. Besides a beating, we would be thrown into a punishment cell for a long time. "Here! Let me have the longest piece," I said. "We're getting out if I have to chew through that bar with my teeth!"

The longest piece of usable blade was about two inches long, and when a new toothbrush handle was melted into place to hold this tiny blade, it took even more of the precious length needed to cut. Only a forward motion could be used. I held the remaining bit of blade in my left hand, then placing my right palm over the stub of the handle, pushed. A few teeth bit into the bar. Lifting the blade out, I set it again and pushed.

After hours of heart-wrenching labor, a thin sliver of metal held us back from victory. Our hands were so sore that neither of us could apply the pressure necessary to push the hacksaw blade. Exhausted, we sank to my bunk and stared at the floor.

All of a sudden Hector jumped up, climbed into the window sill and began kicking the bar with all his might. Grunting and swearing, he unleased blow after blow on the unyielding steel. He rested for a moment, then in desperation drew back and gave a final powerful kick.

The bar parted with a loud bang. For a shocked moment we stared at the bar, then Hector jumped down and together, we danced a jig.

It was late, about one o'clock, but Pandeado immediately tapped for the string to be lowered. He sent up a note: 'I heard the freedom bell ring. Good luck!' He thought we were going to attempt the escape that same night, but this was impossible. The bars still had to be bent.

The following day, January 7th, began with a jubilant, heady feeling in the air. We spent all afternoon watching the guards' movements. We had to know how long it took to walk from point to point. The slant of the roof was checked. Would it be possible to hang there by one's fingertips then pull up onto the roof? That question would be answered at the moment of truth!

That evening Pandeado sent up a note telling me about a man a few cells down from us. He belonged to a secret African cult. God was *Y'fa* and the high priests of the religion were referred to as *Babalaos*. They were supposed to be able to see into the future.

I had heard about them, but I wasn't overly convinced that anyone who claimed to look into the future was sound of mind or serious, especially when he was here, sitting in jail himself. Nevertheless, Pandeado was so adamant, I relented and wrote a note to the Babalao asking the guy just to tell me something about my life and whether I was lucky or not. I mentioned nothing about the planned escape.

A couple of hours went by. The Babalao told me to throw down the cord for an answer. I pulled back a wad of neatly folded papers covered with strange markings. I opened the letter and was stunned by the force and certainty of the message:

"Your sign is fantastic. It's called *Ruler of the Night*. It is very powerful and brings good fortune. It also means that you are a Babalao. Of course to become who you are, you must travel the 101 paths to awareness. The Ruler of the Night was a great king who had the power of divination. At night he could make himself invisible! He ruled a great nation of people. That is your sign. You will have success in all you do!"

What a boost for morale! I slept well that night!

On the morning of the eighth a heavy fog blanketed the prison. It was so thick the wall was invisible. Why weren't we out there now? This was the perfect time for escape. We agreed to sit up that night and wait. If there was the slightest indication of fog in the evening we would make our move. The day passed slowly. From our window we saw a building next to ours being searched. It was just a matter of days, perhaps hours, before our section would suffer the same fate. To make our final preparations, we ripped the stripes from our pants and shirts and lightly restitched them in place again.

Night fell. I was tense and nervous. We had told Pandeado this would be the day and the young killer had wished us luck. The light inside the cell was covered so that the shadow of us working on the bars would not show through the towels blocking the windows. We laced a sheet around one of the severed bars and the bed post which was bolted to the floor. Using a short bar to twist the sheet, the pressure was supposed to force the bar down. As it turned out, it wasn't that simple.

We waited, praying for the return of the fog. We waited all night, then gave up. The rope was left intact. It didn't make any difference. If a search came now, we were doomed.

After putting the cell in order, we dropped off to sleep. While we slept, a repeat performance of the atmospheric phenomenon took place. At lunchtime, when we awoke, remnants of the fog remained. It was maddening!

At about one o'clock that afternoon the prisoners in disciplinary were rocked to their feet by the jangle of keys opening the front door and the shouted order of "Atten...tion!" Officials were coming in. A group of officers, led by one of the prison's most feared security agents, was inspecting the cells!

The agent was Lieutenant Moreno. He was fat, ugly and mean. In his beady eyes was locked the secret of what made this master of intrigue tick. His nickname could not have suited him better. He was called, *"El gordo con trampa!"* Translated, it meant, Tricky fats, or The fat man with a game. He organized snitch teams. He prided himself on knowing all that went on in the prison. He had eyes and ears everywhere. He was hated and feared. Strangely enough, the hacksaw blade we had used belonged to one of his best snitches and the inmate knew what we were doing!

Quickly we checked the strings hiding the cut bars. Nothing else could be done. Anything added would only draw attention. Sure that everything was in place, and trying to look normal, we stood and awaited the dangerous man's arrival.

"Hello, Tony," Fats said. "How's the world treating you?" His eyes flicked over the cell, settled on the two strings, then slid back to me.

I moved directly in front of him blocking his view of the window. "Oh, I'm okay, I guess. Just trying to make it!"

"I'm surprised to see you still with us!" A cynical smile touched the corners of his mouth. "I thought by now you'd be long gone." He broke into laughter. "Not so easy, huh?"

I haven't escaped because I haven't wanted to escape, not because I couldn't escape," I replied.

A fleeting shadow of preoccupation swept across the Lieu tenant's face. His eyes raked over the cell again. Reassured nothing was amiss, he brightened and broke into a new fit of laughter.

"You hear that?" he giggled, pointing me out to the other officers. "He says he hasn't left—just because he doesn't want to! Well, let me tell you something, Mr. Bryant," Fat's voice turned cold and distant, "you haven't escaped from here because you can't. You know something else? You're going to be here for a long time. A real long time!" With that parting shot Fats departed. I sank to my bed with a relieved sigh, wrung out.

The day dwindled and died. Dusk settled. The sharp lines of a faraway hill softened and melted into the approaching shadows. Lights started coming on clearly all over the prison, holding darkness at bay on the other side of the wall. The fog had been beautiful in the morning but we decided this would have to be the night. To wait any longer meant disaster.

Pandeado sent up a note, "Maybe you need a few pep pills."

I felt a compulsion to write to the Babalao again and this time told him everything about the planned escape, everything. Less than an hour passed before the Babalao told me to throw him the string for return mail. I hauled in his answer and started reading. It was brief and concise:

"God says you are going to triumph tonight. He says you will see with your own eyes that nothing will befall you. God says once you start you cannot turn back. God says do not be like the crab; you must always go ahead, no matter what! If you come upon some obstacle and the situation is beyond your control, call on saints and angels. They will come to your aid. This says God."

The message was positive, powerful. Adrenalin began to flow. Hector read the note, handed it back and said, "Well, let's go!"

We draped a blanket over the door, shaded the lightbulb and began a task that took us seven hours. Seven hours! But at last the two bars lay twisted away. The point of no return had been reached. We would soon be caught, shot, or accomplish the impossible!

I kept my eye on a guard on the other side of the prison who kept walking in and out of his post. If he looked up, while I was dangling from the roof, the escape would end right there. We watched and waited. It seemed a guard was always in the wrong spot.

A brilliant full moon lit the sky and clusters of stars sparkled overhead but I stood in my cell praying for rain, the kind of rain that had been falling on us for years. A heavy downpour would give us a good chance to succeed. But the sky remained cloudless.

Precious minutes ticked by and I found myself powerless to take that first step that would lead me into death's presence. This was no game. He was out there waiting!

Time was running out. It was now about 4:30 a.m. Morning count would start in an hour. I stood and looked beyond the destroyed window bars. Not a cloud. Not a single cloud to hide the face of the moon. Nothing! Then, some powerful, unexplainable presence invaded the room.

I heard a voice! The tone was imperious and commanding: "When you hear the rooster crow, God says, go forward!"

I stood there stunned, and in the yard beneath our window a

rooster crowed! It was like nothing I had ever heard before. Normally a rooster will crow once, stop and listen, then crow again. Not so in this case. The sounds rushed out non-stop.

While the crowing went on, a solid force pushed me to the window. A moment later, clinging by my fingertips, I was swinging like a pendulum from the roof's edge. Then, as though it were nothing at all, I pulled myself on top. And the rooster fell silent.

I lay there shaken and trembling. It was too much! Too many things were happening: the voice, the rooster, that force. Then, to top it all, suddenly, out of the clear sky, for about ten seconds, a gentle rain fell on me!

I was shaken from my daze by the sound of our homemade rope hitting the roof beside me. Hector's arm came over the top. I reached down and pulled him floundering to the roof. For a moment we lay there catching our breath, then rolled over. A disagreeable sight met our eyes. White stripes had been painted across the roof so anything or anyone passing over them could be easily spotted.

A searchlight swept by, playing over the window we had just abandoned. Its moving light showed rolls of barbed wire stretched from one side of the roof to the other. Two guards sat behind a twenty-calibre machine gun on the roof of the next building. The gun tower with its bright lights was no more than ten yards away, but we would have to risk edging further toward the center of the roof if we wanted to get away. There was danger of our movements being noticed. But it had to be done.

"Come on," I whispered.

We started crawling. It was slow. We had to go through the wire, inch over the white markings, all as silently as possible. We reached the middle of the building and eased over to the edge overlooking the path used by the guards on patrol. My heart sank. I seemed to be looking down into a mile-deep chasm.

"Maybe," hissed Hector, "we ought to go back and try to get down the other way."

"You know what that Babalao said. We have to go ahead. We

can't turn back. There's nothing there except death!"

We crawled back to the center of the roof to an old, rusty water tank. Its thick legs were perfect for attaching the rope. We tossed the loose end of the line over the side where it wriggled back and forth, etching a moving shadow against the side of the building.

The guard who was supposed to be making his rounds was talking to another in the tower. As long as they conversed, we felt relatively safe; Hector went over the side.

He had almost reached the ground when one of the rope's three strands parted. Hector let go and fell. Unhurt, he rolled close to the building. The two guards stopped talking. They had heard the noise. But after a moment their conversation resumed.

I was in a bad situation. I would have to go down on the weakened rope. There was nothing else to do; so taking the frail rope in both hands, I slid over the side. When my head was level with the second floor I found myself peering into the unbelieving eyes of a Cuban prisoner. By his breathing, I could tell he was an asthmatic. Without a doubt he was returning from the infirmary. That's why he was in the hallway.

"What're you doin' out there?" he stammered. "Who're you?"

"Shh! Don't give me away. My name's Tony. I'm trying to escape."

"But all the people is locked up. What you tryin' to tell me?"

With the guard tower yards away and a guard liable to pass by and spot me hanging there any moment, this wasn't the time for idle conversation. I loosened my grip and continued downward.

"They gonna kill you!" the voice followed me.

True... I expected a bullet to tear into my back at any time. Never in my life had I felt so vulnerable.

I landed as lightly as possible and dropped flat beside Hector. The two guards were still talking. Now would come the most dangerous moment of all.

The stretch of land between the building we'd abandoned and the white wall had to be crossed and the entire area was flooded with lights. Because of the blinding glare of the spotlight it was impossible to see the locations or outline of the guards. But we couldn't just lie there; discovery was imminent.

"You ready?" gasped Hector, his eyes big as saucers.

"Yeah. Let's go. We got no choice!"

We wriggled ourselves into position. Part of our bodies lay on the path, totally exposed. At that very moment I heard the crunch of boots on gravel. Someone was headed our way! There was nowhere to go. We lay there frozen waiting to be discovered.

I closed my eyes and imagined a blanket of darkness covering us. The steps were now almost upon us. Two guards, laughing and talking, were checking the posts to make sure no one had fallen asleep.

I opened my eyes and saw a pair of boots, not six inches away, approach and pass my head. My mind flashed back to the Babalao's words: "You will see with your own eyes that nothing will befall you!"

The two guards walked to the tower, and after hailing the others, continued on their way. It was unbelievable — a miracle!

Hector's eyes bugged out of his head. Awestruck, he whispered, "Now I know we're going to make it. We've become invisible!"

"Come on," I whispered.

We began inching our way across the walkway. I crawled as though in a dream. Surely our bodies scraping over the ground would be seen. It was a milestone when we reached the guard shack used by the patrolling soldier. We had crossed the walkway. "We did it! We did it!" Hector gasped.

We gave each other a quick handshake then, face down, crawled to the foot of the wall. We had to steal alongside it; behind the remaining guards and towers. We still had a couple of blocks to cover inside the prison before we reached the end of the wall, for it was there that we had picked a spot to go over. We snaked our way along the base of the wall, Hector leading the way, and me pulling myself over the wet grass behind.

Suddenly, we heard the sharp crack of a rifle bolt being pulled and released. We lay there petrified, waiting to be shot, our bodies stiffened. But nothing happened! It was just a guard playing with his gun. We continued our struggle.

An ant bed in our path was destroyed and the insects swarmed out angrily stinging us. Hector swore. My stomach and hands were cut and bleeding from dragging myself over bits of broken glass and stones. Blades of grass jabbed me in the eyes and my muscles ached. Then the guards in the buildings began beating on the bars arousing the prisoners. It was count time!

Hurry my mind screamed. Hurry! Hurry!

We were alongside the guards' quarters when the first shriek of sirens began screaming over the prison. Our escape had been discovered!

A group of guards at a dead run headed toward the building where the escape had originated. Time had run out. There was nothing left for us to do except jump to our feet and make a final desperate bid for freedom. Amazing! Guards dashed right past us while the sirens wailed.

Gasping for breath, we reached the farthest point of the prison. In a last futile effort to hold its prey, the barbed wire on top of the wall bit and clawed at us as we went over. It couldn't stop us. We hit the ground running. Dawn was breaking. It was going to be a beautiful day. Another myth had tumbled!

22.
ANOTHER BABALAO

To have just escaped from one of Cuba's toughest prisons, and not from just inside the fortress, but from the maximum security cells, was sinfully heady.

The sun, a brilliant glow in the east, broke majestically over the hills splashing everything in a myriad of colors. The flowers, still fresh with morning dew, sparkled like diamonds and the birds seemed to be cheering us on as we walked, free, down a long railroad track whose rails stretched into infinity. The morning breeze carrying a touch of chill, kissed my body and I thrilled to it. I was drunk with joy.

"Hey, Hector, I would give anything to see Tricky Fats' face now! OooWee!"

Hector gave a raucous laugh. *"Ay mi madre*! Right now he could bite through nails. And when he remembers that just yesterday he was standing right there in front of the cell... *Ay mi madre!*" Hector popped his fingers in a purely Cuban gesture that can mean many things. Now it meant that Lieutenant Fats Moreno was close to apoplexy.

We had run for miles trying desperately to get as much distance as possible between us and the prison. We slowed to a walk only when our legs couldn't take any more and collapse was certain. Since the wail of sirens had long been left behind, we abandoned the railroad tracks and took a dusty road that led to a small village.

We had no money so I gave Hector my cigarette lighter to sell. We only needed 60 centavos to catch a bus that would take us closer to Havana. Hector approached two men working in a field. After giving us suspicious looks, they bought the lighter.

On our way toward the village we passed by one of the highly extolled state schools, its building run down and in need of repair. In a field beside it, groups of children between seven and fifteen years old, chopped and hoed under the sun. Communist newspaper photos always portrayed such children laughing in delight but not a one was even smiling. An older man, an over-seer, stood with crossed arms observing their progress. It looked like another prison farm.

"So this is the free education Fidel is always boasting about," I remarked.

"It's not free at all. These kids work half a day to get half a day of teaching," Hector explained.

So far as I was concerned these children lived separated from their families, lost half their youth digging and chopping in some isolated farmland and were denied the things a child needs most — the warmth and guidance of parents. What seemed to be gratis, had a very high price.

We left the school behind and a short time later were bouncing up and down in an old bus whose shocks had given out ages before and whose driver still didn't believe it. Finally, we reached a fairly large town. It was midafternoon and the sun was trying to outshine itself.

As the bus sputtered away Hector said, "We've got to take a cab from here. When we get to *Parragas* (a section on the out-skirts of Havana) we'll just have to jump out and run."

Miraculously we caught one of the few taxis operating in the rural town. After about a thirty-minute ride the meter had clicked up a sizable bill. I kept my hand on the door handle waiting for Hector to give the word to jump.

He directed the driver down gutted streets lined with houses packed tightly together and just when I thought the moment had arrived to leap out of the cab, Hector shouted to the driver to pull to the curb. He called to a middle-aged woman walking down the sidewalk. A moment later he was giving her bear hugs and whispering excitedly into her ear.

She blanched, then reached into her purse and handed him a small roll of pesos from which he extracted a few and ran back to the cab to pay the driver. "Come on, Tony, let's go."

Our benefactress was a friend of Hector's family whom he had known for years. Providence had smiled on us and placed her in our path. Now there would be no police summoned by an irate taxi driver. She took us to her home, a couple of blocks away. The house was small, old, and crumbling.

While we took turns dousing ourselves with cold water in an outhouse, trying to rid ourselves of sweat and grime, the lady's daughter-in-law scrambled eggs and heated leftover rice for us over coals in a hole outside. They were sharing their dinner with us. It was delicious!

The lady gave us some old pants and couple of shirts, plus a few pesos and an affectionate good-bye kiss. They had taken a great risk already and to remain any longer would endanger them. We thanked her and set off.

Hector wasn't far from his parents' house, but the police would be looking for two men together. The problem was where to leave me while he tried to visit his family.

Luckily, I'd had the good sense to bring along a telephone number I'd guarded for months. It belonged to a guy I'd met in prison. I had doctored him through a serious skin problem and in gratitude he had told me that under any circumstances, if I ever managed to get out of prison, to call him. That seemed to be the solution.

We found a telephone booth and I rang the ex-prisoner. "Wait there," he told me, "I'll be right over."

Night would be falling soon. Not having any identification, we wanted to get off the streets as soon as possible. By now we were being hunted in full force. Never had an American escaped from one of Cuba's prisons, and they were going to take it very personally.

Not a half-hour passed before I spotted my friend, striding toward us. He shook Hector's hand, gave me a big hug, then listened to the problem. "No sweat," he said. "I'll help you. Tonight you can stay at my grandma's. But you'll have to sleep on the floor."

I was grateful. I had a plan. All I needed was time to contact another friend who lived in Havana. We had made a pact to try to escape the island together if I managed to get out of jail and elude the police for a few days. But nothing could be done that evening so after setting up a meeting place for the following day with Hector, my friend and I headed for safety.

We made it to his grandmother's without incident. I thought that I'd be too excited to sleep, but the day's activities had taken their toll. I stretched out on the floor and immediately drifted away.

Next morning, stiff and sore, but still exhilarated, I awoke and lay for awhile listening to the day come alive. My friend's mom came in and fixed us a breakfast of hot milk and crispy, fresh bread. Then, taking her son aside, she whispered adamantly into his ear, pressed some money in his hand, and turned her back.

"You've got to leave," he said, shamefaced.

He gave me the ten pesos his mother had given him and offered to stick with me for the day. I thanked the lady kindly. I understood her fears.

"It's very dangerous!" she said with tears in her eyes. "I wish I could do more, but the risk for my family is too great."

Walking along the neighborhood streets I had the opportunity to observe Castro's terror mechanism at first hand. On every block, at least one house had a bold sign hanging outside declaring its inhabitants members of the Committee for the Defense of the Revolution (CDR).

All the people on the block were under twenty-four-hour surveillance. And since everyone in a block was well known, any stranger drew immediate attention. CDR members hung out of their windows; they made no pretense of not watching one's every move. You were tracked from the moment you entered the block until you left it.

Should you visit a house, note was taken of when you entered and when you departed. If you remained inside more than twenty-four hours, the police were called. The reward for CDR members, at that time, was a thin protective wall that kept back, at least somewhat, the insidious killer force of G-2.

CDR members belonged to a special caste. They had access to a little more food and the chance someday to own a refrigerator, a television or a telephone. Those who belonged to the CDR were despised. They dug and pried into the lives of everyone around them and turned the information over to their masters, State Security. Big Brother was watching constantly. George Orwell's prediction was already a reality.

Chills ran through me, as block after block, we were followed by peering, inquisitive eyes. It was fearful. To be watched on every block, in every city, stripped and examined over and again, day after day, must be a loathsome existence.

My friend and I walked at a fast pace, trying to give the impression that we were on our way somewhere. People strolling casually along drew attention, and consequently, the police.

As we strode purposefully up and down streets, taking care not to follow the same route twice, I told my friend about the strange things that had occurred during my escape from Guanajay.

"I know a spiritualist who lives close by," he remarked, "you want to go there? Maybe she can tell you something."

I really wasn't into spiritualism, but I decided, "What the heck! Why not?"

The plump middle-age woman, head swathed in a colorful bandana, was in the process of cleaning house and begged off. She was too occupied to attend me, but if I wanted, she would send someone to guide us to the home of a Babalao. She disappeared and returned a moment later leading an old, wrinkled, hump-backed man. The old man dragged a deformed leg scraping along behind him. He gave me goose pimples.

I felt a mounting tension as we followed our guide. It was as though I were being swept along by a tidal wave to a foreign land, filled with mystery and unknown.

The old man shuffled up to a small but neat-looking house and knocked on a side door. An elderly lady beckoned us inside. The hunchback turned and dragged himself away.

"Please," said the old lady, "take a seat. My son will be here in a few minutes. Would you like some coffee?" She busied herself toddling here and there fixing a pot of the delicious but very strong brew. The kitchen was neat and clean. A picture of Christ, gazing at his bleeding heart, hung above an ancient American refrigerator.

When the coffee was made, she served us each a cup. Then the bedroom door opened and a thin black man, about fifty years old, stepped into the kitchen. He walked with a lean as if under a heavy load. His skin was leathery and heavily lined. His eyes dominated his entire being. They radiated!

His stare made my skin prickle. He had not glanced at my friend. His first words were directed to me as well. "You are standing in a whirlwind! I see trouble all around you. Death is standing there right beside you!"

At that instant a chicken, trying to imitate a rooster, cackled.

The man turned to his mother and said, "A chicken that crows like a rooster announces its own death. Go chop its head off!" Now humming an eerie melody, he turned to the sink and began to wash his hands. He rinsed his mouth with alcohol, donned a white cap and paying me no attention, entered another room on the far side of the kitchen.

No one had told me whether I should stay or leave, but there was something that kept me glued in my chair. Curiosity? I don't know. My friend told me that he would wait outside and went out. But I remained.

I could hear the old Babalao chanting, and every now and then stop and talk with someone else inside the room. I recognized his voice; it was heavy, almost a growl. The other voice was lighter, more feminine.

Five minutes must have passed before the door slowly opened. The Babalao crooked his finger and told me to enter. I did, and took a sweeping look around the room to see who the other person was. There was no one else and no other exit except the door that I'd just come through!

Hanging on the walls were strange artifacts that, from their appearance, were from Africa. Dolls, skewered through with long needles, hung side by side. Around the floor were altars covered with fruit, flowers, incense and cigars.

I sat facing the old man across a table. I felt strange, not afraid, just strange. I sensed another presence!

The Babalao asked me, "What is bothering you?"

I told him about the escape: everything.

"So you want to know what's going to happen! You want to know if you will succeed in getting off the island. Right?" Without waiting for an answer he began chanting, while at the same time putting pebbles of various weights and colors in my hands. Next he ordered me to put my arms in back of me, jiggle the stones back and forth; then holding one in each closed fist present them to him. Still chanting, he closed his eyes and allowed his own hand to be drawn to one of mine.

The size and color of the pebbles were noted. Then he looked through the pages of a thick, well-worn book at his side. Afterwards, he scribbled on a pad. Finally, he looked up at me and in a drawn voice said: "You are in great danger. You must turn yourself in!"

I returned the Babalao's gaze and shook my head. "No... No..."

"But you don't understand. Death is here with you. He's stalking you. You must go straight back. Get a bus and go back!"

I felt a disappointment. I had anticipated encouragement. "Sir, I've gone through an awful lot to escape. Death was at my side all that time too. I didn't risk my life just to turn around and go back."

His eyes glowing, the Babalao shook his head. "You will not

escape from this island! The revolutionary government of Cuba is going to return you to your country. Listen to me. You must turn yourself in. If you don't, there will be a great suffering for you. Here!" The old man grabbed a tiny packet and began brushing my body with it. "This is why you've come, so that I can do this. He handed the packet to me. "Take this, and when you reach the prison, throw it in the field, and you'll see, nothing will befall you!"

"I'm sorry, sir," I said rising. "I'm not going back."

"Wait a minute!" The old man was angry. He glowered as he walked around the desk. "I've said all I'm going to. Come over here and talk to your protector!"

He led me to an altar that was the largest and most decorated of all. "This is the altar of the Virgin of Charity." The old man bowed to the altar, then picked up a candle and said, "Here is one of your children. He begs you to attend him."

Holding the candle in one hand, he placed a match to the wick. It was no sooner lit than it was snuffed out as though blasted by a jet of air. The Babalao glared at me. "She is angry with you. She is displeased because you are disobedient!" He bowed his head and prayed. Once again he lit the wick. This time it burned with a steady flame. He placed the candle on the altar and turned to me. "Talk to her. She is your protector." He went out, leaving me alone in the mysterious room.

I did not understand what was happening, and if I had not sensed something out of the ordinary, I would have felt foolish. As it was, I bowed and asked permission to speak. "I have risked my life to get out. I'm not going back! Protect me if you wish or let me die, but I'm not going to turn myself in." I turned, opened the door and stepped out.

"Well, what are you going to do?" growled the Babalao.

"I'm not going back," I said, heading for the door.

The Babalao's face twisted in anger. He shouted, "I've told you that you're not going to escape from the island!" He was yelling at the top of his lungs. His eyes flashed fire and he waved his arms. "You're not going to escape! Turn yourself in!"

The man's screaming unnerved me. The CDR was only a few houses down. He must be trying to get me arrested, I thought, as I hurried to open the kitchen door.

"You're not going to make it, I'm telling you. The revolutionary government will send you back to your country. You're not going to make it!" he shouted. The Babalao was raging, and as I rushed through the door and down the steps he ran after me and screamed, "Beware of a woman and a trap! Beware of a woman and a trap!"

The warning rang in my ears like a death knoll. Every nerve in my body was on the cutting edge.

I rushed to my friend, waiting outside, and asked him for a last favor. "Help me get downtown."

I wanted to get to *La Rampa*, a street in Old Havana, I'd heard about in prison. I figured it would be easier to avoid detection there; La Rampa was known as a foreigners' playground.

A couple of blocks from La Rampa my helpful friend and I parted. I owed him a lot. We promised to keep in touch; then alone, at last, I walked over to Havana's Central Park.

Like many big city central parks it was dirty and full of weirdos. There were also a few lovers holding hands and pigeons flocking around anyone tossing them crumbs.

I thought: Well, you're on your own now, in an unknown city in a strange land! I looked around, trying to orient myself. A movie theater sat across the street from the park and close by was an open front cafe. I felt a little hungry and decided to grab a bite to eat; at the same time I'd try to get in touch with my partner.

The small cafe had a few customers sitting around guzzling beer. I walked in and spotted a telephone hanging on the wall. My spirits took a quantum leap when Dormido answered the phone. He told me to meet him at 7:00 p.m. in Central Park. "I'll have an address where it'll be safe for you to stay."

I walked to the counter and ordered rice and scrambled eggs. The waiter held out his hand, and I dropped a five peso bill in his hand. He gave me a funny look. "Hey, I can't take money back here! You have to pay in advance out there!" He pointed to a booth that I had walked by upon entering the cafe. I tensed, a slip like that could draw unwanted attention. I had better be more careful.

Standing outside the cafe a few moments later, I studied the area. It was two o'clock and I had five hours to kill before my meeting with Dormido. I didn't want to spend the time walking up and down the streets. I headed for the theater. You couldn't want a better place to hide in.

The movie was one of those 'Who-Dunnit?' things with no plot and lots of leggy women. I saw it through one and a half times before I slipped out onto the street. It was about six and darkness had already settled over the city. Since it was early there was still life and movement. After ten at night the streets were deserted. Fear of being stopped and arrested forced people indoors early. An undeclared curfew was in effect in Havana year round.

I walked over to the park trying to act as inconspicuous as possible. Revolutionary Police and CDR members were everywhere.

At seven o'clock I met Dormido and walked with him into an alley. Thrusting a piece of paper nervously into my hand, he told me I had to be at the address it contained at ten o'clock next morning. We shook hands and quickly parted.

The next problem was where to spend the night. I was in the center of town and to be seen walking around late meant certain arrest. I decided to walk down to La Rampa. There was the chance that I would meet someone I knew.

La Rampa was a very eccentric part of Communist Havana. Seamen from a dozen countries, prostitutes, hustlers and tourists converged on the area after dark and for a few frenetic hours the four or five blocks shimmered with life.

I shouldered through the sidewalk crush and worked my way over to *La Paragua*, a sidewalk cafe. I had been standing there looking over the chattering crowd only a minute or so when I heard my name called. I turned and saw, Ronco, a thief I'd known in Principe.

"Tony! *Tony el Americano"* he boomed out, throwing his arms around me.

I pulled him to one side and told him not to mention my name, explained why and added, "I need a place to stay."

Ronco promised to help me find a place for the night. He did try. He took me to several friends and relatives, but no one would take the risk of housing an escapee even for one night.

About nine o'clock Ronco told me to wait in the cafe where we'd met while he went to see another friend about putting me up. I decided either Ronco could not find a place and was about to abandon me or he was going to turn me in and wanted to keep me localized. Whatever the reason, I didn't stick around. The area was teeming with police.

I turned onto a side street and headed back toward the park. I was so deep in thought that I didn't notice the police van until I was almost upon it. About five policemen lined the walk from a dimly-lit club to the parked truck. Officers were marching people out and arresting them.

I almost spun around, which would have been a fatal error. Instead I forced myself to act normal and walked straight ahead towards the uniforms.

A policeman at the van door held back one of those arrested as I murmured, *"Perdoname,"* in my best Spanish and slipped by. The hair on the nape of my neck tingled until I safely turned the corner.

Once again I headed for La Rampa, hoping against hope to find someone there who would help me. Ten o'clock was nearing. In a little while the police would sweep the streets clean. I had to find a hiding place.

I was trudging along wondering what to do when again I was hailed. This time it turned out to be Red, a good friend from prison. He had three young ladies in tow who appeared to be prostitutes. I took Red to one side and told him about the escape.

I needed help. Red came up with an idea.

"Hey, man, you ain't got no problem. Just take you a woman and go to a *posada*. At least you'll have a place for the night."

A posada was a state controlled brothel; for a few pesos a couple could stay together the entire night.

"Red, I don't have a woman. I like the idea, though!" I looked at the girls at his side.

"No problem. Which one you want?"

She was from Oriente, a province famous for its lovely women. The strains of Chinese, black and Spanish blood fuse there to create electrifyingly passionate, slant-eyed beauties. We walked two blocks to the *Posada Rex*. The dark-haired girl at my side did all the talking. She paid for the room, and together we took a rattling, creaky elevator to the second floor. Although I was tired the soft body next to me had a rejuvenating effect and in between discussing my plight, we made love.

The following morning at seven o'clock the buzzer sounded. It was time to go. My mind was set on getting to the *safe* house right away.

As soon as we stepped into the lobby I sensed that something was wrong. The cashier behind the desk was extremely nervous. His hands trembled as he took the key; perspiration streamed from his brow.

Perplexed, I stepped through the door onto the sidewalk. I was looking down, deep in thought, trying to figure out what was happening when my mistress for the night gasped and clutched my arm in a tight grip. I looked up and saw why.

The street was empty of people or traffic. a half-dozen police cars blocked the intersection to the right of the hotel. Policemen pointing submachine guns lay stretched across the hoods of their cars. Others with pistols and shotguns crouched from behind staircases. I spun around and the same scene was replayed in the other direction on the street. A massacre had been planned. If I tried to run, I would be shot to death.

"Keep walking!" I hissed to the girl as I stepped away from

her and turned back to the place we'd just left. Maybe she could get away; as for me there was no escape. A flash of anger swept over me. I was only hours away from the *safe* house and to be trapped now was heartbreaking.

Suddenly, the image of the old Babalao smashed into my mind. He was glaring at me and sounded disgusted and angry: "I told you to beware of a woman and a trap! I warned you!" Then the image vanished.

Thoroughly shaken, I stumbled back inside the posada. I walked over to the petrified man behind the desk and taking out a peso, asked for change. I was going to wait for the police there.

The clerk was terrified. The cops might run in shooting, and he was in the direct line of fire. Shaking and babbling nothings he bent over as low as possible, pretending to look in the bottom drawer for change.

I heard the sound of running feet, then the door burst open. A tall, dark-haired guy wearing a Pancho Villa mustache ran up to me, pointed a .357 Magnum at my head and snarled, "Don't move. Don't move a muscle or I'll blow your head off!"

I smiled uneasily, hoping he wouldn't lose control. "Who's going to move... now?"

Just about then a gorilla-type cop punched me in the back, driving me against the desk. My arms were twisted behind me and a pair of thin handcuffs were ground into my wrists. The pain was unbearable. Now the room was full of cops and each one tried to get in at least one blow as I was pushed outside and kicked into a waiting police car.

"So you think you can make a mockery of the Cuban police and get away with it, huh?" growled Gorilla as he slugged me again.

"Hey, catch that whore! She was with him!" Pancho Villa cried. She wouldn't get away either. I found out much later she had been given a year in prison for association and prostitution.

Burning rubber, the car roared away from the curb and sped the seven or eight blocks to the Department of Technical Investigation and slid to a stop. DTI is equivalent to an FBI holding facility in the U.S. — only a lot tougher.

Hauled out and shoved inside the large jail, I was left sitting on the floor writhing in pain while the police stood around and laughed. The handcuffs, digging into my bones, were excruciatingly painful. With the flow of blood cut off, my hands were swollen blobs filled with liquid fire. I was in agony. I begged them to loosen the cuffs just a little.

They laughed and told me they hoped I would have to have my hands amputated!

Just when I thought I'd go crazy from the pain, a different officer walked in and ordered the guards to loosen the cuffs. What a relief! Even months later just a touch on my wrists was sufficient to send electrical currents up and down my arms.

After being stripped, searched and given jail clothes, I was dragged to a cement cell and thrown in. Then its steel-plated door was locked and bolted.

23.
A SPOON, GRIT AND CEMENT

Inside the cell was an old-fashioned iron cot holding a thin, filthy mattress. I flopped down and lay there cursing my luck. I tried to block out the memory of the Babalao's image but I couldn't banish the thought that the old man had foretold all that had happened.

The pain in my hands was beginning to subside and to take my mind off the dull ache that remained, I studied the cell. Nothing unusual here, except a foot-square hole in the ceiling criss-crossed with thick bars. The door had a slot through which the guards could observe the prisoner inside. At the head of the bed, a little to the left, was a shower, and directly underneath it was the ever-present hole in the floor.

Suddenly the slot was snatched open and a pair of eyes stared coldly at me for a moment only to be replaced by a mouth missing several teeth. "When a guard opens this slot," hissed the discolored lips, "get to your feet and stand at attention!"

I was too beat to object. Slowly I straightened to attention. The opening was closed and I dropped back to the bed. The same thing occurred over and over. Each time I was a little slower in getting to my feet. Finally the guard didn't think that my speed was sufficient, and opening the door, ordered me out.

"All right, let's see if we can work some muscles into those legs! Maybe when you finish a little exercise, you'll be able to get up faster!" He pointed to a low bench and ordered me to step up on it, then down, then up, then down. This went on for a few minutes.

The muscles in my legs turned to jelly but I tried not to let the pain show. If another guard hadn't come in announcing lunch, I would soon have collapsed.

Lunch came. It was better than I had expected; rice, bean soup, bread and even a slice of guava was on the tray. After lunch, the trays and spoons were collected on a cart stopped in front of my door. Every ten to fifteen minutes, the slot was snatched open and I had to stand. Sometimes there would be several viewers and I could hear their conversations.

"Yeah, he's the one who busted out of Guanajay. A real tough cookie but he's back to stay now!"

Around three o'clock the cell was opened and a lanky Cuban was shoved inside. As the door slammed shut, he squinted at me and said, "Hey, aren't you *Tony el Americano*?"

I nodded, trying to place the man. Then I remembered we had been in Principe together.

"What," he said, shaking my hand, "are you doing here?"

"They brought me in this morning. I escaped from Guanajay."

"You *what*?" The Cuban dropped to the bed beside me.

I recounted our adventure while he sat thunderstruck. When I finished, the Cuban jumped off the bed and whispered in excitement, "If you escaped from Guanajay, there's no reason why we can't do it from here!"

I stared at him as if he were completely insane, then glanced around the cement vault and laughed, "Why not?" So, aching bones and all, I began planning another escape!

"The first thing we'll need is something to dig with," I said. "This evening when they bring dinner I'm going to try to steal a spoon, then we'll see what this ceiling's made of." I was already studying the barred overhead opening.

After dinner the guard watched closely as I took the trays out of our cell and stacked them with others on the rolling cart. What he didn't see was the cupping of my spoon and its replacement on my tray by another spoon from the tray underneath. Now we had a tool!

Top priority was of course vigilance. How would we know when a guard was approaching the cell? Here in DTI they wore soft-soled shoes to facilitate eavesdropping. Also, they loved the psychological game of keeping prisoners unsure of when the slot would snap open.

We noticed a crack along the edge of the door. Just enough light entered through the crack so that if the thin beam was interrupted, it could only mean that someone was coming. The next time the guard checked, I was certain his shadow preceded him. To be positive, I waited until it happened again. Sure enough, I was right. Now we had a way to watch our captors.

The next thing was to find out how hard the cement was around the bars. I took out my spoon and examined it. It was one of those new stainless steel jobs imported from Russia... tough!

As soon as the guard passed by again, I stood on the bed, and using the spoon like a drill, began the first of many holes.

The ceiling was about five inches thick but not really that hard to dig through. When two holes had been made, we took the head of the bed off, and using one of the legs as a lever, collapsed the cement in between them. Luckily the hole we were making was located over the door. It was impossible to see from outside. But if the guard came into our cell, for any reason, we were in for a heck of a beating.

The method we had devised for watching for the guard was foolproof, and we always had time enough to jump to the bed and be casually talking when the slot popped open.

The day following my arrest I was taken up a wide flight of stairs to a miniscule office. Seated behind a desk that reached almost wall to wall, sat a heavy, middle-aged lieutenant. He was the officer in charge of investigating my case. He looked tired, and as all Latins do, completely out of place and uncomfortable in his starched standard military issue Russian uniform.

He told me to take a seat, then proceeded to compliment me

on the daredevil escape from Guanajay. "That was truly a remarkable achievement," marveled the lieutenant. "Truly fantastic! Tell me something. How did you guys do it?"

I recounted the entire episode, after which the officer showed me photos taken of my old cell; the bars, an angled shot from the bars to the roof, a shot from above of the dangling rope, another at ground level and finally a panoramic view of the wall topped by the barbed-wire fence. They were excellent photos.

As we talked, I wondered what the man would do if he knew that at this moment his own prison was being tunneled through like Swiss cheese.

The lieutenant said, "Your friend Hector has been captured. In fact, we apprehended him before you."

Back in the cell my new-found escape mate and I had a good laugh at the unsuspecting official. We slapped hands and went back to work.

By the third day we had managed to dig one of the bars loose. Now we had a real hole. On the sixth day I could almost get my head through the opening. One more day's work would be sufficient.

On the morning of the seventh day I heard strange noises. There was the scrape of metal being dragged over cement, then the sound of a cell door being opened, followed by clanking and more scraping sounds. Suddenly it hit me. They were dragging beds around. I pressed my ear to the door and my spirits sank. All of the single beds were being exchanged for double-tiered ones. I could hear the prisoners being taken out and the cells checked.

I dropped to the bed and stared numbly at the wall. Each time a cell door opened I prayed with all my might, "Please don't let them come in here. Don't let them open this door."

Lunchtime came and went. My friend and I sat locked in silence. The sound of cells being opened came closer and closer.

I had been concentrating so hard on "Don't come here," that I had almost worked myself into a trance. When the slot flipped open and a guard peered in, I turned to him, and without mov-

ing from the bed, said, "We have two." The guard closed the flap
and told the crew to take the bunks to the next cell. My cell-mate
and I sat there stunned speechless!

There was still a possibility the guard would make a final check.
But when dinner came and no further notice was taken of the
cell, I knew we were home free. The guard either thought he had
seen two beds or he had seen what I had wanted him to see.

While we were waiting to make our final assault on the hole,
we decided to invent some escape clothes. With a hook from the
springs we tore the mattress in half. We took each end of its cover
and put a hole in its top and two small openings on each side
and presto, we had pullover shirts! They were kind of gaudy,
flowers and all, but better than nothing. Maybe folks would think
we were country boys.

About ten that night we were ready to go. Dismantling the bed
once more, we used the leg to bring the remaining portion of the
ceiling crumbling down. We held our breath, waiting to see if the
noise had been noticed... Nothing!

We waited until the guard had passed by again. Then I stood
on the bed and, pulling and wriggling, managed to get the upper
half of my body through the hole and looked around. Instead
of shining stars in a night sky, I was greeted by the sight of a huge
room with large cement blocks for walls. We had dug through
a false roof!

I dropped back and told my buddy to take a look. He did. When
he lowered himself inside again, his eyes were filled with tears.
"What do you think we ought to do?" He was trembling.
"Only thing we can. Go up there and find a way out."
"What about the guard? What if..."
"We'll just have to take the risk that he won't come by while we're
up there, that's all."

We both went up through the hole.

Wearing socks to muffle our footsteps, we moved stealthily over
the tops of the cells underneath. We searched everywhere, found
no escape and grimly lowered ourselves back into the cell. We

had been inside for only a minute or so when the slot was opened and closed.

Back up on the false roof again, we discussed the idea of over-powering the guard as he checked the cells. But we discarded that as being too risky.

The minutes ticked by and I had almost given up hope when I heard something that drew my attention. At first I wasn't sure what it was, then the sound became louder. It was a pinging, like hail striking a metal cover. As we worked our way along one side of the wall the ping grew louder, more distinct. Then, in a flash, I realized what the sound was—rain. The rainfall was striking a ventilator shaft whose opening stood waist high over the false roof. "Listen," I whispered. "If the rain is hitting this thing it must have an exit to the outside!"

Only a few screws held the opening secure. If they could be removed, perhaps the mouth of the shaft could be twisted to one side to give us the space necessary to squeeze out into that falling rain. It was worth a try.

Hope flared anew as we hurried back to round up whatever tools we might need. To be on the safe side, we waited until the guard had made his rounds, then scrambled up through the hole again.

The trusty spoon was not only a good drill, it made a perfect screwdriver as well. In no time the shaft opening was bent to one side and fresh night air poured through the rupture.

We could see the ground about eight feet below. Strangely enough, the rain had stopped. For the last time we descended into the cell. There could have been no doubt in the guard's mind when he opened the peephole and heard us snoring away inside, that we were fast asleep.

A moment after the flap closed we were up and pulling on our *shirts.* We turned our striped pants inside out, slipped them on and climbed to the roof again. Every minute was precious. We went straight to the vent and jumped out!

We landed with a soft thud on the wet grass, took a look around and discovered we were inside a huge patio surrounded by a wall which towered at least twenty feet high. There was no ladder or any other way for us to get over and time was running out. We had one lucky break, though; construction was going on in DTI and the patio was stacked with cement bags.

We darted over and hid behind the bags and mounds of dirt. We saw only one possible way out, straight ahead to a tall wooden door, criss-crossed and held secure by two long poles, one of them, steel. They would have to be removed.

In an office beside the large door I could hear two guards talking. We would have to slip by, only a few feet from these sentries, then lift out the poles. Dangerous! But there was no other way!

Moving from one mound of dirt to another, we finally reached our objective. Every nerve in my body tingled. I thought my heart would burst through my chest. I raised the first barrier, the wooden one, carefully.

My friend grabbed the other, but he was so nervous that the bar chattered against the door. Quickly I leaned my pole against the wall and took the steel bar. Now all of the experience gained from operating under extreme pressures came to my rescue. In one sweep I raised the bar over its supporting hooks and placed it on the ground. With a loud squeak, the door swung open. There, a few inches away, was the sidewalk.

"Hey! Hey, you! Stop! Stop or I'll fire!"

The sharp crack of the pistol only lent wings to my heels. Three people, standing on the corner waiting for a bus, hit the ground and gaped as we streaked by. The night air was filled with the sound of tires peeling away to join the search, as we raced up one street and down the other. I was running for my life. Death matched me stride for stride; I could feel him.

Car lights hit us and shots rang out. Another corner, and this time we split up. The Cuban shot to the right but I was running so fast I couldn't make the turn and kept going straight ahead.

More shots as I turned corner after corner trying to shake my obstinate pursuers. My throat was aching and every breath set my chest on fire. Staggering from exhaustion, I ran up a narrow flight of stairs and out a window onto the roof of an apartment house. I lay there gasping for breath, listening to the progress of my hunters.

More cars and trucks had joined the search party. Every now and again sporadic firing broke out and I heard shots directed at my cell-mate. "Hey, you! Hold it! There he goes! Shoot! Shoot!" He was giving them a run for their money. The chase went on. Finally he must have given them the slip, since I heard no gun-fire for awhile—only the sound of more vehicles.

I peeped over the edge of the roof as a truck full of soldiers careened by. A guard was being dropped off on every corner. They were saturating the area.

A few minutes passed; then a car, microphone blaring, pulled around the corner. A metallic voice was ordering everyone to turn on the lights in their houses and step outdoors. No house was allowed to remain dark. Block after block lit up. My partner must have been well-hidden; even with the intense search being car-ried out there had been no indication that he had been sighted.

Twenty minutes must have gone by, when riding on the cool night air, came the most blood-chilling sound I had ever heard. A horrible generic flashback hurled me back in time and space and turned me into a hunted slave; I could hear the baying of blood hounds!

The howls of the dogs turned into frantic barks and snarls. A moment later the air was filled with shouts and the flat crack of pistol shots. "There he goes — over there! Don't let him get away! Grab him!"

A flurry of sounds, then relative silence. My friend had been captured. Now all of their efforts would be directed to me. I couldn't control the trembling that possessed me. Maybe it was my imagination, maybe not, but as I heard the dogs coming closer I seemed to hear the voice of the old Babalao:

"Don't move. You're not going to get away, but at least they're not going to kill you. Just don't move!"

I settled back and waited, watching policemen with flashlights and drawn pistols moving over the roofs of nearby houses. Not many minutes passed before I heard heavy claws raking over the steps leading to my hideaway.

The choked gasp of a dog straining at the leash and his frantically-gouging nails drew closer. I stood and watched its head come into view.

"Oh, God!" I gasped, "Oh, my God!"

It was a mastiff, a killer, and it had found its prey!

The animal's eyes were blood red and the only sound to be heard, other than the raking claws, was the click of its teeth as it snapped at the air in rage. Silent; savage, silent killer! Coming for me!

As soon as it had enough leash, it charged and exhibiting its excellent training, lunged for my testicles. When my hands went down in a natural reaction to protect myself, the beast leaped for my throat. I cried out and fell.

The soldier holding the leash turned to his companion and shouted, "Should I turn him loose? Should I turn him loose?"

"No," yelled the other. "Don't! It'll kill him."

A shot was fired; a moment later guards streamed onto the roof and under a rain of kicks and blows, I was carried down to a waiting car.

The same officer who had congratulated me so warmly on my escape from Guanajay now sat squarely on my head with both his hands clutched in my waistband. If I escaped again, he'd be with me.

I was hustled back to the prison patio surrounded by a dozen or more guards. The lieutenant turned to me, bewildered, "How did you do it? How'd you guys get out?"

I nodded toward the ventilating shaft.

"Where?" cried the officer. "I don't see anything."

"The vent!" I replied.

The officer gave himself a ringing slap on his forehead.

Chained and handcuffed, I was led to another cell —

disciplinary. I was shoved inside, handcuffs, chains and all. Here there was nothing except cement walls, the steel door and a hole in the floor... nothing else. I dropped to the floor and laughed hysterically with relief, glad to be alive. I fell asleep and dreamed of being chased by rabid dogs foaming at the mouth.

Next day, still in chains, I was taken to see the lieutenant. The poor guy was in a shambles. Dark bags hung from his eyes and his normally well-pressed uniform was wrinkled and dirty. "Sit down!" he said.

I lowered my still aching body into a chair.

"You are a problem," he stated. "Don't you know what would have happened if you guys had gotten away?" I didn't answer. Frankly, I didn't care.

"I, myself, and all of the guards in this section would have gone to jail! A fine officer like me!" He leaned back and studied me for a moment. "You better get something straight! We're not afraid of you!"

His voice rose. "We're not afraid of you. We revolutionaries are not intimidated by you imperialist agents. I just want you to know that." He leaned back and studied me. Then nodding his head up and down, he mused aloud, "You're a tiger all right. But you know what we do to tigers that get out of their cages?" He answered his own question, "We shoot them!"

So another nickname was given to me. The guards referred to me as El Tigre de California, the California tiger! For the seventeen days I spent in DTI, although chained twenty-four hours a day, they treated me with respect.

Day after day squads of *Search and Capture* personnel came by to take a good look at the man who was causing them so much trouble. On about the fifteenth day a well-dressed man in elegant civilian clothes, flanked by bodyguards, stepped into my cell and said, "Tony, listen real close to me. You've caused enough trouble. The very next time you raise your head, we're going to take you out and put a bullet in it." He spoke calmly, as though talking about the weather or the time of day. Then, without another word, he departed.

Two days later, about seven o'clock in the evening, still wearing my *escape* shirt, I was taken to a waiting Jaula. The motor cranked into life and once more I was swept toward the unknown.

24.
THE DEVIL'S CORRIDOR

I wasn't surprised when I spotted the familiar lights of Guanajay. Because I had remained so long in DTI, I knew there had been some question as to where this high escape-risk inmate could be controlled. They were going to try to bury me in Guanajay.

I stepped from the Jaula and faced the rather large assembly waiting for me. My chains were removed; there was no laughing or joking. Everyone was dead serious.

They nodded to me, then firmly took me by the wrists and escorted me to E Unit. This time the stairs leading to the second floor were ignored and instead, a heavy steel-plated door, ten feet inside the building, was swung open. A dismal, long, dimly-lit corridor stretched before me. A solid wall, with a few barred openings was on the left, and lined side by side to the right, cement-enclosed cages.

As we came to a stop in front of a steel door, a familiar face popped up to the food slot of the cell alongside. "Hey, Brudda! Wha's happenin'?" That was one of the few phrases that Pandeado could speak in English. He sounded happy to see me.

The guards removed my handcuffs and one of them must have sensed me go tight. He hurried to say, "Don't worry. We're not going to beat on you. You risked, you played and you won. Now we start all over again. We've got you back it's up to us to hold you. It's a clean slate. Step inside please!"

The door rumbled shut, and I was in pitch darkness.

"Hey, Brudder. Psst! Over next to your bunk. There's a hole in the wall!"

Pandeado had a light burning in his cell, and I spotted the opening at once. "Oh, man, you don't know it but you drove these people crazy! They took everybody's head off from the Warden down!" Pandeado couldn't wait to tell me about all that had transpired the morning of the escape and in the following days.

The little black lieutenant who bummed cigarettes was the one who had discovered the escape. "He was taking count and when he got to your cell and pulled the blanket back from your door you could hear him hollering all over the prison. "Oh! My American's got away on me!" Everybody was locked down tight. The guard that was on duty, you know, the one walking the post that night is in jail, and since then, officials have been coming back here every day. Generals and all kinds of brass, taking photos and interrogating everybody. See, Tony, you don't know it but you escaped on the day that Brehznev was due to arrive in Cuba!" Pandeado burst into a fit of laughter.

I saw the joke right away. "The officials must have thought that I was some kind of black James Bond who had escaped to carry out some dastardly plot against one of the great white masters!" I roared with laughter. "Why else would anyone want to escape on such an important day?"

"Well, in the first place, they mobilized G-2, Search and Capture, DTI, the Coast Guard and all the CDR's in Cuba to get you guys. One general came in and broke up all of the chairs that the guards used to sit in. He said they must have been sleeping or you never would have got away. No guard can sit down anymore on duty — ever. They say it's now a real lousy place to work in. And two — they've put up another fence between the buildings and the wall. Tony, you've changed the whole prison!"

We both fell into paroxysms of laughter. I was pleased. I had struck again. And this time I'd hurt them.

Nothing could have dampened my spirits that night; not the dark cell that echoed my breathing or the cold cement block that bit into my flesh as I stretched out and fell asleep.

"Hey, Tony! *Tony el Americano!*"

I staggered out of bed and put my face to the food slot. A rifle was shoved through the barred window on the other side of the corridor, leveled and the trigger squeezed. The pin fell with a dry click on the empty chamber. They were playing games. I hadn't flinched.

The guard who had simulated the shooting pulled back his gun and shouted up to another in the tower, "You're right. He ain't afraid 'a nothing!"

Yes, I am, I thought to myself. But you people will never know it.

As the sun rose, enough light came through the food slot for me to get a good look at my new home. It was approximately five feet wide by ten long. A double tier of concrete slabs jutted out of the wall to the left. On the right was a toilet and alongside it a wash bowl.

At the rear of the cell, a little higher than was comfortable to see through, were three two-inch-round holes bored through the wall. The wall itself was at least two feet thick. Two naked wires hung from the cobwebbed ceiling supporting an empty socket. Flies, mosquitos and roaches infested the room.

There was a funny thing about this hole. The prison would not issue a person anything — a mattress, spoon or lightbulb. But if by hook or crook a prisoner managed to acquire these items, the officials sometimes allowed them to be kept. In the days that followed I had a thin mattress slipped in, a spoon, a cup, an ever-useful towel and even a tiny mirror.

Guanajay now had two of Cuba's most celebrated inmates: Pandeado and the crazy American escape artist. We were classified as dangerous, problematic and high risks. The order and objective was to hold and destroy us.

Pandeado had been given three death sentences; it wouldn't be difficult to eliminate him. As for me, an additional seven years was being petitioned for the escape. That would give them plenty of time to figure out some way to get rid of me. I was surprised that nothing was said about the break-out from DTI. It must have been too embarrassing to mention.

"I named this place the *Devil's Corridor*," Pandeado told me. "The devil lives here and it's a little piece of hell. I'll never leave here alive!"

The corridor constantly rang with shouted conversations. The walls distorted the voices so badly that verbal messages had to be piggybacked every third cell or so causing a din that made it almost impossible to think. Congregated here were some of the prison's most rebellious inmates. Most were young. The oldest was twenty-four.

The food cart rumbled in twice a day and, under the watchful eye of the guard, trays were served and passed through the slots in the doors. The atmosphere was always tense and often fights broke out in the overpacked cells, giving everyone else the chance to shout down seldom-heeded advice.

Once a day, just to have something to do, those who were in for an indefinite period, patiently took the cups used for the breakfast milk and sloshed water over themselves. Afterward the floor would be dried carefully. It was common knowledge that the dank cells provoked tuberculosis.

At night, after darkness had closed in over the prison, the *Devil's Corridor* echoed with the voices of those seeking relief through song. Most of the tunes were sad—always about some love lost, an unrequited one, or one yet to come. If nobody was in the mood to sing, somebody was ready to stand at his cell door and narrate a movie. All the old Humphrey Bogart movies were told and retold a dozen times. Everyone knew every line, but with each telling, the corridor sat silent as though it was a first. After the movie was over everybody argued, not about the picture, but rather about the narrator's accuracy and portrayal of the script.

February moved into March, and Johnson, a chubby little guy

who claimed to be Jamaican, managed to get me a lightbulb. The light lifted my spirits; I swore never to be without one again.

Sitting in a Death Row cell day after day, with nothing and nothing to do, taught me a valuable lesson. If I could survive without having the basic necessities to help alleviate my existence, there was nothing I couldn't do — if I ever managed to get off this island.

I learned that life is sweet but freedom is sweeter. Some small voice in my head kept telling me not to give up, not to lose my dream...

Pandeado taught me a lot about valor. He kept everyone's spirits up by singing or telling jokes or even by instigating furious arguments between cells. Then, he sat back and laughed his tail off.

Something about the guy made life seem bigger than itself. Maybe because he lived so close to death. He was one of the most liked and feared persons that I had ever known.

Notes slipped down from the Americans kept me up-to-date on what was going on in their section. A new brother named Sunni, a hijacker, had moved in. He had been in Cuba for over three years and had managed to avoid troubles with the authorities and then finally had been throw in jail for breaking the ribs of a cop who had kicked his pregnant wife in the stomach. Sunni kept me stocked with pencils and paper. I started writing songs and poetry again.

I passed the long days thinking, writing and planning. The only time I stepped out of my tomb was if the cell was being searched and then I was surrounded by a dozen or more guards. They made a big production even when they gave me a haircut. I was hand-cuffed and placed in a chair in front of my cell. Then a sergeant, backed by armed guards, took the scissors to my hair. Pandeado and his crime partner, Pipi, underwent the same treatment.

Once or twice a week groups of officials, men and women, came by to gawk. The show started when they reached Pandeado's cell. The new Assistant Warden played *barker* and the circus was on.

"In this cell is the notorious killer Leandro Razo Montalvo, better known as Pandeado. His victims are numbered in scores. At present he is condemned to death... three times over!"

When the Assistant Warden arrived at my cell he threw his arms out, and in true Shakespearian fashion declared, "And here we have the famous escape artist, *Tony el Americano*! The only man ever to escape from Guanajay!"

The group stared at me as though I were some type of rare animal. Sometimes I had the urge to bounce up and down and scratch under my arms or growl or bark at them.

Pandeado asked me to compose a song for him and the girl he loved. She was also a prisoner and lived in the women's quarters in another section of the prison. I wrote a beautiful ballad for them, *Bienvenida Sea*, which roughly translated means, "It's welcome." Pandeado memorized it, and night and day I'd hear him singing.

Late in May Pandeado was taken to court again for sentencing. When he returned he began shouting farewells. He didn't know if they were coming to take him away that night, but he wanted to say goodbye; just in case.

I tried to express to him how important his friendship was to me. I tried to let him know how badly I felt. He sent me a short note:

I don't know why you are sad when I, the victim, am not. I'm going to rest, that's all. You have been a true friend and I have appreciated your friendship from the start. I know that you'll have success with your book. Write all that you know about me in it. Although I have never met them, give your parents my love. Tell all the Americans that I send my best regards and when you write your book, put in there that I directed the firing squad! Your friend and disciple, Leandro Razo Montalvo. El Pandeado.

He sent his personal belongings, his letters and pictures to me.

I don't want them to get hold of any of my stuff, Tony. You and Carlito are my only friends. Give him something to remember me by and you keep the rest.

The next day, just before lunchtime, a guard came and told Pandeado and Pipi to get properly dressed; they were going back to court. Pandeado didn't look up as he passed my cell. He stared straight ahead as though trying to pierce the veil of the unknown and see into the future.

I gave my lunch away. I had lost my appetite. Something deep inside told me I would see my old friend no more.

The *Devil's Corridor* was strangely quiet all afternoon. When dinnertime came and there was still no sign of the two I began to fear the worst; I passed up dinner and sat on the side of my bed grieving. If they did not return before eight o'clock, it could mean only one thing: at nine, when the cannons were fired in the Cabana, they would be executed!

Ten o'clock passed. Around midnight I said a short prayer and crawled into bed. I went to sleep still clinging to a thread of hope that perhaps they were being held overnight somewhere for some unknown reason.

The following morning Sergeant Ciprian came into disciplinary. He strolled to Pandeado's cell, then called me and stood looking up at me waiting for the question he knew would come. It was no secret that Pandeado and I were close friends.

I looked through the food slot, and even though I could see the answer written in the crooked smile worn by Ciprian, I had to ask, "How is Pandeado?" My voice was barely a whisper.

"Pandeado?" The sergeant leaned back, slapped his stomach and laughed a hacking cough, "Pandeado? If you saw Pandeado now, you wouldn't recognize him!" His shoulders shaking with laughter, Ciprian turned away. "Pandeado, huh? He won't be coming back! They executed him last night!" Although I had known it, hearing the official notice caused a depression black and heavy as night to set in. He was dead. My friend was dead.

Later an official who witnessed the execution told me that

Pandeado had died like a lion. Since he was famed for singing to his enemies before attacking them, he was permitted to tape two songs. Just before the moment of truth, he sang his two favorites, *El Ultimo Acto*, and the song I had written, *Bienvenida Sea*. Then he calmly asked them to allow him to direct the firing squad. His request was refused. So walking up to the solitary post where he would be tied and shot, my young friend turned, faced the firing squad and saluted them. He died as he had lived, fearlessly.

I had long since determined that there was nothing more precious than human life. The loss of my friend brought that truth closer to home. To destroy a life was to detract from one's own humanity. Yet I also understood that it was sometimes necessary if the greater good of humankind was at stake. If order, peace and harmony were to be maintained, if humanity was not to be allowed to be dragged into the pits of anomaly, there had to be punishment and even the maximum penalty of death.

I had seen death in many forms for many reasons, and there was a time when I would have killed for the *cause*, but now I felt a deep respect for life. Now I could not understand how anyone could destroy something so precious.

I came to the conclusion that good and evil, as spiritual forces, existed, that there were forces which thrived on conquest and destruction, and there were also the forces of positive and good. Both forces were at war. There could be no compromise; and you had to support one or the other. That naturally provoked the question of how to differentiate between the two. How does one recognize evil? How can one be certain that something is good?

While I lay in my few feet of hell a simple philosophy was born, a simple way for me to determine the difference between Good and Evil. It was, and continues to be, my truth:

The human condition is arrived at by virtue of membership in the universal family, respect for the inalienable rights of any and all members of that family and awareness of and participation in its social obligations. This condition, derived from and thriving on concepts such as those outlined by the *Universal Declaration of Human Rights* is sacred and inviolate, and compels me to believe that this is the state which is the aspiration of all humanity. One day in my cell I sat on the floor, my back against the wall and wrote: *Any and everything that enhances and embellishes the human condition is good. All that detracts from that condition is evil!*

I had been in prison now almost seven years and had used up a large chunk of my lifetime in a Communist hell to formulate that bit of truth. But now, using that knowledge as a base, I could analyze more objectively my surroundings and myself. Also, my recent psychic experiences had made me sensitive to and aware of the existence of powers and forces of good and evil which could not be seen but are nonetheless real.

The racial, social, economic and spiritual problems of mankind had to be addressed and I did not believe that a *turn the other cheek* tenet could bring what was needed. I had developed into something that was the direct result of challenges offered and accepted; I had become a warrior; girded with my truth and a firm belief in God, I was ready to do battle. I had my cause!

Sometimes I would lie in bed, staring up at the ceiling and asking myself, Why me? And the only answer that came was that someone had to be the one. Someone had to come to the outskirts of hell. Someone had to witness the Beast and scream out a warning to mankind. Someone had to die an intellectual and spiritual death, swim through humanity's vomit and return to cry out: *"Danger!"*

A thousand circumstances had woven together to bring me here. Any one of a million things could have been just a breath different and I would not have been here, hands locked behind my head lying on a concrete slab. I was here to see, record and tell the people of America what had been spawned on the earth. I vowed to never pass up the opportunity to talk about the *monster* that I saw so clearly. I realized that humanity was teetering on the brink of something worse than death and destruction. It was poised on the edge of spiritual, intellectual and physical slavery.

What was Communism really about? was the question that I had to answer: Was it, as some say, inevitable, the natural result of certain historic laws? And if Communism's reign is certain, why the need to conquer the world by force? Why the necessity to enclose, enslave and drive with brute power a foreign philosophy down the throats of any people? Why the need to wage war on religion? Why the terror and hunger?

Nothing could make me believe that the purges in Russia and the horror of life in other Communist countries, such as Cuba, were the fault of the United States. There was something different about Communism, something terribly wrong. Communists enjoy killing. They love to watch blood run. I came to the conclusion that according to the Bible, Satan's prime objective had been and continues to be the dethronement of God. When I read that Marx stated that his principal objective was to *Dethrone God and overthrow capitalism*, Satan's eternal desire voiced through Marx, I realized that Communism was of the devil.

Why also the struggle to captivate black people? How could a Caucasian from Russia's Ural Mountains love or care about someone not their color, someone they knew nothing about? And at the same time enslave and murder millions of his own kind? The answer was simple. Since Black America is indeed a country inside a country, if blacks could be persuaded that there could be no hope for them under the system, then they could be used to destroy the U.S. from within and in the process destroy themselves.

The majority of the world's population is non-white and it watches to see which path blacks in the United States will take. And you can be sure the rest of the world's non-whites will follow! This is why a relentless war is being waged against blacks in America. This is the reason our black communities are being flooded with drugs. That is the reason our black churches no longer give spiritual guidance but instead spout phrases like *"We've got to change the system... It's all Whitey's fault... Our time has come!"* Or; *"From the outhouse to the White House!"*

Possibly my internal plunge in search of answers was in a sense an escape from my actual surroundings. But one thing is certain, I found answers. Time will prove or disprove their validity.

Since Pandeado's execution, the *Devil's Corridor* was quieter. I suffered a steady decline of appetite. I felt tired and slept a lot. Word got to prison officials that I was eating only now and then. They took me to the hospital to determine if I was faking or not. The doctor stated that I was anemic and advised them to take me out of the Hole. So, on or about the 4th of August, Sergeant Ciprian and a group of guards came and ushered me upstairs to the foreigners' section. I was to receive sun under guard and take vitamin shots to build up my strength. I was ordered to get better.

I moved into the cell with Sunni. He was a really great guy and looked every inch the sports addict he was. A university graduate, or nearly so, he had gotten involved with some extremist organization and subsequent problems had forced him to seek asylum in Cuba. He brought me up-to-date on what was happening in the U.S. He was sharp, and although admitting that Communism, either Russian or Cuban style wasn't the answer, he debated heatedly on the validity of democracy for black people in a white society.

After our protest on the water tower, conditions had changed somewhat. The cells were open all day so that at least the men could visit each other or just walk the hallway. I heard stories of how certain Americans were collaborating with the guards; also tales of sodomy and rape carried out by these same men. Such things were to be expected in the Cuban section where most were illiterate and spiritually, physically and emotionally starved, but to hear of that occurring within the group of Americans really distressed me.

I felt that since we came from a free country, we had the responsibility of setting examples for the Cuban inmates. Unfortunately it was clear that no matter the race or color, the systematic, scientific pressures utilized by the Communists could turn even

293

the Americans into animals. I noticed a subservience in the group that had not been there before the water tank beating. They were terrified, afraid to assert themselves. They had gotten a glimpse of the monster. They had felt the touch of terror... They had bowed!

Every morning they stood at attention for count. Just for the privilege of walking the hall they acted as though they loved their keepers. The Americans fought over the food, and sniveled if the cell doors were opened a little late or closed a little early. The idea was to be as good as possible and hurry back to the U.S. to continue smuggling drugs or whatever else they had been doing prior to their arrival in Cuba.

They had lost their sense of unity. There was no feeling of togetherness. In just a short while through the Pavlovian application of reward and punishment, fear and hunger, the Americans had become suspicious and distrustful of each other. Some of them had fallen prey to seductive temporary gains in return for services rendered. What does it profit a man to gain the world and lose his soul? Even with my own countrymen I felt alienated and alone. In fact, I felt more comfortable with the Cubans. Many of them had been in prison for years and still maintained a fighting spirit.

The Americans showed their true colors; spoiled, pampered, gutless brats. They represented not only a cross-section of the United States, but a vast segment of humanity as well. They symbolized a portion which would rather crawl than walk; would rather surrender and be a slave than stand and die if necessary to be free.

I watched them grinning and kowtowing to the guards, the same guards who had brutally beaten some of them and killed one of their countrymen.

On September 10th, I was witness to another brutality. Not one American raised his voice in protest. Even I remained silent.

The pump had broken down and water had to be carried from

an open well to the building. Sunni, one of strongest guys, went downstairs to help carry up the fifty-gallon drum. Sergeant Ciprian had given him permission.

It seems that a certain black guard was unaware of the order. Aside from that, he didn't like Sunni because Sunni wouldn't laugh and talk with the guards and he was in prison for fighting with a cop. At any rate, the guard ordered him to take the water back to the well. Sunni refused and told him, "If you want, you can ask Ciprian about it."

The guard pulled a machete.

About then Ciprian walked into the room and Sunni turned to him to explain the problem.

The guard stepped up and swung his machete. The blade sliced into Sunni's head. Like a raging bull, Sunni spun and attacked the guard, giving him a well-deserved beating.

Ciprian drew his machete and stabbed Sunni in the thigh.

I was lying in bed reading when the cell door opened and Sunni, streaming blood, staggered in. White heat swept over me. I jumped up and headed for the door. Sunni grabbed me talking all the while. "No, Tony! It's all right, Brother. Don't go out there. That's what they want. That'll give them the excuse to kill you!"

What he was saying pierced through the anger and I slumped to the edge of my bed staring at his blood spattering the floor.

"I've got to get to the hospital," Sunni said, "and get some stitches. Promise me you won't leave the cell."

Finally I nodded.

He pressed a towel to the wound in his head and left.

I sat there filled with a cold rage, the same rage that turns a man into a killer. I had to do something; if I didn't I felt I would explode. I grabbed a piece of paper, and using my pencil like a sword, slashed out phrases that boiled out with volcanic fury. When Sunni returned about an hour later, I handed him the paper.

Dedicated to Sunny 9/10/76

AGAIN I saw a bloodied head, AGAIN the skin was black! AGAIN the stifled impotent rage AGAIN the force not slack.

AGAIN the blood streamed hot and pure crimson teardrops stained his face and with each drop escaped a moan from the soul of a mighty race.

AGAIN I felt, as though on me, the merciless slashing blows AGAIN I learned to hate anew with an unbridled rage that grows.

AGAIN another black like me was hurried to the test AGAIN was born another giant the past in ashes rest.

AGAIN and yet AGAIN I know our pure black blood they'll seek but though we in our own blood drown they will never find us weak, never AGAIN!

I remained with the Americans for a couple of weeks longer and then was taken under heavy guard back to the death row cells.

25.
SOLITARY

Solitary!

The word itself evokes images of barrenness, of emptiness. It brings to mind a deserted state of being, a place in the wilderness, a mental and spiritual deprivation. It carries the connotation of isolation, of being alone and forgotten.

The wind moans in a special way for those in solitary. It hovers around each nook and cranny, sobbing and grieving over the loss of something irretrievable, something that's slipping away that one can't hold onto. In solitary the winds blow cold and harsh, making you cringe and tremble. In a desperate attempt to escape the solitude, you seclude yourself even more.

When rain falls, it sounds as though someone is crying, someone who loves and dies from wanting you and if your solitary is one of concrete and steel, you count the lines on the floor or the beats of your heart or maybe you lie on a cement bed and watch shadows spring into life as lightning flashes.

A bug crawling across the floor is cause for a close observation of its progress. In solitary you have time to notice and wonder at the most minute of God's creatures and feel desperate to know your place in the scheme of things. The muscles in your body long for the chance to stretch and contract in a run along a wind-swept beach. Your skin hardens; the glow dies. Every animal needs sun. You need sun. But there's no sun in your life.

Solitary!

A place crowded with memories. They all come to visit and haunt you; they all stay too long.

The sweet ones, the memories of love and lost love, are most painful. Recollections of dashing across a sun-scorched field, your dog running beside you barking and nipping playfully at your heels... memories of days gone forever. They all come and station themselves around you, waiting for you to glance at them and give them life. The blows that life has dealt you return to strike over and over again.

You sit in your solitude and wonder what has happened to your soul, and you hope and pray that it too isn't in solitary. You tend to become forgetful. Faces of people whom you knew well become vague and shadowy, and soon it's difficult to even remember how they looked. That frightens you because then you wonder if you're forgetting them because you've forgotten how to love and you wonder if they've forgotten you also.

Solitary makes you doubt everything you once held dear and true. Held in a time lock, a vacuum of dead, irreplaceable time. Your body craves and longs for a caress and the desire is so overpowering that you kiss your own arms and caress yourself. That reassures you... someone loves you.

The days are long, empty and senseless. Night is an enemy that plunges you into abbysms filled with nightmares. Solitary makes you think of life and wish for death!

I was in solitary confinement for one year and two months.

Four austere walls, a steel-plated door and three holes through which mosquitos, cockroaches and other pests entered. What does a man do day after day, month after month? How does he keep his sanity... or does he?

It would be both misleading and presumptuous to assume that a person is not affected by extended isolation from others. One is. There are only two alternatives: learn to live with oneself or go mad. Grow or wither.

I hadn't realized it but I had prepared for this ordeal long before.

While serving time in Soledad Prison in California I had appealed to my mom and dad not to write me. I wanted to learn how to stand on my own.

The lessons in solitude and loneliness now stood me well. What I had learned to do was project myself always into the future — never to live the *now* but always in what would someday be. I survived because I never stopped planning; I never stopped dreaming.

As a young man I had sworn to have a place in history. I vowed to leave some impression of my existence here on earth. I had no idea how that would come about, but I remember telling my wife Eunice, "If I can find a place to stand, I'll shake the world!"

Some of the Americans were released. I didn't envy them. I knew my day would come. I waited and dreamed and made strange friends...

One morning in October, after I'd taken my breakfast nap, I awoke to the feeling of being watched. I opened my eyes and looked around the cell. Everything seemed normal. Then I glanced up at the three holes in the wall and there, head cocked to one side, peering at me, was a prickly-looking brown lizard.

It glared at me for awhile, then suddenly stuck out its red wattle. The red flag went back somewhere in its throat; then the little fellow bobbed up and down like a jack-in-the-box and shot straight down the wall and into the cell.

This tiny remnant of a dinosaur didn't seem to mind my being there. When I rolled out of my bunk and stood, it twisted its neck and looked me up and down as if to say, "All right, where do we go from here?"

He was timid, but I needed a companion. I squatted as close to Willie — that was the name I had given him, Willie the Worm — as he would allow and stuck out my finger in friendship. Willie stood his ground for a minute then flashed to the wall.

"All right, Willie, scare me again, and it's gonna be me and you. Now just be cool. I'm going to kill a big fat fly for you."

Being careful not to scare him, I picked up my towel and started hunting flies. I got one. I thumped it just hard enough to stun it, then while it buzzed in an off-center circle, I pushed it close to Willie.

Willie eyed the *filet* for a moment, then swooped down and gobbled it up.

"Pretty good, huh, fellow? Hey, Willie, what's a good lookin' lizard like you doin' in a place like this?"

That's something that I did. I talked to Willie.

I fixed a nook for my buddy, swatted flies day and night for the voracious *alligator* and always looked down before I rolled out of bed.

As for Willie, all he had to do was watch out for my big feet, and sit and listen to me talk. For that, he had his flies served on a silver platter.

When a search came, I grabbed Willie and stuck him in a tin can. It never failed. Some guard would want to know what I was carrying out of the cell. "It's Willie," I'd tell him.

"Willie? What're you talkin' about? Here. Let me see what's in there."

Then came the startled gasp and a frantic leap backwards, as I removed my hand and Willie's head popped up over the edge of the can. Willie did look like a snake.

They never took Willie. It's good that they didn't try. I was ready to go down fighting to keep my buddy. But as the weather grew colder, the flies disappeared, and I awoke one morning to find Willie had flown the coop too. Even brute creatures dislike poverty and hunger...

In January 1977, Hector and I were taken to court. Three and a half years were tacked on to our original sentences. So, with the one and a half I'd gotten for the fight with the guards, plus this last sentence I had a grand total of seventeen years to serve. I laughed about it. I had no intention of serving the time. I would escape, or die trying!

Early in March the cell door opened; I was told to collect all of my belongings. I couldn't believe my ears. I snatched up my things and rolled them into a bundle, glancing every now and then at the guard to make sure that it wasn't just a dream.

The sun hurt my eyes, but it was warm and so welcome. I could feel my body soaking in its rays like a sponge. I could have yelled for joy; I was finally out of solitary!

26.
ANOTHER TONY

Combinado del Este is a behemoth prison east of Havana.

It sprawls over several acres of what was once swampland. The inmates are housed in three main buildings. Each building is made up of three sections which form a gigantic U. Around the back of these buildings, closing off the U, stretches a tall hurricane fence. The three structures rest on cement blocks, raised two feet above the ground. This makes tunneling out impossible. Due to the design of the buildings, no bars are visible from outside. The walls are chiseled and cut into thick cement bars. Each building is three stories high.

Immediately to the right, after passing through the double gates into the prison, sits Building Number Three. A street over, straight ahead, stands the hospital. A sharp left at the end of the street, and there on the corner, towers Building Number Two, and dead ahead, another two hundred yards or so, sits Building Number One.

At night lights come on under the buildings as well as over, beside and around them. A double row of hurricane and barbed-wire fences surrounds the complex. Police dogs, almost capable of jumping the fences, patrol between them. Sitting on stilted legs, like monsters from outer space, poise the gun towers.

I couldn't keep from laughing when I first saw the place. The buildings were painted pink with dashes of blue and stripes of purple. It was ludicrous. In their attempt to give the prison a benign appearance the keepers had gone overboard. The place looked like a Disneyland playground. But the gaudy paint only hid what one didn't want to see. It could only fool a fool. I dubbed it, *Technicolor Hell.*

The Jaula stopped in front of Building One and we foreigners, tumbled out with our gear. It was suppertime and inquisitive faces of prisoners going to and from the mess hall pushed to the slots in the walls.

As the guards called out our names we walked up a steep ramp to an open door. After being checked off a list we were taken inside and led to a long hallway lined with empty cells. There were about ten two-men cells, a couple of four-men and a large one that was built to accommodate eight. Each one had a shower and alongside it that old hole in the floor. A sink and faucet made it clear this was a top class prison.

The trample of feet on the floor above caused the walls to tremble. Shoutings from one building to the other echoed and died inside the rectangular caskets.

I looked at the other men and asked myself if they realized where we had landed. There were only eleven of us now; the three brothers, Lester, six other guys from different countries and myself. All of the other foreigners had either been released to the streets or, as in the case of the Americans, sent back to the United States.

One entire section of the prison had been cleared for us. We were to be kept as isolated as possible from the Cubans. Since there were so few of us, each had a cell to himself.

Food was sent from the kitchen, and it was the same meal every night thereafter: rice, a dash of fish soup, a bun and big-headed fish. Although the fish was well-fried, there was nothing to it except head! I swore that it had to swim upside down when it lived. There was no way that fish could have kept its head level with its body!

Each of us was issued a mattress, a blanket and, lo and behold, a pillow! They were stuffed with a type of synthetic material which squeaked when you moved your head. They were only soft for a couple of months, then the insides packed together and they turned as hard as rock.

After I had taken a shower and made up my bunk, I crawled under the covers and fell asleep. The next morning I was ripped awake by noisy trumpets blaring out the Cuban national anthem from several loudspeakers turned toward the buildings and set sky-high. With the clashing of cymbals and strident horn playing I could have yelled at the top of my lungs and no one could. have heard me.

When the anthem ended, the prison was immediately shaken by the sound of guards beating on cell doors with iron bars, shouting for the inmates to get up. *"Arriba! Vamos. Arriba!"* That was how each day started. Then, as the water came on, the pipes sputtered and gurgled, adding to the din.

Our cells had no lights and the flashlight held by the guards making count stabbed into my eyes killing the last remnants of sleep. I got up, brushed my teeth, then dropped to my knees and thanked God for being alive. After that year in solitary, I felt as though I had been born again.

The breakfast wagon rolled around with hot milk and a hard bun. Shortly after, I heard what seemed to be happy shouts of men going outside to the enclosed U for sun. They were dressed in yellow. These were the hard-core political prisoners. Waving and calling out greetings, they streamed from the building. It was their day for exercise. Some jogged, some played a type of handball, while others walked at a fast pace around the cement yard.

It was amazing! These men who had suffered incredible abuses, who had been starved, beaten, deprived of the right to visit their families for years at a stretch, these men whom the revolution wanted to destroy, were so plainly different from common prisoners that they seemed to be from another world. They were clean and the expression on their faces was one of personal contentment, of victory not defeat. When they smiled, they lit up.

The Americans drew their attention and many came by to see if we needed anything. I knew quite a few of them, but I didn't see my friend, Tony Cuesta, among them. I was told he would be down in the next patio. The first group frisked around under the sun for an hour, then were ordered back inside.

The second group of politicals swarmed out into the patio. Almost at once I saw my friend towering over everyone else in the yard. Cuesta stood almost six-and-a-half feet tall. He had his hand on his guide-of-the-day's shoulder and was taking such long strides that no one would ever have imagined he was blind.

Someone must have told him an American wanted to see him. He headed my way, and after a couple of shouted directions, stopped in front of my cell on the first floor.

"Hey, Tony," I shouted, wreathed in smiles, "Bet you a hundred bucks you don't know who's talking to you!"

Cuesta's brow wrinkled as he sought to identify the unfamiliar voice. He leaned down and whispered in his guide's ear. Then Cuesta's face lit up. "It's *Tony el Americano*, right? Hey, is it really you? My gosh, I thought you'd be back in the U.S. by now!"

I stopped smiling. It was a bad joke and we both knew it.

"Well, tell me how you've been doing, little brother," he said, realizing the error. "Any fights with the guards lately? Wait a minute, let me get closer."

I studied the man who pushed his guide impatiently forward. Cuesta was a big guy; although his muscles had lost some of their trim, you could tell he'd been athletic in his day. Because his skin was very white, the blue particles of shrapnel imbedded in his face were very noticeable. His left hand above the wrist was missing and the stub too was peppered with tiny pellets. He wore dark glasses so that others would not be bothered by the sight of his destroyed eyes. He was the most respected man in the prison, a living, breathing symbol of what a dedicated warrior is all about.

Antonio Cuesta Valles was born in the province of Oriente on the 13th of June. He would not tell you what year. If you asked him his age, he'd laugh and reply, "It's the same as Fidel's." Then he'd say something like, "Don't you think that's good... to always be the age of your enemy? That way you're always going to be there to see him die!"

While still a youngster his parents moved to Havana. It was there that Cuesta attended high school and college. He loved the outdoors and reveled in the smell of the morning air, in the sounds of the earth coming alive and in nature itself. It was only natural that he studied to become a veterinarian.

He traveled to the U.S., met and married the lovely, dark-haired Cedalia. It wasn't long before a baby girl was born. Cuesta was happy. He worked and built his world around his family. Then fate laughed.

In 1952, Uncle Sam called. Since Cuesta had a resident status, and worked and lived in Miami, he received a draft notice. He explained to the officer, sitting in front of him during the interview, that he could not serve in the U.S. military because, "I am already registered for the armed forces in Cuba!" But *Sam* had spoken. Cuesta decided to return to Cuba.

Cuesta had the gift of gab. Working as a salesman, his talents caught the eye of General Libby of International Telegraph and Telephone, IT&T. He started working under General Libby and rose to the very respectable position of executive vice-president.

During the latter half of the nineteen-fifties, clouds of insurrection loomed over Cuba. Fulgencio Batista's reign was being threatened. The people took up arms to overthrow him. One of those insurgents was Fidel Ruz Castro. Another was Antonio Cuesta. In the mountainous Sierra Maestra something was born in Tony Cuesta. He discovered a cause.

He was a fierce fighter. One had to be, to rise to the rank of captain in the rebel army. There was only one grade higher, commander.

Captain Cuesta fought under Che Guevara; and when the revolution triumphed, Cuesta was awarded the position of Chief of Intelligence of Havana.

Since the U.S. government had done so much to aid Fidel, Cuesta thought that relations with the U.S. would be maintained. The success of his job depended on the amount of information available at any given moment; he came to the U.S. to establish contact with the FBI, a perfectly natural move. All western countries collaborate to some degree to survive in the international waters of intrigue and counter-intrigue. When he returned to Cuba, the wrath of both Fidel and Che fell on him. The three argued heatedly. Cuesta was arrested and fired.

Cuesta tried to slip back into the anonymity of everyday life but news reaching his ears stirred him into action. There were hints and subtle indications that the Communists were taking over. All of the blood spilled, all of the suffering to topple a dictator had been in vain. Cuesta saw another enemy, more deadly than Batista, grasp the governmental reins and plunge the people of Cuba into the beginnings of a nightmare.

He watched the positions of power being awarded to avowed Communists. Although Fidel had not yet openly declared allegiance to the Communist block, those who could read the writing on the wall now began fleeing Cuba.

Cuesta conspired clandestinely, helping to found a resistance movement, MRR (*Movement To Recover The Revolution*). This was a new day, a new type of fight. Before, under the dictatorship, certain rights allowed room to struggle. Now those protections and rights were disregarded totally.

Summary court martial and immediate execution was commonplace. Terror swept over the land and the movement MRR was paralyzed. Cuesta felt his arrest and subsequent execution were imminent. He slipped into the Peruvian Embassy, asked for and was granted asylum. He traveled to Peru remaining only long enough to make the necessary connections which would take him hopscotching over the Caribbean Islands and back into the United States. Then Antonio Cuesta began to conspire seriously against Fidel.

When the Bay of Pigs fiasco occurred, Cuesta was there. Luckily he was a sailor and not one of those who went ashore and was captured. He returned to the U.S.

Now Castro took off his mask and declared Cuba a socialist

state; Fidel and Nikita Kruschev embraced. The ties between Cuba and Russia strengthened.

The warrior in Cuesta impelled him to take up arms again. He had fought against Batista because he wanted to see his people freed from fear, poverty and anguish. Now he would have to fight another dictator who was determined to drown freedom in blood, rule by terror and subjugate the people to a spiritual, economic and moral apathy Batista could never have imagined.

Cuesta founded a militant organization based in Miami, Florida, *Alpha 66*. Its first actions were under his command. He had decided that the most effective way to eliminate the enemy was by direct confrontation. If some type of naval blockade could be set up around Cuba, the stagnant economy would collapse. His idea was both simple and brilliant.

If cargo ships were sunk or placed in danger of being sunk, neither Lloyds of London nor anyone else would insure them. With the waterways closed, the dictatorship would sink like the ships Cuesta intended to attack.

A slip in Alpha's leadership caused internal rivalry. Cuesta left and formed a new action group: *Commandos L*. L was for *Liberation*. The history of his attacks is a matter of record. Carrying out lightning-like strikes, *Commandos L*, always with Cuesta in the thick of battle, sank ships entering and leaving the port of Havana. They shelled the President's own home, forcing him to abandon his seaside resort and seek safer lodgings in the interior. Cuesta led dozens of attacks on the enemy, inflicting costly losses.

He had once enjoyed the protective mantle of the CIA, but after the missile crisis an agreement between the U.S. and Russia was made. No longer would the intelligence corps in the U.S. turn a blind eye on rebels seeking to oust Castro. Those were the terms of the agreement. The missiles had left Cuba on condition that insurgents, such as Cuesta, were smashed. And now, to carry out his missions Cuesta had to elude two forces — the FBI and the Russian gunboats that patrolled Cuba's waters. But after he sank the Russian freighter, *Baku*, an international storm arose over anti-

Castro commandos operating from the U.S.

Until then, Cuesta and his men had opened fire on the ships of many countries, up to and including France, and only a flicker of annoyance had been displayed by U.S. authorities. Sure, they confiscated arms and even a boat or two, but it was after the *Baku* incident that Cuban freedom fighters in the U.S., and mainly in Florida, came under constant and devastating harassment. But Cuesta continued fighting.

Tricking U.S. and Cuban officials, Cuesta and his faithful men attacked Cuban military and economic objectives again and again. Then the fateful day arrived.

Cuesta had infiltrated a strike force on the island of Cuba. They were spotted, and in the ensuing battle Erminio Diaz (he had been with Castro when Fidel was in Mexico) was killed. Erminio was forty-five years old. Along with him died Armando Romero, twenty-five years old. Both were worthy of being Commandos.

Along with Eugenio, his nephew, and two others, Guillermo Alvarez Sanchez and Roberto Anta, Cuesta turned the bow of his speedy light-weight boat toward open sea, and throttle wide open, tried to evade the Russian-built high-speed patrol boats plowing after them. The fighting was bitter. The rebels only had a few small arms and with these they battled the heavily-armed Cuban forces.

The gunboats raked Cuesta's craft with machine gun fire killing Guillermo, who was only seventeen years old. Ironically, he was the nephew of Fidel's First Secretary, Celia Sanchez, the powerful woman I had hoped to see after hijacking that long-ago plane. In the fighting there was no quarter asked and none given. The next to die was Roberto Anta, 19 years of age; warriors all.

Eugenio crumpled in a pool of blood and Cuesta believed he was now the only one left alive. Alone at the helm of his speeding boat, armed only with a twelve-gauge shotgun and a grenade, he fired one last defiant blast. Then, pulling the pin on the grenade he aimed his craft at an enemy ship. There was a blinding flash and Antonio Cuesta saw no more.

Miraculously, he lived through the explosion. The patrol boats fished him out of the water unconscious and blind. His left arm was also missing. Tony Cuesta was rushed to the hospital, the gaping wound in his stomach sewn up, and the veins and tendons of his shattered arm tied off.

Antonio Cuesta woke up in permanent darkness, alone and blind and surrounded by his enemies. When he came to, a messenger from Celia Sanchez was there. She wanted to know what her nephew looked like so she could go to the morgue and identify the body.

"Tell her that he's six feet tall with a bullet through the forehead!" Cuesta replied, coldly.

Eugenio had also survived the blast. Although in serious condition, he was not in danger of dying.

Perhaps the fact that he was maimed and blind saved Cuesta's life. It would have been a black mark against Fidel's machoism to execute a blind man. Aside from that, Cuesta had fought valiantly. So instead of facing the firing squad, as many of Fidel's former friends had done, blind Tony Cuesta was sentenced to thirty years in prison. Young Eugenio received the same length sentence.

All of the loneliness, hunger and desperation that the other political prisoners experienced, Cuesta went through also — only his torment was greater. To hear the crack of machetes on human flesh all around and not know if the next blow would fall on him, to be pushed and shoved by some young punk guard and not be able to see and slap his face, to depend on another to lead him when he had always been the leader, to wonder how he looked as the years passed; all these were Cuesta's torments. Yet it was he who inspired the other prisoners. Even the guards and officials respected him.

The man standing in front of my cell was a living, breathing page of history. More than that, he was a symbol of intransigence, decision and tremendous valor. He was a man of steel. He was prepared to fight, and if necessary, give his life for his fellow man, be he black, white, brown, red or yellow.

For the first time in my life I had a friend who was white and for the first time also I realized that any man can be whatever he wills himself to be. The only limits are those we place on ourselves.

As fate would have it, we two *Tony's* were opposites and alike at the same time. One had leaned to the left and the other toward conservatism. One was black and the other white. One had conspired to overthrow capitalism and the other to save the last stronghold of democracy. Yet we were very much alike. We both hated lies and deceit. We both were ready to fight for a just cause and we both stood ready to die for that cause.

After that first day Cuesta never came to the patio without stopping to converse with me and every now and then getting permission to come by the cell and sit for awhile. Since we both wrote poetry, we criticized each other's works.

Politically, Cuesta was well prepared and he taught me things I needed to know. He took time to explain the whys and wherefores of Communism and its appearance in Cuba. He told me, "It's no accident that Communism is here in Cuba. A lot of people don't know it, but Batista was a leftist. He prepared the groundwork and Fidel completed the task!"

We also talked about the black dilemma and Cuesta said; "Tony, the biggest thing that's holding black people back is themselves! It's the way you think about yourself that makes the difference. A lot of blacks think they're losers and so they're lost! Nobody is any better than anyone else, but black people keep going around telling themselves they're second class — so that's how life looks to them, second class.

"The minute you think you're not equal is when you've accepted you are a failure. Black people have got to learn to walk with their heads up and see the stars of the future and stop looking down at the mud of the past!

"Sure, it's terrible that your people were slaughtered and enslaved, but now there's the opportunity for them to be all that they should be. All they have to do is assert themselves. You should act, not like you're equal, but like everybody else is equal to you! It changes everything. It's all a matter of perspective and attitude!"

I argued with him concerning some points but most of the time I had to concede he was right.

Concerning blacks and Communism, he warned; "Tony, the gravest threat to black people and their freedom is now facing them and they don't even realize it. They don't know that Communism is the last card in the deck to be played to enslave black people forever. They don't know that the objective is to keep blacks from ever finding out who they really are.

"Communists claim to give blacks equal opportunity, freedom and equality. Well, Tony, when somebody gives you something you are always indebted to that person. You don't beg for freedom; you take it! You don't beg for opportunity; you make it! You don't beg for equality; you earn it!

"The Communists aren't worried about anyone as much as they are about blacks. The black they want most is the black American. The black American is the most controversial ethnic group alive. It is the most loved and the most hated, the most known and the least understood. But one thing is certain, the black American is the cream of the world's crop.

"They've suffered through and survived a horrendous experience and now they set the social atmosphere in the U.S. which reflects on every other society on earth. Everything that affects black America is felt around the world. You could almost say that the future of the world will depend on them. That's why the Communists are trying so hard to capture them. If the blacks in the U.S. can be made to believe that the Communists are their saviors, then the rest of the black world will follow their lead and humanity will be swept into the darkest days of its history!"

He told me I would have to go back to America and tell black people about the *Beast*. He said it didn't matter what happened to me, whether I went to jail or not. I just had to go back and tell Americans what I had seen in Cuba, what I'd gone through in flesh and blood. "Tell them to wake up," he urged, "The devil is on the loose."

I listened and debated some but mostly listened and weighed my own convictions against his and found for the most part they were identical.

"There's something I want to tell you," he said one day. "If I get back to the U.S. before you do, just rest assured that when you arrive, you've got a friend. We've got to show people that color doesn't mean a thing. I'm white, you're black, and we're brothers!"

I thought about those words many times. I wondered if I would see Cuesta — if and when I got back. It would be tough. I had a hijack charge and possible life imprisonment to face. But while I was here I meant to study both my friends and foes closely.

My enemies I knew well. But this was the first time that I had the opportunity to be in close contact with those whom I now considered friends, the political prisoners.

About 9:00 a.m. on my first Sunday in Combinado I heard something that moved me deeply. A chorus of male voices from overhead was singing the words, "Glory, glory, hallelujah!" with great exuberance. From other sectors of the political prison various groups holding religious services were lifting their voices in song too. The building seemed to throb and vibrate. It had been a long time since I had heard a religious song or attended church, but the memories were there, and the sound of the politicals worshipping filled me with nostalgia. I felt as though I were sitting in some church listening to the saints praising God.

These men were worshipping God from the pits of hell. Knowing that the Communists were tormented by religious activities and had been known to beat, shoot and kill those participating, they refused to be silenced. It was a great lesson in valor and it taught me that vanity and false pride have no place in a warrior's life.

Those guys singing praises to God were tough and most of them had lived a hundred times over what the normal individual does and yet they did not consider themselves to be too tough or bad to bend their knees in prayer. It wasn't sissy or weak to believe in God. On the contrary, it was a power that strengthened them and gave them courage to face the enemy.

About halfway through the services, the Communists turned on the radio and loudspeakers full blast. The noise was deafening. Five minutes passed, then they were turned off because the blaring radio was bothering the guards too. But immediately, as soon as the radio stopped, the political prisoners' religious services commenced again. The guards had to be amazed at the tenacity and courage of those politicals.

Yellow, in common vernacular, signifies cowardly. Someone should have told the Communists that yellow is also the color of gold. These men dressed in yellow were not cowards by any stretch of the imagination!

Fidel babbled about the future creation of the *new* man. What he didn't realize is that inadvertently he and his fellow animals had already done that. The political prisoner, starved, abused, ground into the revolution's dust, had emerged whole and transfigured! He is that *New* man, I decided, the man to be emulated.

The political prisoners were allowed to take sun two or three times a week for an hour. They always came by to chat.

Ernesto Diaz, a well-known writer and poet of top quality, was one of my friends. He dropped off his writings for me to read. They were flexible, lyrical and awesomely powerful. And then there was Jorge Valls, a thin, ascetic man who was the undisputed philosophical and spiritual guide of the political prisoners. Even more, he was an inspiration to all who came in contact with him. And he was also a beautiful poet.

Martin Perez, a stocky, pugnacious man in his forties, would pace back and forth while we talked. He was a bundle of nerves with the reputation of being really tough. Well-versed in karate, and an expert in guerilla fighting and strategy, he exemplified raw energy.

Dr. Emilio Adolfo Rivero, mathematician, shiny bald head and all, rarely missed the chance to storm, with long-legged strides, up to my cell and crowd in a few minutes conversation. He was a bit hard of hearing, so he bellowed as if I were deaf too. Emilio spoke several languages. He was one of my best and severest critics, and since he was an authority on Shakespeare, his admonitions were well received. When Rivero wasn't laughing hard, he was frowning intensely. He had been beaten too many times. That's how he lost his hearing.

El Jorobado, translated to mean practically anything from hunchback, to twisted or bent, was the one who hung around until everybody else had gone. Then he jumped onto the ledge that ran around the side of the building, and standing on one bare foot like a stork, engaged me in long conversations.

Jorobado wasn't a hunchback; what he had was a stiff, slightly arched neck. To turn his head he had to swivel his entire body around. Jorobado was a farmer, a hillbilly. I swear, he looked like a 65-year-old Tom Sawyer with a heart of gold. He epitomized the simple, hard-working peasant class. He would bring me candy that he'd concocted or cigarettes. It was a rare day when he came empty-handed. It was hard to believe that the knotty-muscled little man, who didn't weigh over 145 pounds, was reputed to be an extremely tough nut. He was a welcome ally in any struggle.

Those and many more made it their business to see that everything possible was done to make my existence less painful.

When Christmas rolled around I received cards with short messages or poems printed neatly on them and cakes or pies that they had somehow, incredibly, made. Some sent cigarettes or cigars wrapped in colored paper. Just about everyone sent their regards.

There were three American political prisoners there at the time also. Larry Lunt, accused CIA agent, was serious and withdrawn. He saluted me as he walked by on his way to a portion of the patio where he paced off the better part of the hour.

And there was Everett Jackson. In the course of our short talks we discovered that we were both from San Bernardino, California, and in fact had lived, at one time, in the same block.

The last was a gray-haired man in his sixties. He was a confessed CIA agent, Frank Emmick. The man had a fantastic memory and told me stories of how he had fought the Communists. He promised to try to help me, if and when I returned to the U.S.

All in all, the political prisoners were the ones who trusted and cared for me most. They were men of ideals, and of them all, Antonio Cuesta was the person I most admired.

The die was cast; my alliances were well defined!

27.
THOUGHTS AND CONTEMPLATIONS

There was a strict policy in effect regarding the Americans and any foreigner who stumbled into Cuba. The object was to keep them out of sight of the main prison population. It was a mistake to allow an outsider to see or know too much; I had been the only American to live and move around like any other Cuban prisoner.

Now, with the knowledge I had acquired, I lived with one obsession: return to the U.S. and tell it like it was. I had seen enough to fill volumes.

I knew one thing, the power brokers of the world were playing a dangerous game. It all boiled down to a matter of balance and power. Keep half of humanity enslaved, ignorant and technologically inferior under Communism and then maintain an almost unchallenged hold on means of production and capital in the free world!

Perhaps that is the reason there was never a serious attempt to enlighten the American people or overthrow the Communists. Instead, at the moment when Stalin was carrying out his infamous purges in which millions of human beings were murdered, the U.S. kept the cruel dictatorship alive by sending it all that it needed to sustain itself.

The American public went about totally unaware that a diabolical force had been unchained. Americans didn't know because they weren't informed. Those who controlled the information reaching Americans didn't want them to know; just as the disappearances of Americans in Cuba and the Cuban reality itself are kept secret.

If the American people understood the nature of the filth sitting only ninety miles from their doorstep, if they knew how deadly Communism is and how it threatens their existence, no president would be elected unless he was an anti-Communist.

The capitalists had diddled and played with the Beastling too long; now it had grown and become a voracious, uncontrollable monster. I was living in the guts of the Beast. I knew that this plague had to be contained and destroyed.

As far as I was concerned, it would be better to sink the world into an atomic conflagration than allow it to drown in the vomit that is Communism. At least you would die with your soul. At least you would not die as a slave.

Black people have a very special knowledge of slavery. We know that it is better to welcome death than live in chains. After four hundred years, we are still battling to erase the stigma of that experience and it was nothing compared to what the Communists plan, not only for black people, but for anyone falling into the muck of Marxist-Leninism.

I still had dreams of escaping from prison but the opportunity did not present itself. So during the next few months I wrote poetry and watched and waited.

In July 1977, the United States Interest Section in Havana was opened. No longer would the Swiss be in charge of American affairs in Cuba. Speculation increased that normalization of relations between Cuba and the U.S. was imminent. The prison buzzed with rumors. The talk was that all of the political prisoners were to be freed, then the Americans, or vice versa.

I will always remember when the Interest Section's representative, Thom Holliday, began the monthly visits to Combinado. The interview took place in the Central Administration Building outside the double fence. We, the Americans, were handcuffed and escorted there by five tough-looking guards pointing machine guns at us. The air tasted a little fresher on the other side of the barbed wire, and I felt a little closer to home.

We waited in a locked hallway for a half-hour, then one by one were taken in to see the representative. I was the last to enter.

A slightly plump man in his thirties, blue eyes peering myopically through his glasses, stood and shook my hand. Two G-2 agents watched closely as the interview got underway.

"All I want to know is," I asked, "is there is a possibility of my going home?"

Thom Holliday could tell me nothing.

That was an autumn of great expectations. We began to believe that maybe, this time, we were really going to leave.

Christmas rolled around again and we still hadn't gone. Everybody sat around drinking a smelly wine we'd concocted.

The political prisoners made and decorated a tree. I could hear them singing carols. A young, new political prisoner came by to visit me. Tears streamed down his face as he listened to the songs.

"Tony, this is the first time I've had the chance to feel free! I've never heard anything like this in my life. His face was glowing. "This is what I've been looking for all of my life... the chance to express myself!"

January was mild in comparison to the first months of the earlier years I'd spent in Cuba. It also brought surprising changes for the Americans. We were allowed to go to the visiting room which sat just inside the fence. It was a long two-story building. On the first floor, lined from wall to wall, were cement seats and tables for the visitors. There was a small space where the prison combo played music. Upstairs was a sort of hotel where the lucky married prisoners had conjugal visits.

The change in treatment indicated something was cooking between Castro and Carter. Giving the Americans a visit or two, while filtering down rumors of our approaching release, kept us hopeful and therefore less likely to cause problems.

On a normal visiting day one to two thousand people crushed into the building. Nobody minded the crowd though; the more the merrier. I had the chance to talked with many families. I tried to learn if they were contented with life in Cuba. They weren't. There was fear in everyone's eyes. When the guards moved through the room, there was a tightening of bodies and people searched for something else to look at rather than look at them. It was around this time that I met political prisoner Eloy Menoyo Guetierrez.

Eloy came up to me while I was having lunch. He had slipped down from the third floor to see me. He was a small man, about five-feet, eight inches and weighed about 130 pounds. He had graying hair and his thin aquiline face was criss-crossed with wrinkles.

"I've heard a lot about you," he said. "I just wanted you to know that you can count on me for anything!"

We chatted for a few minutes, then, like a shadow, he was gone.

Eloy started visiting my cell. Soon we became friends. He was a very intelligent man. Although raised in a socialistic background, he had become a declared enemy of Communism. He was highly respected by the other politicals. He had to be tough to merit the praise given him. I was to find out how tough this little guy really was.

28.
CHANGES

In April, 1978, the foreigners packed up and were moved to Building number Two. By July there existed a definite atmosphere of change.

Listening to American music had been permitted for some time, but never the quantity being piped over the radio as now. There were men hearing American music in prison who had been put there for committing the same *crime* a year or so earlier.

There was a good reason for American music being played in Cuba — money. The economic injection given to the Castro regime by tourism from the States was needed and the tourists wanted to hear American music so... Although Castro hated the United States, he had to bow to the might of the dollar.

A couple of boat-loads of Colombian pot smugglers were arrested. They only stayed in jail a few weeks. Smugglers from that country were rarely locked up long. It was common knowledge that Cuba was involved in the drug racket. Some of the American smugglers smoked some grass that had found its way into the prison and immediately identified it as being the marijuana they had bought in Colombia.

A buzz that some kind of dialogue was going to take place between Castro and 'representatives' of the Cuban community in the U.S. swept the prison. Cuesta told me that Fidel would try to use the politicals as a lever in the talks. If there was to be a release of any prisoners, conversation had to exist. To make the charade sicker, Fidel announced he would not discuss the issue with the United States government, but only with the American Cuban exile community. Just a few months prior to this change of heart, he had labeled the exiles as *gusanos*, worms. Now he called them good citizens and was ready to kiss their butts because it meant money for him.

There were those in the political prison who stood against any type of dialogue and others who were for it. Feelings ran so deeply that old friends became ardent adversaries.

Eloy Menoyo was one of the anti-dialoguists as was Martin Perez and Cuesta. They said that if their freedom depended on relations or dialogue with Castro they preferred to remain in jail.

Speculations and rumors were a dime a dozen. Guards spread lies purposely for the pleasure of watching hope give way to despair. But the effervescence could not be contained. There was something in the air that spoke of change. A little more food, not much, just enough to be noticed, was added to our diet. I awoke every morning tingling with expectation. A glimmer of hope had been ignited... Maybe today... Maybe today...

August and September passed, and Fidel had set the day for the dialogue and supposedly, as a goodwill gesture, was going to release a few internationally known prisoners such as Tony Cuesta.

On the day that conversations between the Marxist-Leninst government of red Cuba and representatives of Miami's Cuban community took place, Tony Cuesta and fifty-four other political prisoners were pardoned and given permission to abandon the island. Date: October 21, 1978.

I was in the patio getting a little sun when someone called me. I ran over to the building and saw my friend Cuesta holding a bag of belongings at his side. "I'm leaving," he said. "I'll be in contact with you as soon as possible. And, listen, if there is anything I can do for you when you get out, just let me know... You hear? I'm going to talk to everybody I can about you." He let his voice drop to a whisper. "There's one thing, Tony. I'm going to be out there pulling for you. You've got to keep out of trouble with these people or everything I do will be in vain. Take care. "

He gave my shoulder a quick squeeze. "Just remember, you've got to go back and tell black people what this is over here. Take it easy and God bless you "til we meet again." The prison rocked with cheers as he walked out of the building. I was happy for him but I had to hold back my tears.

Since the early months of 1978, Americans were being hunted down and hijacked by Cuban naval and air forces. Small planes were forced to land or be shot down. Boats were pulled off the high seas in international waters. *Fido, The Russian Lap Dog,* was going for broke. He wanted to have plenty of bargaining power on hand.

The captured Americans were forced to sign confessions of smuggling dope or of being CIA agents. The Cuban officials let them know that the penalty for spying could be death but if they confessed to trafficking they would be sent home shortly. This gave the Cubans the right to confiscate the boat or plane. It didn't make too much difference if there was a confession or not. The courts always found these people guilty of smuggling or at least of violating Cuban air or water space. Fidel had a double-edged plan that was working. Not only could he play the role of crime fighter, he could confiscate planes and boats for his own smuggling racket.

Innocent Americans were caught up in the slick plan and others from almost every major capitalist country. There would come a time when thirty different countries would be represented in the foreigners' section in Combinado del Este. The only people exempt from Cuban justice were the Russians. They were never seen in jail.

In April of 1978, a quiet Englishman, Terry Childs, was imprisoned and charged with smuggling. Naturally his plane was confiscated. He became one of my best friends. Everybody liked Terry.

Glen Akam and Ray Fitzgerald arrived in April; they suffered the same fate. After them others came pouring in. All were charged with either spying or intrusion in Cuban territorial space. All told the same story of abuse or mistreatment in the State Security Prison. *Fido* Castro was having a field day.

29.
HUNGER STRIKE

A soft rain fell. It was Christmas again, 1978. The year was drawing to a close and the opportunity to escape, legally or otherwise, still had not presented itself. There was nothing to do but wait.

On Christmas night the politicals sang carols as usual and the guards set the radio and loud-speakers to full power to blast them. We Americans, made wine, got drunk and passed out.

In January 1979, all of the foreigners were moved back to Building Number One while repairs were made on Two. It was good to be back with the politicals; it gave me the chance to talk with my friends.

They had a couple of radios secreted in the walls and every day they sent down the latest news. Naturally, most of it was about the release program. There was no doubt about Fidel keeping his promise to let the politicals go. We were going crazy with excitement and hope. We were positive we would be among those freed. Since we were back in Building Number One, we took this as a sign we'd be included in the package release.

In March and April more political prisoners were released and *Fido* was making a swaggering show of the procedure. Castro was in the world spotlight and loved it.

Newsmen from the international press were allowed to visit with some of the politicals in the administration building. They interviewed Eloy Menoyo and asked his opinion of the dialogue. Eloy told them, "In any other country, when amnesty is given to political prisoners, there is no dialogue about it. Only Fidel Castro has to have one. He's trying to take advantage of a common situation to draw closer to the United States. I am against any kind of dialogue. You don't dialogue with a tyrant!"

Naturally, Fidel didn't like that. His henchmen were given the order to eliminate Eloy Menoyo Guetierrez. First Eloy had to be isolated. The guards and officials began harassing him, looking for any excuse to throw him in the Hole where he could hang himself. Eloy had an explosive temper, but he was cunning. He knew he was in trouble and had to do something quick. Then, came the episode of *La Guitarra*, The Guitar.

On the 4th of May, prison officials confiscated Eloy's guitar, a guitar a friend had brought for him. Not only did they take the guitar but they refused to allow it to be returned to Eloy's friend. They hoped to provoke him into doing something rash, but he outwitted them. Eloy announced he was on a hunger strike and denounced the Cuban government for plotting against his life. His attack quickly drew international attention.

The charges were serious. The prison officials gave the order and Eloy was taken to the Hole. That same day, Guillermo Rivas, an ex-newsman, Ernesto Diaz and six other political prisoners joined him on strike. That way they could make sure that Eloy wouldn't be killed without someone knowing and they would let the world know if the plot was carried out.

That evening, about seven o'clock, I was told to go down to the Day Officer's section. Menoyo wanted to talk to me. The guard on duty allowed us to converse privately.

Eloy's thin face was creased with worry and his voice strained as he shook my hand. "Tony, I need a favor. You know I'm on a hunger strike. Fidel is in the middle of his release plan and he doesn't want anybody to rock the boat, and I'm going to do it! They took me over to the Hole but they brought me back to talk these other guys out of going on strike with me. I'll do nothing of the kind. I told them that I would, so that I could get back over here and talk to you. Listen, you're going to see the Interest

Section tomorrow... Right?"

"Yeah. What can I do for you?"

"Here's a list of names of people on strike. I want you to get it to the diplomats. Don't let the guards catch you with it." He didn't have to tell me why; I didn't relish beatings either.

"Tell Mr. Holliday why we're on strike and give him the list. Once he's got it, it'll be too late for them to do anything and I doubt if they'll take it out on you. They'll be mad enough to kill, but..." Eloy shrugged. "That's tough. Will you do it?"

"Sure, I'll take it," I answered. "But you know what he's going to say. He'll tell me they can't become involved in a problem that's Cuban. As long as no American is mixed up in the deal they can't even ask questions."

A plan formed in my mind. "Say, Eloy, I've got an idea. Tell you what I'm going to do. I think we have to force the U.S. State Department to take notice of what happens to you!" I was about to drop a bomb. The other strikers who were waiting to be taken to the Hole crowded around. "I'm going to declare myself on strike in your support. That way, because I'm an American, the U.S. government will have to make inquiries. It will give them the right to probe."

The following day I smuggled the list out. I told the Interest Section that I was on a hunger strike also. Immediately upon return to the building, I was ordered to get my towel, toothbrush and spoon and report to the Officer of the Day. They were hopping mad!

The Americans couldn't understand why I was getting mixed up in something that wasn't my business. The blacks couldn't fathom my putting myself out for a white. I wasn't too sure of my reasons. I remember telling myself that it was just another chance to strike at my enemy, but maybe I was growing up.

I was marched to the Hole. The guard slammed the iron gate, set the lock, then stepped through a wooden door into the hallway and closed it behind him.

They had permitted me to bring a sheet. I spread it over the cement slab and sat listening to the din created by the men shouting back and forth. The sounds seemed to be amplified by the cement walls. I could hardly hear myself think. But somehow I heard my name being called.

"Hey, Tony! *Tony el Americano*!" It was Ernesto's voice.

"Yeesss!" I answered at the top of my lungs. "What's happening?"

"Did you get the message to the counsel?"

"Yeah!" I shouted back. "How's Menoyo?"

"He's fine. They put him farther away. I'll call and tell him you're here. He'll be glad to know!"

I heard Ernesto call, then faintly an answering voice. Eloy sent greetings and thanks. Now the battle had begun in earnest.

When the normally shouting common prisoners became aware the politicals were on a hunger strike, they lowered their voices in respect or stopped talking when we shouted out a message.

The isolation cells in Combinado del Este Prison were much harsher than others. There was a certain difference, something that threw everything out of kilter. The slab lacked that soft spot. The cell was prefabricated. Natural cement had warmth to it. This didn't; it was cold and alien.

The following day, after my refusal of lunch, a group of officers opened the outer door and crowded up to my cell. They wanted to know why I was on strike.

"Because Menoyo is my friend," I answered.

They laughed. "Now look, Tony," said one, "we know he's a friend of yours but what you're doing can be harmful to your health."

This wasn't a warning about smoking cigarettes. And I wasn't sure if it was a threat, but he didn't have to tell me about hunger strikes. I had seen men left blind, crippled or dead by them.

They had never been concerned about my health before. Why now? They weren't; it was that my move had put them in check! Fidel's attempted portrayal of the good guy was in danger of being marred by something distasteful — like an American dying on a hunger strike while protesting a plot to murder a helpless prisoner. Too, with me on strike, the Interest Section would request a daily report on my health and the progress of the hunger strike. I had put my keepers in a bind.

They kept trying to talk me out of it. To end the conversation I told them, "I don't intend to stop until Menoyo does. So there's really nothing for us to talk about."

They glared at me and stalked out. I could hear them cursing as they huffed down the hall.

It would take a couple of days before the news of the rebellion made it to Miami, but when it did there would be a hue and cry from the exile community that would reach the four corners of the globe.

The third day, four more Cuban strikers joined the group. All of them were tough and hard. Their many years in prison had taught them the weak die young.

The situation was serious. The officials knew this group would not give up without a victory. The protest could easily produce a death or two. Fidel would be enraged about any situation that besmirched the image of Third World Leader he was trying to project.

After seven days I no longer felt hunger pains. By the tenth day more political prisoners had joined the strike. The total was now twenty-one. The Voice of America was broadcasting our plight. We heard that an American Archbishop had rushed to Rome for talks with the Pope who conveyed a message to Fidel pleading for our lives. The exile community in Miami was in an uproar, we were told, as scuttlebutt filtered in from outside.

Menoyo sent word to the other political prisoners not to join the strike. He did not want a massive protest because that could harm the release program. Yet he did want to draw attention to his situation.

We strikers got a pleasant surprise when Jorobado joined the strike. His arrival brought a big cheer from all of us. The tough little hillbilly had gone up to thirty-eight days without eating and to see him involved was tantamount to saying, "This could be a long one!"

On the fourteenth day of the strike I was sick. My back bothered me, and I felt weak and drained. My appetite had long since died. Now all I had was a numbness in the pit of my stomach.

I wasn't afraid they would let us die. A few years before when I had worked in the infirmary at Principe, I had helped carry out on a stretcher the dying body of Pedro Luis Boitel. He was in a coma. He had lasted fifty-four days. All of the while he was in a coma, the guards placed a tray of food at his head and said, "If he wants to eat, he'll eat!"

That had happened a few years ago, but today it was a different story. Cuba was in the spotlight; deaths from a hunger strike could not be permitted.

I didn't know how or when they would do it but something had to be done and fast. Some of the strikers were elderly. Their bodies, weakened by prior hunger strikes and the long years of prison, couldn't take it much longer. Menoyo had two bleeding ulcers and others were in similar condition.

A doctor began coming by to check on us each day. After the fourteenth day of our strike, his expression was worried.

On the sixteenth day of the hunger strike, a group of officers went to Menoyo's cell and offered to take him and four others to the hospital. But the rest of us would have to figure a way to get ourselves out of the mess we were in.

"We came here together and we'll leave here together—dead or alive, but together!" Menoyo replied.

That occurred about 9:00 p.m. Around fifteen minutes later, I heard a muffled shout, the sound of a scuffle, then Menoyo's cry, "Rivas, Ernesto! They're taking me by force!" Then the voice was choked off.

A motor roared into life; the squeal of spinning tires sounded. Then silence... then pandomonium.

The politicals started banging the cell locks. "Killers! Assassins! Red murderers!" The common prisoners followed suit. Our bit of hell, dubbed the *Human Rights Building*, shook. But at the sound of another cell being opened, the noise died.

Again the scuffle. It was Rivas this time. That set off an ear-shattering din; and suddenly I got a bright idea.

Getting everyone's attention wasn't easy, but finally I did it. "Listen," I shouted, "I've got a suggestion. Let's not bang the locks. If we're banging, we can't hear when they come in to drag someone out. Instead let's just wait and every time they come in to get someone," I paused to let my words sink in, "let's all sing the Cuban national anthem!"

The national anthem of Cuba is a song of war. It's a tribute to battle and encourages the motherland's children to fight to the death in her defense: *"Morir por la patria es vivir!"* To die for your country is to live! Now we had a weapon.

The next time boots sounded in the corridor, the building was strangely silent. Another cell clanged open. I took a deep breath. "Political prisoners... Attention!" and I started singing. The political prisoners joined in and a moment later even the common prisoners were singing.

This was like igniting dynamite. The man the guards went in to get fought like crazy. Sounds of battle raged down the hallway and outside.

A few minutes later the guards returned, opened another cell and subdued, by brute force, another of the strikers.

I called, "Attention!" again, and once more the building swelled with Cuba's ode to battle. The guards were in a frenzy. They stormed into the common prisoners' cells beating the inmates into silence.

I heard them stop in front of my cell. A voice demanded: "Who's in there?"

"The American," someone answered.

The boots departed followed by the clank of a cell alongside being opened and the slap of machetes on flesh. The political prisoners continued singing.

The soldiers left. The men over in Building Number One had

heard the ruckus. They were shouting, wanting to know what was going on. The prison was on the brink of a riot. The soldiers did not return.

The next day a colonel, flanked by three other officers, came to my cell. For once I was humorless. All night long I had been hit by hot and cold flashes, and the pain in my back was intense.

The colonel said, "Menoyo is eating now. You come on and get off the strike."

"I don't believe you," I answered. "I'd have to hear that from Menoyo. If you want me to break the strike, bring Menoyo here and let him tell me. Until then — nothing!"

"Why is he involved in this?" the colonel asked the others with him. "This is a Cuban affair!"

"He says he's Menoyo's friend," dourly answered one.

"Listen, Americano, don't you realize that this looks bad on your record? I'm asking you to stop for your own good! I'm telling the truth. Menoyo is in the hospital, and he's doing fine. He sent word to tell you guys to come off the strike!"

I told him to go talk to Ernesto Diaz and if they took Ernesto to see Menoyo and he returned telling us that Menoyo said to break the strike then I would. Other than that they were wasting their time.

They left and went straight to Ernesto's cell. Ernesto was taken to see Menoyo and returned half an hour later. The same officers brought him down to my cell.

I remember how Ernesto stood and stared at me for a moment, a look of wonder in his eyes. He had looked at me many times, but now, for the first time, he was seeing me. He stepped up to the bars and said, "Eloy wants us all to come over to the hospital so that we can be together. He's still on strike."

I shot a glare at the lying colonel. He didn't blink an eye! "So we'll go over there," Ernesto said. "But we hold to the same position that we've had until now. Okay?"

We were all shuttled by jeep to the hospital. Under heavy guard we were taken to an isolated ward on the third floor.

The hospital was locked down. On the first floor were prison guards. The second was controlled by G-2 agents and on the third landing, leading to the ward, stood counter-intelligence personnel. They gave me a scary feeling as I walked by.

When I stepped into the ward, Menoyo greeted me with a bear hug. Words weren't necessary. I had made another friend.

Several doctors scuttled around examining us. We were put to bed and given intravenus fluids. Then, the adverse reactions hit. The rich liquid injected into our bodies caused some of the men to vomit over themselves. Some collapsed into a coma-like sleep and one went temporarily blind. I had a kidney infection. All that day and night antibiotics were pumped into me. Menoyo was the only one who stayed on his feet and went around giving out encouraging words.

I felt content with the role I'd played in the drama. My fellow strikers wrote a song in my honor. I felt a sense of pride in who I was.

My seventeenth day on strike Menoyo received word that his father had died. He went off by himself for awhile, then called everyone around and said, "I had planned to call off the strike today because I think that we've won. But I don't want these people to think that the news of my father's death weakened me. We'll go on until tomorrow!"

The next day the strike was halted. For the first time in eighteen days we ate: tea and soup.

Somehow, incredibly, Menoyo had a small radio smuggled up to us and at night we listened to the Voice of America which was giving a day by day report on the progress of the strike.

During the ten days which followed, we were handled with kidskin gloves. Juices and meats were plentiful, but the atmosphere, although relaxed, was one of waiting for something yet to come. Then one morning the doctor in charge of the ward walked in. With a contented smile, he started reading off names from a list. My name, along with seven others, was called. "These men can now consider themselves released from the hospital and must return to their respective buildings and cells!" He barked it off like a declaration.

Menoyo stood and holding up both hands said, "Hold it! Hold it right there. Don't anybody move." He turned to the doctor. "I told you people once. We came together and that's how we'll leave! We didn't ask to come here. You brought us by force. Now you're going to tell us to leave? You can't tell us how to terminate our protest!"

The doctor's mouth dropped.

Menoyo rushed on, "I still haven't talked to anyone in reference to my charges that the prison officials, acting on higher orders, have a plot to kill me. And until I have a meeting with someone from the Ministry who assures me that my life is no longer threatened, until then, we're still on strike. We just aren't on hunger strike. It's our way of saying that we are prepared to take the first step toward reaching some kind of understanding!"

The doctor spun around and stalked off.

The Warden sent orders that the men whose names had been called must abandon the premises. We refused. The prison went into complete lockdown. Doors to the hospital wards were closed and the hallways filled with rifle-toting guards.

Peeping from the window, I saw truckloads of soldiers unloading below. I told Menoyo but he shrugged it off. "They know that if there's a fight here, the prison will go up in flames. They've got something else in mind!"

He was right. Word came that Colonel Lemus would be here shortly to talk with Menoyo and the strikers.

Lemus!

That name brought back to mind a scene that was scorched into my brain. I remembered the young escapee as he was blown away from the sacks by the firing squad. I saw him again as he lay face up, tied hands held chest high, as though in prayer, jerking spasmodically.

Lemus!

336

He had stepped across the body, placed his gun behind the left ear and fired.

Lemus!

He had kicked the cadaver's face, then turned and strolled away!

Lemus!

I was watching the window when Lemus arrived and stepped out of a chauffeur-driven car below.

I heard the tramping of boots and a moment later Lemus, now elevated to colonel, backed by two bodyguards, strode into the ward. His vicious dark eyes flicked over the men who were getting to their feet. "Good evening, gentlemen. I trust that you're all better!" A sardonic smile played over his face. "Where's Menoyo?" he said, glancing at his watch.

"He's in the toilet," someone answered. "He'll be out in a moment."

I took the opportunity to move closer to the men guarding Lemus.

The one to his right resembled a beady-eyed hog. A stubby bristle covered his face and his lusterless eyes were two pinpoints of darkness. His right hand was curled around a half-exposed pistol and as his eyes darted over us, his body strained forward as though held back from attack only by a word.

The other guard had a reptilian face, devoid of feeling. He stared at us as though completely unattached from all that was going on around him. He was a machine that moved and killed.

Lemus, the man in charge of prisons in Cuba, appeared to be around thirty-four years old. His dark hair receded slightly. He moved about constantly, as though unable to control his body. He swaggered when he walked. An extreme vanity was reflected in his every move.

Menoyo appeared and walked calmly to where we stood, and after saying, "Good evening," to Lemus, sat down on a bed and crossed his legs.

Lemus, preening himself, addressed all of us: "I understand you have a problem. I understand Eloy has a problem. I'm here to solve all problems." His face became granite. "And I'm going to do it one way or the other. You know you're breaking the rules. We can't allow you to tell us when you'll come in and leave the hospital. We run this place, not you!

"We've been patient and generous with all of you, but our patience has run out!" His voice rose to a shout. "This is a State institution and we won't permit you to tell us what you will or will not do. Now those of you whose names the doctor called on the list... leave!"

Menoyo stood and took a step toward Lemus. "We didn't ask to come here and we're not saying we won't abandon the building. What we're saying is that we'll abandon it together and we'll return to our place of origin — the Hole — together!"

Lemus shook his head. "That's out. You can't remain here and you can't go back to disciplinary."

"And we're not going back to the building!" Menoyo softly said.

The two men stared each other down. Lemus' goons danced with anticipation.

"Eloy," Lemus' voice was brittle, "I want you to consider what you're saying. We both know that if we don't reach an agreement, the inmates are going to riot. That would stop the prisoner release program. I don't want to do it, but, " he paused to let his words sink in, "...if I have to I will give the order to subdue you. I have a plane waiting. All I have to do is give the order and all of you will disappear. No one will ever know what happened to you!" The colonel's eyes raked over us, then back to Menoyo. "There are men over there in Building One waiting to be released. They're friends of yours." Now his words were measured with care. "I have the authority to cancel further releases. If we can't reach an understanding, I'll give that order and your friends will continue serving time. You will have been the one responsible for the collapse of the prisoner release plan. Think it over!"

Lemus had scored a heavy point. He was the top man in the prison system. He had the power to do whatever he wanted.

"The guilt would be yours," Menoyo replied. "We're only exer-

338

cising our right to protest. But you're right," he conceded. "There's no reason why we can't reach an agreement. But first of all you've got to promise me that there'll be no more plots to kill me."

Lemus shuffled his feet; a sly smile flicked over his face. "Now, Eloy, you know nobody wants to harm you!"

"That's the first condition," Menoyo reiterated.

"All right! I swear there'll be no more plots against your life. You have my word!"

"And no reprisals against the men who were with me? No reprisals of any kind?"

"There won't be any action taken against any of you. There will be no reprisals!" He smiled. But as all good Communists do, he had lied.

A couple of months after the strike, Menoyo and all the other men who had participated in the hunger strike, except me, were shipped out in the dead of the night to the dreaded prison, Boniato, where up to this day, years later, they still languish.

30.
NEW ARRIVALS

In May 1979, a lanky New Yorker, Michael Seitler, arrived and told everybody to call him *Zip*. We found out later that nicknames ran in his family.

The Cubans had actually gone out past the twelve-mile limit to drag Zip and his two shipmates back into Cuban waters where they were arrested and their boat confiscated. A few days later the authorities said that they had found bales of marijuana floating in the ocean and charged Zip and his buddies with trafficking in narcotics.

Poor Zip didn't know what to think of it all. This wasn't his cup of tea. Zip came from a middle-class background. His mom, Isolde Seitler, was senior vice-president of a large advertising firm in New York. They lived in a comfortable home in Glen Cove, Long Island, with sisters Penny and Shawn. Dad was an artist and teacher. As time passed, Zip and I became good friends.

As soon as Zip's mom found out where he was and learned about the trumped-up charges that had gotten him fifteen years, Sunny — that was her nickname — began moving heaven and earth to get her son out. Her efforts were to benefit me greatly also.

She contacted the families of prisoners in Combinado and formed the movement, *Ad Hoc Inside Out Committee*. Next, she badgered Carter government figures about the lack of interest shown for Americans captured and imprisoned in Cuba. Sunny and her committee classified us as hostages. And it was true. We were being held on ice to be used or traded off as best suited the Communists.

While the committee's prime preoccupation was getting Americans out of Cuban prisons, they battled to be allowed to send us dried foods, canned meats, fruit and other wonders. Their persistence finally paid off. Some kind of deal was struck, and for the first time American prisoners were permitted to receive packages of food.

If, in a land of starving, a loaf of bread makes you a prince, then we American prisoners were now kings in Cuba. Everyone wanted to do business with us. I could understand why. Some of the freezer-dried products completely blew my mind; and I was American!

The first black pepper I had tasted in over ten years came in Zip's first bag from home. That simple addition to the prison fare made it edible and made me homesick.

Zip always shared his food with me. He was a friend indeed.

In the middle of June another curious pair arrived. One was a Frenchman, Jean Claude LeSage. He spoke with such a heavy Parisian accent that his English was unintelligible. The other guy was a hillbilly with an accent that dripped molasses. His name was John Dacus. He was nicknamed Ridge Runner. Jean Claude was tabbed, *The Frog!* Both were pilots.

A funny situation brought about their arrival. It seems a company that wanted a plane delivered with its cargo in the Caribbean, contacted the two men for the job. The flight was going to be risky. Why these two were picked is a mystery.

They met at the airport for the first time in their lives. Neither of the two could understand the other. But the mail and private enterprise must go on. So, somehow they managed to get it together and took off.

Although they didn't hold long conversations, the flight was an uneventful one until upon their return, after having been battered by a storm, something went wrong. Their plane began losing altitude. They had run out of gas, and there below, like a sleeping alligator, sprawled Cuba. Why they weren't spotted and shot down by a MIG jet is another mystery.

The two rattled pilots spotted a field. It looked smooth enough to land on. Now if they could just miss those cows. The flaps came down. Suddenly the Frenchman cried out, "Vach aot for zee feens!"

Dacus looked over at him and drawled, "What chall saay?"

Jean Claude didn't have time to repeat the warning. About then they were dragging parts of the destroyed fence behind the skidding plane.

When they slammed to a stop, Dacus looked at the Frenchman, shook his head and groaned, "What we got heah is a lack of communication!"

Jean Claude LeSage and John Dacus brought a laugh into the prison. A much-needed laugh.

On September 1, 1979, all the foreigners were moved back to Building Two. Individual cells were out for us this time. We were all crowded into three ten-man rooms. Rumors of more Americans coming were constant.

On September 7, 1979, at four o'clock in the morning, I was shaken from sleep by the Assistant Warden who was escorted by a couple of other officials.

"Wake up and be as quiet as possible," they whispered. "Don't wake the others. Get your belongings. You're leaving!"

I thought I was dreaming. They had to tell me again before I realized what they were saying. I leaped out of bed, my heart was thumping wildly. My mind was spinning. Unable to speak from the shock, I began stuffing my things into a bag I'd made.

Lester woke up and started waking everybody else. Then to add to the confusion, three other Americans were brought in. There was just time enough to shake their hands.

"My name's Bill Dawson," said one of the men. "This here's my partner, Austin Householder, and that peanut head over there is my other buddy, Doug Miklos. Hey, Doug," he shouted, "come over here and say goodbye. This guy's on his way back to the States!"

I couldn't believe it! The words, "I'm going home! I'm going home!" raced around inside my brain. "I'm going home!"

I floundered in a daze. It was all so sudden, so unexpected. I was led downstairs and my belongings taken away. I didn't care; I was going home!

The guards took me outside to a waiting van. Seated inside were Larry Lunt, Everett Jackson and a guy called, *Puerto Rico*, all alleged CIA agents.

There had been talk of an exchange of four Americans for the release of Lolita Lebron. She'd been in an American prison for a quarter of a century for the attempted assassination of former President Harry S. Truman. It was apparent that an agreement had been reached. Here were three alleged CIA agents and myself on our way home. We pulled up to the administration building.

"I can't believe it!" I whispered to Larry as we stepped from the Jaula. I don't know why I whispered. Maybe I was afraid that if I talked too loudly I'd wake up and find it had all been a dream.

Larry Lunt, always reserved and cool, replied, "I think it's for real. But you can't ever trust these Communists. I won't feel safe until I'm in the air!"

All of us felt the same.

We were taken to the rear of the building, and one by one dressed out in civilian clothing. This took about an hour. When we had finished, they let us stand on a veranda-like porch that ran along the front of the building. From there we watched the prison come alive.

The sun rose, turning everything bright and new. My body tingled with anticipation. I was anxious to be on my way. The four of us sat around talking and trying to mask the excitement we all felt.

A couple of hours passed and we were taken out back of the building and told to wait. Someone was coming to pick us up.

We had lunch; rice and Russian meat from the guards' kitchen, and then we sat locked in our own thoughts and waited. The hours rolled by and still no one had come to pick us up. My feelings of joy were giving way to uncertainty. With each passing moment I felt less and less certain that I would leave.

Toward six o'clock, the Assistant Warden walked up to me and smiling crookedly, like it hurt, said the words that destroyed all my illusions about home. "Looks like a false alarm for you, Tony. It's back inside again!"

I was stunned. I was not leaving! There had to be a mistake! Surely they couldn't make such a big mistake. Is it a mistake? A thousand thoughts flashed through my mind. But finally just one remained. I am *not* going home!

"Must have been a mix-up or something. But the orders are to take you back inside until further information is received."

They led me inside the clothing room, and once more I slipped on the ugly prison uniform. Another political prisoner, Cuban-American, ex-CIA agent, Juan Tur, was the fourth American leaving, not me.

The walk back to Building Two and up the stairs was the hardest journey I'd ever taken. Everybody grouped around and I told them what had happened.

I was depressed. I dropped down to my bunk and started taking out my personal effects.

Bill walked over and sat beside me. "Hey, look, Tony, sorry to see this happen, ol' buddy, but you wanna know sumthin'? I already found out that being in Cuba is like being in a sub with a depth charge tickin' off the seconds. You know what the chances of gettin' out are?" He looked me in the eyes. "Slim and none!" And he fell back laughing his fool head off.

I couldn't help but join in. He was a saving grace at a bad time.

When Christmas arrived, we celebrated in the usual way. All that I could think about was home. The wine we drank only made me feel gloomier.

New Year's rolled by without celebration for we had no future. But then, in May, 1980, an unheard of event occurred in Cuba

345

and startled the world. We wondered if the crisis at hand would affect us.

It did!

31.
A STAND

Cuba, like other countries has foreign embassies of other nations. These embassies look after the interests of their citizens while they are visiting Cuba. They also issue visas for individuals in Cuba to travel to the embassy's homeland.

Foreign embassies are also a place of refuge, a sanctity for those seeking political asylum. In Cuba foreign embassies are guarded by soldiers or police. In most countries this is done to protect the embassy. But in Cuba, as in other Communist nations, the guards are set up to prevent citizens of the Communist nation from seeking political asylum.

On one fateful day in May of 1980, Fidel Castro changed the history of Cuba, Miami, Florida, United States immigration policy and the political future of President Jimmy Carter. It began when Fidel ordered the removal of guards from the Peruvian Embassy. In just minutes the embassy was swamped by Cubans seeking asylum. Within hours ten thousand people were packed inside, terrified souls fleeing for their lives.

No so-called U.S. revolutionary protested, defended or stood up for those people who were running from something they considered worse than death itself. No words or broadcasts from Jane Fonda, nothing from Angela Davis or Gus Hall. No so-called defenders of the proletariat voiced even a whisper of concern that something was wrong enough in Cuba to force ten thousand people in a matter of minutes to abandon their homes, their loved ones and even their own country. All in a matter of minutes— and no one protested!

The image of those refuged in the embassy had to be stained. It looked bad for Cuba. And so Fidel labeled all those seeking asylum as criminals, agents and saboteurs of the revolution. Then a cunning idea took form. He'd make those seeking asylum look bad, hurt the United States and trick President Carter into accepting an internal Cuban problem — all in one serving.

In a brazen, historically unprecedented move, he ordered Cuba's prisons and mental institutions emptied and began shipping some of the most criminal and problematic elements of Cuba to the United States in what soon became known as *the Mariel Boatlift.*

To show support for his action Fidel called for the largest gathering of Cuban *Patriots* in the history of the island. Of the nine million people in Cuba, he demanded that five million be in the streets for massive marches all over the island on the 17th of May.

"They're overdoing it!" said Bill. "Who in their right mind would believe that five million people want to be out in the hot sun protesting because somebody wants to leave the country! I mean, that's unbelievable. Who cares if they leave?"

To keep us separated from the Cubans, the prison had put a television set in an empty storage room. We were allowed to watch it for an hour or so each night. I went in to see what the final outcome of *Fido's Folly* would be. The TV room was full. So I watched from the windows as busloads of Cuban prisoners were taken away.

All of the Americans were angry. Our government was allowing thousands of refugees, among them hundreds of criminals and madmen, to enter the United States and it still would not ask for the release of Americans locked up in Cuban jails!

I tired of watching the shouting groups of departing prisoners and turned to the TV. What I saw boiled my blood!

A large group of people, about two thousand, were being led in a chant by a Cuban official. It was the same slogan I'd been hearing for the past two weeks: *"Carter loca a Cuba no se toca!"* "Carter, crazy bitch, hands off Cuba!"

That did it. I left the TV room and went back to my cell. When sleep came, I had already decided what to do.

The next morning Terry, the Englishman, brought the milk. "Throw mine in the trash!"

Terry looked at me surprised. "Why? What's the matter? You not hungry?"

"Never felt better in my life. But today I don't eat this filthy Communist food. Listen, you've been hearing how they've been talking about Carter. I don't like the fool, but as much as I dislike it, he *is* representing the American people, and when Fidel talks about Carter or any other American president, he's also addressing the American people. Fidel is talking about my mother, my father and all of my people when he calls the President a crazy bitch. I'm not going for it. I don't care what anyone else does, but as for me, I'm going to protest by refusing the food. For at least one day, I won't eat their garbage!"

Terry walked away shaking his head.

The news of what I had planned quickly spread. By lunchtime four other Americans joined me. We threw our food into the garbage. That created a stir. Everybody else crowded around wanting to know what was up.

I told them. Just about all of them felt the same as I did and agreed that we would all throw away our food at the evening meal.

Someone pointed out that if just a few Americans, or even all of them, threw out the food, the prison officials would simply let us go hungry. "Now, if we could get the rest of the foreigners to go along with us and throw theirs out too, that would make a splash."

That would be hard to achieve. It wasn't their president who was being slandered. This was our problem and we had to handle it.

"I've got an idea!" I told the others. "I'm going to talk to all the non-Americans and ask them to allow us to throw their food away. They can pretend that they didn't know anything about any protest and demand that more food be sent. The prison will be forced to acknowledge our strike!"

Everybody throught it was a good idea so I talked to each foreigner and explained the situation. They were all for it. Only three Americans didn't participate, Bartos, Finney and Hill.

When the food arrived that evening a group of us calmly lifted the barrels containing our meal and turned them head-first into the garbage.

Lieutenant Calzada, one of the rankest guards I'd ever known, gaped for a minute, then hurried to the telephone.

I called everyone and told them to get back into their cells. "They're going to come looking for somebody to beat on and if we're out, they're going to whale on our heads. Everybody in! Let's go!"

We had been in our cells for only a few minutes when streams of guards in riot dress, wielding bayonets and rifles stormed into the corridor. I heard someone say, "Call *Tony el Americano*. Go get him!" They knew that I had something to do with the incident. My cell door was opened and I was ordered out. The voice broke in again. "Bring 'em all. Get 'em out here! All of 'em!" The voice belonged to the Assistant Warden.

After we were all packed in the TV room the Assistant Warden, face splotched with anger, beckoned me over to him. "What's the meaning of this? Who started all this?"

"I can only speak for myself," I answered. "I threw my food away because I don't like your people referring to the President of my country as "loca!"

"What! What!" The lieutenant's eyes bulged and the veins on his neck seemed sure to pop. "So you don't like it, huh?" His voice rose to a scream. "Well, that's what he is — LOCA! LOCA! LOCA! Take them to the Hole. All of them. Don't let them get anything from the cells. Take them just like they are!"

We were hustled into the Human Rights Building and paired off two to a cell. Edward King, a newcomer, landed in the stripped cell with me. All that the poor guy had on was shorts. The mosquitos were going to eat him up! All of us had come in partial undress. I only had pants on.

I had expected much worse and to tell the truth, I felt proud of the way everyone had conducted themselves. We had walked the razor's edge and come away unscathed.

To challenge Communists unarmed, alone and without recourse is tantamount to playing Russian roulette with five or six chambers loaded. You escaped by a miracle.

After three days of fighting mosquitos and roaches, Ed King looked as though he was stricken with the pox. Others called over and said they were in the same shape. We had to do something. Now was the time to use our American products. The guards were always ready to make a deal.

A Jamaican, Yuma, who had lived with us since the days of Guanajay was already in the Hole when we arrived there. Yuma was the epitome of bad news. He lied, wheedled, tricked, snitched and could even be a good guy when it got him what he wanted. I didn't like him and once awhile back, I had pulled a knife and threatened to kill him. Yuma had gotten thrown in the Hole for stealing a watch from a Colombian during some kind of deal and had been sentenced to an indefinite period of time. He finagled his way into staying outside of his cell most of the day and even briefly at night. He worked with the police. He was their eyes and ears in our section. He lived openly with a young homosexual and the guards let him do as he wished. He would be our middleman.

Yuma and a couple of guards started going to the building at night and bringing back personal items for us. Naturally it cost. The guards took advantage of the situation to get their hands on cologne or toothpaste or anything — just as long as it was marked: Made in the U.S.A.

Ed had American cigarettes and it only cost him a carton of Mores to have his pants and shirt brought over. At the time, a pack of American cigarettes sold for twenty pesos. But what are two hundred pesos when you're talking about putting something between you and hard cement plus protection from the insects? Yuma and the guards did a thriving business. By the fourth day in the Hole, everyone had clothes. It was a good thing the Assistant Warden didn't come to check on us.

I had pencil and paper smuggled in and on May 24, 1980, I wrote the following letter which was sneaked out of prison and back to the United States:

TO WHOM IT MAY CONCERN.

"This letter, written on a cement floor in a stripped cell in the punishment section of the prison Combinado del Este is a valid and just rebuttal to any and all forces that think to make might the essence of truth and right.

"Once again, we the American prisoners held hostage in enemy territory, hope to bring to the attention of all freedom-loving people the dreadful situation that confronts us. Not only are we subjected to a constant barrage of anti-American propaganda which encourages attempts on our safety and well-being, not only are we denied opportunities that other prisoners enjoy, not only do we suffer abuses due to our national origin, not only are we reduced to the status of sub-humans, due to our living conditions, but now we find ourselves subjected to cruel and inhuman punishment simply because we object to our President and our nation being slandered. In protest to the slogan, *'Carter loca a Cuba no se Toca!'* (Carter, crazy bitch, don't touch Cuba!), which we consider as vile, slanderous and insulting, we, a group of twenty-two North Americans, threw the garbage that they give us as food into the garbage.

"We feel that such slogans are directed to every North American and we refuse to allow the dignity of our homeland attacked without an adamant protest.

"For that protest, for that action which we carried out, we have been thrown into stripped cells, not allowed to bring a toothbrush, soap, toilet paper or towels with us and many were brought here wearing only shorts!

"We have not been told how long we will be here and some even fear that there will be an attempt to bring charges against us for "rioting" although we have done nothing except throw away the food given us. We have done nothing more than defend the honor and dignity of the concepts and precepts upon which our forefathers founded the only true revolutionary country that exists.

"We will continue to defend our country's honor at all costs even though that price be written in blood!"

"This letter is no plea for sympathy, but rather a cry for unity to the citizens of our country in the face of the enemy and also a warning to that enemy that there are still those who will not sit close-mouthed and allow them to spread their vomit unchecked. There are still those who are proud to be called North Americans and any attack on one will be considered an attack on all. We believe that an official apology is in order.

"Thank you for your attention.
Twenty-two Americans in Cuba.
Celda de castigo, Combinado del Este, Havana Cuba.
    Anthony Bryant
    Edward King
    Michael Seitler
    Lester Perry
    William Dawson
    Louis Moore
    Douglas Miklos
    Henry Jackson
    Austin Householder
    Raymond Fitzgerald
    Richard Baker
    Glen Akam
    Lorenza Maulden, Jr.
    Lance Fyfe
    John Gaynor
    Robert Bennett
    Larry Masters

John Dacus
Melvin Bailey
David Rodriguez
Mark Contino
David Keene

We stayed in disciplinary for seventeen days. Ed King and I got to know each other pretty well. Ed was to play a very important role in my life in the future. For now we spent seventeen days breathing the same air and dreams of escape.

While we were in the Hole, the remaining foreigners were moved to the opposite side of the building into four-man cells. When we returned we were paired off. Everybody tried to get in the same cell with a few friends. I ended up with four of my best buddies, Bill Dawson, Zip, John Dacus and Jean Claude, the Frenchman. All in all, we got along fine.

To divert ourselves we tried to throw monkey wrenches into a couple of the guards' lives. We didn't play around with the dangerous ones, but if we found out a guard was a dunce, we leaped on him with all four feet.

Lechuza was one of our favorite jokes. Lechuza means owl. That's what he looked like, so that's what we called him, Lechuza. We drove him crazy.

As soon as the shifts changed and Lechuza walked in, we'd let out a series of hoots. That would be sufficient to start the comedy. Lechuza would set off at a dead run trying to catch the hooter who always seemed to be in the next cell. I can recall watching him with the tip of my mirror as he tiptoed from cell to cell trying to catch anyone acting suspicious.

Our cell was always catching flack. We hooted and he knew it was us, but no matter how he ran, he always found us engaged in serious conversation or sleeping.

One day we cut a picture of an owl from a package of freeze-dried food. We posted it where Lechuza had to see it. We were still in the dining room eating dinner when he spotted it. The shock was too much. After coming in he closed the gate behind and stood there rubbing his chin. His eyes had a strange faraway expression and his face was blank.

It was after we were locked up and he'd gone to look at the bird again that he turned a deep purple and started raving. "It's a lack of respect! That's what this is — a lack of respect!" He was ready to explode. "I wish I knew who was responsible for this, I'd..."

"Whoo! Whoo!"

"Hah!"... at a dead run "...You see! You keep looking for trouble!" He crept around corners, slunk past cells and finally crawled up on the roof trying to bust the hooters. All to no avail.

He couldn't take it. Lechuza wrote a report denouncing "the lack of respect." This made the rest of the guards notice that he really did look like an owl and pretty soon they too were calling him Lechuza — behind his back.

He asked for a transfer. Refused! He started coming in only when it was lock-up time. He'd be off like a streak almost before the last cell door clanged shut. Lechuza was a laugh. But others were not so funny.

Lieutenant Carlos reminded me of a slug. He was messenger boy for the brass out front. He never knew anything about anything and his fondest dream seemed to have been to make things as unpleasant for us as possible. He hassled us constantly. For the slightest infraction it was twenty-one days in the Hole. He rained searches on us and stole our products. He was a cowardly ass...

And there was the head of the floor, Lieutenant Calzada. Calzada was black. I don't know what America had ever done to him but he hated us. He bragged about how many Americans he had killed in Angola. He and I were slated to be enemies. We couldn't stand the sight of each other and our conversations always bordered on the edge of insolence and insults.

One day he took me to the end of the hall and told me, "You're our little problem child, Tony. You think you're smart. You think you can make fools of all of us." He paced back and forth, a crooked smile etched on his lips as his eyes stabbed me. "But it's just a matter of time and intelligence. We know how to handle you. When I sit down and get this to working..." He tapped his forehead, "...we'll see what happens." It was a threat.

From that point on, I would have to watch my step. Someone did not want me to leave Cuba alive. One of the last things Jose Manuel, the medic, had told me before his release, "They've got something in mind. Be careful and watch your back!"

After Jose left there wasn't anybody to fill his place as medic. I took over his job, nothing more than escorting the foreign patients to the hospital to keep doctors' appointments and handing out medicine. The job did give me more movement, and I was able to wheel and deal for extra food for us.

Rumors flew thick and fast: the Americans were going to be released soon. Zip's mom sent news that things were moving in our favor. Her Inside Out Committee was shaking up Capitol Hill. Others too had joined in the fight to obtain our release. One of her supporters was M. M. Carson of Canada. Ms. Carson was a determined woman. The one-time holder of international womens' flying records, bombarded the Canadian government with letters, telephone calls and petitioned private interviews with members of Parliament. She forced the Canadian government to take a closer look at the Cuba to which Canadian tourists were flocking. There was talk of a possible trade reduction between the two countries. That may have been a decisive factor in events to come.

I felt that if we were to ever get out of Cuba it was now or never. The heat was on Fidel; moreover, elections were coming up and Castro was willing to do anything to keep Carter in office. There was a hue and cry over the Iranian hostages, and Carter's image was sagging. Since Fidel definitely didn't want to see Reagan in power, there was speculation that our release might bolster Carter's popularity and help him maintain residence in the White House. Yes, if we were ever to get out, it would have to be now.

32.
THE HUNTED

I continued working as a medic for the foreigners. But as rumors of our leaving intensified, I grew slack and started doing business left and right. If I were going to be released, we couldn't take any of our products with us, so everyone tried to get rid of them in exchange for alcohol. I was the 'runner.'

A guy nicknamed Judoka set up the deals for me. I didn't know it at the time, but Judoka was one of the key players in a plot to murder me.

Why kill Tony Bryant?

He had seen too much. He knew too much. He planned to write a book, produce a record. He could be a threat. By all indications, the Americans would be leaving soon and the officials did not want that threat to escape from the island alive.

But how to kill me and not have it appear as an assassination was quite another thing. Cuba was in the public's eye. There could be no cold-blooded murder—at least not openly. So the Communists prepared a plan to eliminate me in such a way that no one could point an accusing finger at them.

Judoka was in charge of the infirmary on his floor. He started doing me odd favors and always seemed to have alcohol around. That was the bait. He gave me single shots of it at first, then small bottles. And then pints and quarts of alcohol became available to me. Judoka took care of our cigarette trades, some of which came to stop in the prison officials' hands to be used against me.

Then I was introduced to the supplier who worked in the hospital; I began buying from him. The trap was set. I had taken the bait.

The supplier had a dangerous reputation and it was well known that I was involved in wheeling and dealing. If anything hapened to me, it could be ruled off as a squabble.

On September 20th, the trap was sprung. Judoka told me that the supplier had a batch of alcohol. For a few pesos and American cigarettes, a deal could be worked out. I should have known that something was up. It was too easy. An old gray-haired guard escorted us to the hospital and turned his head politely while I turned over the required amount to the supplier.

I had bought the alcohol for some of the Americans who were in the hall celebrating our hoped-for release. I'd had a couple of drinks when Judoka sent word for me to come down to the second floor where the principal infirmary was situated.

He had a quart of alcohol. I thought it was really generous, and in the course of our chat, the contents of the bottle disappeared. Judoka invited me to come over to his section where he had an additional supply. I drank more; then when the bottle was finished, in a swift change of attitude, Judoka told me that things looked a little hot on the floor and that I'd better leave.

The guard let us both through the door again, and I headed upstairs to my cell. Judoka went down to the Officer of the Day's office and the trap closed.

I had scarcely reached my cell and gone inside when a guard came up and told me to report to the Officer of the Day.

The O.D., a squat sergeant, squinted evilly at me and said, "Take a seat," as he closed the door. He wasted no time in getting down to business. "We have been told that you've been drinking. You were seen on the second floor near the infirmary and then on the other side in Judoka's section." The man had been well informed. I smelled a rat.

A lieutenant came in and began interrogating me. "Where did you get the alcohol?" The fact that the man questioning me had come in from the administration building told me that they had something special prepared for me. I tried to wiggle off the hook.

"All right," I said. "It's true. I have been drinking!"

"Hold it. Let me get this in writing. Okay. Go ahead!"

"Well, I've had this sore throat and I've been using a mouthwash that's got a little alcohol in it. I took a few swallows."

"You expect me to believe that? Who'd you buy the drinks from?"

That wasn't any of their business as far as I was concerned. I had admitted drinking and all that was left was to send me to disciplinary. I could see that there was something else they wanted.

"You expect for me to believe that?" he repeated.

"Yes. That's what I have to declare. And you know something else? It didn't taste too bad either!"

The lieutenant glared at me as he wrote down my answer.

It was kind of funny; they wanted anything that could be used to incriminate me and justify their next step. I had a strong hunch that a setup was in progress, but at first I thought that it was only a plot to get me thrown into the Hole; a sort of personal revenge perpetrated by the floor chief, Calzada.

The events that followed awoke me to the full degree of the danger I was in.

The lieutenant told me to wait while he went out and supposedly questioned Judoka. He returned. "Judoka confessed. He says you bought the alcohol in the hospital."

I denied it and stuck to my flimsy story about the mouthwash.

"Come on," the officer scowled. "We're going over and let a doctor check on you!"

The setup was beautiful. They had brought a few political prisoners to pick up medicine for asthma and had stationed them where they could clearly witness the drama.

The lieutenant sent for a key and ordered the supplier's office opened. After a minute's search, they came up with the money and cigarettes I'd brought there that day.

I was handcuffed and a guard put over me.

"Don't let him move an inch!" the lieutenant said.

A few minutes later, the supplier was brought in wearing handcuffs. He gave me a long questioning look. I shook my head — no.

Nonetheless, when the lieutenant took the man aside, he told the supplier I had snitched on him.

The doctor checked me and stated I had been drinking but was not intoxicated. I was taken back to the building to pick up my personal items, then escorted to the Human Rights Building. It was about 8:00 p.m. Sunday evening when the cell door slammed shut and I found myself again on a cement floor.

The supplier was not brought in that evening. Judoka never was. The supplier did show up, however, the next day around one o'clock. He had been given a prefabricated trial and stripped of all the benefits that had made life easier for him, his wife and children. His job, which paid him eighty pesos a month for the upkeep of his family was taken away. So were his conjugal visits. On top of these horrible punishments he was sentenced to twenty-one days in disciplinary. He would surely hate me.

The trial had been well prepared. In the hospital auditorium, filled with civilian personnel, doctors, nurses and guards, the conspiracy took full form.

Lieutenant Carlos testified that I had confessed to him to buying alcohol for the Americans and that I had furnished the name of the man who sold it to me. A black lieutenant testified to the same effect.

Lieutenant Salcines, the officer in charge of all foreigners, had told him the same thing and held up a piece of paper alleging that it was my confession.

There it was! The complete setup. Now a knife in my back; and who would blame the supplier for doing it! After all, that was the prison code. I was being set up for a revenge murder.

When the supplier arrived, he was brought to my cell. That in itself was highly irregular. It was meant to incite my future assassin even more.

When the outer door opened and I saw my ex-business partner standing there, I realized that the situation was critical. It was in the next few seconds that the supplier would decide to extract revenge or not. My life was on the line.

I stood and walked over to the bars, not taking my eyes from his. "How's it going?" I asked.

"Everybody's saying you busted me, Tony. Is that the truth?"

"Do you believe that?" I countered.

"I don't know what to believe. In the trial everybody said that you set me up."

I stood a long minute peering into his eyes. "It's all lies. I never mentioned your name. I took all of the blame so that you wouldn't get involved. I'm not a snitch. I couldn't inform on you or anybody else. Believe me."

The supplier searched my face for a trace of guilt or fear and evidently not finding any, gave a sigh and dropped his head. "I believe you."

"Come on!" snapped the guard. "Let's get to your cell!" He wasn't pleased. The expected threats and shouted curses had not materialized.

I sent a note to my ex-associate asking him to explain all that had occurred. At the same time I wrote a letter to the political prisoners alerting them to the plot. Another went to the Americans. I sent word to Bill and Zip that when the Interest Section came for the monthly visits, to tell them I had to see them urgently, that there was an official plot to kill me.

The supplier sent me a note in which he named the officers who had testified at the trial and what each had said.

I wrote him another note explaining that I intended to denounce the prison officials and that the letter he'd sent me was a very important piece of evidence. "It may mean they will take it out on you in a bad way," I told him. "But they have to be exposed, and I need this letter. Let me use it!"

Heroes come in strange and varied forms. The poor man must have wrestled with a thousand fears but finally, a few hours later, he answered my note and told me to go ahead!

The hunted had become the hunter!

Again I sent word to the politicals for help. Wheels began to turn. A common prisoner who swept the floor and passed out the food came to my cell and opened the outer door so any disturbance inside could be heard. He told me he would be keeping an eye out for me. If there was the hint of anything unusual, a strike would explode; the prisoner release program would grind to a halt and the world would know of the plot.

I hid the note the supplier had given me. It was to be taken out when the Interest Section came to visit.

Seven days later the supplier was released from Human Rights. I wasn't. This was to give my assassin time to set up the kill. The officials didn't know he was on my side now.

Bill and Zip had seen the Interest Section representative and given him my message. He had requested and was denied permission to see me.

Zip wrote and told me the prison was buzzing with talk about my cop out on my former partner. Even other civilians were involved who were also supposed to have been mentioned in my confession. All in all, the Communists had concocted a perfect atmosphere for my execution.

After fourteen days in the Hole, I was released and taken back upstairs. The next day, Lieutenant Carlos stopped by my cell. He swaggered in and, looking at the ceiling, remarked:

"I hear you're making wild accusations about the officials here wanting to kill you!"

"Carlos, you stated at the fellow's trial that I had confessed to you that he sold me alcohol."

Carlos jumped. He hadn't expected me to know about his role.

"Did I ever tell you I'd bought anything from him?" I asked.

"Yes. You did tell me that!" he blustered.

"You're a liar," I ground out. "Are you willing to repeat that in front of the Interest Section representatives?"

"Why not? I'm a man. I'll say it anywhere. We're not afraid of your Interest Section." But sweat beaded his brow and he had a worried look in his eyes when he left.

The Interest Section came to visit us in early October. I rolled the note from the supplier into a tiny wad, covered it with cellophane to keep it dry, and stuck it in my mouth.

Following a quick search, ten others and myself were bussed to the administration building. When there was no danger of being seen, I took the note out of my mouth and threw away the cellophane.

Finally I was taken inside the visiting room; I found to my surprise not one, but two U.S. representatives there. Lieutenants Salcines and Carlos were present plus two G-2 agents.

I didn't wait for the visitors to say anything. "I have a serious accusation to make!" I blurted out as soon as I sat.

Salcines straightened in his chair and Carlos eased closer, peering down at me.

"The prison officials here in Combinado del Este are plotting against my life!"

The G-2 agents were busy writing.

"You say officials. Specifically, which officials?" enunciated Salcines slowly.

I slipped the note from my pocket and handed it to the representatives. "Will you please read that? There you'll see where Lieutenant Salcines stated that I had signed a confession accusing my partner of selling alcohol." I then explained to the representatives all that had transpired. Turning once again to Salcines, I asked, "Do you still maintain I signed a confession?"

"Of course I do," Salcines snapped. "We don't have any reason to lie. You signed a confession and you told me the other guy was the one who sold you the alcohol!"

I turned back to the visitors. "Gentlemen, this is very serious. This is one of the officers who has taken part in the plot to have me killed. If the man who wrote that note had not believed me I would be dead today because even if he just stabbed, or cut me, I would not emerge alive from the operating room! You've read the note and you've heard this man swear I signed a confession. Gentlemen, ask to see that confession!"

Salcines squirmed. He was trapped.

"May we see the declaration signed by Mr. Bryant?"

"Well, it would be difficult to get a document on such short..."

"Gentlemen," I pressed the attack. I wasn't going to let him get away. "Don't give them time to fabricate one. If he can't produce the confession by the time you leave, then I suggest you inform the highest levels that you can reach about this."

Lieutenant Salcines sprang to his feet in a rage. "You'd better mind how you talk. That's slander. You better shut up or we'll have you back in front of another tribunal!" Like most dangerous animals, he was ferocious when mortally wounded.

I disregarded his open threats and said to the Interest Section representatives, "You have the note written by the man they planned to use to kill me and if he didn't fulfill the job, they had another guy called Judoka who was to stab me. Plus you've heard him admit or allege he has a signed confession from me. All I want you to do is force him to present it!"

One of the representatives, a thin-lipped, icy-eyed young man looked piercingly at Salcines and said, "If there is an attempt to take Mr. Bryant to trial for the charges he's made, we, as members of the United States Interest Section, will be there to testify on his behalf. Also, if you cannot produce that signed confession, we'll have to report it to the Ministry."

I then turned on Lieutenant Carlos. "Now, Lieutenant... have you ever heard me confess and accuse my partner of selling alcohol?"

Carlos blanched. He had seen what had happened to Salcines. It was now every man for himself. Fidel didn't like bungling. "Unh... No. I've never heard you say anything like that but..."

"Then why did you testify in front of all those people and tell that guy I had?"

"Uh, well, I heard... you know... everybody was talking..."

I turned to the representatives. The thin-faced one spoke:

"We'll take it from here, Tony. We'll turn in a full report as soon as we get in. Now listen. There is a real possibility all of you might be leaving soon. Try to stay calm for just a little while longer. Keep your cool! Don't blow it!"

Sweet is the taste of victory! I didn't even glance at my two victims as I left.

There was a bit of unfinished business before I could savor complete victory. About five days later, I struck.

I signed up to go to the hospital. Lou, Flip and Melvin came to watch my back. They knew what I had in mind. There was the usual crowd waiting on the first-floor landing to go to the hospital. I searched the assembled group over until I found my prey.

Judoka heard me charging and spun away just as I swung. It was a glancing blow that caught him high on the cheekbone. He didn't wait to see if anything else was coming behind it and took off running. Try as I might, I could not catch the fleeing medic.

I thought I'd trap him at the end of the hall, but he suddenly dropped to the floor, spun around and was gone again the same way we'd just come.

Flip stuck out a foot and tripped Judoka trying to give me enough time to arrive. But scrambling on all fours, Judoka shot through the crowd into the O.D.'s office.

One of the guards I knew grabbed me and held me back. "All right. You've made your point. Let him go. I know all about everything and all I can say is if you want to kill him just don't do it in here in front of me. Okay?" He released me, and with a grin that turned into a laugh, added, "I thought Judoka was a judo expert. He ran right past his judo!"

I had to laugh. This was better than beating the man up. Judoka had a reputation of being tough. Well, I had destroyed another myth.

My victory was now complete. *Tony, el tigre de California,* smiled and thought to himself: when the hunted becomes the hunter, the prey rarely escapes!

33.
A DREAM COMES TRUE

"You will not escape from this island! The revolutionary government of Cuba is going to return you to your country!" The old Babalao's voice seemed to carry on the wind hissing through the slatted walls of Combinado. *"The revolutionary government of Cuba is going to return you to your country!"*

It was true!

A week earlier, on the 20th of October, we had been told we were to be released. The Cuban authorities claimed it was a humanitarian gesture by the government. They told us we should be thankful to them because if it had been left up to our government, we would have stayed in Cuba and rotted. I knew through long experience that the Soviet-Cubans did nothing out of the kindness of their hearts, but, for whatever reasons, they wanted to expel us.

I was ready to go.

But there still remained the vivid memory of the last time the Communists had told me that I was going free and my heartbreaking return inside the prison. I tried hard to keep my emotions under control. I had learned never to trust what a Communist said. But all indications pointed to our release. It was difficult not to jump and shout to heaven above the overpowering joy!

All written material, poems, letters from anyone other than family, and addresses, were confiscated. I lost dozens of poems and two short stories. They didn't want us to carry anything out of the country that might let the world know about Castro's murderous regime.

Then on the 26th of October, 1980, each of us was interviewed by a Cuban major, acting the part of an affable politician. We were given three options: return to the United States; go to a third country such as France or Algieria or remain in Cuba.

I didn't know what to expect if I returned to the United States; prison or a death sentence. It really didn't matter. The only thing that occupied my mind was the desire to go home and give the warning to my people — the American people, all my people, white and black. What happened to me had no importance. I had to return and unmask Communism's plague to the U.S. citizenry.

I had come to Cuba hating white America. But in Cuba my life had changed. Now I had friends who were white and enemies who were black. I had risen above the color barrier.

There was an enemy greater than any one ethnic group; I saw an enemy who enslaved and mutilated both body and soul. I had come face to face with Satan and learned that evil comes in all colors. Yes, it was time to go home. Freedom was only hours away. The old Babalao had been right again.

Although it was early in the morning, around two o'clock, everyone was up, talking and planning. We had long since packed, and now it was simply a matter of waiting, simply a matter of waiting...

I did not feel as happy as I should have been. Too big a part of me was being left behind. Some parts buried in unmarked graves, others spattered against bleak walls pocked by bullet holes. I had developed strange ties with that island. I had found my dearest friends and greatest enemies on it.

October 27, 1980, at around 4:00 a.m., Lieutenant Salcines and a flock of other officials invaded our section. There was no need for them to say anything. We all let out a shout and grabbed up our belongings. As usual, the Communists were moving us under cover of night... It was normal; they feel at home in the dark.

Seated in the bus, I took a long last look at *The Technicolor*

Hell where I'd witnessed a bestial savagery that numbed my mind.

How could I ever forget the time I spent locked in disciplinary, listening to a man a couple of cells down moaning and pleading for a doctor all night? The guards had come and could be heard beating and kicking the man. We all beat on our doors trying to divert their attention. But they wouldn't stop.

The body was discovered at breakfast time. There was a mad rush to close all of the doors so no one could see what had been done to the man. But later, when the deceased's cell was being hosed out, my door was opened again. Clots of blood swirled past as a prisoner lazily swept the crimson water down the hall.

How could I forget the day I saw a guard stamp into the infirmary and knock a sick patient down, then kick him unconscious?

How could I forget when Lieutenant Calzada led a cowardly charge on about twenty Cuban prisoners seated in the patio in a silent protest? The guards beat and chopped the men as though they had murdered someone. Heads fractured, pierced bodies, arms and legs broken and one dead inmate was the day's toll.

The stink pouring out of cells built to house forty inmates, with up to a hundred and twenty inside could not be forgotten. None of this would ever leave me.

The bus cranked into life. As we passed the visiting area I remembered scenes of grief-stricken mothers, wives and children who found out that their loved one had been taken without notice from prison, transported to Mariel harbor and shipped to the U.S. The shock and grief disfiguring their faces would be impossible for me to describe or forget.

The bus rumbled to a halt between the double gates and a quick check of the underside was made. A mixture of envy and wonder was stamped on the guards' faces as they watched us pull away. We were bound for a paradise forever forbidden to them. They were staying on in hell. The gates slammed shut and already perdition and its keepers was behind us.

We were again taken into an auditorium in the administration building, searched one last time, then issued shorts, slacks, shirt and shoes. I was in a daze. One part of me was convinced I was leaving, but there was also the unbelieving cynic's cave within me waiting to comfort and hide that other part should something go wrong. I would not be able to believe I had escaped from Cuba until I was in the air above it.

The *Owl* was spotted heading up the stairs to an overhead office. Immediately the building was filled with hoots.

Lechuza stopped and gave us a withering glare.

To let him know that it had all been in fun, we gave him a round of applause.

He blushed, threw a half-hearted wave goodbye, then trudged up the steps. The Owl would never get to leave Cuba.

The perennial milk and bun came. I was too nervous to eat. I think everyone felt the same. There would be a rash of conversation, then a dead quiet would blanket the auditorium. A guard, his submachine gun pointed at us, sat on the stage gaping. He probably wished that he were with us.

"Hey, guys, look! There's a bus... No, two of them!"

A shout went up as we packed the window. Outside was a beautiful scene. Two busses crammed with camera-clutching American reporters had pulled up to the building.

Someone inside the vehicle filmed the prison. A guard ran up. Beating on the bus window, he waved his arms — no!

The Assistant Warden, Lieutenant Salcines, and a group of officers came in. We were told to take a seat. Then, they came... all those free members of a free press of a free nation.

The reporters poured in like a tidal wave. The guards would have had greater success trying to hold back the ocean than stopping the unruly capitalist newsmen who paid no attention to the cries of Salcines forbidding the interview of any prisoner in private.

There was bedlam. Cameras flashed and everybody talked at the same time. The newsmen and women had brought American life and all its hustle and bustle into the room.

Guards were bumped out of the way by busy camera crews, and if an officer ran up to protest an interview, the reporter spun away adroitly and grabbed someone else on the other side of the room.

After awhile, a semblance of order was restored and we were interviewed one by one. I was asked how conditions had been. How had conditions been? My mind was flooded with scenes convulsing like worms over one another—terrible scenes that would have taken hours to describe.

"Conditions?" I answered. "Horrible!"

All of us agreed our release was a political ploy by Castro to help Carter in his re-election try.

To the reporters and to most people who saw those anti-Castro shots on Television, the denunciations might not have had any great meaning. But had they realized the danger involved in making them, we would have been applauded.

The cameras could have been confiscated, the reporters expelled from the country and we Americans taken back inside the prison. There would have been no protest except from people like Sunny Seitler, Ms. Carson and a few others who were fighting for our freedom. Yes, it took courage to say something like that in Communist Cuba.

An hour later, the newspeople packed their equipment and boarded the busses again. We were taken out back where another waited for us.

As the bus turned onto the street leading from the prison, I took a last look, then closed my eyes. I was trying to block it out of existence. When I opened them, the prison was gone and we were going down a narrow road lined on each side by leafy trees. I felt something breaking around me. Walls were falling down.

The ride to the airport was short. People along the way stopped and stared at the procession. Some waved. They seemed to know that someone was escaping from hell.

Jose Marti Airport had undergone some changes since I arrived on my hijacked Flight 97. The runway looked in better shape than it had when I came in at pistol-point almost twelve years before.

371

After a short while, we were taken to a waiting plane and one by one unloaded from the Russian bus. We were photographed by Cuban photographers at the jet's entrance, then led to a seat by watchful United States federal marshalls. They looked mean and beautiful.

The hijackers, the three brothers and myself, were put on one side apart from the others. We were handcuffed and a chain run through the cuffs and around our waists.

The jet taxied to its take-off point, sat poised for a moment, then with a roar leaped ahead as though anxious to shake off Cuba's dust.

As the tires broke contact with the ground the terrible feeling of depression that I'd felt since my 1969 arrival in Cuba dropped away. It was an incredible sensation of freedom. It was as though a heavy weight had been lifted.

The sky was overcast, but as we circled suddenly a break in the clouds appeared. The pilot headed for the opening and slipped through into a brilliant sun.

I was glowing. I had to write something. I had to jot down something about this most important plane ride in my life. I managed to pull a pencil from my pocket and on a piece of napkin wrote:

Fly Free

A roar, a whistle of wind
And like an arrow escaped
Towards a patch of blue
That opened before heaven's portals,
We slipped!
No! We raced!
Cuba, the crimson laboratory
dropped away beneath us. God's
Breath pushed us higher until,

The cumolo-nimbus
Became the carpet on which homecoming
Hearts skipped.
Escape! Escape!
Escape from hell, from sorrow, from
Death to
Fly, fly, fly, fly
Free!

34.
THE RETURN

But I wasn't free. I was returning to face one of the toughest charges of our times — hijacking! Not only had this crime forever changed my life, it was a phenomenon that plagued the U.S. and other free world countries and forced agreements between enemies in an attempt to stem its outbreak.

The Communist countries had no real problem with skyjackings. In Russia or Cuba it's almost impossible to seize an airliner. The cockpit is sealed and armed guards open fire on anyone attemting to deviate the flight. Such was the case of two young men whom I had met in Principe.

The would-be hijackers, armed with grenades and a pistol, boarded a flight from Santiago, Cuba to Havana. Knowing it would be impossible to gain access to the cockpit, they waited until the plane gained altitude then pulled out the grenades and threatened to blow the airliner up unless they were taken to the U.S.

A security agent drew his gun and began shooting over the heads of the terrified passengers. One of the youths panicked and dropped his grenade. A soldier threw himself over it to muffle the explosion and was killed. The pilot made an emergency landing, and while the plane was still moving at high speed over the runway, the two 'jackers' leaped from the airplane.

When I met them in the prison hospital, one of the youths had to be carried to and from interrogations on a stretcher. He was taken before the firing squad the same way, taken off the stretcher and tied, slumped against a target pole. The other hijacker's father, a high Cuban government official, signed his own son's execution order and watched him die.

An officer who witnessed it told me that it had been a messy affair. The firing squad botched it. When the official walked over to administer the coup de grace, the kid was still alive and grappled with the gun pointed at his head until his strength ran out.

In the 1960's there had been another famous attempt by a man named Betancourt. He got into the cockpit, probably the reason it's sealed now, and demanded to be taken to the U.S. The pilot circled and changed routes making Betancourt think that the plane was headed for Miami. Instead he landed again in Havana. Immediately Betancourt discovered the trick and shot the pilot to death. He eluded the police for a few days, then was captured and executed. That was how Cuba treated its own hijackers.

I didn't think I'd be executed but my past record was so bad that I expected anything to happen. The three brothers, also returning to face hijack charges, sat quiet and subdued. They too must have been wondering what fate had in store. But the other Americans were in a party mood. They laughed and made plans for the good times awaiting them.

I remember looking down at the chain around my body and thinking: What a way to come home! Returning in chains! I hope Mom and Dad don't come to meet me. I wouldn't want them to see me like this.

A momentary wave of regret swept over me. Maybe I should have gone to another country. Was I heading back to years of prison? But I pushed that thought from my mind as I remembered what I had said to Lester Perry: "I've got to go back and face whatever's waiting. You should too. Even if you have to go to jail, man, you've got good food and liveable conditions. You'll for sure eat better in a U.S. prison than you would out free in the streets in Cuba!"

There was a long silence, then Lester had said softly, "Tony, I've been in a lotta joints and a prison with bars of gold is still a prison!" Lester was wanted in the States for hijacking and he didn't want to face serving more time even in America.

What Lester said was true, but it didn't matter. I had to come home. If it meant coming home to a prison, then let it be, but I was coming home.

The plane banked to the left, then gently to the right. An airstrip came into view. As we made the final approach, I saw a crowd of people waiting below, many wearing yellow ribbons and carrying welcome home signs. The guys on the plane cheered... I did too.

The plane touched down and rolled to a stop. Within seconds my ex-cellmates and close friends were in the arms of their loved ones. My dearest friends cried, kissed and hugged people I'd never seen before and then walked away without a look or a goodbye wave to me. I wondered if I'd ever see any of them again.

We, the hijackers, were whisked off to The Federal Correctional Institute in Homestead, Florida. The barbed wire surrounding the compound gave me a constricted feeling in my chest. Yes, a prison with bars of gold is still a prison!

I had never been in a federal prison before. I had heard that their living conditions were a lot better than those of state institutions; however, I wasn't ready for the 'executive retreat' awaiting me.

Our Cuban clothes were taken. We were issued coveralls that resembled jumpsuits, towels, toothpaste, and whatever other paraphernalia we might need.

The first night we stayed in isolation, but the next day we were led into a split-level room. It was huge. Cells on the two tiers ran side by side forming a large circle. Two pool tables and a section for playing cards or chess faced each other. The cafeteria-style kitchen, with an adjoining dining area, was a little to the right. The smells drifting my way had me going out of my head. Flip and I were placed in a cell together, and Lou and Melvin in another.

After a dinner of fried chicken, mashed potatoes, brown gravy, and peas, topped with a wedge of apple pie, I collapsed happily in a real bed with American springs. I listened to the music I had missed so much, the music I once had played, and fell into a deep and contented sleep.

Compared to what I had just left, this was a country club. It's true, Lester: a prison is a prison even though the bars be gold, but if I had to be in prison, then let it be where I was not stripped completely of my human condition.

The following morning I was presented before Federal Judge Charlene Sorrentino in the federal courthouse in Miami. I had no funds to afford an attorney and so a young, clean-cut guy named Larry Rosen was appointed to represent me.

Larry looked like he was old enough to shave... maybe. But he had bright intelligent eyes; the other thing I liked about him was his respectful air. He asked that the bond hearing be postponed until he'd had a chance to talk to me. Judge Sorrentino set the hearing for Friday, October 31st.

I was so happy to be around familiar sights and sounds that a smile kept breaking over my face.

The judge noticed and smiled. "You certainly appear content, Mr. Bryant. Happy to be home?"

"Yes, Your Honor, deliriously!" I leaned over and whispered to my newly-appointed lawyer, "I'd like to make a statement. It's important."

"What kind of statement?" Larry asked, chewing his lip nervously.

"Well, I made a promise to myself that every time I had the chance, I was going to expose Communism. I want to keep that vow!"

My lawyer turned to the judge. "Uh... Mr. Bryant would like to say something, Your Honor... not concerning his case."

Judge Sorrentino nodded.

I cleared my throat. It was my chance. "First, I would like to thank you for allowing me to address the court." The courtroom audience sat quiet and expectant. "Communism is humanity's vomit!" I blurted. "Wipe it out!" I turned and walked out of the electrified courtroom.

TV cameras tracked us until the van pulled away. As we weaved in and out of traffic, I strained my eyes at a world that to me was twelve years new. The women were fresher, lovelier. Cars, sleek and shiny, resembled rockets skimming along the ground. But something tugged at my mind. I noticed a sense of urgency in the air. A desperation. Everything seemed to gyrate so urgently. That was my first return impression of life in the U.S.

I had a visit with Larry that same afternoon. He informed me that I had a $500,000 surety bond imposed, which is to say, I needed about $75,000 to make bail. My indictment originated out of New York and that's where I would have to stand trial. We discussed asking for a change of venue on the grounds that a possible guilty plea might be entered. Then, Larry could ask that I be released on my own recognizance. It was a long shot, and the decision was mine. Larry warned me my chances of pre-trial release were slim.

I didn't have to think about it. The few friends I had were in Miami. If I was to have any chance at all it would be in Florida. I agreed with the strategy. As an afterthought I told him, "And you know what else, Mr. Rosen? I'm walking out of there on bail!"

Larry looked at me as though I were insane. He hunched his shoulders and said, "We'll give it a try. That's all we can do."

That night I called my mom. When I heard her voice I wanted to shout. Just the sound of it, and all the lonely years melted away.

At first she didn't know who I was. "Who is this? Is this you, Chuckie?"

"No, Mama. It's Garnet."

For a moment there was absolute silence, then I heard her crying and trying to talk at the same time. "Oh, Garnet! My son, my baby. Oh, Garnet! Where're you at, sugar? You need some money? Mama'll send you your bus fare. How much do you need? Oh, thank God! I'm so happy. Lord, my son is home! Boy, you don't know how much I've prayed for you. I knew you was comin' back. The heavenly Father told me you was comin' back!" Then she broke into a flood of tears, and I was crying too.

Finally, both of us managed to control ourselves, and I explained the situation. I hurried to assure her that I would be home shortly. I couldn't tell her otherwise; it would have broken her.

She called my step-dad, Jim, to the phone. He and I talked for awhile, then Mom came back on. I promised to call every day and with her final, "I love you," ringing in my ears, hung up.

I had to wait in line again for another turn at the phone. I telephoned my dad. My step-mom answered, and when she realized who it was she gave a shout and screamed, "Daddy! Daddy! Come quick. It's Garnet! Hurry! Hurry!"

My dad came on the line crying. He kept repeating over and over, "Oh, praise the Lord! Praise the Lord!"

They were ecstatic. We talked for the fifteen minutes allotted. I felt downright happy. I barely slept that night.

Larry returned the next day and told me he'd gotten in touch with Tony Cuesta. "He's agreed to testify on your behalf at the hearing, so we're sending a car to pick him up Friday morning."

My spirits took a leap. Cuesta had promised to do all that he could for me. Most jailhouse promises are cheap. I knew from experience that they're forgotten as soon as freedom is attained. But somehow I believed in Cuesta.

"Look, Tony," Larry continued, "you've got some real tough charges facing you. I'm going to need all the ammo I can get. I want you to tell me more about you. The other day you said you had a mission in life. Care to tell me what you meant?"

It would have been impossible to explain in a few minutes, but if I were to make people believe in me, I had to start right there with my lawyer. "Well, first of all, I want you to understand something. I committed the crime and I don't deny it. I do have a mission; to tell the people about what happened to me and what it means to their lives. I can do that more effectively free, but if I have to go to prison, I'll do it from there!"

Larry questioned me closely about my past, my stay in Cuba

and about my future plans, if I didn't go to jail.

"I'm not going to prison, Larry. God is on my side. You see, I went to Cuba not believing in anything. Now I know there's a God and I believe He's with me."

I know that Larry must have thought I was trying to play some kind of game with him. Almost every prisoner claims to have been 'born again' if it will help to escape judicial wrath, but what I felt was too private and too real to exploit. Rarely did I discuss my personal beliefs on religion. I only knew that I had gone through hell on earth and come out whole, and the only reason I could accept was that God must have wanted me to carry the message of Satan's plague, Communism, to the people.

"I don't want to go to prison, but my main objective is to warn the people. If I have to yell out that message from the depths of the sea then I'll do it. You see, it's time to take a stand and either be for or against the anti-Christ!"

Larry laughed and turned the conversation to more mundane matters.

That night I called my mom again. Practically the whole family was there waiting to talk: Terron, my little brother; Anita, Luita, my two smaller sisters; and Chuckie... all of them except my sister Rommel; she was having another spat with Mom. The two of them were too much alike, strong-willed, lovely ladies. James, my older brother, wasn't present either. He was tied up with an organization that he'd co-founded in Los Angeles.

"I don't know what that mess is," Mom said. "Somethin' about anti-Communism. I tol' that boy to forget about all that dooky an' git hisself a job!"

I thought I would die laughing. It was the first real laugh I'd had in years. That's how Mom was; she made me feel good.

I was awake early the next morning, tense and nervous. After a quick breakfast, the three brothers and I were dressed in civilian clothes, loaded into a waiting air-conditioned van and whisked downtown to the courthouse. I couldn't help comparing it to the Russian-built jaulas that had carried us in Cuba. We were taken upstairs to Judge Sorentino's courtroom. It was half-filled with reporters, but there was no sign of my prison friend, Cuesta. I saw Larry sitting in the first row and caught his eye. He shrugged and shook his head. My spirits sank.

A few minutes later, Judge Sorrentino entered. After everyone was seated quiet settled over the room. Court was in session.

The three brothers went before the judge first. They were in the process of answering her questions concerning bail when a slight disturbance at the door drew everyone's attention. I looked over and my heart bounded.

Entering the courtroom, led slowly by Jose Manuel, a friend I'd made in Cuba's Combinado Prison, was Antonio Cuesta. The blind veteran found a seat, and all eyes turned once again to the judge.

I felt a tingle in my stomach, like when you're going to fight. The three brothers were led away and my name called.

Judge Sorrentino nodded and gave me a brief smile. "Will you please state your name to the court?"

I did, almost in a whisper.

"I'm sorry, but you'll have to speak up a little louder."

I tried again and did better. My throat felt dry. My nerves taut.

The preliminaries over, Larry asked that I be released on bond. He told the judge that he believed I was a changed man and that since I had returned voluntarily to confront justice, I should be given the opportunity to be free until sentencing. "Mr. Bryant is requesting a change of venue and we are contemplating entering a guilty plea." Larry pointed out that after twelve years in jail, I deserved the chance to prove myself. He explained my belief in my mission.

Then, a sharply dressed, typical All-American boy about thirty years old stood up. He was Wes Currier, Assistant United States Attorney. His lips were curled in a slightly sardonic grin. In a voice polished and smooth, he said:

"If it pleases, your Honor, I think that bail for this man is unthinkable. Not only are the charges very serious, almost as serious as they can be, but the man's past is horrendous! Besides, what's to say he won't decide that his mission, whatever it is, is more important than keeping his promise to the court. Not to mention the twenty-year minimum staring him in the face. I don't think that bail should even be considered and the government would certainly appeal such a decision!" He kept on smiling.

Judge Sorrentino listened to his arguments, then said, "I'd like to talk to Mr. Bryant." She took a deep breath. "Mr. Bryant, I want you to tell me about yourself. Where did you say you were born? Oh, I see. California. Have you ever been married?"

"Yes, Your Honor. Twice..."

"Do you have any children?"

"Yes, I do, a son."

"Does all of your family live in California?"

"Yes, Your Honor."

"Tell me about the times you've been arrested, Mr. Bryant." Her voice was probing, yet gentle. "Let's start with the first time. What happened?"

I told her all that I could remember about my life of crime, the heroin, the armed robberies, the time spent in prison, all that I could think of at the moment. It wasn't a pretty story.

Have you ever worked, Mr. Bryant? What kind of jobs have you held?

"I've worked, Your Honor. I used to be a professional musician!"

"What instrument did you play?"

"Flute and saxophone."

"C-flute?"

I had to laugh. It seemed that the judge and I were alone in the courtroom talking — communicating. Two people from completely different worlds had met and were saying, "I'm okay, and you're okay, too."

"I see that you're a musician also," I remarked.

"What kind of flute do you like? The Dubussy?" Then, as though realizing that there were duties yet to be performed, she asked me about my mission.

I told her how I felt about my commitment. I told her that I would honor my word to the court. I said, "Seated here with us today is a living legend, Your Honor. That man you see there," and I pointed to Tony Cuesta, "is one of the greatest men alive!" He's a giant. I could never disappoint him. I would die for him. If you'll allow me to go out on bail..."

"Mr. Bryant..." Judge Sorrentino rubbed her chin. "Do you have any friends here in Miami?"

"Yes, Your Honor. The man I've been talking about is my friend."

The judge sat thinking, then heaved a sigh and opened her mouth to say something when my lawyer interrupted her.

"If it please, Your Honor, there are two people here who would like to speak on Mr. Bryant's behalf."

The judge nodded and leaned back in her chair.

Tony Cuesta was helped to his feet and led to where I stood. We threw our arms around each other slapping each other's backs. It felt good to have my friend standing there. Somehow I knew that the tide had turned in my favor. Wes Currier, the Assistant U.S. Attorney, wore a slight frown.

"Your Honor," Larry said, "I'd like to present Mr. Tony Cuesta. He's a good friend of the defendant. They knew each other in prison and he's come to offer testimony."

"Good morning, Mr. Cuesta!" said Judge Sorrentino.

"Good morning, Your Honor. I am very happy to be here to be able to see my good friend Tony Bryant!"

"Mr. Cuesta, I'd like to ask you some questions."

"Ahh... Your Honor, is there a translator here? My English is not too good and I think to express myself better in my native tongue..."The U.S. District Court translator, Luis Nigaglioni, was called and started off so smoothly that Cuesta laughed and said, "Ah, we have a wonderful interpreter here!" and he took the opportunity to play politics and advocate bilingualism which was a hot political issue in Miami at the time.

Judge Sorrentino almost smiled, caught herself and said, "Fine, Mr. Cuesta. Now will you tell the court how you met Mr. Bryant and under what conditions?"

"I met Tony Bryant in the prison El Castillo de Principe many years ago. It was a very hard jail and you had to be strong to survive. Tony was one of the strong ones. He never gave up. He was an inspiration to all of us there in Cuba.

"I would like to add that I owe a great debt to this country. When I needed refuge I found it here. I am here to pay part of that debt. I'm here today because I believe that justice must be done and it would not be just if Mr. Bryant was not given the chance to show who he is now." Cuesta took a deep breath. "When I first met Tony, I could not feel any sympathy for anyone who had violated the laws of this great nation..."

The judge seeing that Cuesta had long wind and was about to take the whole court on a journey, stopped him. "Mr. Cuesta, try to be a little more brief!"

"Uhm! Well, Your Honor, after seeing how Mr. Bryant carried himself over the years, not only myself, but all of the political prisoners learned to love Tony. I remember one day when he fought seven guards who had insulted the President of the U.S. and just let me add that he's a good man and justice would not be served if he were put behind bars again!"

The judge asked him if he owned his own home.

"No, Your Honor, I live in an apartment. I collect disability."

"Would you be willing to let Mr. Bryant stay with you in your home if he were released on bond?"

"In my home? It would be an honor."

"Mr. Cuesta, would you be willing to sign a bond for half a million dollars knowing that the courts would hold you personally responsible?"

"Your Honor, I would be willing to do more than that. I would give my freedom in this country if he fails to comply with the court's order. If he flees, I will go to jail for him!"

A rustle of excitement swept the courtroom audience.

385

"Mr. Cuesta, you understand that if he should fail to appear that you would be liable for $500,000. You understand that?"

"Yes, Your Honor."

"And you're willing to sign?"

"Yes, Your Honor!"

"Thank you, Mr. Cuesta. You may be seated."

I felt a great pride for this man who had shown everyone what the word 'friend' really meant. He was placing his reputation and freedom on the line simply because he believed in me. There was no talk of color or thought of what was in it for him, only his belief that I was worthy of his trust and faith. The judge had to be impressed. Not many blood relatives would offer to do what he just had.

"Your Honor, I have another witness," said Larry. "Mr. Jose Manuel Perez. He also knew the defendant while in Cuba."

Jose Manuel strode up and gave me a bear hug.

"Mr. Perez, where did you meet Mr. Bryant?" asked the judge.

"I met him in Cuba in the prison Combinado del Este."

"When was that?"

"In 1977. I was working as a medic for the American prisoners."

"What is your impression of Mr. Bryant? What was he like in jail?"

"Tony Bryant is a wonderful person. What called my attention to him was the dignified, clean, honest way he carried himself while in prison. He was admired by everyone. I believe that he is a different person than when he went to jail!"

"Would you be willing to sign the bond if Mr. Bryant were released?"

"It would be a pleasure and I too would go to jail for him if necessary!"

"Do you have a home or an apartment?"

"I rent a house, Your Honor."

"Would you be willing to let Mr. Bryant live with you?"

"Yes, I would, Your Honor."

By now, Wes Currier was sitting on the edge of his seat.

Larry made a brief summation and pointed out that he'd been in touch with Marilyn Barnes, the United States Attorney in New York, and that they had agreed to a change of venue with the possibility of me entering a guilty plea. Since I did have friends in Miami who were willing to back me with a place to stay, Larry asked again that the bond be changed and that I be allowed to go out on my own recognizance.

Judge Sorrentino sat locked in thought for a while. When she spoke her voice was soft. I strained to hear her next words. "Mr. Bryant, I'm hereby ordering that the surety bond be changed to a personal one." She paused for a moment. "I'm going to place you on bail on your own recognizance. Mr. Cuesta and Mr. Perez will be required to co-sign and I must warn them that should you not comply with the court's orders, they will be charged with contempt of court and face a jail term. Is that understood?" She drew herself up and her voice turned cold. "Mr. Bryant, if you disappoint this court..."

I was stunned... The impossible had happened! Reporters scratched out hasty notes.

Wes Currier sat straight up in his chair. He stood and informed the judge that the government would appeal her decision. Since Judge Sorrentino was appointed to her seat by federal judges, the United States Attorney could ask for a decision on her ruling before a judge appointed by the President of the United States.

Judge Sorrentino shot the Assistant Attorney a sharp look. Then she turned back to me. When she spoke, her voice was soft again. "Mr. Bryant, I'm going to sign the order for your release. The Assistant Attorney has stated that he will appeal my decision so I'm giving him until four o'clock this afternoon to submit that appeal. If he doesn't have a ruling by then, you'll walk out a free man!" Again a quick smile that seemed to say, "I trust you," skipped across her face. "Good luck, Mr. Bryant!"

I could hardly speak. I managed to choke out, "Thank you! Thank you so much!"

Larry Rosen, a little shocked himself, stammered, "Th... thank you, Your Honor!" He turned to me and whispered, "This is incredible, Tony. Fantastic! We'll still have to wait and see what Wes Currier's going to do. I know he's going to appeal but if he doesn't do it by four ... you're home free. Listen, I'll tell Cuesta to wait and maybe you can leave with him. Here's hoping!"

I didn't know it then, but Larry had just graduated from law school, and he was as nervous and excited about the way things were going as I. In Wes Currier, he was up against a polished and dangerous adversary who was an old hand at putting people away. The dice had been thrown. Fate would decide who would win this battle.

I was escorted to a medium-sized cell where other federal defendants were pacing. I began pacing too and hoping.

MacDonald's Cheeseburgers, french fries and cokes came for lunch, and although my nerves were stretched to the snapping point, I had dreamed too many times, while on hunger strikes in Cuba, about this very meal. I forced myself to sit and savor one of my dreams come true.

When the other prisoners learned of my situation, I had an immediate fan club. Everybody pulled for me. It was as though I represented their hopes to beat the system. I only wanted freedom.

As the minutes turned into hours and four o'clock drew near, everyone began keeping tabs on the time. I couldn't keep my eyes from straying to the clock every minute or so. I didn't want to spend the rest of my life in some cold, sterile cell. Only if you have waited at the portals of life or death can you understand the agony of those slow-moving minutes.

Ten minutes to four! Countdown: Nine minutes... eight... seven... six... five... four!

Everybody was smiling. They crowded around slapping me on my back and congratulating me. Then a U.S. marshal walked up to the cell and said, "The United States Attorney has filed an appeal, Mr. Bryant. I'm afraid you'll have to go back with us!"

At four minutes to four I was made to understand that I would have to defeat the powerful United States Attorney just for the opportunity to combat the enemy.

That night, in the cell, I said to Flip, "I'm still leaving. If I had walked out today, the victory would have been too easy. There wouldn't have been any drama. Everything's going like it's supposed to. Now it's become a story right out of Hollywood. You'll see! I'm walking out of here Monday. I told my lawyer the same thing. You watch me!"

The Miami Herald was keeping abreast of the unusual activity being generated around the black ex-hijacker who claimed to have been a Black Panther. There was full coverage of the bond hearing and of the dramatic statements made by Tony Cuesta and his guide, Jose M. Perez. A story was in the making.

Here was an anti-Castro freedom fighter defending an ex-militant advocate of the violent overthrow of the government of the United States and its system. On top of that, one was black and the other white. And they were both named Tony. No matter what happened, a beautiful example had been set by Cuesta's trusting gesture.

Saturday afternoon my young lawyer came to see me. He seemed pleased but very reserved about the outcome. "Look, Tony, I found out that Monday you'll be going before a federal judge named Eugene P. Spellman. I hear he's the best there is, I can tell you that if I had to go before anybody I'd want it to be him. He's tough but understanding and the man is brave!" Larry gave a short laugh, "I mean, if he wants to let you go, he'll do it just like that!" He snapped his fingers. "But you've got to make him believe you and believe in you. Don't worry about Wes Currier. You just concentrate on trying to convince the judge that you've changed."

I tried to memorize all the things I wanted to say that night. It was better than counting sheep.

Monday, the 3rd of November, I was snatched awake by the alarm clock that I'd bought the day before at the prisoner PX. It was 5:30 a.m. I turned it off and lay there thinking about the events to come. This would be one of the most important days of my life. There could be no mistakes, not even a negative thought, if I were to have a chance against the power wielded by the United States attorney.

My indictment read, "The United States of America against Anthony Garnet Bryant," and Wes Currier was carrying out the will of some 230,000,000 Americans who made up the United States of America. At least that's the way Wes Currier probably saw it.

I only knew one thing...

Myths were made to be destroyed!

35.
EUGENE P. SPELLMAN

My handcuffs were removed and I was ushered into a large, solemn courtroom. It was blanketed by a heavy silence. This was the realm of the Honorable Eugene P. Spellman. The room demanded respect as did the man who presided over it. The long rows of high-backed oak benches resembled church pews.

The place where Judge Spellman sat, a little elevated above the rest of the room, inspired dread. The U.S. marshal and everyone who entered spoke in whispers.

I sat down in the front row, unnerved. I couldn't take my eyes from Judge Spellman's seat. In that tiny spot in time and space lay my destiny.

Larry Rosen walked in followed by Tony Cuesta and Jose Manuel. I gave Jose Manuel a quick wave, then went into a huddle with Larry.

"Tony, today is the day. You have to go out there swinging! Wes Currier's going to be tough but all you've got to do is be truthful and act like you have up 'til now. This is your chance!"

Across the way, on the other side of the courtroom, poised like a cobra, stood Currier, glacial and distant.

The courtroom door opened again and who should walk in but my friend, Ed King. He threw me a clasped-hand wave.

"Who's he?" whispered Larry.

"He's a buddy of mine who was in Cuba with me. We once spent seventeen days in the Hole together."

"Would he be a character witness for you?"

"I think so," I answered. "Sure. He'll testify for me!"

Larry slipped over and talked with Ed who gave a strong affirmative nod. The plot was thickening!

Newspaper reporters began drifting in. After things settled down, the bailiff stood and intoned, "Will everyone please rise?"

A business-like man, bristling with energy, entered through a side door and walked to his seat.

"The Honorable United States District Judge Eugene P. Spellman. Court is in session. Please be seated!"

"Okay, Tony, this is it!" whispered Larry. "There's the man who can set you free. Don't get rattled and above all be truthful!"

I studied the composed man in black who sat peering intently at everyone and everything around him. My name was called; and Judge Spellman's eyes swept over me like searchlights, probing and astute.

There was no doubt in my mind that seated before me was a highly intelligent person. There could be no tricks, no games. I looked at the judge head-on. I tried to see into the mind of the man who held my destiny in his hands. It was strange. The first feeling I received: We like each other. It was so fleeting and brief that I wasn't sure if it was my imagination or not.

The judge had a strong yet compassionate voice. "This court is here today to rule on Judge Sorrentino's decision which was appealed by the U.S. Attorney." He studied a sheaf of papers spread out before him. "I would like to hear both points of view concerning the matter. Now... who would like to start first? You, Mr. Rosen?"

Larry leaned close to the mike and in a quiet earnest voice explained to Judge Spellman the reason why Judge Sorrentino had changed my bond to a personal one. He underlined that three people in the courtroom were prepared to testify to my character.

"And, Your Honor, there is no reason why my client can't be afforded all the benefits of bail. The law states that the only persons not eligible for bail are those accused of a capital crime.

I humbly submit that Mr. Bryant is not to be tried for a capital offense! I have talked to the defendant many times, Your Honor," he continued. "I believe he's telling the truth. He has changed and all he wants is the opportunity to prove it."

Wes Currier stood and with the trace of a smile addressed the court. He was eloquent and his almost casual condemnations hit harder than if he had shouted. He cited my FBI rap sheet. It was three pages long. As far as he was concerned, there was no doubt that I should be behind bars and he meant to put me there.

"This man is dangerous, Your Honor. He's a convicted armed robber. He's been involved with drugs, and to top all that, this man hijacked an airliner and robbed the passengers. I can sympathize with the fact that he spent nearly twelve years in Cuban prisons, but — the truth of the matter is that he must still stand trial for those crimes!"

Pacing slowly back and forth, Currier pressed his attack. He classified hijacking as one step from a capital offense. "There is no way, under any conditions, that the defendant should be released on bond!"

Some of the things he had said were true. I had been an armed robber. I had become involved with narcotics. I had been all of the things Currier had accused me of being. But Currier was nearsighted. He couldn't see beyond the cold glacial exterior that separated him from the rest of the world. He wore a cloak of superiority which did not allow him to feel or perceive any use for justice except for the edge of her sword.

As I listened to him speak, I wondered what fears he harbored that made him so cold, so determined to punish.

When he sat down, the judge glanced over the stack of papers on his desk, then swung his gaze to me. His eyes were piercing.

"Mr. Bryant, there have been few times that I've seen a record as bad as yours. Why do you think that this court should allow you to go out on bond?"

I struggled to collect my thoughts. It was now or never.

"Your Honor," I said, "in twelve years we have traveled hundreds of millions of miles through space. Everything around us has changed. The man standing before you has too. There is not one molecule, not one cell in my body that has remained the same!"

I tried to organize my jumbled thoughts as I gazed into the judge's eyes.

"I am a different man and all I ask of the court is to permit me to prove it. I haven't returned to the United States asking for pity because I spent twelve years in prison. I don't want pity. I want the opportunity to prove I've transformed. I have a message to give, and if I have to deliver it from inside a prison, then I'll do it. I have placed Tony Bryant's welfare on a secondary level. I can't think about Tony Bryant per se; that's why I returned. If Your Honor will give me the chance, I promise that I will not defraud the court. I'll keep my word. It's all I've got!"

Larry took over and called Tony Cuesta to the stand. He again testified to my character, reasoning for the judge that I was a credit to my country. In closing Tony said: "I am here precisely because I am convinced that justice in this great country is based on the regeneration of a man, not on his destruction!" In a voice ringing with sincerity, he continued, " Those twelve years in prison have made Tony a U.S. citizen worthy of the opportunity to prove he's changed. I believe in him. That's why I've come here today!"

Wes Currier stood. "Mr. Cuesta, you stated that you are willing to sign a half-million bond for this man. Is that correct?"

"Yes, that is correct."

"What kind of security do you have? Do you have a bank account?"

"I have no bank account. I receive government assistance."

"Your Honor, I respectfully submit that this witness has no way of responding to the bond. He's on welfare and has no assets!"

He whirled on Cuesta and in a derisive tone snickered, "How would you pay the court — if your friend ran away? You have, by your own admission, no money!"

Cuesta straightened to his full height and in a hard tone rebutted the Assistant Attorney with the same answer he'd given before. "What I offer is worth more than money. I offer my own freedom in this country to guarantee that Mr. Bryant will face his responsibilities. If he does not — then I will go to jail for him!"

Wes Currier's mouth dropped open. His line of questioning had backfired. He looked as if the world had gone mad. "No further questions," he snapped and sat down.

"Mr. Cuesta," queried the judge, "do you realize that if this court were to release the defendant into your custody and he did not comply with the court's orders that you could be cited for contempt of court and sentenced to jail? And the court would do so."

"Yes, Your Honor!"

"Do you understand that a lien could be placed against you and everything that you own, perhaps for the rest of your life?"

"Yes, I understand, Your Honor!"

The gauntlet had been tossed.

The judge studied the man standing in front of him for a moment, then in a voice soft and respectful said, "Thank you, Mr. Cuesta. You may be seated now."

Larry called Jose Manuel who reaffirmed his desire to sign the bond and if necessary keep me in his house.

Wes Currier fought back tooth and nail. "You don't have any money! You have no assets with which to respond to a half-million dollar bond. Your Honor, these people, as generous as they are, do not possess even the minimum requirements to substantiate the release of this defendant into their custody. I have nothing more to say. The facts speak for themselves!"

Jose Manuel returned to his seat.

The judge was about to speak when Larry said, "Your Honor, I have one more witness for Mr. Bryant."

Judge Spellman nodded and leaned back in his padded chair.

Edward King was sworn in.

"Mr. King," Larry said, "how did you find out about Mr. Bryant's hearing?"

"I heard it over the news."

"So no one asked you to come. You came to offer testimony for the defendant on your own. Is that right?" questioned Larry.

"Yes, sir. I decided to come and see what I could do for him."

"Mr. King, from where do you know the defendant?"

"I met Tony Bryant in the prison Combinado del Este."

"Will you tell the court what impression you have of him?"

"Tony and I lived side by side for a long time. He was always trying to help the rest of us. I know one thing. I believe he is one of the most patriotic Americans I have ever seen!"

"Would you be willing to sign the bond for Mr. Bryant's release?"

"Yes, sir, I would!"

Larry stepped back. "That's all, Your Honor!"

Wes Currier tried to dig into Ed's past activities.

"I'm an ex-fighter pilot. I fought in Vietnam!"

There was nothing left to say. Wes Currier sat down.

Judge Spellman sank back in his chair and gazed up at the ceiling. He twisted his chair slowly back and forth. The room was dead quiet. The reporters sat with pencils poised.

I tried to swallow and failed. It seemed that time had stopped. I waited and dripped sweat. For all of my life I had been a rebel. My childhood and home life had lacked the ingredients necessary to produce a sturdy character and instead I had been pulled from one extreme to the other by my bickering parents. I had sought to blame all of my failures on 'Whitey,' and now all of those who had come to my rescue were white.

I had once been willing to die for the revolution. Now I was ready to live for it. Not the false revolution of death and destruction, but rather for the only revolution that is real... the individual revolution of concepts and values.

At last I was ready to help others seeking to find the right path. How effective I could be depended on the man who slowly swiveled back and forth staring at the ceiling.

"Mr. Bryant...," the judge turned and fixed his eyes on me.

I pulled myself up straight. I remember thinking I had to stand tall, no matter what the decision. I had been so certain I would be released, but now in the moment where my life was at stake, I lost faith. The room seemed dimmed by a heavy, dark cloud.

"Mr. Bryant, this court is going to uphold Judge Sorrentino's decision! This court is going to give you the opportunity you've asked for!"

Few times in life does a person stumble across pure unadulterated joy. I felt like turning a backflip and running all around the courtroom. I could feel tears burning my eyes. If I hadn't thought that it might be considered a lack of respect, I would have shouted at the top of my lungs.

"You will be released on your own recognizance. However, if you deceive this court...," Judge Spellman's eyes turned hard. "If you deceive this court, you'll wish you'd never seen me!"

These were the conditions of my release: I had to report to him every Monday at 9:30 a.m. along with my three co-signers, Cuesta, Perez and King; I had to report to U.S. Marshal Jim Simmons by telephone twice a week; and Judge Spellman wanted a day-by-day record of my activities kept and read to him each Monday. "All right, Mr. Bryant... You have your chance. Good luck!" The judge allowed a fleeting smile to cross his face as he stood and strode out of the courtroom to his chambers.

My three friends ran up, hugging me and beating my back to a pulp. I caught a glimpse of Wes Currier's face. It was mottled and red. The smile was gone.

36.
FREEDOM'S TASTE

I waited for a hand to grab my shoulder and point me in a direction; towards a door, a corridor, a jaula, a cell, the Hole... but the hand was missing. I paused for a command; silence. For the first time in many years I was master of my own body and could walk where I chose ...

My feet floated over the courtroom floor and down the wide cement stairs that sprawled onto the sidewalk's edge. I was holding Tony Cuesta's remaining hand. We were leading each other and shaking with excitement. Teams of television reporters were waiting for us. They crowded around peppering me with questions I'd waited so long to hear. "Mr. Bryant, tell us how you feel. How does it feel to be free after twelve years in jail?"

How could I possibly answer? I was effervescent. Words had lost all meaning. They could not describe the sensations that raced over my entire being. I threw my arms up and with a grin that must have stretched from ear to ear, shouted, "I can taste freedom. It's wonderful!"

A story was in full bloom. The press would certainly follow my activities very closely. A battle was in progress. There was still a war to be won... or lost.

The United States Attorney had opposed me from the outset and had suffered a defeat but he would surely try to bury me. Could I find some way to overcome the expert Assistant Attorney, or would Wes Currier send me back to prison? For the moment

I pushed the thought aside. I was too happy to let anything sour this day. I was ecstatic.

"We did it, Tony! We did it!" Ed King was jumping up and down. "I told you back there in Combinado that I saw you coming down a long flight of stairs laughing. Remember? Remember?"

"This is a great day for Democracy!" Cuesta crowed, slapping me on my back. "We've scored a victory over the enemy. You can bet the Communists don't like it. Now it's a matter of history that blacks and whites can unite as one in a common struggle for a common cause. We've got the enemy on the run, and I've got me a $500,000 chauffeur!"

We had lunch together. Sounds simple, but it was the first meal I'd shared with close friends of a dozen years that wasn't supervised by guards. Then the small group that had united to save a friend in distress disbanded in freedom. Ed gave me a final hug and headed for his car, able to drive wherever he wanted. Jose Manuel drove us to Cuesta's house in Hialeah, promised to keep in touch and left.

My first day of liberty is nothing more than a collage of sounds and images that will forever sweep through my memory. My first month was fast and furious.

I had come out swinging. During my first weeks out of jail, I had not even taken time to talk to a woman... not on an intimate level. Then, on Sunday, December 30, 1980, I met Janie...

I had gone to talk with a reverend about speaking in his church. While waiting for him to emerge from his office, I saw a lovely woman standing in the church dining room. I struck up a conversation and the next night when I took her out to dinner, she gave me my first *in the United States kiss*... on the cheek.

We started seeing each other. She was always there when I needed someone. Our relationship was deep, but never demanding. It was one of the nicest friendships I've ever known. Janie Lewis was wonderful and she promised to help at my trial.

I met many interesting people in that first fantastic month. One was a big, husky, tough-looking cop named Kemper.

400

Sergeant Kemper was an ex-Green Beret. He was now a member of the Hialeah, Florida Police Department. Ironically, we had missed meeting many years before.

"I was supposed to be on that plane you hijacked," Fred told me, "One of us is lucky 'cause at the time I wasn't born again!" He rubbed his chin and laughed. "God must have been working. If I hadn't missed that flight, one of us would be dead because I'd have jumped you!"

I made another interesting friendship. Jim Hayes was an ex-FBI agent who for twenty years had fought against crime. He had soft blue eyes and a kindly smile that didn't quite fit the pattern of *the heartless pig*. He had a lovely wife, Nancy, who was as sweet as honey. This loyal paladin of the law befriended me and declared his alliance in the fight to win my freedom for me.

If my first month out was something, my second thirty days of freedom clearly showed Wes Currier and the world that I was there to fight and if possible... win!

A funny thing happened to me on my first flight since returning home to the U.S. Judge Spellman had given me permission to travel to California to visit my relatives. It happened that John Dorschner, a writer for *The Miami Herald's Tropic Magazine*, was finishing up a story about me. He decided it would be an excellent time to get some photos for the magazine's cover. Since taking pictures inside a plane by newsmen required special permission, John had to inform the airlines of the nature of the story and who the personality was that would be gracing their plane.

It took me a while to figure out why every time I got up to go to the bathroom, four or five big, beefy guys had the urge to go too. They had hard looking faces and some kind of hearing impairment. Every one of them wore a little hearing aid-type earpiece with a wire running down into his jacket. It was really funny. These guardians tripped over my heels going and coming!

I landed at Los Angeles International Airport around 9:00 p.m. The air was crisp and fresh as mint, the sky plastered with stars.

I called my brother and he met me thirty minutes later at the

Greyhound Bus Station. We spent the night at his place and the next day my Uncle Ed drove me to San Bernardino.

The day was ideal. San Bernardino had changed completely since I'd last seen it. But there was something that enveloped me. It was something that is found only in the land of one's birth. Something that says, "You're home." California and freedom is a heady mix. I was drunk on joy.

The outskirts of San Bernadino were different and yet the same. Descendants of wild, prickly weeds which had plagued me as a boy still reigned king. They covered the ground where old Mill School used to stand. Given time they will someday cover me.

Uncle Ed's car eased into my mom's driveway and pulled around in back of the house. She came to the door and stood there looking at me. Then, with a sharp cry, ran sobbing into my arms. "Oh, my son! My son! Oh, God, thank you for letting me see my child again."

We stood there and cried and kissed and cried. It was good to be home.

Still clinging, we entered the simple house that my mom had helped build with her own hands. The same familiar smells were there, soft and full of memories. The old piano, loaded down with pictures of the family looked just the same. It was there where my sister Rommel had practiced her lessons. It was there too where mom would sit and drink a little wine 'for the stomach's sake', and sing hymns until her eyelids drooped. Everything was still and quiet. Nothing had changed.

Jim, my step-dad, came out of the bedroom, and throwing his arms around me chortled, "How're you doin', fella? Shucks, you ain't changed a bit. Looks like you just need a little fattening up, that's all!"

That was sufficient to set Mom in motion. "Boy, you ate anything?" And without waiting for an answer she scurried to the kitchen. "You just sit down. Mama's gonna fix you some biscuits an' brown gravy. You want some grits, child? Honey, we got turkeys, chickens, ducks and a whole bin of vegetables. We got to put some meat on them bones, boy. You skinnier than them worthless roosters out back!"

There was no saying no to the plate of steaming food put before me. I ate every bit. Nobody could cook like Mom.

"How's Dad?" I asked, between bites.

"Don't mention that nigga's name in this house. Old buzzard, I wish he'd drop dead!"

No, nothing had changed. They were still battling.

Despite my mother's warning that Dad would get me in the house and set me up so that someway I'd be sent to jail, I went to see him. I knew my mom could no longer rationalize when it came to him. They despised each other.

Reporters were waiting when I arrived at the home of my father. I gave them a brief interview, mainly to please my dad. But in spite of the temporary interruption, it was great seeing people whom I loved; and I finally realized I loved my father.

Cousin Loise heard I was there and rushed over in time to be included in the newspaper photos. She was ecstatic. After we'd run ourselves down talking, she left, but promised to return shortly. She did, driving a new Lincoln Continental for me to use while I was in town. That was it. I hit the road!

First I drove back to Mom's, then followed her over to my youngest brother's home. I was shocked! Terron, the little kid I'd last seen years ago, was now a good-looking, husky man taller than I. We called the rest of the family over and partied. Did we party!

The time passed too quickly but it will not be lost. Until those San Bernardino weeds cover me I'll remember the sight of Mom standing on the front lawn, fighting back tears and staring at the ground as I left.

Cousin Loise drove me back to the airport in Los Angeles. A quick hug and I went running down the corridor just in time to catch the flight back to Miami... back to the battle!

I began gaining greater access to the media and on every occasion talked about the disturbing things I had noticed in the attitudes of Americans in general and blacks in particular.

During an interview with Ben Kinchlow on the *700 Club* over the *CBN Christian Broadcasting Network*, I explained to millions of Americans, "When you live with someone and see them every day you don't notice if they are getting old, or fat or thin. But when you leave and you come back after, say a year or two, then you notice the changes very easily. Well, I was away from home for twelve years and I've come back and I see the terrible changes that have taken place in the United States."

The defeatest attitude of black America was disheartening and struck me first. One of the earth's greatest peoples had been reduced to the level of accepting charity. Black America had been given and had accepted a welfare mentality. Time and time again I warned, "The uniting factor that cheap politicians use is welfare programs. Those who mislead the people are traitors. They lie and trick the people insinuating that it's *Whitey* and *The System* that's to blame for everything negative that happens in black lives." I pointed out that black on black crime was reaching astronomical levels. Black America was destroying itself!

My voice was ignored when I warned of Communist takeovers in community leadership roles. I cautioned, "If your pastor or civic leader tells you 'We've got to change the system,' just ask them, 'What system are we going to put in its place?' And if they imply a Socialist or Communist state, get away from them. They intend to lead you to destruction!"

The black Miamian was ripe for Communist infiltration. I found myself fighting two battles at the same time—to keep my freedom and awaken my people.

I was told that to use the name Ronald Reagan in the black community was like waving a red flag in front of a bull! I thought it was pathetic. "Reagan is a great President," I said, " but we have been so crippled by liberals, leftist and welfare programs that when he tells black people to get up and walk, they don't believe they can. There is a hue and cry for the return of their crutches.

"As far as I am concerned, the President had paid us a compliment when he slashed welfare programs to the bone. He was telling us, Black Americans, 'I believe *you* can do it! I believe that you are as intelligent as anyone else. All you have to do is assert yourselves.' The one thing we haven't learned to do is to stick together and really help one another!"

My messages were firmly rejected. The blacks seemed to be the only ethnic group against itself. Shamefully, we are the most uneducated and consequently the poorest.

During this period I met 'Sunny' Seidler, mother of my white cellmate 'Zip', the lady who had organized the Ad Hoc Committee.

Sunny now returned to me a copy of a letter I had written to the American Congressional Black Caucus and which she had courageously smuggled out of Cuba after visiting her son.

I held it now in the safety of America. It was a sad message from black American prisoners in Cuba to black American power wielders; sad because with all the terrible risks we had taken, blacks and white lady courier too, the letter had gone unanswered. There had been no reply or offer of help from America's black leaders.

I'll give this letter to my son someday as a reminder that all of his enemies are not white:

June 20, 1980

Gentlemen Of The U.S. Congressional Black Caucus:

The letter that you are about to read has been sent clandestinely with a great amount of danger for the persons involved in its writing as well as for those who have made its arrival to you possible.

Only a dire necessity could have impulsed us to take such extreme measures. We hope that you will take into consideration not only the fact that we — the letters authors — are black North Americans who have suffered brutally during the eight to twelve years of our imprisonment, we wish for you to consider not only the hapless situation in which we find ourselves, but perhaps above all, we hope to impress upon you the terrible fact of our existence in a living hell where the 'Human Condition' is nothing more than a play of words whose context is lost in the misery of the reality in which we are forced to live.

No other prisoners have been subjected to that which has been the black North American's plight. No others have been so savagely tortured, starved, beaten and abused as we have; in the vain effort to divest us of our dignity and break our spirits, but we have maintained an attitude which history will record as "admirable."

We received the news that you, the members of the Black Caucus are planning to visit Cuba within a short time. This notice has been received by us with great joy and the hope that during that visit you will ask the Cuban Government to accord you an interview with us.

Only then, when you witness with your own eyes, the abject conditions in which we live, when you can look and see for yourselves the scars that mark our bodies and souls, only when we can talk to you face to face and let the truth be known, only then do we believe that you will make an adamant demand for our expulsion. According to universal precepts, any country may ask for its citizen's expulsion when it is apparent that his trial was a mockery or when mistreatment and/or abuse can be proven.

We know that if you accord us an interview, you will leave here convinced that all that we would have time to tell you; although superficial, would leave you horror stricken and duty bound, as fellow Americans and as human beings, to struggle for us and our freedom from this, one of the most racist and cruel dictatorships that history has known.

We beg of you to attend us and to seek by any and all measures to obtain a visit with us. We doubt highly that they will allow you to see us. We don't believe that they have the valor to allow us to speak to you and unmask them as the sub-beings that they are.

We will anxiously await your arrival to this country and con-
sequently your visit to the prison 'Combinado Del Este'
Thanking you beforehand,
We Remain,
Anthony Garnet Bryant
Lewis Douglas Moore

The total lack of reaction to the letter simply reinforced what
I had come to believe: communists, power seekers and racists were
hard at work using divisionary tactics to polarize ethnic groups
across America and particularly in Miami. The latest cry was that
Cubans were taking away all the *black jobs*.

I tried, through radio and TV, to put things in their proper
perspective. I said, "The one who is causing black unemployment
here in Miami is not the man or woman who has been forced
to flee from Cuba! They're human beings. They want to live just
as you do. The one who is guilty of helping create black unemployment here is Fidel Castro and Communism! If there were no Communists, no Fidel Castro in Cuba, these people would not be here.
They've fled for their lives and come to America for asylum. They
have to work. Naturally, they are going to take jobs, but if you
want your jobs back again, then help overthrow Fidel's dictatorship and these aliens will leave and you'll have your jobs again!"

I was rebuffed by the black community. Blaming the Cuban
refugees was a lot easier.

It was frightening! The black giant was teetering on the brink
of an abyss. The result of the Communist effort in the black community was horrible. Girls — black babies, ten, eleven years old,
were already seasoned prostitutes. Along Miami's 79th Street and
Northwest 7th Avenue, hordes of black women exposed themselves
to passing motorists, selling their bodies to the first taker.

Our young black men were being destroyed by drugs and crime.
The precious black home had disintegrated. The *thing*, or style,
was to look as dirty and mean as possible. To be courteous was
a sign of weakness. Black women had no respect for black men

because they had none for themselves. The black community was being destroyed.

The Communist plot was so apparent I couldn't understand why others couldn't see it. Capture black America, if possible, and if not, destroy it!

I tried to cry out the warning, but found myself alone. Since my message was not 'Down with Whitey!' or 'Burn, baby, burn', because my message was, 'We can do it ourselves!' and 'Black-Latin collaboration!' I was given the cold shoulder by black leaders and in many instances, by the black people.

The social fabric of white America was putrid also. The change that had taken place in a dozen years left me thunderstruck. The *Beast* was on the rampage! Pornography was corroding and distorting all sense of decency and respect for the human body. Herpes was at epidemic levels and *Gay Liberation* marched neck and neck with so-called *Women's Liberation*. A new disease from which there was no escape was rearing its ugly head: AIDS. White America was sick. Its music reflected a rejection of role model and mannerisms, a rejection of identifiable sex. It beat out tunes reeking with sexual innuendo and double entendre. There was a need for me; I had to stay out of prison!

I started fighting harder than ever. It looked like a long, tough battle ahead. In spite of all the blank walls of silence that I ran up against, the truth of it is: I was enjoying the uneven struggle! For this was America.

Home life, most of the time, was orderly and calm. I was usually the first to get up. A steaming pot of Cuban coffee to open our eyes and over breakfast Tony and I would map out the day's plan.

After a long day of lectures and interviews, we would head home for the kitchen where my tall friend would demonstrate his culinary expertise. He'd tell me what to put in a certain dish. The only problem we had was that they could rarely be repeated. Cuesta changed, by design or bad memory, the mixture of the dish each time. But as exotic as the food tasted, it was always good: maybe because it was shared by brothers.

Wes Currier was also on the move. He sent out flyers all over the U.S. to see if I had any outstanding warrants on me: I didn't. There could be no parole violation either; my parole had expired. The Assistant U.S. Attorney would get no outside help. The battle between us would be fought in the confines of Judge Spellman's courtroom. There would be no quarter asked... and none given!

Every Monday morning, Cuesta, Perez, King and I were in court to salute the judge and inform him of my progress. Judge Spellman seemed to be becoming more impressed with us each passing week. We were on a blitzkrieg. My life hung in the balance!

It was around this time that I gained another ally. It happened during the airing of the *Marvin Dunn Talk Show* from Miami. Following a question and answer period between Dr. Dunn and me, the telephone lines were opened and I found myself talking to a man who identified himself as the Reverend Clennon King. By his articulate expressions I could tell that I was talking with an extremely intelligent person. Before the conversation ended, I had the reverend's telephone number and address. I wanted to meet this black man who spoke with an Oxford accent.

I gathered, from our short conversation, that because Reverend King's message too was one of self-help and less government control, he was not liked by his constituents. I heard later that he had made headlines when he tried to integrate President Jimmy Carter's all-white church.

I liked the reverend. He was a fighter!

January was not particularly exciting but like a good boxer, I kept slugging away... rolling up points.

And then the indictment arrived from New York.

37.
BEGINNING OF THE END

The indictment arrived on the 20th of January, 1980.

UNITED STATES DISTRICT COURT

EASTERN DISTRICT OF NEW YORK

—–—–—–—––- X

I N D I C T M E N T UNITED STATES OF AMERICA :
Criminal No. *__69CR__99*
-against- : Title 49, U.S.C., 1472(i)
(1) (2) (j) and 1472 (e) GARNET ANTHONY BRYANT : (i)
(k) (1) (2); Title 18,
661 and 113 (b)
Defendant :
—–—–—–—––- X

THE GRAND JURY CHARGES:

COUNT ONE

On or about the 5th day of March 1969, at John F. Kennedy International Airport, Queens County, within the Eastern district of New York, the defendant GARNET ANTHONY BRYANT boarded an aircraft owned and operated by National Airlines, Inc., a domestic carrier, scheduled for a flight from New York to Miami,

Florida, known as National Airlines Flight No. 97, and after the aircraft was in flight, in air commerce, and en route to Miami, Florida, carrying the defendant GARNET ANTHONY BRYANT and other passengers, the said defendant GARNET ANTHONY BRYANT did seize and control the flight with wrongful intent, by threatening with violence and intimidating the crew consisting of a pilot, co-pilot and stewardess of the aforesaid aircraft, at gun point, and by threat of force and violence and at gun point, directed the pilot to fly to Havana, Cuba, and interfered with the performance by said pilot, co-pilot and stewardess of their duties and lessened their ability to perform their respective duties, and the defendant GARNET ANTHONY BRYANT, in the commission of the act of aircraft piracy as aforesaid, used a deadly and dangerous weapon, namely: a loaded revolver.

(Title 49, United States Code, 1472 (i) (1) (2) (j).)

COUNT TWO

On or about the 5th day of March 1969, at John F. Kennedy International Airport, Queens County, within the Eastern District of New York, the defendant GARNET ANTHONY BRYANT boarded an aircraft owned and operated by National Airlines, Inc., a domestic carrier, scheduled for a flight from New York to Miami, Florida, known as National Airlines flight No. 97, and after the aircraft was in flight, in air commerce, and en route to Miami, Florida carrying the defendant GARNET ANTHONY BRYANT and other passengers, the said defendant, at gun point, perpetrated an act of robbery on three of the passengers of the aforesaid flight, from whom he took a total sum of Seventeen hundred and Fifty Five Dollars ($1,755.00), that in the commission of the act of robbery as aforesaid, the defendant GARNET ANTHONY BRYANT used a deadly and dangerous weapon, namely: a loaded revolver.

412

(Title 49, United States Code, 1472 (i) (l) (k) (1) (2) and Title 13, United States code, 661.)

COUNT THREE

On or about the 5th day of March 1969, at John F. Kennedy International Airport, Queens County, within the Eastern District of New York, the defendant GARNET ANTHONY BRYANT boarded an aircraft owned and operated by National Airlines, Inc., a domestic carrier, scheduled for a flight from New York to Miami, Florida, known as National Airlines flight No. 97, and after the aircraft was in flight, in air commerce, and en route to Miami, Florida, carrying the defendant GARNET ANTHONY BRYANT and other passengers, the said defendant assaulted three of the passengers on the aforesaid flight, at gun point, with the intent to commit the act of robbery, that in the commission of the said act of assault as aforesaid, the defendant GARNET ANTHONY BRYANT used a deadly and dangerous weapon, namely: a loaded revolver.

(Title 49, United States Code, 1472 (i) (1) (k) (1) (2) and Title 18, United States Code, 113 (b).)

A TRUE BILL.

VINCENT T. McCARTHY

UNITED STATES ATTORNEY

GEORGE T. SLATTERY, FOREMAN.

....

413

It looked bad. Nothing was mentioned in the indictments about the swarthy white passenger from whom I'd taken thousands of dollars and who was described by Cuban G-2 agents as a revolutionary agent of Havana; the man who had been forced into hiding from the Federal Bureau of Investigation, the man Captain Hernandez told me was part of a Cuban spy network in the United States. That man was the reason I'd been considered a CIA agent by Cuban intelligence and because of him I'd been forced to serve twelve years in Castro's prisons. The indictment did not say I had given passengers back their money when I found the treasure trove in the Cuban agent's briefcase. News reports I'd recently seen about the 1969 incident reported I'd given money back. But this wasn't mentioned in the indictment.

It looked really bad!

Judge Spellman informed me that the court was prepared to set a date for plea. Larry stood beside me listening closely to the instructions. Later we had a short but decisive talk.

"Tony," Larry said, "there's a decision that has to be made. You're charged with three crimes. You're sure you want to plead guilty to one of them?"

"Yep. I'm sure!"

"If you plead guilty to air piracy, it's a twenty-year minimum sentence. But, and I think I'm right, the judge can give you probation if he wants to; any offense without a life top or where no homicide has been committed is comprehended within that statute!" He raised a hand. "Don't think that I'm encouraging you to do that, because the possibility of your getting probation is almost nonexistent. But I'm letting you know what all your options are.

"I've already told you that if you plead guilty to one of the charges, the others will be dropped. Right? Of course, we'll discount the arms violation. I don't think the U.S. attorney would accept that as a very fair exchange. So that leaves the armed robbery of the passengers, which carries from one to any number of years. Plus — the hijacking.

"I want you to weigh the distinct possibilities very carefully. I think that the judge is favorably impressed with you and I know that he wants to do all he can for you. But, if you plead guilty to the hijack charge, the odds are not in your favor. In fact, Wes Currier has publicly stated the government would agree not to recommend a sentence, but it has reserved the right to appeal, and would do so, if the judge awarded you probation. See, that would take it out of Judge Spellman's hands and place you at the disposition of others who don't know you so well. So think about that!

"Now, let's say that you plead guilty to the charge of robbery. Here the judge can be extremely generous and sentence you to, say, a year, and maybe with good time, you'd be out in nine months. I don't think that Wes Currier would appeal any jail sentence. Well, what do you think?"

"Larry," I answered, "I'm not going to prison ever again. Not for a year, one month or even a day. That's all over! I'm going to plead guilty to the hijacking because it's the only charge that offers a chance for probation and freedom!"

"Listen, Tony," Larry insisted. "Do you understand what a twenty-year minimum sentence means? It means that if for any reason the judge can't give you probation, he would be forced by law to apply the twenty-year minimum. Are you sure you understand what I'm saying?"

"I understand and I've made up my mind. I'm destined to walk out of that court a free man. God is on my side. You'll see!"

The following week, I entered a guilty plea to hijacking.

Judge Spellman was firm and a cold glint of resolve flickered in his eyes. "Mr. Bryant, I'm quite sure that your counsel has fully informed you of all the ramifications of that plea, and if he hasn't, I'm going to make sure that you are aware of all of the possibilities. The U.S. attorney has openly stated that should this court hand down a sentence — and I'm not saying that this court is even contemplating such an idea, but should this court deem it proper to award you probation, then the U.S. attorney would indeed appeal the decision.

"Mr. Bryant, the law states that if I cannot give you probation, then I must impose a minimum sentence of twenty years, and I would do so. Understanding that, Mr. Bryant, do you still wish to maintain your plea of guilty to the charge of hijacking?"

I could almost feel the silence in the courtroom as everybody waited for my answer. "I maintain my plea of guilty to that charge, Your Honor!"

A date for sentencing was set.

Miami, and especially Miami's Cuban section, was buzzing with talk about the drama. Some of Cuesta's friends told him that he was crazy for taking a notorious criminal into his house and then dropped him. But for every one who discredited him, two came to his side showing their respect by bringing me new clothes or food and sometimes, the more affluent ones, like Jorge Mas Canosa or *Papo*, would drop by and leave some badly-needed cash. The majority of the exile community was with us.

Jim Hayes, the silvery-haired ex-agent, moved heaven and earth to help. He was a great ally and friend. The head of ALPHA 66, Nazario Sargen, promised and gave all his support to me. These were the kinds of people who were attaching themselves to the fight to win me my freedom.

Some of the members of Reverend Southwell's congregation like *Chicken George* were urging me to become a born-again Christian, but I felt that to do so might be construed as a trick on my part to sway the judge. Besides, I knew that God was with me and I wanted people to understand that it wasn't necessary to be a member of any organized religion or church to do Christian works or believe in God.

Toward the end of the month, I gave a lecture to a group of airline sales representatives and received a standing ovation. All in all, February was a good month packed with activity.

The few times that I saw Wes Currier, the assistant U.S. attorney had an odd look in his eyes.

March! The most enigmatic month of the year for me. It was my nemesis. March had always brought me down. Most of the major events in my life had occurred during the reign of Mars and now once again it was in the transcourse of March that my life would be forever affected. March 27th was the date set for my sentencing.

It was in March that I'd gone to Cuba. It was in March that I'd been returned, after my last escape from prison in Cuba, to spend more than a year in solitary. It was in March also that I had gone to prison for my first time. There were many minor events which occurred during that accursed month too, such as the fight I'd had with the guards at Principe for insulting Richard Nixon. I had never approached March without feeling a prickly sensation invade me and never had I faced a March that meant as much to me as this one.

A regulation sanity hearing was held and I was deemed able to understand the difference between right and wrong.

Never once did I even think of running away. All I had left, after passing through the Communist cataclysm, was my word and no matter the consequences I would not break it. Had I been out on a paid bail, I might have considered absconding, but now there were unbreakable chains of trust, faith and friendship that bonded me to my destiny.

If I said that I did not feel apprehension and fear, I would be lying. I was living under tremendous stress. I lost my appetite. My stomach was jittery and nervous most of the time. There were occasions when I'd be walking along and suddenly my legs would go weak. Yes, I was unsure, nervous and afraid. Life and all that makes it so beautiful lay in the balance of justice.

The taste of air that has not blown around rusted bars, the feel of grass and earth instead of concrete beneath my feet, the touch of a woman, her fragrant body, to see all of a star-crusted sky and not just a square patch criss-crossed by bars; Beautiful things were out there in the free world and I was in danger of losing them. Of course I was afraid!

The judge informed me that I didn't have to bring in a weekly report anymore. There was no need. The cards had been played.

March brought something else too that I hadn't counted on. I leaned over the side of my bed and picked up the receiver to the ringing telephone. "Hello."

"Hello, Daddy. This is your son, Anthony!"

It was impossible for me to answer. All the years of wondering, of imagining, now resolved themselves in a voice that said, "Hello, Daddy!" Many times in Cuba, I had sat in the darkness of dismal isolation, mental and or physical, and tried to imagine how my son was, how he looked and sounded. My voice sounded strange in my ears when I answered, "I can't believe it! My son!" Then came a deluge of questions and answers. He was twenty-one. He'd gotten married and was trying to make a go of it.

His wife's name was Gladys. She was Puerto Rican. My daughter-in-law and I chatted for a while in Spanish, and then my son came back on and I asked him the question that had haunted me for so many years. "How's your mother? Has she remarried?"

"Oh, she's fine. No. She hasn't ever remarried!"

After we hung up, I sat thinking about the woman I had loved and lost. I hadn't known how to demonstrate my love. I thought it was weakness to show affection. Now after years of separation I was going to hear her voice. My son had told me that she was going to call. I sat there wondering what I would say. The phone rang again.

"Hello... hello, Garnet. This is Eunice!"

The same soft voice. How could the past come garbed so sweetly and bring so much remorse?

I tried to say, "I'm sorry," without the words. There was no way to do it. While we talked, memories of those bitter-sweet years plagued me. The night we eloped. The funny-looking little house where we had lived and gone hungry together. The tears and hurt looks in her eyes each time I left her or did something wrong. Her voice brought it all back.

Eunice told me that she would fly down for the sentencing. I was euphoric.

Although tension-filled, the days that passed were beautiful. Then on March 20th Larry called me.

"Hey, Tony," he sounded excited. "I don't want you to get too optimistic now, but I've got some good news for you!" He paused for a long moment. "The U.S. attorney has informed the judge that he won't appeal whatever sentence the court hands down! Isn't that great?"

Great! It was more than that. I could have shouted for joy. My chances for a victory had just shot sky high.

Eunice called me the next day and told me that she would be in Miami for sure for the sentencing. I felt happy and blue at the same time. I didn't tell her, but my horoscope said that an old love would return briefly to my life, then disappear forever.

Eunice arrived two days before the date set for sentence. As usual the airport was abustle with incoming and outgoing passengers. When she walked down the long corridor into the waiting area, I was struck numb. She was beautiful! The skinny girl I'd left behind had blossomed into a smooth, cultured woman who attracted attention at every step. She gave a soft cry and ran into my arms. The hours passed and soon that was all that separated me from my destiny... a few hours.

The morning of the 27th of March broke a little hazy. The hesitant chirping of early-rising birds, welcoming another day, filtered into the apartment as I stumbled around the kitchen making coffee. There was no need to wake anyone. None of us had slept too soundly. We ate a subdued breakfast, then took the elevator downstairs.

The ride to the courthouse was a silent one. Eddy Bello drove. Cuesta sat chewing stubbornly on his pipe and in the back seat, Eunice held my hand, giving it an encouraging squeeze from time to time. Would I return this way again?

A hundred thoughts crowded my mind. It all seemed like a dream!

We pulled up to the toll gate. The dime's tinkle as it struck the metal basket marked the point of no return. We were only a couple of miles from the courthouse. Even if I wanted to, it was too late to run now.

TV cameras whirred as we made our way past banner-waving members of ALPHA 66 and into the courthouse. After going through the metal detector, we crowded into the elevator along with others whose faces were as serious as mine.

Larry Rosen greeted us solemnly, then we had a last minute conversation.

"How do you feel?" he asked.

"I'm okay, I guess." I could hardly talk.

"Is there anyone else here who might speak on your behalf?" His eyes wandered over the rapidly-filling room.

"Well, there's Eddy Bello, the guy sitting beside Tony, and that guy over there. His name's Jose Luis. They'll testify."

"Okay. I'm going over to talk to them and then..." He threw his hands up. "There's nothing else to do except wait."

Wes Currier came in and took his usual place. Cool and distant, he studied the full courtroom. If he was surprised by the number of supporters I had, he didn't show it.

Other than Janie Lewis, Reverend King was the only other black who had come out to speak in my defense. It was truly paradoxical; the whites, the very ones I'd wanted to see destroyed, now stood beside me ready to plead clemency on my behalf.

The courtroom doors closed and as the bailiff stood a tense hush fell over the crowd. A side door opened, and wearing a long, black robe, my fate walked in!

38.
THE END

The Court was called to order. After the crowd rustled into silence, I was told to approach the bar. Judge Spellman was completely unreadable. His face was impassive and his eyes held their normal tinge of formality. How could I have ever thought he liked me?

The preliminaries over, my lawyer informed the judge that several people wanted to testify on my behalf.

Judge Spellman nodded and leaned back in his seat.

Jim Hayes, ex-FBI agent for twenty-five years, stepped forward and said, "I believe Tony Bryant, Your Honor. I've had the chance to be around him and we've come to know each other well. I truly believe he's a changed man. I beg this court to give him the opportunity to prove it!"

Ms. M. M. Carson, a well-known Canadian who spent her winters in Florida, stated that she believed firmly in my transformation. She told how news filtered back, through families who visited their loved ones in Cuban prisons, about a hijacker, a black man named Tony Bryant, who in spite of his past, had gained the respect of the other Americans and was considered their leader.

Then, the striking figure of a tall black man dominated the scene. The Reverend Clennon King praised me in glowing terms. "This man is a hero! Not just for the black community but the white community as well! This man is as great a hero as Jackie Robinson—maybe even greater!" His voice carried a note of awe. "What we have here is an anomaly! What we have here is a *black anti-Communist!*"

Eddy Bello, Cuesta's bodyguard, who was later shot and wounded in Miami defending the blind anti-Castro guerilla, testified on my behalf, then Ed King ratified all he'd said at the first hearing. He stuck with me all the way. Janie Lewis added her voice to the others. She had promised to always be there and she was.

Larry was using his forces like a general at war. He had the initiative and he was determined not to lose it. Jose Manuel Perez was called as witness and after being sworn in, was examined and testified through an interpreter.

"I met Mr. Bryant when I was at Combinado Del Este Prison in 1977."

"Describe to the Court the conditions in the prison, the conditions you lived under and how Mr. Bryant conducted himself while in prison."

"Well first of all, conditions varied in different prisons. The last prison in which I met Mr. Bryant, was a prison for political and psychological use because the Cuban Communist Government had prepared an amnesty plan for American prisoners to reach an agreement, a rapprochement with the Government of the United States.

"The material conditions of life in that prison were quite good in comparison with the other prisons in which we had lived. But, naturally, they were at no time the minimal conditions in which a human being should live.

"We lived in that prison practically without any medical attention in spite of the fact that the government of Cuba had built a hospital nearby.

"I was a student of medicine and had the opportunity to work in this field and I had under my responsibility nearly 400 persons, among them Bryant.

"We lived in the same galley and I lived exactly next to the cell of Mr. Bryant and I knew the most intimate ideas of this man from the very first moment due to precisely the need of medical attention that he had and that the directors of the prison denied him. I had to make direct contact with him so that under my responsibility I could help him.

"The conditions in general were bad. There was hunger, an enormous amount of hunger. I still remember the pieces of old bread which Tony Bryant and I ate at the time where there was no other food.

"In that prison during the time that we were together, there was very little physical contact with others. But, as medical workers, simply by crossing our building to another which contained the common prisoners, we could hear and see the inhuman and criminal way in which these poor boys were being hit, were being massacred and were being physically tortured, as we had been in previous years before we arrived in this prison.

"Because it was expected that the Cuban Government would release a group of political prisoners and allow us to go to the United States, guards now were forbidden to beat, kill or torture us; and so we were taken out of the regular program.

"But we were tortured psychologically by means of hunger and lack of medical attention. There were men who suffered from cancer, tuberculosis and different types of terminal diseases.

"Bryant at all times maintained a strong position in the jail. At all times, he defended his country. He defended his President. He defended his ideals. He defended his principles and at no time did he give up.

"And the person who is speaking to you now had the opportunity to have a close friendship with Tony Bryant and to respect his ideals. When he is released to accomplish them they will be the same ideals he put into practice in prison in Cuba — to defend the Democracy of this country, to defend his people and to struggle against Communism.

"Finally,... We want to tell your Honor that at this time when the Court pronounces its final verdict, you should know that you have a man who is dedicated in body and soul to defending our institutions, our churches and our Democracy. If it's true that Tony Bryant needs his freedom; then freedom also needs a lot from Tony Bryant."

What a beautiful tribute! I felt my face glowing. No matter what, I knew I had found real friends.

Then the head of Alpha 66, Nazario Sargen, was called.

"How do you know the defendant, Mr. Bryant?"

"I know him by two ways. One, I received letters from the political prisoners in Cuba... Ernesto Diaz Rodriguez, the poet, and from the former commander, Eloy Guiterez Menoyo. Besides, I know all that has been published about him and I have had personal contact with him since he arrived in this country."

He told the court he was and had been director of Alpha 66, Communist Cuba's greatest enemy, for twenty years, that his organization has thirty-three delegations in the United States and in Europe.

Sargen told Judge Spellman he had a great deal of experience dealing with thousands of men who had been under his command. "...and others that I have observed in political and social life, and I have seen Mr. Bryant expressing himself in a very clean and clear manner in relation with human life... and with his view-points about integration amoung all human beings.

"Recently, I have witnessed him trying to unite the black people in the community with the Cubans and the Anglos so that they can live in a social normal way. His efforts are sincere.

"I think that in my opinion when a person has difficulties in life and rectifies them, society has the opportunity to see an example in him."

Tony Cuesta was led carefully forward. Jose Manuel walked him to my side then quickly seated himself. After being sworn in Tony was examined and testified through an interpreter, describing how he had wound up in a Cuban prison.

"Well, we were in our thirty-third mission. When I say 'mission,' I say war mission. I had an unfortunate combat with the enemy. And when I considered that my whole crew was dead, I decided to blow up our own vessel which was already on fire before being captured by the enemy. And in that way, I lost my left hand and my eyesight.

"Up to that time, I considered that mission unfortunate, but thanks to the way in which I remained, it was why I was not sent to the execution wall. And I had the opportunity to live in prison, in the Cuban political prison and to know men in a positive way and among them I met the man that has brought all of us here today."

"Mr. Cuesta," instructed Larry Rosen, "tell the Court the conditions under which Mr. Bryant lived."

"A very brief example would be to take a Nazi German concentration camp or a Japanese Second World War concentration camp, and then we would have something similar to what the Cuban prison is today.

"The scars that are on the body of Mr. Bryant are much more eloquent than anything that I can say here.

"And in order to finalize this matter of the Cuban political prisoner, I want to point out that I myself, blind and maimed, did not receive any special treatment because of my physical condition, to live in that hell.

"If the Tribunal allows me, I would say that I had the opportunity to meet Bryant almost from the beginning when he arrived in Cuba and for more than twelve years in the hell that the Cuban political prisoners face. A very special place in which no man can remain neutral. There you become a despicable human being or a superman. And I don't think that Bryant is a despicable person.

"In that place for many, many years, we saw the conduct of Mr. Bryant, and neither I nor our companions have anything to criticize. Of course, the enemy thinks very differently than we do.

"Now I, as a simple observer of all these matters, asked myself this question. The Cuban political jail is easily three times harder, more inhuman that a common prison in North America.

"Bryant, in this case, because of the hardship, served probably thirty-six real years in jail. Of course, that is if you accept my calculations.

"Well, I wish to say this, and I will again try to clarify that

I do not wish to set rules for this Court. But I wish to point out that Mr. Bryant, according to reports I have had and I think this Court has also, did not commit a crime against the Cuban authorities.

"Then what did Mr. Bryant serve those hard thirty-six years for? This is a question that I wish to leave in the air. But I also wish to point out that we do know the great crime Mr. Bryant actually committed was against the Communist community in Cuba; simply not to be one of them.

"Today I am here with a tremendous happiness in my heart. I do not know what the result is going to be, but I do present to this Court an extremely revealing fact.

"When we were here about four months ago, there were three of us speaking on behalf of Mr. Bryant. And now, after a quarter of a year in which Bryant enjoyed a freedom with certain restrictive measures, I find that we are not alone defending Mr. Bryant, the future Mr. Bryant.

"Men have come here who not only represent themselves but also organizations of hundreds, perhaps thousands of men and women, and this for us is very encouraging.

"And I would like to finish clarifying for this Court that we have lived under the same roof. We have shared the same food and the same dreams in the last 124 days with Mr. Bryant. And we feel even more sure of him today than the day in which we came here before to tell this Court that if the United States justice system was based more on the rehabilitation of human beings, then in the court's discretion Mr. Bryant deserves, as many have said, his second chance.

"I thank all of you, especially this Court. I don't want to exclude anyone, for what we have observed up to today, and whatever the result might be, I believe that we have given a lesson for the whole world of how justice is administered in the United States of America."

Judge Spellman thanked the blind commando politely and looked toward the Assistant United States Attorney.

Wes Currier didn't try to harass anybody. He asked a couple of questions of each witness, then dismissed them. He seemed to be waiting for the chance to present his final arguments. He realized that no matter what, these people were going to stick by me.

Larry paused, nervously rubbed his forehead, looked up at the judge and said, "Your Honor, at this point Mr. Bryant would like to speak to the Court."

"All right."

The moment was here. Whatever I said now would forever affect my life. I stood up beside Larry and our shoulders touched briefly. I felt some of his strength. Maybe it would give me luck. I needed luck. Whatever happened today my young lawyer would walk out free. He wasn't on trial for hijacking.

A pause to clear my throat. Thoughts scampered around in my head like leaves on a windy day. I really didn't know how or where to start. Then I opened my mouth and the words flowed.

"Good morning, Your Honor. First of all, I would like to express my sincere and profound gratitude to everyone who appeared and spoke on my behalf. For me, that alone is worth everything. All that a man could want as far as achievement is to have other people think well of him and believe in him and his cause.

"The question that is most important here, the question on everyone's mind is: What happened to Tony Bryant to make him change? Has he really changed and what is he going to do in the future?

"These are the basic questions and they are the questions I would like to answer: As Tony Cuesta just stated, the conditions in Cuba's prisons were sub-human. Each of us faced an individual hell. For me it was lesser or greater. I don't know.

"I only know that it is impossible for any man to go through the same situation I endured, those same circumstances I suffered through for twelve years and not change. Impossible. That is impossible!

"Therefore, we are dealing with the fact that there has been a change because it would be virtually impossible not to change. You either become a sub-human being, you bow, you bow down, you sell your soul for a little rice because you are hungry twenty-four hours a day, or you stand up and fight and you die, if necessary.

"Myself, I chose to fight; and if necessary, to die!

"My attitude has not changed at any moment from the time that I first decided that Communism is diabolical, that it is humanity's vomit. I decided then that I would fight and, if necessary, die but, most important of all, I would try to live and come back and expose what Communism really is, what it does to human beings, what it is doing to humanity, how it enslaves and deprives us of our human condition.

"It was very difficult for me at first to accept the fact that the Cubans did not believe me or accept me as a revolutionary. And then I began to understand they could not believe me and accept me because of the fact that they, the Cuban Communists themselves, are counter-revolutionary.

"When Mr. Fidel Castro speaks of the counter-revolutionaries and when he refers to the United States as *an imperialist counter-revolutionary country*, I think he is really referring to himself. Because this is the only country where there is a constant revolution of new ideas; where a man can interject a different way of life and be respected in the community and give it support and be a part of the community... Ideas. It's all ideas, whether they're new or different. This is the only country in the world that is really revolutionary.

"In Cuba, I have been on many hunger strikes, been beaten many times. I have been shot at and they have tried to assassinate me. I lived a true hell. It was impossible for me not to change.

"But I have always thought there was another factor in my change, the most influential factor of all; the fact that I found God in Cuba. It was necessary for me to see the devil to believe that there is a God.

"I touched the wounds of Christ's hands. I believe in Christ because I have seen the devil. I saw a diabolical society trying with all of its efforts to subjugate humanity and enslave it.

"I suffered greatly in Cuba but that is not the important factor. What is important is what I have learned and I've learned a lot.

"The most important lesson is that this is the greatest country in the world, that it deserves defending, that it deserves that we fight for it. And that is why I, from the beginning in Cuba, placed my personal well-being in second place. I stand on that today, your Honor.

"Whatever the Court decides, I will continue. Whether it be from prison or whether I will be able to continue in the streets. But I will continue to fight.

"There are certain organizations here, as your Honor has heard, who have already spoken with me concerning plans to travel all over the Latin Americas giving lectures.

"And, of course, I am going to write the book that I think should be written. I do have a great amount of support from the Cuban community, from the Latin community, but I have also been able to break the ice in the black community, which is very, very difficult.

"As I said before, I am dedicated to this cause. I believe it is worthy of everything that I can give it. It does not matter what happens to Tony Bryant but it does matter what happens to the community. It does matter if we allow Communist infiltration or allow division, if we allow breakdown in the moral fiber of the United States of America.

"In the past, I was never really interested in the moral aspect of the community. I think my past record shows that... But since that time, since what I experienced in Cuba, seeing to what levels a society can be brought down, I have decided that this is my object. I decided to return to the United States even if it meant going to prison.

"I think you remember sir, when I was here the first time, that I said I would keep my word, that I would not do anything I thought would place the Court's position in danger or the word of Tony Cuesta and others that signed that half million dollar bond, I still stand on that same position, your Honor.

"I am not a liar. Some people find it hard to accept some of the things I say. But if this Court does allow me now to continue in the path that I began: I will continue to conduct myself as I have been doing and will do so in an even greater way because I think with greater freedom of movement I will be able to do a better job; fulfill the task that needs to be fulfilled.

"I don't know if I am the only person capable of it. I'm not saying I am. But I know I am one of a few to have lived through an experience that requires you to be a survivor. It demands an intestinal fortitude that we all have, but must find... and I found it.

"Your honor, I am very thankful to this Court for the opportunity that it gave me. And thank you for putting your trust in me."

"Thank you," said Judge Spellman, his face, cool, distant and indifferent.

Now Larry spoke. If he was nervous, he hid it well, and his voice, though low at first, gained in intensity and fervor as he spoke. He rattled off case after case where probation had been given in serious offenses. Brilliantly he argued that "imprisonment for any term of years or for life, precluded probation," because, "a defendant may be placed on probation only when he has been convicted of an offense *not* punishable by death or life imprisonment." He handled himself like an old pro.

"In summary, Title 18 U.S.C. Section 3651, explicitly states that a sentence of probation may be given, except where the offense is punishable by death or life imprisonment; second, the interpretations by the Supreme Court and of the Fifth Circuit of a similarly worded statute concluded that either the sentence is not mandatory or that if it is mandatory, probation is nevertheless available; third, where Congress has decided that probation should not be available, it has explicitly prohibited probation, as Congress did in the now repealed Narcotic Statute; fourth, in all the decisions considering probation for air piracy, every court has concluded that probation may be given. Mr. Bryant respectfully submits that the court has the legal power and ability to put Mr. Bryant under supervised probation. It is his sincere expectation that the court will also have a factual basis for giving him probation! Thank you, Your Honor."

A tense silence settled at the end of his arguments.

Wes Currier seemed to have lost some of his fire. His address to the court was lackluster, but he was dogged. He pointed out my nefarious past and asked that I be sentenced to a minimum term of twenty years in prison!

Judge Spellman listened attentively to Currier, then in the silence following the plea, he swung his chair to one side and, lost in thought, stared up at the ceiling. He remained that way for several moments, then he turned quickly back, like a gunfighter taking aim.

When Judge Spellman swung around it was a replay of all times I'd stood before a judge listening to a sentence being handed down...

"Airman Bryant, this court sentences you to six months in the stockade with a two-thirds loss of pay!"

"Mr. Bryant, this court has no choice but to sentence you to six months in the county jail for violation of Section 11500 of the Health and Safety Code!"

"Mr. Bryant, you are sentenced to an indeterminate term of five years to life to be expedited in a state correctional institution!"

"Mr. Bryant, you have been found guilty on all five counts as charged. This court sentences you to five years to life on each count. The sentences will run concurrently. You are hereby ordered to serve a prison term of ten years to life!"

"Senor Bryant, here are your papers. You have been sentenced to twelve years in prison!"

"Senor Bryant, you are sentenced to one year and a half for aggravated assault on military personnel!"

"Senor Bryant, we find you guilty of escape and of destroying State property. You are sentenced to three years loss of freedom. The sentence to start upon completion of present sanction!"

"Mr. Bryant..." Judge Spellman's voice was clear and firm.

Under no circumstances must I collapse, I thought, steeling myself for the worst.

"Mr. Bryant, I'm not as impressed by what you've done since you've been back as I am by the transformation you showed while in Cuba. The transformation is evident!

"Mr. Bryant, there comes a time in every man's life when he comes to the crossroads!" Judge Spellman paused and peered intently at me. "You've reached those crossroads. From here on out, it's up to you what you do with your life.

"I know there are some who will not be in agreement with me. But this court is going to give you that second chance. This court sentences you to five years probation. Good luck, Mr. Bryant!" He smiled.

I almost dropped ... I had won! What a difference from my trial in revolutionary Cuba! What a difference between Communism and a Democracy! We had won!

A burst of applause rang out from the crowd. Reverend King, tears streaming, rushed from the courtroom.

I had been born again!

I was swamped by backslapping well-wishers, and as I stumbled out into the glow of a radiant day, I felt the last remnants of fear fall away. At last the nightmare had ended. I heard someone say, "It's over. Let's go home!"

It will take a while to forget, but in time — like the scars on my body — all the wounds will heal. Someday only the shadows of memories of Communist Cuba will remain; that land where nightmares begin at dawn... where the myth was destroyed.

THE BEGINNING

As seen on
the CBS Television Special:
Coming Out Of The Ice
starring John Savage and Willie Nelson.

COMING OUT OF THE ICE
by Victor Herman

This astonishing true story is the tale of a young American man who was sent to the Soviet Union with his parents by the Ford Motor Company to set up an auto plant. He was eventually thrown into Soviet prisons and could not return to America until forty-five years later.

During his life in and out of Russian prisons, he met and fell in love with a beautiful Russian gymnast who followed him into exile and lived with him and their child, for a year in Siberia in a cave chopped out under the ice. Theirs is the compelling story of a romance destined to thrive under even the most desperate conditions.

It was 1938 when Victor Herman was inexplicably thrown into prison, after he had become a celebrity in the Soviet Union, having won acclaim as 'the Lindbergh of Russia' for his flying and world-record-breaking parachute jumps. But what happened to him was a common nightmare during the Stalin years: those who survived imprisonment and torture were sent north to hard labor in the icy forests and mines, or into exile. Victor was one of the very few who survived.

What kept him alive for eighteen years was an overwhelming, unshakable belief in his own invincibility, and the desire to return to America and tell his story. After Stalin's death he was 'pardoned' and allowed to live quietly until he began petitioning to go back to America. Years of persistence despite endless frustrations paid off when, in 1976, Victor Herman was finally allowed to come home

This eloquent, unflinching true adventure recounts a scandalous and little-known episode in Russian-American history. It gives vivid testimony to the boundless faith of a human being who refused to be defeated.

Another book by an American in Communist captivity published by FREEDOM PRESS:

$14.95 in hard cover, $6.95 in soft cover, $2.00 postage and handling.
To order TOLL FREE by telephone simply dial:
1-800-GET BOOK or 1-800-438-2665.

To order multiple copies telephone: (305) 565-2665 or write:
ORDERING, FREEDOM PRESS INTERNATIONAL,
3223 N.W. 10th Terrace, Suite 607
Fort Lauderdale, Florida 33309, U.S.A.   ISBN 0-915031-00-0